black,
quare
& then
to
where

Religious Cultures of
African and African Diaspora People

SERIES EDITORS: Jacob K. Olupona, *Harvard University*
Dianne M. Stewart, *Emory University*
and Terrence L. Johnson, *Georgetown University*

The book series examines the religious, cultural, and political expressions of African, African American, and African Caribbean traditions. Through transnational, cross-cultural, and multidisciplinary approaches to the study of religion, the series investigates the epistemic boundaries of continental and diasporic religious practices and thought and explores the diverse and distinct ways African-derived religions inform culture and politics. The series aims to establish a forum for imagining the centrality of Black religions in the formation of the "New World."

duke university press durham and london 2023

black, quare & then to where

theories of justice
and black sexual ethics
jennifer susanne leath

© 2023 Duke University Press
All rights reserved
Project Editor: Liz Smith
Designed by Aimee C. Harrison
Typeset in Untitled Serif and Fraunces (typeface designed by
Phaedra Charles and Flavia Zimbardi) by
Westchester Publishing Services

Library of Congress Cataloging-in-Publication Data
Names: leath, jennifer susanne, [date] author.
Title: Black, quare, and then to where : theories of justice and Black sexual ethics / jennifer susanne leath.
Other titles: Theories of justice and Black sexual ethics | Religious cultures of African and African diaspora people.
Description: Durham : Duke University Press, 2023. | Series: Religious cultures of African and African diaspora people | Includes bibliographical references and index.
Identifiers: LCCN 2023011444 (print)
LCCN 2023011445 (ebook)
ISBN 9781478025146 (paperback)
ISBN 9781478020165 (hardcover)
ISBN 9781478027140 (ebook)
Subjects: LCSH: Maat (Egyptian deity) | Sexual ethics. | Religion and ethics. | Womanist theology. | Black people—Sexual behavior—Moral and ethical aspects. | BISAC: SOCIAL SCIENCE / Black Studies (Global) | SOCIAL SCIENCE / Gender Studies Classification: LCC HQ32 .L3925 2023 (print) | LCC HQ32 (ebook) | DDC 176/.4—dc23/eng/20230516
LC record available at https://lccn.loc.gov/2023011444
LC ebook record available at https://lccn.loc.gov/2023011445

Cover photograph by the author.

To the Divine spark and stardust of us all
To Maât and for maât
To the Nubians
To Hatshepsut
To Mama and Mimi, Poppie and Papa
To Mom & Dad
For Axé

Preface ix

Acknowledgments xiii

Introduction. Introducing Maât 1

Part I quare-womanist-vindicationist movement

one A Prolegomenon to Justice Hermeneutics and Black Sexual Ethics 17

two Naming (and Transforming) Justice. (Re)Imagining Black Sexual Ethics 35

Conclusion. Re-covering Maât 245

Notes 255

Bibliography 293

Index 313

contents

Part II justices

three Flying Justice. Sun Ra's ~~Sexuality~~ and Other Afrofutures 71

four Heterexpectations. Jumping the Broom, Marriage, Democracy, and Entanglement Theory 101

five Dancing Justice. Just Black HomoSexualities 137

six Ancient Mixologies. Joel Augustus Rogers and Puzzling Interracial Intimacies 167

seven Black Web. Disrupting Transnational Pornographies for Post(trans)national Humanalities 205

preface

Sometime in 2018 I had an idea for a sermon series: Second Sunday Sex Sundays. At the time I was serving as the pastor of Campbell Chapel AME Church in Denver, Colorado. About fifty-five people came to church each Sunday; there were about 135 members. About two-thirds of this predominantly Black church were over seventy years old. I am still not quite sure why I could not shake the burden of preaching this series that would address various aspects of sexual life, Black experience, and Christian teachings. It was not merely that I am quare or had some need to work out a reconciliation of my own beliefs and practices with respect to sexuality. It was not merely for the challenge of addressing muted issues.

Something would not release me from the assignment. Even when members complained, when my presiding elder and bishop urged a different course, when my mother pleaded that I stop, when counselors and colleagues questioned my agenda, when I experienced an unanticipated spiritual drain, when I found myself the target of unsolicited interest: even then I still felt obligated to preach. The topics for the ten months during which I preached through this series were: "Opening Conversation: Let's Talk about Sex," "Sexual Abuse," "Sex outside of Marriage," "Sexual Orientations," "Gender Identities," "Put a Ring on It: Marriage," "Hold Up: Fidelity," "Polyamory," "Sex? (Meh) Over It," and "Pornography and Fantasy Lives." To this day, those sermons were the hardest I've ever had to prepare and preach. Most

Sundays, I offered members handouts of the series to aid in teaching and preaching on these subjects; I met with the Sunday School to engage in more dialogue about these subjects as well. Over the course of this period, a basket of candy and condoms was kept outside of my office (a member's idea). I set up a box that invited comments about the sermons. By the end of the series, I was grateful to have survived—and grateful for those who took this journey through to the end.

A woman in her early nineties had written a comment: "My son and I have no problem with gender." It is hard to explain how and why, but this note touched my soul. It felt like an inexplicable affirmation. Though she named gender, I knew and could feel that she meant more. It was about the series. It was about my preaching. It was about me as her pastor. It was about sexuality. It was her way of saying that she had love for me, for her church, and for others, regardless of their sexual orientation and/or gender.

"No problem": what does it mean to have "no problem"? Perhaps it meant that she felt there had been no harm done, no violation of rights, no infringement on rights, no recognized injustice, no desire to create or participate in an injustice. To me, "no problem" also recognized the spiritual work at hand. Maybe she was saying: Because this is not a problem, I/we do not know why it's necessary to address these matters. Maybe she was saying: Because this is not a problem, I/we do not mind you addressing these matters (and, perhaps, are glad that you are doing so). "No problem" was such an interesting phrasing because in so many ways the series was a problem for many. It exposed and parsed some of the most private, wounded, rewarding, and complex aspects of Black life, community, and faith. And whether my congregants recognized this or not, I intended it as an exercise in spiritualizing sex as a matter of personal and communal justice.

Around the same time, I designed and taught my course Queer Theory, Religioethics, and Activism. Each week, students not only read the work of queer theorists of color but also encountered sacred texts of various religious traditions. I asked my students to read these texts queerly, meaning from the perspective of queer theory. I had drawn the sacred texts from Hebrew and Christian, Hindu and Buddhist, Ifá and Muslim traditions. By the middle of the quarter, it was clear that students were having spiritual experiences and divine encounters in the classroom space. In a sense, this was an exercise in sexualizing spirituality (i.e., an inverse echo) as a matter of personal and communal justice.

In both the ecclesial and the academic space, there are constant reminders that handling sex and gender, religion, and race is handling the holy. Handling these together is like pursuing a glimpse of G*d. Speaking to these matters at once as a matter of personal and community ethics—and hearing the cries for justice seeping from the interstices of this discourse—is like singing with the Divine. Together, sex and gender, religion, and race do not make sense. Apart, sex and gender, religion, and race do not make sense. And so stories of sex and gender, religion, and race often go untold. The ethics and theories of justice that might help describe, define, and refine approaches to sex and gender, religion, and race (especially for Afrodiasporic people and communities) often go uncharted. "No problem" is a problem when individuals and communities have no way to harness the power of sex and gender, religion, and race for purposeful living; it is a problem when rigorous, explicit conversation, teaching, preaching, and praxis with respect to these subjects is always eschewed, verboten, taboo, disgraced, and out of reach.

Others have thoroughly rehearsed the difficulty of discourses on sexuality in society and in ecclesial spaces. However, the relationship of these discourses to deeper questions of justice through the lived experiences of Afrodiasporic people—and the ethical approaches of Afrodiasporic people—has been largely unexamined. This book revisits Black sexual ethics as a pathway into the rhizomatic sphere of justice theories. With great hope for just spiritualizations of sexuality and sexualizations of spirituality within and beyond Afrodiasporic contexts and communities, I embark upon this quare-womanist-vindicationist journey. For those who say "no problem," I hope this book is confirmation and embrace of all we can be when we allow new (and old) visions of justice to take root in and branch out of us.

acknowledgments

To G*d—the Supreme Being who lovingly calls us into being—be every acknowledgement!

To the ancestors and saints who have kept watch over me, inspiring me and giving me strength, especially Hatshepsut, Richard Allen, Jarena Lee, Rebecca Cox Jackson, Denmark Vesey, Henry McNeil Turner, Daniel Alexander Payne, Zora Neale Hurston, Audre Lorde, James Baldwin, August Wilson, and Toni Morrison.

I honor and thank Harold Benson Jones, James Franklin Leath, Josephine Sykes, Bertha Leath, James Franklin Leath Jr., Juanita Jones, and Harold Wells.

I honor and thank Rosa Bridges, Everett and Constance Chandler, Annie Epps, Martha Lang, Frank Smart, Robina Wimbush, Vuyani Vellem, and Agnes Abuom.

I honor and thank Richard Allen Chappelle, Sr., Sarah Frances Davis, William Phillips DeVeaux, Zedekiah LaZett Grady, Richard Allen Hildebrand, Frederick Hilborn Talbot, and Richard Franklin Norris.

I honor and thank Cheryl Irving, Vincent Harding, James Hal Cone, Delores S. Williams, Charles Long, and Katie Geneva Cannon.

I am grateful to and for the Orishas I have met along the way, especially Elegba (whom I saw first through St. Anthony), who has found me at many crossroads. Ogun, Ochossi, Shango, Yemanja, Oshun—and all who point me toward the One some have known and called Olorun.

My parents and siblings are my lifeblood: Susan Venida Jones Leath and Jeffrey Nathaniel Leath; Victoria Nicole and Jeffrey Nathaniel II with Shamaiah and my dear nieces Lamai and Jade. Thank you for your unconditional love and for the ways you remain my steadiest and most positively challenging discursive partners.

To my family, and especially Dennis Jones, Barbara McCauley, Paul Jones, Karen Coleman, Caprice Buskey, Natasha Shepherd, and all their families, with special love for my goddaughter, NaRiah—and my cousins David and Fred, Carson, Byron, Nick, Lauren, Allison, Paul, Grant, and Nia, Corey, William, Breea, Amika, Chanté, Akim, Hu Caleb, Tres, Sarai, and Michelle: thank you.

Thank you, Carolyn Love, Kay Farley, Carroll Watkins-Ali, Naomi Harris; Timothy E. Tyler, Nita Mosby Tyler, and Sheriolyn Curry Hodge; Rachel Harding and Jonathan Harding; Caran Ware Joseph, Terrence and Rachel Hughes, Brydie and Xian Harris-Brooks, Marsha Evans, and Danielle Abrams for the family and community, teachers and mentors you were to me in Denver.

To those who have shown special care for me through childhood and beyond: Sylvia Lett and family; Mary Mansfield and family; Juretha "Dee" and Henry Murray and family; Helen M. C. Jones and Wilberta Jackson; Vernon Ross and Anthony Stevenson; Steve, Charmaine, and Sean Lewis; Janie Busch and family; Brenda, Melvin, and Tanya Phillips and family; Louis Smith and family; Phyllis Tann and family; Gloria Oakley and family; Sharon Custis and family; Thalia Harris and family; Roberta Alford and family; Dolores Lyons and family; Susan Jones and family; Gwendolyn Bright and family; Jerome and Kim Stembridge; and a multitude of other family and friends, especially throughout the First, Fifth, and Fourth Episcopal Districts: thank you.

Thank you for friendship, Tiffany Martin, Sherisse Butler, Craig Robinson, and Shakira Sanchez-Collins; Tiffany Willoughby, Ravi Perry, Oluwadamilare Ray, and Omari Aarons. Thank you for the "New Guard" vision of ecclesial family, James Simmons and crew.

Thank you for the ways you model ministry: Virginia Sanders, Jocelyn Hart, Kimberly L. Detherage, Erika Crawford, Miriam Burnett, Francine Brookins, E. Anne Henning Byfield, Carolyn Tyler Guidry, and Vashti Murphy McKenzie. Fierce.

Thank you, Henry Allen Belin III, Rita Sinkfield Belin, Roderick Dwayne Belin, and Toni Belin Ingram for the ways you love the church, love the people, and follow the lead of the Holy Spirit as best you can; thank you for the wisdom you impart through your love of G*d and joyful celebration of life. Thank you for always inquiring with genuine interest and encouragement about the progress of my scholarship.

Thank you, Garland Pierce, for the ways you lead with integrity and for the friendship and support you have offered along the way. Thank you, John Thomas and Teresa Fry Brown, for modeling excellence—and what it looks like to open doors so we can feel a fresh wind of Holy Spirit. Thank you for the ways you model scholarship, innovation, and pastoral presence in the AME Church: Jacquelyn Grant, Reggie Blount, Mark Kelly Tyler, Esther L. Seales, Marsha Foster Boyd, Nicholas Tweed, Karla Cooper, and Brenda Hayes. Thank you, Jacquelyn Dupont Walker, Nikia Robert, Anita Peete, Bria Belim, William H. Lamar IV, Brandee Mimitzraiem, and Simeon Rhoden. Thank you for the ways your welcome to the Fourth District helped me through the finish line with this project: Kenesha Blake-Newell, Tracey Thomas, Denise Johnson, Joelynn Stokes and Alicia Skillman, and Stacey Smith.

Thank you, bishops of the AME Church and your families, for the ways you carry the torches of Richard Allen and Jarena Lee, strive to cultivate a church of integrity—sincerely in love with G*d and G*d's incarnate reflection in the least among us, and nurture the spiritual and material gifts of the communities you serve that justice might be realized for people of African descent and all who share in systemic dispossession. I am especially grateful to the following episcopal families who, in different ways and times, have inspired these commitments in me: the Primm, Bright, Adams, Hildebrand, Talbot, H. H. Brookins, Anderson, James, Cummings, Cousin, Ming, Senatle, Belin, Byrd, Bryant, Thomas, Chappelle, Young, Webster, Grady, Henning, DeVeaux, Kirkland, Richardson, Norris, McKenzie, Ingram, Williams, Messiah, Kawimbe, Guidry, J. L. Davis, Daniels, Green, S. F. Davis, McCloud, McCallister, White, Fugh, Jackson, Seawright, Mitchell, Byfield, Brailsford, Wicker, Reid, Beaman, Zanders, F. A. Brookins, and Wright families.

Bishop Yvette Flunder and Mother Shirley Miller: we thank you, we look to you, and we pray your strength.

I give thanks to and for the ecclesial communities that have kept me whole: Tanner-Price AME Church (Windsor, ON), Grant AME Church (Toronto, ON), and the Canada Conference, Campbell Chapel AME Church (Denver, CO), Allen AME Church (White Plains, NY), Campbell AME Church (Media, PA), First AME Church: Bethel (New York, NY), Bethel AME Church (New Haven, CT), and, my home forever, Mother Bethel AME Church (Philadelphia, PA). And I thank The Fellowship of Affirming Ministries and AIC Tanzania—and a host of Baptist, Pentecostal, Lutheran, Anglican, Catholic, Evangelical,

United Church of Christ, Metropolitan Community Church, nondenominational, and United Methodist churches that helped my spiritual development through and beyond my undergraduate university years along with several AME churches in the Cambridge/Boston area: St. Paul, Charles Street, Bethel (Mattapan), and Grant.

Thank you to other communities that have inspired and encouraged this project: the Youth Theology Institute (now Initiative), the Fund for Theological Education, the Mellon-Mays Fellowship, Kivulini, the Womanist-Buddhist Consultation, the Brazil Travel Seminar, the Roundtable on the Sexual Politics of Black Churches and (later) the Center on African American Religion and Sexual Politics, the Harvard Divinity School Seminar for Debates on Religion and Sexuality, the World Council of Churches, Oikotree Roving Faculty, Sudipta Singh and the Council for World Mission: I offer my sincere gratitude. Thank you to the Women's Studies in Religion Program at Harvard Divinity School and Ann D. Braude. Thank you to Nancy Lynne Westfield, Timothy Lake, Donald Quist, and the Wabash Center.

To scholars without whom this project would not be—and most especially Emilie M. Townes, who still teaches my mind to dance—I express my deepest gratitude. I am also grateful beyond words for these scholars who carry a unique flame and blaze a trail as translators of Black spiritual life: Terrence L. Johnson, Dianne Stewart, Tracey Hucks, and Jacob Olupona. Thank you, Evelyn Higginbotham and Diana Eck; Charlie Hallisey and Janet Gyatso. Thank you, Marcia Riggs, Traci West, Monique Moultrie, Janet R. Jakobsen, and Mark Jordan. Thank you to those who shaped me as a scholar, encouraging my curiosities and discipline: Jafari Allen, Margaret Farley, Willis Jenkins, Gene Outka (in fond memory), Jennifer Herdt, Fred Simmons, Gerald Jaynes, Kathryn Lofton, Crystal Feimster, Hazel Carby, Elizabeth Alexander, Jonathan Holloway, Elijah Anderson, and Chris Rhomberg. Thank you to scholar-teacher-colleagues who showed interest in the earliest stages of this quare work: Cathy Cohen and Corey Dolgon; Gary Dorrien; Layli Phillips; and Josef Sorett, Brad Braxton, Michael Brown, Barbara Diane Savage, Mandy Carter, Dennis and Christine Wiley, Keri Day, and Monica Coleman; Stacey and Juan Floyd-Thomas; Pamela Lightsey; Stephen Ray, Lee Butler, and Alton Pollard.

Thank you to my siblings in the academy: Kathryn Ott, Melanie Harris, Jennifer Harvey, Eboni K. Marshall Turman, Monica Maher, Sofia Betancourt, Leonard Curry, Shatavia Wynn, and Courtney Bryant. Thank you for what we share.

Thank you, Sharon Fluker, Matthew Williams, and Stephen Lewis. What you have given to the future of Black religious scholarship is unparalleled.

Thank you, Stephanie Crumpton, Shively T. J. Smith, Kimberly D. Russaw, Kimberleigh Jordan, and countless sister scholars for your accompaniment and encouragement; thank you, Nikotris Thelathia Young, Benae Beamon, Ashon Crawley, Emerson Zora Hamsa, Elyse Ambrose, Annemarie Mingo, Antonia Daymond, and Melanie Jones for fellowship; Jalylah Burrell and Adom Getachew, thank you for blessing me with a most patient form of sister-scholarhood. Thank you for existential conversations, commitments, and connections that keep my mind-heart pumping to this day: Robin Hayes, Nicole Ivy, Jamicia Lackey, Stephanie Greenlea, Sarah Haley, Calvin Warren, Carlos Miranda, and Meredith Coleman-Tobias; Chelsey R. Carter; Vanessa Agard-Jones, Darnell Moore, and Derrick McQueen; Asante Todd and Angela Cowser.

I am grateful for gracious colleagues at Iliff School of Theology who generously read, responded to, and encouraged my work on many occasions: Tink Tinker, Miguel De La Torre, Kristina Lizardy-Hajbi, Albert Hernandez, Eunjoo Kim, Edward Antonio, Katherine Turpin (through the finish line!), Amy Erickson, Tony Alumkal, Boyung Lee, Carrie Doehring, Cathernie Kelsey, Eric C. Smith, Jacob Kinnard, Mark George, Pam Eisenbaum, Philip Butler, Michele Watkins, Ted Vial, and Tom Wolfe. I am grateful to have been at home with you, on walks with you, in dialogue with you, in classrooms with you, and on Zoom with you.

Thank you to new colleagues at Queen's University and in Canada: M. Shobhana Xavier, Chloe Savoie-Bernard, and Natasha Bissonauth; Katherine McKittrick, Sailaja Vutukuru, Daniel McNeil, Vanessa E. Thompson, Dalitso Ruwe, Kesha Fevrier, Bianca Beauchemin, Juliane Okot Bitek, Joseph Kang-mennaang, Qanita Lilla, Denita Arthurs, Amarnath Amarasingam, Dustin Atlas, Sharday C. Mosurinjohn, Richard S. Ascough, Tracey Trothen, Forough Jahanbakhsh, Jorgé Legoas, Aditi Sen, Adnan Husain, Pamela Dickey Young, Allison Gowanlock, and Levanna Schönwandt. Thank you, Marsha Monique Hamilton, Taylor Cenac, and LaShae Watson.

Thank you to my ecumenical friends and colleagues, among them Evelyn Parker, Shazetta Thompson-Hill, Vanessee Burns, Traci Blackmon, Bernice Powell Jackson, Cheryl Dudley, Tyrone Pitts, Larry Pickens, Jerry Pillay, Rogate Mshana, Fulata Moyo-Mbano, Faautu Talapusi, Tara Tautari, Doug Chial, Cecil Mel and Patsy Robeck and the Joint Consultative Group of the WCC; thank you, Kyriaki Avtzi, Martin Robra, and Peter Cruchley; thank you, Chola Sim, Christina Biere, Iosif Bosch, Itayi Ndudzo, and so many other cherished Echos colleagues. Thank you, Iva B. Carruthers and Martha Simmons. Thank you, Seong-Won Park, Angelique Walker-Smith, Karen Georgia Thompson, Fernando Enns, Kathryn Lohre, and Michael Blair.

To friends who have kept me grounded for decades: Aishah Shahidah Simmons, Camele-Ann White and Latrisha Chattin—and my little brother Anthony Phillips, one of my first Maât instructors.

I am grateful to each of you for being ever-present with unconditional love and abiding friendship: Rachel Rutishauser, Kristin Naragon Gainey, Sae Takada, Monica Castillo, and Michelle Kuo. Thank you for your friendship in some of the earliest iterations of this work—and for the ways our bond remains: Aida Hussen, Erica McClendon, Emily Feirman, Kendrick Sadler, Gerald "Jay" Williams, Anthony Long, and Marcel Anderson.

To countless students I have met along the way: I am grateful to each of you; you have taught me—and yet teach me—so much. And to members of congregations I have served: thank you; *you* have taught me the most!

Thank you: Miriam Angress, Liz Smith, Paula Durbin-Westby, and the editorial team at Duke University Press.

To Ona Osirio-Maat, Charmaine Jackman, and my friends at Serenity—with and through whom I understand the world more clearly: thank you. To my beloved Familiar whose ways of knowing teach me: thank you.

This project would not have been possible without Katherine Turpin's ever-present working companionship, encouragement, and generous reading, Imani e. Wilson's spiritual wisdom, encyclopedic knowledge, prescient discernment, social witness, and love of Black people and culture, Joseph Lamar's musical tether to eternity, and Tef Poe's realness—and the abiding friendships I share with each of them.

Thank you, Aida Kane. Je t'aime plus que les mots ne peuvent l'exprimer dans toutes les langues. Merci de m'avoir ouvert ton cœur et pour tout ce que tu m'apprends si généreusement sur la vie et l'amour.

And to so many more whom I cannot name or number—whose generous intellectual, spiritual, and material contributions I have received: thank you. To you whom I remember (whom I never knew)—and to you through whom I will one day know (better): thank you.

Asante Sana. Nashukuru mno!

Amen. Axé. Hotep.

I last wrote from land stolen from the Arapaho, Cheyenne, and Ute, as well as the Mississaugas of the Credit, the Anishnabeg, the Chippewa, the Haudenosaunee, the Wendat peoples and land that remains home to many other diverse First Nations, Inuit, and Métis peoples. And, too, I have contemplated and written parts of this text in various geographical places on at least five continents over many years—all places where indigenous cultures have been systematically obliterated. Justices are yet unrealized—especially for these named and countless unnamed indigenous peoples and people of African descent. I strive against my own complicity in cultural genocide, leaning toward justices with the full weight of my being.

introduction   Introducing Maât

Names and purposes are entangled matter. How we are named and how we name ourselves impacts who we are and anticipates what we do. Names can be invocations of purpose. Names can be expressions of intention. Through names and purposes, we ask these two fundamental questions: Who are we, and why are we here? For Afrodiasporic people, the answers to these questions are especially complicated. Without clarity about origins, the process of naming and discernment of purpose is compromised. Still, we undertake the creative processes of naming, purposing—and (re)situating. This book is quare—and a quare testament. *Quare* is, first, a transliteration of E. Patrick Johnson's US southern Black grandmother's way of saying *queer*.[1] And *quare* is an appellation of what Afrodiasporic culture expresses when it is also self-affirming as queer (i.e., gender and sexually variant). This book is womanist—and a womanist testament. Womanist is, first, as Alice Walker put it, "from the black folk expression of mothers to female children, 'You acting womanish,' i.e., like a woman."[2] This book is vindicationist—and a vindicationist testament. Vindicationist is, first, concerned with the Wynterian and Fanonian projects of expressing the full, agentive dignity, integrity, personhood, and humanity of Afrodiasporic peoples while grounding this expression in African sources. This book is a call to transdimensional justices through the filters of Black sexualities. This book is a vocation—and a vocational testament. As I am called (also) to be a quare-womanist-vindicationist,

I.1: This image of Maât is found in Nefertari's tomb in the Valley of the Queens. The hieroglyphs drawn across the top of this image that sits atop a threshold in the tomb show the cartouche of Nefertari followed by a narrative; the iconic single feather of Maât that is worn as part of her headdress evokes the Hall of Judgment and the significant role of Maât and her single feather in weighing the heart (symbolizing the morality) of the deceased. Maât's wingspan suggests both what she is and represents (justice) and how she functions as herself, embodying that which she represents. *Source:* Jamie Marriage, "Almighty Women: Indomitable Goddesses," Geek Girl Authority, February 14, 2017, https://www.geekgirlauthority.com/almighty-women-indomitable-goddesses/.

these names align with my purpose through this book: shining light on Afrofuturist possibilities for thinking through and practicing cultivation and maintenance of justices in the glow of African origins, Black women's lived experiences, and persistent insistences to be free, and Blackqueer "acting up."[3] To understand *justices*, the first task of this text is an introduction to one whose name means justice and whose purpose is to cultivate and sustain justice: Maât. If you share in the vocations of Blackness, Africa and its diaspora, womanism, or quareness, this book (re)considers Maât and *maât* (i.e., Maât's conceptual correlate) as offerings to be received and shared for fresh manifestations of justice—in all the places, in all the ways.

Maât, the ancient Egyptian *nṯrt* of justice and truth, she who bears a feather as her headdress, the oft-winged feminine manifestation and adjudicator of right order, is the first fruit of this quare-womanist-vindicationist project.[4] References to her in "Maxims of the Prime Minister Ptahhotep" (circa 2450 BCE) are among the earliest and most prominent philosophical and material manifestations of Maât. Maât is at the heart of "wisdom literature, instructions, maxims, teachings . . . cultivated in ancient Egypt from the Old Kingdom (2780–2260 BCE) to the Late Period (1085–333 BCE)."[5] Théophile Obenga describes and defines *maât* as "the combination of Justice and Truth, the supreme moral law."⁶ And, as Obenga explains, *maât* is part of a framework of virtuous living where "virtue can be taught" and the "discipline for teaching it embraces both science and conscience, knowledge and consciousness, a consciousness inseparable from the responsibility of governing the polity."⁷ Obenga writes:

> Egyptian morality lacks neither high purpose nor nobility. It is a moral system which . . . aimed at shaping the good [person]. . . . It was a practical morality, or to be more precise, an "eclectic morality." It began by recognizing responsibility, then moved on to offer the training required to fulfill it. Its goal was the strict duty of living in tune with *Maât*. . . . Egyptian morality was . . . civil and secular, profoundly focused on the life of the community. Its moral foundation, of course, was an imperative law, that of *Maât*, Truth-Justice. *Maât*, a transcendental law, also taught human beings, in practical terms, how to live as dutiful members of their communities, how to assume future political and administrative responsibilities, how, in short, to behave as social beings.⁸

As such, those who aspire to be attuned with *maât* are vocationally accountable and responsible to community—and, more precisely, a community of right order.

If *maât* (as concept and applied principle) begins with a framework of community, my primordial premise is that gender diverse and sexually diverse Afrodiasporic communities (co)exist within broader cultural community contexts. Gender variance and sexual diversity are givens in all cultures—even nonhuman cultures. However, this diversity has historically been used as leverage—intraculturally and interculturally—for establishing and maintaining hegemonic power. If, instead, a community of right order built on the premise that empirical (i.e., what is) gender-sexual diversities are also normative (i.e., what should be) gender-sexual diversities—there would be provisions at every level and in every context for the fact of such diversities. Thus, the question this project seeks to answer with respect to *maât* is not simply about what *maât* is, but what *maât* is in a queering project. And, more precisely: What is *maât* in a quareing project—a quareing project as one that begins with the celebrated fact of melanin, gender, and sexual diversity? So what distinguishes a quare approach from a queer approach? While a queer understanding of *maât* might emphasize theories and practices of gender-sexual conscious justice, a quare understanding of *maât* might draw from the lived experiences of those who honored and practiced *maât*. In this quare (read: already womanist, vindicationist, *and* Blackqueer) spirit, I invoke Hatshepsut, the woman pharaoh who reigned from 1473 to 1458 BCE, adopted *maât* in the title she took upon her coronation, and disrupted the theological order by situating Amun as one who upholds and answers to Maât.[9] Obenga further explains *maât* in this way: "On the universal level, the concept of *Maât* 'expresses the harmony of the elements as clearly established each in its right place.' This is the concept of the ordered Whole, the cosmos." *Maât* operates on universal, political, and individual levels and is "order, harmony, and supreme wellbeing."[10] In this way, Maât invites those who would learn of her—and apply the principles she is and represents—to everyday life in community, to harmonious and holistic order through complementary balance. This suggests that we all have roles to play, cosmic assignments to fulfill—and that, although we may have individuated responsibilities as we play our roles and fulfill our assignments, these responsibilities are not discrete. Our roles and assignments are acted out in relationship with others and the roles and assignments of others. Collectively, Maât invites us to cooperative complementarity. In a queering project, readers might get squeamish with worry that calls for complementarity might lean into inversion theories' traps of dualistic, cisgender-reifying, heteronormativities. After all, Maât is reputed to have been Djehuty's consort—and pharaohs who invoked Maât modeled their sexual praxes according to the drive to produce a viable male offspring by any means necessary.[11] In this quareing project, however, there are other expressions of Maât's complementarity. In new and quare ways, Hatshepsut puts Maât on the sociopolitical, geographical, and moral map. Hatshepsut was a pharaoh who thought, felt, and acted—and sometimes acted up; a pharaoh who loved her culture and community and oriented herself with respect to gender and sexuality in ways that stabilized and promoted the social organization and governance that were the bedrock of her culture and community.[12] She cultivated and sustained balance insofar as she leaned into a path that was "odd or slightly off kilter." "On the political level," Obenga notes, "the concept of *Maât* works against injustice. It is in the name of *Maât* that the pharaoh subjugates rebels and dominates foreign lands."[13] Queerly, Maât offers the pink-washing language and persona of a flailing—though, by some measures, sexually liberated and aesthetically robust—monarchy. Quarely, for Hatshepsut, the concept, *maât*, and name of Maât are deployed for shade throwing and gender role disruption that challenge the unequivocal inevitability of male leadership. Building on Michel Gitton's work, Obenga notes that "on the individual level, '*Maât* embraces specific rules for living in concert with moral principles.' Whoever lives according to these rules and principles achieves universal order in his or her own life, in practical terms, and lives in harmony with the ordered Whole."[14] Queerly, there is virtue in what others may deem too marginal. Quarely, the pageantry of the stage together with the practice and performance of religious, social, and physical rituals becomes the bedrock for claims of moral agency and political potency in the persona of Hatshepsut. She plays by the rules, acting in the play of pharaonic regency; through her diligence, she establishes balance. As Obenga explains of pharaonic inscriptions, "The most accomplished, useful and appropriate human actions are circumscribed in the cosmological order, as symbolized by the way the pharaoh's name is written inside a circular cartouche, a perfect geometrical shape representing the vitalizing sun."[15] And for Hatshepsut, suspected of having a long-term affair with one of her male architects after the death of her husband-brother, *quare* may not be found in queer sexual acts characterized by sexual desire for one's own gender but rather is circumscribed in her cartouche through which Hatshepsut lays claim on Maât—and claims Maât has laid a claim on her—as she has become. And is it not also quare that Hatshepsut and Amun's priests in her day declare Hatshepsut as the offspring of Amun and her earthly mother and that Hapshepsut is "Maatkare (The Soul of Re Is Truth)" (i.e., Hatshepsut's self-selected throne name)?[16]

Maât as a concept is distinct from, but also comparable to, the idea of justice that has been inherited from "the Homeric Greek concept of *dike*." As Maulana Karenga puts it, *dike* is similar to *maât* "'insofar as it functions as a regulating force of the natural order.' But it differs from Maat in that it is a fatalistic, restrictive and 'negative force, one that prevents change or development and holds the cosmos in a static situation.' *Dike* also contrasts with Maat as a 'positive moral force working to right wrongs and to maintain a moral order.' *Dike* was originally amoral and developed later with essentially the role of punishment."[17] And the images of justice do make a difference. Consider justice as the blindfolded woman with scales—and the history of this image. Interestingly, the blindfold was not always a part of the image of "lady justice." It seems that her blindfold appeared in time to keep her from seeing much of the transatlantic slave trade.[18] In *More Beautiful and More Terrible: The Embrace and Transcendence of Racial Inequality in the United States*, Imani Perry quotes Langston Hughes's poem "Justice":

> That Justice is a blind goddess
> Is a thing to which we blacks are wise.

> Her bandage hides two festering sores
> That once perhaps were eyes.[19]

Even as the "blind goddess" does, so too the image of Maât—with her outstretched wings and decisive feather—transforms the experience of justice. Maât opens new quare-womanist-vindicationist possibilities for this research because her impact is multidimensional, and she offers relevant guidance for discerning and embodying right order. Maât is a hermeneutic (of) justice: interpreting right order according to the gravity of cultural context and the mass (or energy) of the heart.[20] Maât is performative justice: visually rendered and embodied in ways that evoke action, movement, and multiplicity. Maât is constructive justice: the companion of counsel to the wise, the offering of the righteous for the sake of social order, to the glory of the Divine, and in the name of eternal posterity. Maât's right order is balance.[21] Too, Maât's right order is a balance of interpretation, action, and creation.

Movements with Maât: Chapter Outlines

Having introduced Maât and the potential of a Maâtian theorization of justice as the foundation for a new direction in Black sexual ethics, *Black, Quare, and Then to Where* opens with part I, "Quare-Womanist-Vindicationist Movement." The chapters in this first part of the book provide descriptions of, definitions for, and connections between quare, womanist, and vindicationist. These first two chapters, chapter 1, "A Prolegomenon to Justice Hermeneutics and Black Sexual Ethics," and chapter 2, "Naming (and Transforming) Justice: (Re)Imagining Black Sexual Ethics," frame these connected terms of the discourse and situate them in relation to three other key conceptual categories—justice being the most significant, alongside politics and physics. Part II, "Justices," explores various doings and beings, theorizings and practicings of justices. The chapters in this section are 3, "Flying Justice: Sun Ra's ~~Sexuality~~ and Other Afrofutures"; 4, "Heterexpectations: Jumping the Broom, Marriage, Democracy, and Entanglement Theory"; 5, "Dancing Justice: Just Black HomoSexualities"; 6, "Ancient Mixologies: Joel Augustus Rogers and Puzzling Interracial Intimacies"; 7, "Black Web: Disrupting Transnational Pornographies for Post(trans)national Humanalities"; and "Conclusion: Re-Covering Maât." Each chapter in part II of *Black, Quare, and Then to Where* moves with Maât and *maât* (i.e., justice/s) in different ways. However, each of these chapters consistently integrates an intersection of Black sexual lives and experiences, vindicationist voices, the political implications of this analysis of Black sexual ethics as it reorients justice, a scientific connection that can be made through the study of physics, and a way that these elements altogether might change the thinking-doing-being of *maât* (i.e., justice/s).

Chapter 1 introduces womanist, quare, vindicationist, Black, Black religion, and physics as co-constitutive terms of discourse in this book. Interlocutors in this chapter include Alice Walker, E. Patrick Johnson, W. E. B. Du Bois, Charles H. Long, Barbara Holmes, and Chanda Prescod-Weinstein. The close relationship between womanist and quare (as its heir)—as well as their rootedness in Blackness, religion, and physics suggests that quare theory and praxis may be an important foundation for contemporary theories of justice dedicated to Black futures. Maât is a critical aspect of vindicationist histories—redactions of which are promising for a fresh perspective on Black sexual ethics. The groundwork is laid for how justice performs and is performed as a wonder of physics, religion, Blackness, sexuality, and gender.

Chapter 2 presents and evaluates various theories of justice—and approaches to (doing) justice. The themes of quare, womanist, and religion are more tightly woven and threaded through the needle of justice. Acknowledging the vindicationist voices of Yosef Ben-Jochannan, John Henrik Clarke, and Frances Cress Welsing—and tempering these voices with that of Cheikh Anta Diop—this chapter disrupts heteropatriarchal trends in traditional vindicationist approaches. Diop's appeal to "sovereign experience"—and its complementarity with the womanist imperative that situates Black women's experiences as the primordial noetic sources—is explained. Through a reoriented vindicationist appeal to Maât, possibilities for justices are imagined and given new theoretical and practical life. Maât is reconsidered in terms of what she actively, presently does (personified and as a concept)—and what it means for those who pursue a righteous path to do *maât*.

Chapter 3 takes up ~~sexuality~~ as an aspect of Black sexuality and the musician Sun Ra as a primary vindicationist voice for this discourse. I introduce the term ~~*sexuality*~~ as a way of signifying both the tranversing and transcending of sexuality that is characteristic of Sun Ra and others who understand their vocational paths to include chosen celibacy, induced or natural asexuality, and variations of gray asexuality.[22] Sun Ra's voice is supplemented with some of the writings of Cheikh Anta Diop, Ayi Kwei Armah, and Théophile Obenga. With Sun Ra, born of Saturn, the chapter considers the role of order in black holes as a way of helping to think about political organization and democracy in extraterrestrial terms. Cosmic order, movement, and contents are aspects of physics that intrigued Sun Ra and inform the possibilities this chapter imagines for flying justice.

Chapter 4 takes up marriage as a site for Black sexual expression and engages the vindicationist voice of Frances Cress Welsing. This chapter explores the fluidity of entanglements that characterized the lives of enslaved people of African descent in the United States. The impossibility of marriage for so many—or the ritualized reduction of marriage to broom jumping—is evaluated as a parallel to the impossibility of (full) democratic citizenship for people of African descent. The institution of marriage is considered as a "heterexpectation" that becomes the foundation of the nation-state.[23] Entanglement theory gives spring, bounce, and direction to the possibilities of jumping justice.

Chapter 5 takes homosexualities, explicitly quare sexualities, and post-heterosexualities in Afrodiasporic experience as its point of departure. With an emphasis on Black churches as primary sites of moral formation and implicitly and explicitly specified sexual ethics, this chapter reviews some of the recent work of the artist Joseph Lamar. Joseph's contemporary vindicationism complements the earlier vindicationist voices of George G. M. James and Aimé Césaire. This chapter gestures toward the ways that Black churches' (mis)handlings of sexualities, in general, and homosexualities, in particular, create stressful conditions of intrainstitutional politics and compromise the relevance of these churches to broader national and transnational political contexts. This chapter imagines individual and collective moral agents who dare to say: I do not just want to participate in "the power," I want to transform it. The relationship between classical and quantum mechanics is invoked and evaluated with new rhythms of dancing justice.

Chapter 6 listens for the vindicationist voice of Joel Augustus Rogers in thinking about interracial intimacies and racially hybrid identities. The voice of Frantz Fanon is also introduced as a vindicationist interlocutor through the lineage of Négritude. Linking antebellum interracial violences with the evolution of the carceral state, this chapter pushes back against Rogers's defense of interracial intimacies with an acknowledgment of the ways that sexual violence and "systemic sexual surveillance" have been pillars of white supremacy and white heteropatriarchal expressions of hegemony. Anarchy is presented as an incomplete, but relevant (and potentially necessary) political rejoinder to contemporary US governance that renders democracy perennially anemic. Anarchy signifies a tragic hybridity—and, perhaps, hybridity calls forth a tragic anarchy—neither of which can get a handle on justice completely. The complexities of electromagnetism help convey puzzling justice.

Chapter 7 takes a close look at pornography and, to an extent, sex work in the lives and experiences of Afrodiasporic people. Being and coding justice becomes a way of thinking about globalization, transnational discourses, and the need for post(trans)national discourses. A *dunia* terraspheric orientation enables fresh imagination about how to be moral, how to be human, and how to think, talk, and be about the metaphorical and physical resolutions of "tantalizing tensions."[24] Through his narrative research approach to Maât, notwithstanding the deeply disturbing accounts of his sexual history, Karenga provides a foundational vindicationist voice for this chapter because of his unparalleled study of Maât.[25] The philosophical work of Sylvia Wynter provides a foil for Karenga's vindicationist approach, extending the spirit of Négritude. Together, Karenga's emphasis on Maât and Wynter's humanism recode and ontologize justice/s.

A layered conceptual approach that expands the applications of Kimberlé Crenshaw's intersectionality far beyond critical race theory and Hortense Spillers's interstices far beyond the discipline of English and "Papa's Maybe" informs the analysis presented in this book.[26] Attention to categories of race, class, gender, sexuality, capital, empire, and domination are fundamental to the work of cultural and religious institutional critique; *Black, Quare, and Then to Where* endeavors to critically apply these categories to cultural and religious institutional spaces with balance. The political implications of such critique are dramatic challenges to the very organizational structures of governance in specifically secular and religious spaces.

This book is for students, scholars, and researchers of Black religion interested in more thoroughly destabilizing occidentalism and reclaiming Egyptian vindicationist contributions. This book is for Black church members and leaders who are interested in discerning ways to pursue sexual holiness while dropping sexual piety, false modesties, and hypocrisies, who are interested in being politically (terraspherically/*dunia*) relevant, and who are interested in cultivating actualized and whole conspirators for justice/s. This book is for Black sexual beings who want to do justice/s both in the streets and in the bed (i.e., sex, sexual intimacies, and relationships). This book is written for theorists of justice who are unashamed to prioritize Black outcomes and impacts as a first concern for theories of justice—and who recognize the value of doing this. This book is also for theorists of justice who are able and willing to identify and respond to epistemic and material spaces of great(est) human contribution and vulnerability (i.e., sex). This book is written for other leaders of religious and academic institutions who are invested in disruptions of fundamentalisms. Above all, this book is written for people who love Afrodiasporic people and culture in ways eternal, unconditional, and beyond words. If any or all of these audience descriptions include you, know that I am writing to you. This book should empower you to cultivate and express moral constellations and sexual ethics. These constellations and ethics should be (1) liberative, (2) epistemologically shrewd, and (3) true (in a *maâtian* sense). Thus empowered, you can redefine justice/s such that our transformed theories of justice/s reflect (1) cultural context, (2) personal and collective inspiration and complementarity, (3) postconservativism, and (4) dynamism with perpetual maintenance.

(And Then) To Where?

Maâtian justice/s are doing and being a lot here. And, frankly, Maât is neither top nor bottom, but versatile as she, too, is doing and done to, and regards the equitable beings and doings of others. Maâtian ethics as they are presented in this book on theories of justice and Black sexual ethics are altogether quare. Quare justice/s may have grammar, vernacular, and code, but they are also switching as needed for the dignity of the persons and communities sheltered in the shadow of Maâtian wings. José Esteban Muñoz speaks of queer theory and queer identity as fundamentally futuristic. It releases the "here and now" and focuses with intention, devotion, and perseverance on the "then and there."[27] Unlike a Moltmannian Christianity, there is no preoccupation with the "already" that is "not yet."[28] There is only and always a steady gaze on the future. In concert with the wisdom of ancient Egypt, this is a focus on "the rising sun," the "new day begun," and the ultimate sign of eternity.[29] This is the "morning by morning new mercies we see."[30] A quare Maâtian utopia is always on the horizon as the dynamism and maintenance of justice/s are honored—and blackqueerness and queerblackness, quareness, and Blackness and queerness "keep on keepin' on" in fantastically transformative style.[31]

Where this text takes us is not about geographic location. This book has a moral destination. This book is not about diverse Black sexualities uncovered and legitimized as much as it is about how we name, tell the truth about, and

I.2: This photograph taken on August 7, 2021, at the Temple of Seti I depicts a common representation of Maât. Maât is in the hands of a royal person, in this case Seti I, for whose honor the temple was built; Seti I is offering Maât to Amun Ra. It is common for Maât to be depicted in the hands of pharaohs, queens, nobility, and others for whom these ancient artifacts were built. The offering of Maât reflects honorably on the one who offers her, the one to whom she is offered, and Maât (i.e., the offering) herself. The one who makes the offering is concerned with and committed to justice. The one who receives the offering is concerned with and committed to justice. Justice is a good in and of itself. This image is especially powerful because the kneeling Maât not only wears her iconic feather but also herself offers the only symbol (and principle) more substantive and prominent than she is with respect to morality and righteousness: the ankh, a symbol sometimes called the key of life, a testament to the connection between the Kushite sources of the Nile and the river that flows through Egypt, a tribute to the very heart of the human, the manna of everlasting life. *Source:* Photo by author.

honor our "sovereign experiences."[32] I am after a justice that takes "sovereign experiences"—especially the most intimate experiences of our sexual selves—as primary source material for theorizing about justice. When we acknowledge the most complex aspects of our sexual circumstances, we uncover implicit and explicit moral constellations and ethical codes. Our sexual ethics manifested in and through our sovereign experiences are not to be policed or baptized in a Christian wash of occidental Victorian bath salts. Politics of respectability are not for (all/any? of) us. Our sexual ethics manifested in and through our sovereign experiences teach us right from wrong, just from unjust, true from untrue, a light soul ready for eternity from a heavy soul that can bear existence no more.

Maât's measure is her own. Far be it from me to say how her feather handles the dust, the grime, the stickiness, the excretions of hybridities born of oppression. I cannot know how her feather manages the matter of equity in unequal and inequitable circumstances. It is clear, however, that Maât's feather does imply that we each answer for ourselves—and that we must be preparing and prepared to do so. Maât's truth does imply that the answers our lives yield personally are inextricably linked with how we show/ed up in community. Maât invites us to watch and guard and take care with respect to our moral consumptions.

The work of Maât in each of us who accepts our role and responsibility as a moral agent is a new balance. For those of us who continue to research, write, learn, and teach: it is the responsibility of the Western academy to stop lying about its roots and to acknowledge the lies that are at the core of its roots. We must be on task, assuring a reorientation—and, perhaps, multiplication—of epistemic center/s. For those of us working out our soul's salvation (also as sexual beings) in religious and secular institutions, variously interested in the existence of Afrodiasporic people: Maât invites us to lay aside the shame that does not register on her balance. For those of us recovering from our judgmentalism and learning to love a fuller version of our Afrodiasporic sexual selves: Maât invites us to concentrate on our own sexual and relational health and to discern ways that we, ourselves are and should be accountable as sexual and relational beings in community.

Instead of writing of justice, *Black, Quare, and Then to Where* speaks of justices. It is so that there are higher justices to which this project appeals—justices that can be arranged in relation to one another, contingent upon particular contexts and conditions. Unlike offensive rankings of oppression, certain appeals to certain forms of justice attain more than and/or in ways that others do not. This book takes up the question of how the priority of some justices vis-à-vis other justices might be adjudicated. Not all justices, not all claims to justice, not all appeals to justice are (created) equal. For those of us who carry the revolutionary spirit of forerunners like Malcolm X who insisted that our justice be realized "by any means necessary," Maât adds "for as long as necessary."[33] She tells us that we must continue to assert our dignity. Truth and justice/s begin with the integrity of our being, our personhood, and our communities that affirm our being and our personhood.

quare-womanist-vindicationist **movement**

Part I

A Prolegomenon to Justice Hermeneutics and Black Sexual Ethics

Womanist is to feminist as purple is to lavender.
—Alice Walker, *In Search of Our Mothers' Gardens*

Quare is to queer as "reading" is to "throwing shade."
—E. Patrick Johnson, "'Quare' Studies, or (Almost) Everything I Know about Queer Studies I Learned from My Grandmother"

And womanist is to feminist as quare is to queer. As such, quare—like womanist—is a space-time discursive and practical possibility, a line of patches in a quilt, on a spectral journey of justice—especially as it pertains to race, class, gender, and sexuality. The working of justice, the justicing of justice/s, begins with the agentive works of naming. In her essay "Gifts of Power: The Writings of Rebecca Jackson," Alice Walker makes it plain that she is "questioning . . . a nonblack scholar's attempt to label something lesbian that the black woman in question has not."[1] Walker writes, "I simply feel that naming our own experience after our own fashion (as well as rejecting whatever does not seem to suit) is the least we can do—and in this society may well be our only tangible sign of personal freedom."[2] If nothing else, Walker signals a right to self-naming (and to describe one's own existential predicaments) as a minimal self-determinative act. Situating *womanist* relative to *lesbian* here, she writes:

> The word "lesbian" may not, in any case, be suitable (or comfortable) for black women, who surely would have begun their woman-bonding earlier than Sappho's residency on the Isle of Lesbos. Indeed, I can imagine black women who love women (sexually or not) hardly thinking of what Greeks were doing; but, instead, referring to themselves as "whole" women, from "wholly" or "holy." Or as "round" women—women who love other women, yes, but women who also have concern, in a culture that oppresses all black people (and this would go back very far), for their fathers, brothers, and sons, no matter how they feel about them as males. My own term for such women would be "womanist." At any rate, the word they chose would have to be both spiritual and concrete and it would have to be organic, characteristic, not simply applied. A word that said more than that they choose women over men. More than that they choose to live separate from men. In fact, to be consistent with black cultural values (which, whatever their shortcomings, still have considerable worth) it would have to be a word that affirmed connectedness to the entire community and the world, rather than separation, regardless of who worked and slept with whom. All things considered, the main problem with Lesbos as a point of common reference for women who love women is not, as I had once thought, that it was inhabited by Greek women whose servants, like their culture, were probably stolen from Egypt, but that it is an island. The symbolism of this, for a black person, is far from positive.[3]

Black, Quare, and Then to Where is about naming. Yes, this book is about naming as a primordial transformative work of justice—as it was also in my sermon series.[4] The workings and doings of justice/s in Black existential space-time is always quintessentially self-determinative work. A most tragic aspect of antiBlack terror is the stripping of Black sexualities and spiritualities as conceptual landscapes for self-determinative naming. Black sexualities and spiritualities thus become "strange fruit" ripe for the transformation of resurrection by a new name. Quare is such a name. Like womanist, quare is a name I choose. Quare is a name I invite others to choose with me.

As a womanist conversation that addresses all the things boldly and frankly in a Blackwoman, Blackqueer way, *Black, Quare, and Then to Where* presents a multidirectional critique of Black religious institutions and contemporary US culture from inside and outside of those social locations. Not only does this book present a Blackwoman, Blackqueer discursive way, it also presents a Blackwoman, Blackqueer discursive content. Specifically, this book asks and answers the following questions: How does reading Black sexual ethics and theories of justice as inseparable threads in the lives of Black people in the United States from a quare (i.e., Blackqueer-womanist-vindicationist) ethical perspective transform these threads, liberating Black sexuality and justice alike? Beneath this question are these underlying questions: What are the empirical and normative theories of justice that have operated in Black religious institutions and popular US culture, respectively? What are the empirical and normative Black sexual ethics that have operated in Black religious institutions and popular US culture?[5] What are the politics that attend to such discourse and praxis? How do these threads of Black sexual ethics and theories of justice shape space-time quanta and continua/spectra—or the gravity with which space-time remains in conversation?

Furthermore, this book offers ways forward for those committed to the heart and soul of Blackness through spiritual rootedness, moral integrity, geographic flexibility, and sexual freedom. *Black, Quare, and Then to Where* is for those haunted by a "politics of respectability" and on a lifelong quest to discern, embody, and promote an effective "politics of deviance" that dismantles the intersecting evils that populate the "fantastic hegemonic imagination."[6]

There are spectra of meanings that terms like *Black* or *queer* signify. The tasks at hand are acknowledging the intersecting and layered discursive spectra in play, acknowledging the movements along those spectra, and moving from point to point on the spectra. There are ways that spectra of Black have attempted to hold spectra of queer at bay—as we saw in the responses of my congregation even to the announcement of my sermon series. However, there has always been some Black in queer and some queer in Black (and quare is but one indicator of this). While acknowledging this may seem conceptually recent, as with the fashionability of Black (and quare), quare is not the last of the new (and acknowledged) categorized diversities that exist in spectra of Blackness. Likewise, quare is not the last expansive stop for queer.[7] Quare (and queer) are places on (i.e., spans of) womanist spectra too—as Black (and womanist) are on spectra of quare (and queer), and quare (queer) and womanist are on spectra of Black. Taking Black, womanist, and quare together—and considering their movements and significance in the lives of people of African descent in the United States, "quareing justice" emerges as a different account of Black and womanist terra-story.[8] What is it to quare justice? It is awakening visions and expressions of justice that insert off-kilter blue notes, troubling epistemological and ontological certainties or arrogances (a) with primary perspectival regard for the subjectivity of LGBTQ persons of color who love other people and appreciate Black culture and community, (b) in ways that are holistically committed to struggles against all oppression, (c) organically connecting spirituality, gender, sexuality, race, class, age, ability, region, and all points of intersection between social identity and power, (d) and engaging *deeply*.[9] Quareing justice happens through readings of Maât and translations and interpretations of khemetic literature. Justices quared present expressions of Black sexuality through futurized Maâtian eyes—assessing the ethical dimensions of ~~sexuality~~, heterexpectations and marriage, interracial sexual intimacies, homosexualities, and pornographies.

Map Key: Discursive Terms

I begin with expanded definitions of Black, womanist, quare, vindicationist, politics, and physics to establish a common sense of the terms of this discourse and its trajectory.[10] These terms constitute the conceptual threads woven together throughout the chapters of this book. Moreover, I offer a womanist Black queer (i.e., quare) way of being, thinking, and doing in ways that are spiritually mindful, concerned with the religious, and hold the sacred in highest regard. Blackness has always been a religious subject.[11] Religion has always been a Black subject—though we must acknowledge the ways in which Black people have been the implicit and explicit colonized subjects of religion.[12] Quare qua womanist—and womanist qua quare—come into focus through evolutions of Blackness. Vindicationists and their thought—which I present as a US-oriented expression of Negritude—are vehicles through which to think about the academic study of Blackness; they make a necessary connection between scholarship taking place within academic institutions and the streets, between discourses and praxes.[13] Politics are about the social relationships of people, the organizational patterns of human sociality, and how these patterns are governed. Physics is about the ways that matter acts in the cosmos and why it acts in the ways that it does. Maât, the *nṯrt* and symbol of justice, becomes a way of understanding justice and justices that organically connects these terms. And each of these terms is about relationship. They are all fundamentally relational terms, and an exploration of the relationships that exist within each of these terms and between each of these terms enables new possibilities for virtues of joy, reciprocity, mutuality, wholeness, purpose, and what Ayi Kwei Armah might call "the way" to be more fully manifest in the worlds that we inhabit (and the worlds that inhabit us). As these terms are considered together, we can see how gender identities, sexual orientations, political positionalities, and scientific references are mutually implicated.

Indeed, these are not the only mutually implicated categories, but this set reveals helpful bridges over the choppy waters of sexuality (and gender) under parallel, contiguous arcs that are often set against one another (e.g., culture [specifically politics] and science [specifically physics]). What makes sexuality such dicey terrain? There are many answers to this question, but one plausible response might be: the tension between the unambiguous universality of sexuality as the quintessential vehicle for transgenerational human existence (e.g., the chemical interaction of sexual organs or their contents) and a perennial ambivalence about the value and significance of human existence. Why focus on sexuality? Perhaps because, inevitably, sexuality applies to us all. Imani e Wilson notes: "Sexuality is a defining fact of life, central to our design as a species."[14] As such, anything that can be said about sexuality in theory navigates through "lived sexualities, ethical questions and answers, [and] intimacies"—"crawling back" over diverse cartographic terrains to the very existential praxes of humanity.[15]

Black is a term that is used to refer to people of African descent and Afrodiasporic people. Black (and Blackness) are historic, linguistic, and psychological—and therefore also cultural.[16] I offer *Black* as a self-determined term of racial recognition and of pride. It is a conscientious appeal to the power, moral agency, and value of Blackness, notwithstanding the ways that consciously and unconsciously antiBlack people use *Black* as a racial and moral putdown against people of African descent. *Black* is a term that has cultural fluidity, the currency of which shifts in different cultural contexts, in Britain at times including all people of color (not just people of African descent) and excluding "colored" people (often distinguished both by their mixed-race appearance and Afrikaans as their mother tongue) in South Africa. Black, in fashion, has also come to signify a permanent place of honor such that "the new Black" signifies the powerful advent of an indomitable style. The popularity of applications of this meaning (with the intended double entendre of race) birth such cultural gems as *Orange Is the New Black* or rhetorical questions such as "Is Queer the New Black?"[17] Unless otherwise indicated, throughout the book I use the term *Black* to signify people of African descent in the United States. However, I use it interchangeably

A Prolegomenon   21

with *Afrodiasporic* and *people of African descent* (again, based in the United States, unless otherwise noted).

Shifting from *Black* to quare, in his essay "'Quare' Studies," E. Patrick Johnson offers the following definition of quare:

> Quare: Quare (Kwâr)
>
> n. 1. Meaning queer; also, opp. of straight; odd or slightly off kilter; from the African American vernacular for queer; sometimes homophobic in usage, but always denotes excess incapable of being contained within conventional categories of being; curiously equivalent to the Anglo-Irish (and sometimes "Black" Irish) variant of queer, as in Brendan Behan's famous play, The Quare Fellow.
>
> —adj. 2. a lesbian, gay, bisexual, or transgendered person of color who loves other men or women, sexually or nonsexually, and appreciates black culture and community.
>
> —n. 3. one who thinks and feels and acts (and, sometimes, "acts up"); committed to struggle against all forms of oppression—racial, sexual, gender, class, religious, etc.
>
> —n. 4. one for whom sexual and gender identities always already intersect with racial subjectivity.
>
> 5. quare is to queer as "reading" is to "throwing shade."[18]

Johnson's definition makes direct reference to Alice Walker's 1983 definition of *womanist*, the form of which it also echoes:

1. From womanish (Opp. of "girlish," i.e., frivolous, irresponsible, not serious.) A black feminist or feminist of color. From the black folk expression of mothers to female children, "You acting womanish," i.e., like a woman. Usually referring to outrageous, audacious, courageous or willful behavior. Wanting to know more and in greater depth than is considered "good" for one. Interested in grown-up doings. Acting grown up. Being grown up. Interchangeable with another black folk expression: "You trying to be grown." Responsible. In charge. Serious.
2. Also: A woman who loves other women, sexually and/or nonsexually. Appreciates and prefers women's culture, women's emotional flexibility (values tears as natural counter-balance of laughter) and women's strength. Sometimes loves individual men, sexually and/or nonsexually. Committed to survival and wholeness of entire people, male and

female. Not a separatist, except periodically, for health. Traditionally universalist, as in: "Mamma, why are we brown, pink, and yellow, and our cousins are white, beige, and black?" Ans.: "Well, you know the colored race is just like a flower garden, with every color flower represented." Traditionally capable, as in: "Mamma, I'm walking to Canada and I'm taking you and a bunch of other slaves with me." Reply: "It wouldn't be the first time."
3. Loves music. Loves dance. Loves the moon. Loves the Spirit. Loves love and food and roundness. Loves struggle. Loves the Folk. Loves herself. Regardless.
4. Womanist is to feminist as purple is to lavender.[19]

Both of these definitions respond to the inadequacies of categories originally offered as radical and revolutionary correctives to hegemonic and conservative ideologies. Feminist (and feminism) emerge as correctives for sexist (and sexism). Queer emerges as a corrective for heterosexism (and surpasses gay, lesbian, bisexual, and transgender discourses). However, these categorical options—feminist/feminism and queer—are inadequate for addressing racial diversity in general, and the particularities of Black identities and experiences more specifically. Walker and Johnson carve out new definitions from the truths they experience, encounter, and perceive in their own communities. Quare is not just a Black version of queer any more than womanist is just a Black version of feminist. Quare and womanism are part of a vernacular of Black(ness). Quare and womanist/womanism are reflections of what we (Black people) do (and how we are) that feels unique to us and our experiences, that we do not perceive and experience when we are in other coded cultural spaces. And we can lean into not only quare's inherent Black(ness), but also its inherent womanism.

Concerns with Black experiences and their epistemic relevance are at the heart of vindicationist scholarship. In his book *Black Folk Here and There*, St. Clair Drake uses the term "vindicationist" to denote a "style of scholarship, variously expressed in such theoretical designations as Egyptology, Pan-Africanism, and Afrocentricity."[20] Ethicist Peter Paris, borrowing the "vindicationist" term from Drake, identifies "the vindicationist style" as "the predominant form of African and African American scholarship" since the mid-twentieth century.[21] Paris describes the vindicationist style: "This style aims at overturning the findings of all colonialist and racist scholarship by bringing an African and African American perspective to bear on its subject matter. The most distinguishing characteristic of this style is its search for an independent form of knowledge emanating from the African and African American historical perspective."[22] Paris contrasts this with what he calls the "traditional style," explaining, "In the traditional style various dimensions of African life (whether on the African continent or in the African diaspora) are subjected to the traditional methods of mainstream scholarship for the following reasons: (1) to demonstrate the many and varied commonalities between African and Caucasoid peoples by analyzing the nature of social and environmental forces and their determinative effects on the life-changes of human beings; (2) to make visible the many and varied cultural contributions African peoples have made to human civilization."[23] While Paris notes that there have been some, like W. E. B. Du Bois, who have employed both the traditional and vindicationist styles of scholarship, it is clear that the traditional style has largely prevailed in terms of academic reception and influence. The reasons for this are obvious.

Unapologetically focusing on vindicationist voices concerned with ancient Egypt and pairing this focus with an emphasis on womanist and quare methodologies, sources, and sensibilities, *Black, Quare, and Then to Where* presents a marginalized epistemological approach. In some ways, there is an irony in this endeavor: notwithstanding the whiff of essentialism and fundamentalism among some vindicationists, my project reclaims vindicationism as an important part of the constellation of beliefs and methodologies rightly subjected to the reasonable critiques of modern relativism.[24] No one may boast of objectivity and/or perfection. And no way of thought should be summarily dismissed without adequate engagement, attention, analysis, and critique. The commitment to retrieving a vindicationist perspective on theories of justice and Black sexual ethics is not a way of commending ancient Egyptian mores as superior. The commitment to retrieving a vindicationist perspective on theories of justice and Black sexual ethics is a way of expanding the data points relevant to the discernment, adjudication, and praxes of justice and Black sexual ethics. Ancient Egypt does not save the day; it is not an epistemic savior. After all, ancient Egyptian beliefs and culture are riddled with some of the same oligarchically set sexism, homophobia, and heterosexism that can be traced to and through other epistemic centers. Yet plumbing the depths of ancient Egyptian beliefs and culture, however, does help to broaden our perspective and approach. The very appeal to this horizon—this then and there—is a quareing of the subject of Black sexualities.[25] The primacy of Black women's voices and experiences throughout this project makes this a uniquely and distinctly vindicationist-womanist—and, subsequently, quare—project.

I argue that politics—from the Greek word *polis*, developed in Aristotle's *Politics* (Πολιτικά, *Politiká*), translated "affairs of the city"—is (broadly) about the organizational patterns and consequent governance of people. There are, of course, a variety of ways to think about politics beyond this simple definition. However, this definition suffices as a starting point for discussing the plethora of reasons for which those who might be included within or are otherwise interested in a "black intelligentsia" should be concerned with politics and with the political.[26] Yes, in 1967 Harold Cruse wrote of "unfinished business," decrying a "black bourgeoisie" that is "self-seeking but in a shortsighted, unsophisticated, unpolitical and cowardly fashion."[27] And in 1995 Manning Marable advocated a "transformationist" alternative— abandoning the dualistically opposed political frameworks of integration or separatism.[28] However, the contemporary political demands of the Black Lives Matter movement and of other racial justice organizers who situate themselves in the lineage that flows from the Civil Rights Movement and Stonewall through the Black Power movement carry these historic dilemmas with a revived juxtaposition of democracy and anarchy. And these modern Black politics are both proBlack and dedicated to dismantling all things anti-Black before all else. There is no regard for questions of democracy, anarchy, or any other strategy of sociopolitical organization that precedes this two-pronged concern. Politics must serve Blackness, Black people, and our best and ideal future—not the other way around.

Blackness and Black people do not have an identity outside of religion. I mean this in two senses. There is the sense in which religion as a category is being developed as conceptualizations of race and Blackness are taking shape; the formation of religion as a discipline is grounded in the transatlantic slave trade and all the tentacles and forms of colonization. Then there are the ways in which Blackness and Black people have integrated what has been categorized as religion and/or the religious for survival and flourishing. Whether or not we call "the way" religious, Black people have been adopting it in forms that would be categorized as religious in modern terms.[29] If, in these senses, Blackness and Black people do not have an identity outside of religion, then we also do not have an identity outside of politics. And as I present it, the juxtaposition of democracy and anarchy benefits from a moral, if not religious, lens, but these are not the starting points.[30] As Du Bois suggests, it is the sincerity of intracommunal Black religious experience that could yield to the political possibility of anarchy. And for Du Bois, the choice for people of African descent is between anarchy and hypocrisy (i.e., a form of opportunistic assimilationism). With respect to democracy, Du Bois is, at best, suspicious of its potential for Black people in the United States. He writes, "Deeply religious and intensely democratic as are the mass of the whites, they feel acutely the false position in which the Negro problems place them. Such an essentially honest-hearted and generous people cannot cite the caste-levelling precepts of Christianity, or believe in equality of opportunity for all men, without coming to feel more and more with each generation that the present drawing of the color-line is a flat contradiction to their beliefs and professions."[31] Democracy (coupled with a form of the religious) is the heritage of "the mass of the whites." The hope of democracy for Black people (as Du Bois puts it in *Souls of Black Folk*) is that the pejorative pathologizing of Black people is an inherently dissonant—read: (anti)Christian—Christian religiosity. Thus, the hope is not so much in the political priority, privilege, correctness, and supremacy of democracy as in what democracy can require of Christians and in what Christians should be demanding from democracy. So, Du Bois juxtaposes anarchy and hypocrisy (among Blacks) and democracy and (anti)Christian religiosity (among whites). However, the comparative analysis I offer is, perhaps, more modern and has yielded to the forces of popular social discourse: between anarchy and democracy. It is between Black Lives Matter activists and sympathizers who refuse the ballot as a viable form of social protest and transformation and advocate a deconstruction of existing political institutions and those who insist upon the ballot as one of the most important tools for justice and a reasonable form of social participation.

Terrence L. Johnson expands upon the Rawlsian notion that "politics is the engine of progress" in the quest for "social cooperation" rooted in "equal access to public rights and equal economic opportunity," suggesting that beyond a "focus on our political commitments" there is likely some value in turning "to religion to solve social crises."[32] At the very least, Johnson agrees with Martin Luther King Jr., whom he paraphrases: "a political vocabulary of rights and equality alone cannot legislate or create a just society."[33] When Johnson argues that "tragic soul-life is the story of how former slaves retrieved hope alongside suffering, death, and despair to achieve human fulfillment within the boundaries of an unjust society," he is pointing to the religious (as it is politically implicated and implicating) in general terms and to the precise theodically and existentially concerned nature of Black religion (such as it is). Here, hope and faith are the better angels of religion. This is a hypothesis that warrants testing. And just as Johnson demonstrates the ways that politics must include astuteness about the religious to be relevant in Black public spheres, Du Bois has first clarified that Black religion must be political for it to be positively relevant in the lives of Black people and communities. Du Bois writes, "But back of this still broods silently the deep religious feeling of the real Negro heart, the stirring, unguided might of powerful human souls who have lost the guiding star of the past and seek in the great night a new religious ideal. Some day the Awakening will come, when the pent-up vigor of ten million souls shall sweep irresistibly toward the Goal, out of the Valley of the Shadow of Death, where all that makes life worth living—Liberty, Justice, and Right—is marked 'For White People Only.'"[34] The souls of Black folk depend on the political direction of our religion. Through this book, I tease out what might constitute fruitful and healthy relationships between Black people and communities, religion, and politics, specifically as we affirm our diversities of sexual orientation and gender identity.

As I write about it, politics concerns the social formations and organizations of Black people. However, politics invites our consideration of the "affairs of the city" as well. I am not specifically interested in a focus on so-called urban spaces and the ways that Black people migrate to and from US and global metropolises. I am much more interested in the city as organized and organizing geographic space. In *Significations*, Charles Long evaluates Mircea Eliade's concept of "center as religious reality": "Accessibility to the center through the construction of domes, temples, and other architectural forms is given as evidence of the pervasive notion of centered existence as denoting the religiously real. Again, the prestige of the beginnings in Eliade's thought is predicated on his conception of the center as symbolizing the beginnings, representing the novelty of creation to a human community. In traditions emerging after the rise of cities, a return to the beginnings through cyclical rituals is at the same time a return to the center. The center for Eliade is the locus of revelation par excellence."[35] And Long accepts an "empirical historical verification to the religious meaning of the center," recalling that

> cited traditions begin as ceremonial centers which later develop into embryonic cities. It is not that ceremonial centers always develop into cities; it is simply that before there can be a city there must first be a ceremonial center. The ceremonial city is the symbol of the metaphysical notion of effective space. The discernment of the sacred in the ceremonial center is a recognition of a surplus of power (Eliade's kratophany), and from this

place power may be allocated. The power and prestige of the ceremonial center are transferred to the city, and thus the early, and for that matter all, cited traditions express centrifugal and centripetal dynamic forces; they tend to bring power into their centers and redistribute the power from the center. One might say that there tends to be an imperialistic principle inherent in even the earliest cited traditions.

This pattern may be observed in the economic, political, and military structures of cited traditions. It is equally documented in rituals and ceremonies. Social relationships are of a hierarchical nature in these traditions. The sedentary, agricultural, allocative, centripetal-centrifugal character of cited traditions stands in marked contrast to the nomadic egalitarian traditions of the hunters and gatherers of pre-cited cultures.[36]

Long continues:

It was in the context of a nonegalitarian cited tradition that the critique of myth in the classical Western tradition by Aristotle and Plato expressed a new meaning of the center as human reality. This critique, which generated the pervasive and persistent understanding of rationality, of the concept and the category, formed the epistemological structure of Western philosophical thought. It represented the meaning of rationality and logic, the possibility of a *common* mode of knowledge in all human knowing. This common mode, expressed through the form of an epistemological center, was correlative to an ordering of consciousness. It is highly significant that this order of the knowing faculty was formulated within the context of hierarchical cited traditions. It is presupposed in the mystery of the "other" to be known, which is at the heart of every problem of knowledge; yet it is equally presupposed that the issue of knowledge itself was part and parcel of a class structure and a privileged position, not only in regard to rationality but also and simultaneously in regard to sociological context. The criticism of myth in the classical Western tradition is at the same time the criticism of and the beginning of the deterioration of the city as center of a ceremonial order—an order that is homologous with cosmic and biological structures of nature. This development is the beginning of the institutionalization of a notion of the irrational.[37]

I quote Long at length because through this essay, "Human Centers: An Essay on Method in the History of Religions," in *Significations* he offers a definitive explanation of the relationship between religion and politics insofar as politics can be understood in terms of the affairs of the city. Cities have been established on ceremonially significant centers; city plans reflecting dynamic convergences and sprawls often reflect the centripetal-centrifugal sociopolitical power of these centers. Long also makes a critical connection between "the city" (with its implicit relationship to a center, centering, and centered reality) and others, "the opaque," and peripheries. The city is not just about space (and sacred space); it is also about knowledge and knowing, about people, and about hierarchy. As Long suggests, irrational ideas and people are those who do not fit neatly into the city/center. As a methodological organizing principle for space, time, being, and knowing, the city/center also contrasts with non-cited cultures. And the contrast is political—and not just in the sense of it being about cities or not about cities. Politically speaking, Long observes a contrast between "egalitarian" versus "nonegalitarian" organization. Egalitarian forms of human social life are less cited, less centralized, but not necessarily less sacred or relevant to the sacred. If we accept this claim, this simultaneously disrupts (the aspirations of) Western political structure (i.e., politics as city affairs) and belief systems (i.e., religion and its philosophical foundations).

For Long, I think it is also appropriate to acknowledge that the city is about physics. The city is about the relationship of matter in time and space. This, I think, is why Long writes of the "centrifugal and centripetal dynamic forces" and the "ceremonial order—an order that is homologous with cosmic and biological structures of nature." And herein lies a critical connection between physics, politics, and religion as I offer an approach to justices steeped in the complexities of Black genders and sexualities. What is being orbited is critical for Long. And as he elucidates the dispersed aspects of others, "the opaque," and peripheries before and as a result of the transatlantic slave trade and colonization, he is calling into question the ways we have thought about the orbits of which we are a part, whether these are city orbits or planetary orbits.[38]

When I write about physics as a scholar of religion, there is a temptation to direct this writing away from material concerns—and the matter of physics. To wrestle with topics of metaphysics—the first principles of things and abstract concepts such as space and time, being and knowing—would be unsurprising. However, connecting this research with a material regard for how Black people and communities organize and move ourselves, how we relate (sexually and otherwise) to ourselves and the physical world(s) around us, and how our material being impacts and is impacted by the pluriverse(s) or multiverse(s) of which we are a part is not only a distinct approach but also one that makes a case for applied physics as an additional analytical tool, mediator, and even layer of intersectional Black lives and living, oppression and identity. How we Black people, Black communities, and even Black scientists are thinking about quanta, gravity, entanglement, dark matter, orbits, chaos, electromagnetism, rare B-meson decays, and/or the relationship between quantum electrodynamics and quantum chromodynamics, and likewise what we think about these subjects matters. That we center ontological and material commitments to Black people and Black communities and our flourishing does not negate or diminish the quality and validity of our observations.

And when we do this, scholars like Barbara Holmes expand our conceptualizations of both physics and culture. In *Race and the Cosmos*, Holmes writes, "Social theorist Iris Marion Young sets forth five categories of oppression: exploitation, marginalization, powerlessness, cultural imperialism, and violence. I am adding my own category of cosmic myopia, which takes into account the influence of science on the discussion."[39] Holmes responds to Young's account of marginalization as a form of oppression, writing, "This is a familiar social description that does not take into account the scientific theory of omnicentricity that centers each living being. Margins aren't relevant concepts in this theory. Instead, each of us exists in a center or sphere of reference and relationships that cannot be redefined by systems of domination. Theologian C. S. Lewis agrees. 'There seems to be no plan because it is all plan: There seems to be no center because it is all center.' If we take the findings of quantum physics seriously, the language of marginalization and its effects will be discarded."[40] Again, pushing back on Young's categories of oppression, Holmes further explains her definition of "cosmic myopia" as a missing category of oppression: "I define this as an exclusive focus on closed social and religious systems that negate options for freedom and limit our awareness of intrinsic and cosmic connections. People who are conscious of their connections to the cosmos will not be deterred from full explorations of their gifts, because true liberation includes the ability to conceptualize freedom beyond social configurations. Although freedom is difficult to conceive or embrace when fixed determinatives predominate, quantum physics speaks in a very different way about location and determinism."[41] Holmes not only invites a move away from identity politics discourses through a departure from center-margin frameworks but also destabilizes the sacred, center, city as Long presents it. In so doing, she also challenges approaches to politics and religion correlated with the sacred, center, city. Moreover, Holmes models an alternative approach to cultural studies while presenting innovative, unusual, and new ways of thinking in physics—ways that assume countless worlds and orbits, ways that suggest that matter moving in space-time is likely tethered according to orbital dimensions and nuances that we may never be able to describe with complete accuracy.

But what is physics? It is "a science that deals with matter and energy and their interactions."[42] Physics, as a key discursive strand of this book, is incorporated as an extension of the work of Barbara Holmes, who integrates an analysis of race and the cosmos. Like Holmes, I seek to avoid "misappropriations" of science and "obsolescence"—and: "I hope that ordinary people like me will hear the powerful metaphors, symbols, and 'words of power' that emerge from physics and cosmology as a clarion call to broaden our thinking about origins, endings, and the process of moral fulfillment."[43] With Holmes, I also believe that the possibilities implicit in quantum physics point toward some of our most hopeful, fulfilling, and fulfilled cosmic and moral futures.

She explains the areas of classical physics that quantum physics transforms: "mechanics, which is the study of force and motion; electromagnetism, which focuses on the attributes of light; and thermodynamics, which focuses on energy, its change from one form to another, and the properties of heat." She notes that "each area of interest presumed cause-and-effect relationships in a deterministic model," but "the quantum world doesn't work in that way.... In the quantum world, electrons jump and leap without rhyme or reason and get more and more active if the space they are in diminishes.... Elements in the quantum world have a chaotic existence and can be said to be both here and there."[44] Grounding this book is both a curiosity about modern trajectories of physics like these that Holmes pointed out in 2002 and a recognition that discourses about people of African descent have always been physical grounds.

Before Black Lives Matter, Black people have mattered both in the sense of having significance and in the sense of being (Du Boisian) "problematic" material. And the problem of Black materiality in the latter sense has always been tethered to the problem of Black materiality in the former sense. Because of the "essential" features associated with Black (material) bodies as matter, these same bodies do not matter in terms of ontological (i.e., metaphysical, philosophical) significance. More precisely because of the significance ascribed to the "essential" features associated with Black (material) bodies as matter, Europeans and other complicit parties have been able to negate the ontological significance of Blackness (and Black people). What was the significance ascribed to Black (material) bodies? Their energy ... for physical labor. And if "work" can be understood in terms of a change in "energy," (i.e., $W = K_i - K_f$ or $W = \Delta K$), Black (material) bodies are ideal for work inasmuch as their energy seems (or is made to seem) endless, eternal, unextinguishable, inexhaustible, and impossible to deplete. Returning to the standard definition of Blackness: when Black bodily matter is assessed with respect to energy, the interaction between the two is reckoned invaluable, priceless. In terms of human potential, no combination has been more commodified or commodifiable. (Wait, you say: what of stereotypes about "lazy" Black people? These are a convenience for enterprising capitalists interested in maximizing this tried and proven Black potential, historically harnessed by the application of force. These are bad jokes to those who resist their own exploitation.) Black people, Black bodies, Black communities have often become a first-order physics problem that capitalist social systems must solve. Proactive, agentive approaches to physics, especially quantum physics, reveal new options, revelations, and opportunities for transformative resistance and creation for people of African descent.

Particle cosmologist and theoretical physicist Chanda Prescod-Weinstein—who is also a Black queer woman—describes the work of physicists. According to Prescod-Weinstein, physicists "study systems as they change in time and look for patterns or make predictions about patterns in their behavior."[45] Prescod-Weinstein explains:

> We used to think that absolute predictions could be made if we had sufficient information. One of the toughest lessons of the twentieth century was that this is not the case—our world is at base quantum physical in nature.
>
> For our purposes here, quantum physics (which physicists call "quantum mechanics") means that the fundamental properties of particles are such that we must now understand that each event in the universe is but one probability among others. Some events are more likely, but everything is possible. The probabilistic nature of quantum mechanics is particularly noticeable in the land of particle physics, where the fundamental objects are very small and more evidently governed by quantum rules. We can never really predict exactly what particles will do, but we can calculate the likelihood that something will happen and the timescale over which we expect it to occur. The quantum world of particles requires a kind of stretching of our scientific imagination into our scientific reality: things that do not seem intuitive are now what is real. The existence of any given object in our everyday life seems definitive, guaranteed. The table my feet

are resting on is there—except there's an incredibly small, almost zero probability that in a moment it won't be.[46]

In a sense, quantum physics offers a curving correction to the linearity of Newtonian physics that builds on Euclidean geometry. However, as Prescod-Weinstein demonstrates, this correction is not necessary when mathematics (and physics) begin with a "curvilinear" approach. She explains, "The Palikur people of the Amazon see it rather differently. Their geometric system, which more accurately describes the movement of stars across the night sky than the Euclidean one, is what we would call 'curvilinear.' Understanding stars moving across the sky requires a kind of intuition for curves—something that's hard to gain when you're always thinking in Euclidean terms. The Palikur system seems to train the mind to think in terms of curves from the very start, rather than using straight lines as a jumping-off point to curves."[47]

Prescod-Weinstein shows how space-time and matter manifest in ways that are rendered invisible not only because of our cultural points of origin but also because of cosmic (and physical) complexities. These complexities have a great deal to do with the uncertainties and infinite possibilities to which quantum mechanics points. Prescod-Weinstein writes:

> Raising questions about the supposedly intuitive, universal Euclidean geometry also leads me to wonder about the scientific presumption that time flows forward, uniformly and independent of observers. I promise, this is not a joke about CP time. But every person has their own internal clock, and our cultural contexts around the counting of time vary. The prevailing Western wisdom is that we individually and collectively typically experience time as a one-dimensional phenomenon that always moves forward. Yet the Maya had a concept of cyclical time, and this shouldn't be so counterintuitive for someone like me. I experience menstrual cycles that are roughly the length of a lunar month. As anyone who experiences menstrual cycles will know, they are rarely identical, either; as we get older, they change. When my cycle starts, it usually feels like time has rebooted, right back to the beginning all over again. And it is not just the same moment, but in the same place. Again, my uterine lining and blood are being shed through my vagina. Yet I also know that my body is aging forward in time, my eggs are getting older, and that with each period, I get closer to my last one. After my last one, my vagina will likely change. Do we really even perceive space and time as separate when we mark time by events that occur in locations? Blood flowing out of our vaginas—the

moon appearing to have a certain shape in the sky. Which sense of time is the correct one? The one that marches forward and never repeats, which seems to be organized around the universal guarantee of decay, or the one that centers and recognizes repetition?[48]

Yes, these could be read as materially reproductive applications of quantum physics. However, put differently: in this passage, Prescod-Weinstein evokes race, gender, and sexuality. Prescod-Weinstein helpfully notes, "the separation of space and time is a lie, even from the point of view of a clock."[49] And "spacetime tells matter how to move, and matter tells spacetime how to curve."[50] Prescod-Weinstein explains that Einstein's genius is traditionally understood in terms of his insight that "the speed of light implied radical new ways of looking at space and time, introducing the basis for arguing that space and time are in fact one four-dimensional phenomenon."[51] Yet Prescod-Weinstein also shows how Einstein's work—along with the work of others, including his wife—helps uncover yet another challenge beyond the four dimensions of "spacetime": gravity. Gravity centripetally pulls (more) matter into its path while spacetime manifests as a centrifugal haunting—revealing omnicentric, curvilinear epistemologies that deny a singular, teleological justice or way of being Black and sexual. The heavens (and earth) are telling of recalibrated theories of justices and Black sexual ethics. Here in the chapters that follow, justices begin with holistically engaged, integrative work. Primordial ways of being and doing—other (even African) indigenous approaches—can teach us at once about physics, sexual ethics, and justices.

Naming (and Transforming) Justice

2

(Re)Imagining Black Sexual Ethics

Justice holds us accountable to the demands of living in a community of responsibility and one that fosters self-worth and self-esteem for others and for itself.
—Emilie M. Townes, *In a Blaze of Glory*

Justice can be named and explained in many ways. With respect to Black sexual ethics, I offer two initial approaches to justice by way of introduction:

- Approach One: Black sexual ethics must complement working theories of justice in the lives of Black people.
- Approach Two: Working theories of justice must complement Black sexual ethics.

The first approach may strike us as more comfortable and familiar. However, the second approach has more quare potential.

The first approach centers justice and emphasizes its gravitational pull. If justice is at the heart of normative (i.e., ideal) moral reasoning and ethical interactions, then ways of being Black (and) with one another as materialized sexual beings (i.e., in our sexual orientations and gender identities) must answer to demands of justice. Justice is the standard. Our everyday lives—our moral reasoning and ethics in practice—must align with justice or what is just. We can acknowledge that there may be problems with the way we name what is just, and so justice may need to be transformed. We can acknowledge that there may be problems with the way we pursue what is just, and so we may need to reimagine how we arrive at what is just (or apply our moral reasoning). This approach suggests that we first set a standard and then (aspire to) live (up to) it. This seems innocuous enough. However, this approach also suggests that a standard can be set in an a priori, supposedly neutral and/or objective way. This is rarely innocuous and indeed often deliberately shows preference to one group over another.

The second approach assumes that there are just Black sexual ethics already being practiced. The second approach suggests that justice can (and, perhaps, should) align with the ways that Black sexual ethics are playing out (in just ways) in everyday life. For sure, there are countless ways that sexual immorality, abuses, and unethical behaviors are expressed among Black people and in Black communities. While I name some of these terrors, I am also concerned with what Black ways of being (and ways of being Black) with respect to gender and sexuality are already manifesting as justice/s. There are Black ways of being (ethical) with respect to gender and sexuality that can (re)teach and transform justices. There are *alreadies* and *not yets*. The strength and the weakness of this approach are the same: the approach is subjective.

However, such subjectivity is essential. It is, in fact, advisable. This subjectivity is a concern with the particular and particularity. Too often quare subjects or people are rendered inherently unethical and/or immoral—especially with respect to sexuality and sexual ethics. Quare is an erased particularity, especially within Black life. This subjectivity, however, is rooted in "sovereign experience."[1] The "counter-normalizing" and, consequently, normative (i.e., ideal) potential of the empirical (i.e., actual, everyday, lived) experience of quare or "black queer" people is fundamentally grounded in the subjectivity of "sovereign experience." Thelathia Nikki Young makes a strong case for this: "I argue that black queer people practice disruption as we critically reflect upon, narrate, and subsequently construct our own ideas and implementations of family. I argue further that processes of normalization, through which we have established norms of race, gender, and sexuality to govern ideas of family, ought to be fully engaged, re-thought, and re-acted to make space for new, irruptive norms to exist in families. These new norms exist as products of counter-normalization that queer the concept of normality and make space for unknown potentialities."[2] Young describes this work of dismantling reflection and narration followed by (counter)normalizing construction as "disruption-irruption," writing, "The dually operating strategy, of disruption-irruption comprises two dynamically interacting elements. The first element is rational and deconstructive, as it works to destabilize and dismantle norms and the technologies and disciplines that stabilize them. The second element is nonrational and constructive, as it reappropriates components of norms and reconceptualizes norms in general."[3] It is true, the empirical and the normative do not and will not always align. However, emphasis on what is right, what works within the empirical experiences of Black queer people, can reveal an alternative and/or multiplying "center" around which justices can reorient themselves. There are already Black familial spaces of "*accountability, accommodation,* and *innovation.*"[4] The creative and transformative spaces of irruption can include various arts of resistance—including deviance.[5] Through strategic intentional, inspired, improvisational, and/or impulsive responses to the disruption of primary and secondary forms of marginalization, irruption occurs.[6] Such irruption can be observed in some of the transformative social acumen and trendsetting artistic gifts of quare people in community.[7]

Womanist ethics also begins with sovereign experience and, namely, the sovereign experiences of Black women.[8] In *Womanist Ethics and the Cultural Production of Evil*, Emilie M. Townes explains a way in which womanism privileges the particular in its approach:

> The womanist dancing mind ... has before it an enormous intracommunal task. One in which we are trying to understand the assortments of African American life. If I do this task well, I will realize the ways in which Black life is not my life alone, but a compendium of conscious and unconscious coalitions with others whose lives are not lives solely in the Black face of United States life.... It is ... in taking seriously my particularity—not as a form of essentialism, but as epistemology—[that] I can meet and greet others for we are intricately and intimately interwoven in our postmodern culture.[9]

Townes recommends the cultivation of countermemory to follow the justice work of dismantling evil. Through countermemory, she reconnects particularity with "the universal": "Countermemory begins with the particular to move into the universal and it looks to the past for microhistories to force a reconsideration of flawed (incomplete or vastly circumscribed) histories."[10] And it is here—with "disruption-irruption" and countermemory—that *Black, Quare, and Then to Where* picks up and carries forward a thread of womanism. The dismantling work of reflection and narration flows into the constructive work of countermemory and counternormalization. Specifically, this book turns to the particular, the microhistories, the counternormalizing possibilities of justice/s through the Maât of ancient Egypt. And we can (re)-assess the universalizability of a way of theorizing justice—if not a theory of justice/s—once we have reconsidered the particularity Black sexual ethics expressed in the fullness of our gender and sexual diversities.

In her 1996 essay "What's in a Name? Womanism, Black Feminism, and Beyond," Patricia Hill Collins offers the following critique of womanism as Alice Walker defines it: "Walker's definition thus manages to invoke three important yet contradictory philosophies that frame black social and political thought, namely, black nationalism via her claims of black women's moral and epistemological superiority via suffering under racial and gender oppression, pluralism via the cultural integrity provided by the metaphor of the garden, and integration/assimilation via her claims that black women are 'traditionally universalist' (Van Deburg 1992)."[11] While this is not the only critique of womanism Collins offers, this critique is important to the work of *Black, Quare, and Then to Where* insofar as Collins identifies the centralization of Black women's experiences within womanism as a part of its philosophical "black nationalism." I reject this part of her critique on two counts: (1) Walker and subsequent womanists who flow from her lineage are interested in Black women's experiences as foundational to womanism, but not only or even especially Black women's experiences of suffering; in fact, a denunciation of redemptive suffering is at the heart of womanism as theologians like Delores Williams explain it; and (2) Walker and womanists of her genealogical tree do not explicitly promote the "moral and epistemological superiority" of Black women; at most, Walker's womanism could be interpreted as claiming a "preferential option" of Afro-indigenous morality and epistemology for people of African descent—not because it is superior, but because it does less (or no) harm and includes healing capacities; Walker's womanism inherently resists the kinds of hierarchies that produce and reproduce superiority and inferiority.[12] More than Black nationalism, I would identify Walker's regard for Black experience as a branch of vindicationism. Beyond these two counts, I also reject Collins's assertion that "Walker's definition thus manages to invoke three important yet contradictory philosophies." While Collins has magnificently parsed Walker's womanism, revealing what she identifies as "black nationalism," "pluralism," and "integration/assimilation," I assert the following: (1) these philosophies with reference to Black social and political thought are more aptly identified as vindicationism, pluralism, and (universal) liberation; and (2) these philosophies are not contradictory. To my second assertion, vindicationism, pluralism, and (universal) liberation are each edified, and perhaps even perfected, by the other/s. Taken together, these philosophical strands become the better forms of themselves: vindicationism is better with pluralism; pluralism is better with liberation; liberation is better with vindicationism; pluralism is better with vindicationism; liberation is better with pluralism; vindicationism is better with liberation.

Womanist approaches to justice and sexual justice are varied. However, the fundamental contribution of womanism to theories of justice is that applied ethics can inform what is just. Womanists like Keri Day theorizing justice recognize that "one's perspectives and beliefs depend on one's positionality or situatedness, that one often cannot see the perspectives and beliefs that are furthest from one's own" and that "epistemologically, virtue cannot be understood outside of social processes and institutional structures of power that disenfranchise."[13] Justice (detached) does not always present the a priori standard for what is moral, ethical, and/or right. Universalized or generalized moral reasoning is not the only way ethics can inform justice. Normative ethics that have not passed through the refining fires of empirical experience and particularity are often inadequate for adjudicating justice. Approach Two is valid. From this point, *Black, Quare, and Then to Where* embarks on a journey of naming (and transforming) justice, (re)imagining Black sexual ethics.

From Black: Vindicationist Visions of Maât

The retrieval of Egyptian Maâtian ethics reflected in artifacts from the 2500s and 2400s BCE—and the unequivocal assertion of Egypt as part of what is called modern-day Africa in terms of its historical geographic and cultural posture—is a recovery of Egypt's religious, philosophical, social, and political contributions and a disruption of antiBlack epistemological patterns.

From a philosophical perspective, this retrieval work addresses the similarities, differences, and comparative potential of sexual ethics and theories of justice as categorical forms. From a historical perspective, this retrieval work invokes the vindicationist projects of Ayi Kwei Armah (chapter 3), Frances Cress Welsing (chapter 4), George G. M. James and Aimé Césaire (chapter 5), Joel Augustus Rogers and Frantz Fanon (chapter 6), and Maulana Karenga and Sylvia Wynter (chapter 7) to contextualize, explore, and explain the appeal of khemetic culture to people of African descent in the United States during the twentieth century.¹⁴ From an ethical perspective, this retrieval work offers a critique of the ethical principles to which people of African descent have been held with respect to sexuality, justice, and sexual justice. Critiquing both the heteropatriarchal commitments of Western philosophical and social commitments and the heteropatriarchal commitments of many of these vindicationists, I offer a Maâtian alternative of justice-based virtue ethics.

Outside of religious studies, Afrodiasporic scholars who have committed themselves to the study of khemetic (i.e., ancient Egyptian) religious and moral traditions have often been dismissed. These scholars have often explicitly and implicitly taken an oppositional stance vis-à-vis traditional Western frameworks for philosophy, religion, and ethics. Many of these scholars have unequivocally expressed their suspicion and distrust of the theories (and practices) born of epistemologies of the West. To be precise, for the purposes of this project the West includes ideological claims that take ancient Greece as their points of origin—and center whitewashed Christian theological traditions (e.g., de-Egyptianized Augustine and Aquinas) that simply expound upon the works of Aristotle and Plato, the Constantinian empire, Enlightenment philosophers, and European Christian reformers. Perhaps khemetically oriented scholars are dismissed because of the ways they challenge accepted truths about the Western foundations of the modern liberal arts project—refusing to attribute this pedagogical framework to Greek philosophers.¹⁵ These scholars may also be dismissed because they are perceived to be "playing the race card." These Black scholars are implicitly and explicitly naming what they perceive as a characteristic antiBlack racism (as antiBlackness) in academia. When white scholars focus on ancient Egyptian texts and traditions, they too are criticized, but the grounds, content, and quality of that critique are different.¹⁶

The implicit, lurking (racist) question asked about Afrodiasporic scholars studying African sources is: Are these Black scholars studying and attempting to recover African sources and origins—and even Egypt as African—to assert and/or defend their personhood?¹⁷ The haunting accusation behind that question is: the Black scholars are studying and attempting to recover African sources and origins only because they are (attempting to) assert and/or defend their personhood. The especially nefarious element of this question and accusation is that it is a shadow side of other racist logics:

- that the quality of Black people's scholarly work in fields of study that white people have dominated is rarely if ever on par with others (i.e., white scholars) in those fields;

- that it is reasonable for (and to expect) Black scholars to be experts in white scholarship and all things pertaining to race and people of African descent;
- that "Black stuff" (i.e., scholarship on, by, or about people of African descent) is not as difficult to learn or master, not as objective, and not as well/rationally researched as Eurocentric subjects in fields of knowledge that white people have dominated;
- that Black scholars should, if anything, attempt to study and master Eurocentric subjects—and should write about these in ways that utilize the lingua franca of those fields and build upon and respond to the traditions of and contemporary debates in those fields;
- that Black scholars (already do and should) self-impose a "twice as good as" standard on ourselves and attempt expertise that exceeds that of our peers in our fields on any given subject and demonstrate expertise on multiple subjects; and
- that Black scholars should "play it small" and downplay their knowledge on their subjects—never wanting to appear arrogant, too knowledgeable (i.e., smart), or more knowledgeable (i.e., smarter) than their colleagues.

And Black scholars in the field/s of knowledge coded and colonized as classics are so unusual that these logics rarely need to be applied directly against Black scholars from these fields. The work of Black scholars that intersects with classics is largely ignored and dismissed as irrelevant and unsophisticated among those trained in the classics through predominantly white institutions.

It has largely been left to Africana studies (and Black studies and African American studies) scholars and scholars of Black religion to take up vindicationist work and to study the work of vindicationists—especially those vindicationists who take interest in khemetic knowledge and wisdom. Within the field of religious studies, scholars who have specifically taken up Egyptian contributions to some extent include Peter Paris and Barbara Holmes.[18] Other scholars of Black religion have also engaged Egyptian philosophical and moral contributions, but their agendas have been more Christocentric—and most engaged with a latter (Judeo-Christian) antiquity.[19] In many ways, this is where an intraracial intrigue begins. Notwithstanding the honor of this scholarly mantle, many scholars of Black religion and philosophy, womanists, Black feminists, and African Americanists have missed an opportunity to transform contemporary scholarship, public discourses, and policies as a result of a premature dismissal of African epistemologies. More precisely, many scholars of Black religion and African Americanists have largely ceded khemetic (i.e., Egyptian) space and noetic possibilities because those studying khemetic (i.e., Egyptian) sources as foundational Afrodiasporic epistemological material, their interpretations of that material, and (perhaps) the material itself are (or at the very least seem to be) decisively misogynist and heterosexist.

A critically important exception is found in Delores S. Williams's *Sisters in the Wilderness: The Challenge of Womanist God-Talk*, published in 1993—following only two other womanist monographs: Katie Geneva Cannon's *Black Womanist Ethics* (1988) and Jacqueline Grant's *White Women's Christ, Black Women's Jesus: Feminist Christology and Womanist Response* (1989). In *Sisters in the Wilderness*, Williams re-presents the biblical narrative of Hagar—the Egyptian woman enslaved by Abraham and Sarah and forced to serve as a surrogate. The appeal to Hagar's experiences in the wilderness becomes a womanist alternative to the Black liberationists' appeal to the Israelite Exodus from slavery in Egypt as the most apropos biblical correlate to modern US Black experiences. For Williams, Egyptianness is the key to understanding Hagar—and the unique encounter she has with the God she names "El Roi" (i.e., "God of Seeing").[20] She notes that "Hagar's naming of God gathers additional meaning when we look at her action in relation to Egyptian traditions as well as Hebrew traditions. In the context of Egyptian myth the deity's eye (sight) has been involved in the creation of humanity only incidentally and not through planned choice. The parallels here between Hagar's experience with God in the wilderness and the work of Ra's Eye are considerable."[21] The power of naming, the promises she receives from God, her independence and power as a woman and single mother, and even the ways that the Egyptian creation story connects to Hathor—another Egyptian feminine deity who symbolizes fertility and justice—all redirect our attention to the significance of Hagar as an Egyptian. However, neither the Egyptian Africanness of Hagar nor the Egyptian moral and religious constellations from which she hailed have been explicitly emphasized in womanist theology and ethics.

Instead of focusing scholarly interest on Egypt, scholars of Black religion and scholars of womanism and womanist scholars—along with Black studies and African American studies scholars interested in the feminist and queer directions of their fields—have most often turned to West Africa and West African traditions (and sometimes South Africa and South African traditions) if they have turned to Africa at all.[22] Neither Egypt nor khemet are part of the African story for many contemporary scholars of Africa and its diaspora.[23]

Reflecting upon what might explain the interest of queer Afrodiasporic practitioners in Candomblé and some other African traditional religions rooted in West African Yoruban cultures that utilize Ifá divinations, Rachel Harding hypothesizes that (1) the gender-nondiscriminant ways that Orisha may mount people regardless of the gender identity of the Orisha or the gender identity of the person mounted as well as (2) the gender fluidity and metamorphoses of some of the Orisha themselves may account for the complementarity of some of these African traditional religions with Black queer people and communities.[24] Complementary theses are even further developed in the work of Roberto Strongman, Elizabeth Pérez, Omise'eke Natasha Tinsley, and Lyndon K. Gill. Still, a broad diversity of perspectives on gender and sexuality is reflected in the spectrum between the spiritualities and praxes M. Jacqui Alexander describes in *Pedagogies of Crossing* and the spiritualities and praxes Tracey Hucks describes in *Yoruba Traditions and African American Religious Nationalism*. Another explanation of the general interest of scholars of Africana, Black, African American, Black religious, and womanist studies in West Africa and its religious and philosophical heritage can likely be attributed to ancestral and geographic connections that can be made between Afrodiasporic peoples and the points of no return on the Atlantic coast of the African continent.

I contend that a properly critical approach to religion, or to particular religious traditions, practices, and ideas, draws from the perspectives of those in diverse social locations with respect to religion, or to religious traditions, practices, and ideas. In other words, the perspectives of those who claim and/or are claimed as belonging more and less are important to the work of critique. This project explores the metaethical value of authenticity in the attempt to properly locate oneself and/or others as belonging or not belonging. Though the gatekeepers of khemetic knowledge within Africana and Black studies have been drowning in their misogyny and heterosexism, khemetic knowledge and wisdom do not belong to these gatekeepers. Moreover, the same critiques of fundamentalism and essentialism that obtain with respect to religion (qua Christianity), gender, sexuality, and race in critical comparativist religious studies, ethnic studies, and women, gender, and sexuality studies can (re)read and conscientiously draw from khemetic literatures and traditions (without compromising the integrity of those sources). To put it differently, a quare reading of khemetic literatures—and Maât—is possible.

More has been lost than the richness of a khemetic moral constellation; more has been lost than the value of knowing that Africa is more than a conquered, underdeveloped continent of peoples who succumbed to enslavement or colonization; more has been lost than the location and identification of primordial human rationality in a Kushite person; more has been lost than the confidence of genetic connection to original thought responsible for critical aspects of human formation and social organization through the present day.[25] Freedom codes have been lost. Justice languages and logics have been lost. Discourses on how to improve the life experiences of Black people have revolved around justice. Many scholars of Black religion and philosophy, many womanists, Black feminists, and African Americanists have missed an opportunity to redefine and reorient justice discourses through a more deliberate reorientation around African epistemologies.

In this book, most documentation about Maât is drawn from the work of scholars who were not formally trained in academic institutions as Egyptologists, but who are experts in their fields of training and have taken up autodidactic commitments to understanding and teaching about ancient Egyptian histories, languages, figures, beliefs, cultures, and concepts. While subsequent research may engage original hieroglyphic, Coptic Egyptian, Greek, and Arabic source material along with various forms of secondary source material, as far as the subject of Maât is taken within this book, a key epistemological foundation is what have been called "black books."[26] A "kind of shorthand for works on a constellation of related subjects and issues," Mitchell Duneier argues that these "books may be geared toward helping people of African descent understand where they fit in; codifying the achievements of people of African descent; uncovering the history of African Americans and of white racism; or helping African Americans develop the knowledge and pride necessary to participate in the wider society."[27]

This is an intentional strategy to simultaneously engage most ancient African epistemic resources and to engage more contemporary Black epistemic resources. Methodologically, this is a way to honor the hybridity about which Charles Long writes. There is, here, a refusal to fetishize the most ancient for being most ancient; there is, too, an insistence on honoring the (more and) most ancient insofar as it is relevant to what is current and contemporary. And not just what is current and contemporary, but what is profitable to and for Black people—and especially those dispersed in the United States as an inheritance of the transatlantic slave trade.

To explore the concept of justice, it is helpful to consider dominant theories of justice within the US academy. However, a foundational theory of justice will be drawn from the Maâtian concept developed in black books.

The composite theory of justice that surfaces in and through these black books is echoed in the voices of some scholars of Black religion, culture, philosophy, and political theory. Some of these echoes will be noted here. However, it is also necessary to acknowledge the ways the Black liberation and womanist conceptions of justice are not only part of what Charles Long identifies as "theologies opaque" but are also the unequivocally hybrid fruit of modernity—including the dominant genetic material of Eurocentric corruptions of more ancient, though ethnically and cultural conquered, epistemological cores.[28] To begin an exploration of theories of justice as they relate to Black sexuality—taking modern black-book invocations of ancient Maâtian ethics as a starting point—Joel Augustus Rogers (1880/3–1966), born in Jamaica; George G. M. James (1893–1956), born in Guyana; Aimé Césaire (1913–2008), born in Martinique; Cheikh Anta Diop (1923–86), born in Senegal; Frantz Fanon (1925–61), born in Martinique; Sylvia Wynter (b. 1928), born in Cuba; Frances Cress Welsing (1935–2016), born in Chicago; Ayi Kwei Armah (b. 1939), born in Ghana; and Maulana Karenga (b. 1941), born in Parsonsburg, Maryland, are the primary thinkers with whom this book theorizes. I also engage the work of Molefi Asante (b. 1942), born in Valdosta, Georgia, alongside Maulana Karenga; Marimba Ani (b. Dona Richards) alongside Frances Cress Welsing; Théophile Obenga (b. 1936), born in the Republic of the Congo, alongside Ayi Kwei Armah. The recovery of these figures is what might be called a revivalist approach to the dilemmas of justice, Blackness, and sexuality.

Four central claims and contributions of the vindicationists are important to note for this book:

- vindicationists often argue that Egypt has primordial standing in human civilization and modeled all forms of social life for Greece and its descendants; Egypt was "the quasi-exclusive teacher of Greece";[29]

  - this social modeling included relational (i.e., gender, sexual) life;
  - this social modeling included political organization;
  - this social modeling included scientific knowledge;
  - this Egypt-Greece, pedagogue-pupil, social modeling included philosophical and moral instruction.

The latter four points are implied in the first point but are specified as such for emphasis and clarity. While this social modeling is a compelling reason to explore ancient Egypt on its own—and, perhaps, even to do so with vindicationists as our guides—for many of these vindicationists, homophobia and heterosexism are baked into their claims. One might wonder: How is it possible or even advisable to engage vindicationists in a quare theory–oriented book on Black sexual ethics and theories of justice?

After all, with a legitimizing tone, Diop notes in his account of the Moroccan degradation and destruction of Timbuktu: "Kâti and Sâdi agree in situating at this time the corruption of morals and, especially, the introduction of sodomy into Black Africa."[30] In his essay "Erotics of Aryanism/Histories of Empire: How 'White Supremacy' and 'Hellenomania' Construct 'Discourses of Sexuality,'" Greg Thomas notes, "Diop's vast, multidisciplinary corpus manifests a positive politics of sexuality with a sustained affirmation of 'matriarchy,' as Ifi Amadiume reminds us in *Re-Inventing Africa* (1997) and elsewhere."[31] And Thomas goes on to argue a connection between matriarchy and sexuality, citing Diop to support this claim. Is Diop off the hook for homophobia and heterosexism? Absolutely not. Diop provides the foundation for vindicationists and an Afrocentrism that proffers a weak feminism (at best) with a deep-seated homophobia and heterosexism at its core. His matriarchal model does not cure Diop's heterosexism—rooted in a procreative, fertility-oriented view of sexuality. While I believe that Diop's appeal to the "sovereignty of experience" may well have led him to a different perspective on creativity, procreation, and queer sexualities, this is not where it led his pupils and contemporaries.[32]

Born in 1918, Yosef Ben-Jochannan, known to most as "Dr. Ben," wrote forty-nine books focused in various ways on the early Nile civilization contributions to Western cultures. He builds in many ways on the legacy of Rogers, the contributions of Diop, and the teachings of his friend and intellectual colleague John Henrik Clarke (1915–98). In *The Need for a Black Bible: The Black Man's Religion, Volume III*, Dr. Ben writes:

> We notice that most of the GOD-HEADS of the world that preceded Ywh, Jesus Christ and Al'lah were from such places as Ethiopia, Egypt, Punt, Nubia, Meröe, and other High-Cultures along the Nile Valley and the Great Lakes regions of Alkebu-lan, also in other areas of Asia and the so-called "Americas." But the "Negro" CLERGY cannot see this fact, because they do not want to see anything that does not wholly [*sic*] conform with their adopted MYTHS and ALLEGORIES in the European and European-American VERSIONS of the Old Testament and New Testament that allow them to BLAST OFF into euphoric trips just prior to the hour of their call for the FINANCIAL OFFERING, which they always precede with . . .

"IT IS BETTER TO GIVE THAN TO RECEIVE,"
in their respective churches. For this same reason they have failed to understand the...

SEXUAL CONTRADICTIONS
between the <u>Adam and Eve anti-procreation syndrome</u> and the allowable...

HOMOSEXUALITY
within the so-called "<u>Holy Scriptures</u>," as shown in JUDGES, Chapters 19 and 20.

The BLACK BIBLE, as I see it, cannot tolerate the <u>contradictions</u> we have been examining throughout; neither the <u>distortions</u> in the TEACHINGS of the ancient and glorious traditions of the Africans of the Nile Valley and Great Lakes regions of Alkebu-lan; nor the prohibitions against normal male and female copulation at the expense of support for UNNATURAL UNISEXUALITY.[33]

For Dr. Ben, Black clergy in 1974 are not homophobic enough, are money motivated, and blind to the Egyptian (i.e., "the Nile Valley and the Great Lakes regions of Alkebu-lan") roots of deity. And this is but a portion of his critique.

While John Henrik Clarke's audience and the day of this address are unclear, a video records him saying:

> See, we have had a healthy attitude toward things other people made unhealthy and made filthy and dirty.... Show me one case of prostitution before the coming of foreigners, show me one case of sexual deviation before the coming of foreigners [claps, "ouch, ouch"].... And yet you've got people, whole radio programs, talmbout Africans and the Greeks were both homosexuals. Africans could have introduced it to the Greeks [audible sigh/gasp in the audience].... Now, we ain't have no *confusion* [laughter/applause/"help yourself, docta"].... We've been confused on many things [laughter, "but not on this one," "not on this one"].... But not that. Yeah. We know the difference between mother and father and what each one of 'em's s'posed to do.[34]

"Sexual deviation" is offered as a euphemism for homosexuality. Clarke takes a shot at both prostitution and homosexuality. In so doing, he not only makes these tantamount (and likened) to one another but also dismisses homosexuality and sex work, respectively.

And among the primary vindicationists I engage, no one is more vocal than Frances Cress Welsing about homosexuality. With respect to Black gay men in particular, she writes:

> Black male homosexuality and bisexuality are only the long-run by-products of males submitting in fear to other males in the social arena; they fail to resist because death is the result of resistance.... One method I have been using with all Black male patients—whether their particular disorder be passivity, effeminization, bisexuality, homosexuality or other—is to have them relax and envision themselves approaching and opposing, in actual combat, the collective of white males and females (without apology or giving up in the crunch). The fear of such a confrontation is at the basis of most of today's Black male pathologies in patterns of logic, thought, speech, action and emotional response as they participate in all areas of human activity.[35]

In many ways, Welsing's response to "Black male homosexuality and bisexuality" builds on her broader theory. She writes, "According to the Color-Confrontation theory, white supremacy culture degrades the act of sex and the process of self-reproduction because for whites both are reflective of whiteness and, in turn, their inability to produce color. This self-deficiency clearly is despised and is stated most explicitly in the religious and moral philosophies of the white supremacy culture. Yet, this manner of degrading the sexual act is not found in non-white cultures."[36] Under the cloak of Albert Einstein's determinacy and a complementary "unified field theory," Welsing argues a logical continuity that is in stark contrast with that which Greg Thomas and Ifi Amadiume intimate. Welsing writes, "It is clear that current Western psychiatry's inability to identify the interrelationships existing between racism, homosexuality and sexism... is due to an inadequate conceptual and theoretical approach."[37] Homosexuality is on the same level as racism and sexism; all of them are reproachable. Of course, there is a logical consistency here: if sexism is a disruption of a matriarchal model that prioritizes women's fertility and bodily reproduction, if homosexuality is a disruption of procreative possibilities, and if racism is about the all-encompassing annihilation of nonwhite people (including a disruption of their reproductivity), these three can hang together. Welsing holds, "*Homosexuality and sexism* are necessary derivatives of this energy field and, just like all other significant behaviors in the global and local white collective, can be understood as derivatives of this finite unified behavior-energy field."[38] Welsing's, thankfully, is not the only approach.

Why would we want to reimagine any of these individuals from a quare theory vantage point? How are these theorists important to the futures of quare theory? Is this project to recover those who attempted to recover khemet just a terrible idea? Greg Thomas does not think it is a terrible idea. In his "Erotics of Aryanism" essay, Thomas levels a strong critique against some of the most notable names in queer theory and sexuality studies—including John Boswell and David Halperin, among others. He writes that "they frame a spurious debate between 'genetic essentialism' and 'social constructionism' (17) in which all parties involved restate the basic dogma of Occidentalist historiography."[39] He challenges, "An anticolonial analysis can easily destroy this stale dichotomy between 'biological essence' and 'social construction,' not to mention the other major, unquestioned dichotomy here between 'homosexuality' and 'heterosexuality.' By and large, however, a racialized conflation of Occidental specificity and 'Universal Humanity' determines the fashion in which the historicity of erotic identification becomes intelligible."[40]

And finally he holds:

> The shape and substance of sexuality is certainly contingent upon time and space, or history and culture. The History of Sexuality canonized by Europe and North America claims to make this point in theory. However, the concept of historicity employed normalizes the time-space of Occidentalism as the only imaginable mode of sociocultural existence. "The Rise of the West" is thought to permit "European History" to stand as "Human History." The bourgeois standard for "socially constructed" sex, whether "heterosexual" or "homosexual," stays basically the same as the standard for "biologically essentialized" sex. Hence, sexuality is never in fact "de-naturalized" by this "historicist discourse" of "de-naturalization." "Queer Theory" is not very "queer" at all.[41]

For Thomas, whether vindicationists are misogynist or heterosexist is beside the point when queer theorists are all too eager to reify the racist historical agendas of Mary Lefkowitz and company. That queer theorists cannot find their way to an acknowledgment of the histories—and sexual histories that not only predate Grecian sources, experiences, and positions but may even also inform Grecian sources, experiences, and positions—is an offense. Thomas is rightly disturbed by "how the categories of sex and sexuality function in a way that routinely erases the history of race and empire from their system of reference."[42] For the sake of a quare theory and for the sake of the vindicationist project, it is essential to consider more closely how sex, sexuality, and queer/quare sexualities do manifest in ancient Egypt and in the histories of Black people, and how ancient Egypt and the lives of Black people do manifest in epistemic origins and centers of sex, sexualities, and queer/quare sexualities. Quare disrupts difference. Queer theory lacks integrity partnered with Mary Lefkowitz. Vindicationists lack integrity, erasing "sovereign experiences" of queerness in Africa that predate European invasions—and the value of Black queer experiences and cultural contributions through the present.[43] Langston Hughes, Audre Lorde, James Baldwin, Lorraine Hansberry, Countee Cullen, or Pauli Murray should neither be dismissed from the vindicationist project nor their expressions and expansions of Blackness questioned, on account of how they produced and reproduced revolutionary Black culture and people (as LGBTQ or sexuality-ambiguous Afrodiasporic intellectuals). Reconciling these two deficits—quare/queer theory without vindicationists and vindicationists without quare theory—is the fundamental task of *Black, Quare, and Then to Where*. Here I argue that vindicationist projects must be wrested from homophobic and heterosexist commitments in ways that do not deny the holistic, intersectional contributions of ancient Egyptian culture. I make a distinction between cherry-picking—an allegation that progressive and conservative Christians direct against one another as they read sacred texts that also might be made with respect to readings of ancient Egyptian culture and texts—and applications of sovereign experience. In different ways, addressing these two deficits grasps at the wings of justice, demanding her strength to carry their weight in flight.

Justice Is, Justice Ain't

We might ask if justice can or should have to carry such weight—and balance such concerns. The esteemed Black gay poet, activist, and filmmaker Marlon Riggs challenged us to consider—and reconsider—what Blackness is and what it "ain't" in his 1994 documentary *Black Is . . . Black Ain't*. He not only challenged essentialist interpretations of Blackness, but he also clarified the belonging of Black LGBTQ people within the category of Blackness in no uncertain terms. This book not only asserts the belonging of Black LGBTQ people as a fundamental and central concern for any contemporary justice discourse (i.e., what justice is) but also makes it clear that theories of justice that are not obviously relevant and applicable to the everyday life and sexual experiences of Afrodiasporic people in the United States are not justice (i.e., what justice ain't). What is justice? This is a central contemplation of this book. Related to this central question are other questions: How do we define justice? What are the forms of justice? What is the relationship between moral reasoning and justice?

Notwithstanding the limited perspective of most vindicationists when it comes to sexual diversities, I begin evoking a conversation between quare theory, vindicationism, and womanism with a turn to George G. M. James, who offers the following explanation of ancient Egyptian religion and morality: "The ancient Egyptians had developed a very complex religious system, called the Mysteries, which was also the first system of salvation. As such, it regarded the human body as a prison house of the soul, which could be liberated from its bodily impediments, through the disciplines of the Art and Sciences, and advanced from the level of a mortal to that of a God. This was the notion of the summum bonum or greatest good, to which all men must aspire, and it also became the basis of all ethical concepts."[44] He goes on to argue that Plato's cardinal virtues—justice, wisdom, temperance, and courage—are reflected first in the teachings of the Egyptian mystery system. While chapter 5 further explores James's claims with respect to the teachings on virtue in the Egyptian mystery system, James writes, "Justice meant the unswerving righteousness of thought and action."[45] James suggests that, in khemetic culture, it is the ways we align our thinking and action for the sake of the greatest good that constitutes justice.

James expands on this notion, backing into Egyptian mystery moral codes from the Greek theorists to which they have been falsely ascribed. Wresting the concept of the summum bonum from Pythagoras (along with Socrates, Plato, and Aristotle), James writes, "This is an attainment, or transformation which is the harmony resulting from a life of virtue. It consists in a harmonious relationship between the faculties of man, by means of which his lower nature becomes subordinated to his higher nature."[46] To attain the highest good is to become godlike in the ancient Egyptian system. The highest good is experienced within and attained by the individual (not to be confused with utilitarianism) but is also attained by the habituation of virtues that relate to community (i.e., how individuals relate to one another in and through community). One, therefore, cannot attain the highest good without the righteousness (i.e., consistency and organic reconciliation) of virtuous thought and action. One cannot attain the highest good without justice. Moreover, James maintains that Plato's suggestion that virtue (which includes justice) is to the soul as justice is to the ideal state—and the charioteer Allegory Plato uses to explain this—is a close parallel to the ancient Egyptian descriptions of the Day of Judgment.[47] However justice is theorized—with respect to the individual moral agent or with respect to the state (i.e., the society in which we find ourselves)—there are ancient concepts of justice that are both useful for modern theorizations of justice and foundational for those theories of justice. The challenge becomes whether or not (and how) the greatest good can be realized in the lives of Afrodiasporic people and communities—including LGBTQ people, cisgender, transgender, and gender nonbinary. What kinds of virtue habituations are im/possible, im/probable, cultivated, or inhibited in the lives of Afrodiasporic people—especially when it comes to our lives as sexual (and sexualized) beings, especially once we have accounted for our lives as sexual (and sexualized) beings?

Modern Eurocentric Translations of Justice

What theories of justice directly respond to and improve the everyday life experiences of Afrodiasporic people? Modern justice discourses often engage the following questions: How do we reason through the questions of what is right and what is wrong—and why or why not—that come before us? What determines how we reason what is right and wrong? Are there any rules or guidelines that help us to make this determination? Are there consistencies or inconsistencies that characterize this determination? What accounts for those consistencies and inconsistencies? There are different claims of right and wrong—and right thought and action—that can govern the ways that individuals and communities answer these questions. When race, gender, and sexuality are introduced as terrains that require fairness of thought and action, they can appear to be complications, to say the least. This book begins to articulate a theory of justice that constructively builds upon the sexual moral codes of Afrodiasporic people already in conversation with ancient khemetic forms of moral reasoning. With Maât as a guide, virtue and consequentialism are blended, calling forth social and political communities that support the cultivation of moral agents who reflect such a blend.[48] These forms of reasoning become foundational for the discernment and pursuit of justice. In metaethical terms, this book calls for a restorative justice that begins with an epistemic reorientation and unequivocal affirmation of the de facto morality and moral agency of Afrodiasporic people and communities (as human). The need for such restorative justice becomes clear through a closer consideration of modern occidental theories of justice and approaches to moral reasoning.

Modern occidental ways of reasoning about what is just and what is unjust include the following: (1) Consequentialism: this is outcome-oriented reasoning (i.e., utilitarianism or teleogical); adjudication of the goodness of an action is based on what the action produces. Consequentialism may ask: What is the greatest good for the greatest number of people? (2) Nonconsequentialism: this is prior principle-oriented reasoning (i.e., deontological); adjudication of the goodness of an action is based on a predetermined rule. Nonconsequentialism may ask: What is the right thing to do regardless of the outcome of that right action (and regardless of the context out of which right action is being discerned? (3) Virtue: this is a personal and/or community type-oriented reasoning (i.e., ontological); adjudication of the goodness of an action is based on whether and the extent to which an action confirms the best quality or character of a person or community. A virtue ethicist may ask: What is the best course of action in terms of its consistency with who I am/we are, its consistency with who I am/we are habituating ourselves to be, and/or its consistency with who I/we want to be? (4) Intuition: this is a type of reasoning often set aside as unreasonable, responsive to what one feels or senses in one's soul, gut, bones, heart, and/or body. It is when "ma spirit n'tek" or "ma spirit tek" a person or thing.[49] If consequentialism, nonconsequentialism, and virtue are the ways we decide right from wrong, just from unjust, fair from unfair, alignment from hypocrisy, we rarely apply these with consistency or purity. Often, intuition is erased from deliberations on moral reasoning. However, each of these is often mixed up in our minds and in our praxes. There are times when we deploy a consequentialist form of moral reasoning—and times that we focus on virtue. There are contexts in which a deontological premise prevails and times when we set this aside for a utilitarian principle. There are times when virtue trumps an a priori principle—or they completely correspond with one another. It follows that there are more and less thought-action-reconciled ways of applying these forms of moral reasoning. A person can be unjust in their discernment of right and wrong by virtue of which form of moral reasoning they apply, how they apply that moral reasoning, and the choices they make to follow the same code of moral reasoning (or not) in different contexts. Do we judge ourselves more harshly than others? Are we more permissive with ourselves than we are with others? Are there certain others with whom we apply one type of reasoning and certain others with whom we apply another type of reasoning? Are there some whom we always (or usually) find a (moral) reason to condemn? Are there some whom we never (or rarely) find a (moral) reason to condemn?

Other questions include: How do we express, live out, and practice our discernment of what is right and what is wrong—individually and collectively? What determines how we believe right and wrong are best expressed? Are there any rules or guidelines that help us to make this determination? Are there consistencies or inconsistencies that characterize this determination? What accounts for those consistencies and inconsistencies?

Close at hand when thinking through these ways that we discern right and wrong are questions about the different forms that justice in action (or enacted) can take. I recall some of these here: (1) distributive justice, which is primarily concerned with the equal balance of goods or rights; (2) procedural justice, which is primarily concerned with the process by which goods or rights are ascribed or attained; (3) restorative justice, which is primarily concerned with the rebalancing of goods or rights according to those goods or rights that have been denied or lost; and (4) retributive justice, which is primarily concerned with the punitive consequences resulting from the denial of goods or rights.

Including the retributively oriented aspects of the modern carceral state, I reject retributive justice as a just form of justice. Retributive justice often reifies the very social and moral ills it seeks to punish; retributive justice adds momentum to cycles of violence. Procedural justice raises concerns as well. To demand procedural justice often means an implicit acceptance of the laws, a respect for the legal systems, and a legitimization of the state according to which these laws and legal systems operate. For many Afrodiasporic people, the only procedural justice is the justice that leads to, establishes, or maintains anarchy; justice is the procedural work of tearing down as much of the system, its foundations, and its laws as possible. For many other Afrodiasporic people, procedural justice continues to be the establishment of laws that proactively and reactively protect the rights of marginalized people. Similarly, distributive justice must be set aside because of the ways that such discourse tends to imply materialistic forms of ownership and property that are endemic to the very injustice that fueled the transatlantic slave trade, colonialism, imperialism, and the ongoing sociopolitical oppressions that are the legacies of these. This is not to say that the material needs and rights of people are irrelevant. This is not to say that equity with respect to resources and opportunities is not a fight worth fighting. Ultimately, *Black, Quare, and Then to Where* is most concerned with restorative justice—and with the repair and reparations restorative justice implies.

This is, however, to say that what is in need of repair and restoration is inclusive of and also beyond goods and rights. The just (i.e., equitable) distribution of goods and rights cannot be discerned without a prior restoration of goods and rights lost, stolen, promised (but not fulfilled), and accorded as debt. Moreover, the primary restorative justice this book demands is of an epistemic nature. There is a need to restore an acknowledgment of Egyptian moral and philosophical sources at the foundation of our modern sociopolitical, moral and philosophical contexts. There is a need to restore Egypt as the de facto center of modern research and knowledge. Epistemically oriented restorative justice means that white (and Black) scholars all acknowledge the African roots—persons, minds, and pigments—from which so much of contemporary social structures (and social promises) come. This is a for-better-or-worse prospect. For indeed, ancient Egypt and its contemporary legacies are not all so noble. However, if a fraction of the romanticization of ancient Greece was redirected toward (more) ancient Egypt, the scaffolding of contemporary white supremacies, xenophobias, and the social oppressions that follow would stand on shaky ground. Secondarily, the restorative justice this book demands is the de facto morality and moral agency of Afrodiasporic people and communities (as human). The ontic goodness and value—and the universal assent to this goodness and value of Afrodiasporic people and communities—is a matter of justice. It is a starting point for the doing of justice. And where better to begin contemplations of how to understand and apply such justice than one of the intersections of Afrodiasporic identity that remains most surveilled and contested: sexuality? The goodness—and sexual goodness—of Black people must be restored (and affirmed) in the minds, in the intellect, in the intuition, in the rationale, and in consequent human behavior.

Consider some other modern occidental treatments of justice. Philosopher Michael Sandel explores justice as an evolving concept. He proposes an initial way of distinguishing ancient theories of justice and conceptualizations of a just society from modern theories and conceptualizations: "ancient theories of justice start with virtue, while modern theories start with freedom."[50] Expanding a bit, Sandel argues, "Modern theories of justice try to separate questions of fairness and rights from arguments about honor, virtue, and moral desert. They seek principles of justice that are neutral among ends, and enable people to choose and pursue their ends for themselves."[51] Sandel's approach, along with those of other philosophers such as Alasdair MacIntyre, Charles Taylor, and Michael Walzer, pushes back on Rawlsian liberalism and enters the modern justice discourse with an emphasis on the ways that communities shape moral and political judgments.[52] They attempt to reconcile rights and virtue to an extent. Notwithstanding their regard for the particularities of community, they still move too swiftly toward generalizing theories disconnected from everyday Afrodiasporic communities. Shatema Threadcraft establishes that the contexts of Black women's lived experiences matter to the theorization of justice.[53] Accordingly, she puts Tommie Shelby and Charles Mills, among other Black political scientists, in conversation with Moira Gaten, Nancy Hirschmann, Martha Nussbaum, and Iris Marion Young, among other feminist philosophers and political scientists. With an interest in retheorizing justice complementary to this book, Threadcraft writes, "As the sphere of intimate relations is a significant realm in which black women experience injustice, it is critical that scholars develop theories of corrective racial justice that explicitly attend to the history of racial injustice on both sides of the public/private divide and address the legacy of racialized disadvantage in the black intimate sphere."[54] While Threadcraft is concerned primarily with racial justice and continues in conversations with Eurocentric scholars of justice, she helpfully (re)theorizes justice with regard to Black women (and people) and sexual intimacies:

> Any theory of corrective racial justice inspired by Rawls, whose theory of justice focuses on establishing fairness in man's efforts to control his political and then his material environment, must include at minimum explicit additional provisions designed to establish justice within the black intimate sphere. It must acknowledge that our sexual, reproductive, and caretaking capacities are not natural—that they, too, require resources, protection, and support as well as social contexts in which they can be developed and exercised—and that black intimate capacities have been profoundly diminished under racial domination in ways that theories of corrective racial justice must explicitly address.
>
> Justice requires that no one's intimate capacities be unduly constrained and that all live within contexts that support and enable equally the exercise of their intimate capacities, social contexts that provide equal opportunity to develop and exercise those capacities. Justice requires that racial-group membership must never determine whether or not one has to create intimate and caring relationships amid disproportionate violence, nor should the exercise of intimate capacities themselves expose one to interpersonal and institutional violence, as has been the case for black women throughout American history.[55]

In light of this kind of contemporary analysis, treating ancient khemetic sources and their vindicationist allies is a considerable task. While these ancient sources and the vindicationists who highlight them promote matriarchy and value women's sexuality, fertility, and reproductive capacities, they tend to essentialize Black women as sexualized beings in a romanticizing way. In contrast, the scholars Threadcraft challenges to critically and correctively engage "the black intimate sphere" tend to ignore, erase, and/or fetishize Black women's sexuality (i.e., slightly different forms of essentialization). Moreover, in contrast with vindicationists—and many womanist scholars and scholars of Black ethics—Threadcraft does strike a rights-oriented tone and steers clear of some of the debates around virtue ethics. This is understandable considering the problematic moral(izing) (virtue critical) attacks that often attend to treatments of Black sexuality. A vindicationist, womanist, virtue-oriented rejoinder to modern occidental translations of justice—that also takes rights discourses seriously—opens the door for new theoretical possibilities of justice.

And new theoretical possibilities of justice are important because the language of justice (i.e., discourses that invoke justice or injustice) largely dictates the naming of right and wrong, good and bad, ambiguous but acceptable, and ambiguous and undesirable in private and public spheres. Notwithstanding clarifying discourses that help define a normative justice, injustice is no less prevalent. Why, then, is justice discursively important? Though injustice persists, justice discourse still gives us ways to name and defend moral positions and codes. In terms of sociopolitical organization, justice discourse is important because it has become the terrain through which (implicit and explicit) social contracts have been asserted and reasserted from Thomas Hobbes onward in terms of modern occidental thought. Notwithstanding considerable critiques, Rawls's contractarian theory of justice still drives willful blindness with respect to mitigating factors that render the veil of ignorance irrelevant.[56] Whether or not one is justly governed, whether or not one cedes one's sovereignty, how one relates as an independent moral agent in the context of political and social governance, and even how one relates to matters of privacy and property all turn on questions of what is right or fair. These matters are embodied in the experiences of Afrodiasporic people once considered property themselves. Though not enough of us yet perceive it, justice with respect to sociopolitical organization is a matter of planetary survival. In terms of the cosmos and organic, biological, and scientific organization, justice is important because of the ways human existence now rests in the balance of human capacities to self-regulate. The balance is not level between corporate greed and community need—and Black peoples are suffering disproportionately. This is not, however, a discourse for Afrodiasporic peoples alone. Again, justice with respect to scientific organization is a matter of planetary survival. Justice continues to matter in terms of discourses on race and Blackness. Justice continues to matter in terms of discourses on gender and women and transpeople. Justice continues to matter in terms of discourses on sex and sexuality—and queer and quare people, normative sexual deviants and those rendered sexually deviant.[57]

(Crawling) Back to the Future

Theorists of justice have largely participated in the erasure of African sources of philosophy and moral codes. What would crawling back to a khemetic philosophical and moral framework look like or mean?[58] How can this be done effectively and thoughtfully—especially among those who will have to teach themselves? How can the intellectual prowess of Wynter and Karenga be cultivated in new generations of scholars of Black religion and theorists of justice? I believe Charles H. Long helps to point the way. While acknowledging a modern Western standard for moral inquiry and reasoning, and theories of justice, *Black, Quare, and Then to Where* centers an ancient Egyptian principle, Maât, as an epistemological point of origin. This approach is not distinct from traditional academic discourse insofar as it offers "an interpretation" of a "primitive and prehistoric religious" culture and may contribute to the problem of a "continuing and inordinate concern for the data of primitive religions and methods growing from their interpretations."[59] However, this approach is distinct insofar as it does not reify the inferiority of what Charles Long calls "empirical others" and defines as "a cultural phenomenon in which the extraordinariness and uniqueness of a person or culture is first recognized negatively."[60]

In his seminal text, *Significations: Signs, Symbols, and Images in the Interpretation of Religion*, Charles Long's concern is not explicitly or first with justice; his starting point is religion and the sacred. However, the plurality of religion or religions in his work lays the groundwork for the plurality of justices. Of religion, he writes, "For my purposes, religions will mean orientation—orientation in the ultimate sense, that is, how one comes to terms with the ultimate significance of one's place in the world."[61] Of religious experience, he writes that it "apprehends and discovers the sacredness of the forms of the world."[62] Elsewhere, Long writes that the "theoretical and methodological bases" for his work are evident in "two formulations of the meaning of religious experience": "First, religious experience is a primordial experiencing of that which is considered ultimate in existence.... Second, implied in this notion of religious experience is that of human orientation—the meaning that human communities give to the particular stances they have assumed in their several worlds."[63] And of the religious heritage of people of African descent, Long writes:

> The Christian faith provided a language for the meaning of religion, but not all the religious meanings of the black communities were encompassed by the Christian forms of religion.... The religion of any people is more than a structure of thought; it is experience, expression, motivations, intentions, behaviors, styles, and rhythms. Its first and fundamental expression is not on the level of thought.... Americans of African descent have been forced to deal with several heritages.... And they have had to deal with these realities always under a situation of oppression and duress.... For the majority culture of this country, blacks have always been signified. By this I mean that they have always been a part of a cultural code whose euphemisms and stereotypes have indicated their meaning within the larger framework of American cultural languages.[64]

In other words, the religious experience of people of African descent is "experience, expression, motivations, intentions, behaviors, styles, and rhythms" (beyond thought) hewn from "several heritages" and a "situation of oppression and duress." Such is a way of understanding the religious experience of a signified/signifying people. And it is through Long's conceptualizations of religion, religious experience, the sacred, and people of African descent that (injustice and) justices are signified. For Long, injustices of "oppression and duress" mingle with cultural particularities to catalyze the hybrid evolution of "opaque people" (i.e., those who endure "oppression and duress") as fully human and dignified subjects—and religious subjects.[65] And that evolutionary process and its products are dynamic liberation and justice in motion.

Of course, such an account begs several questions: What would justice be if it were not for injustice? How can justice be defined independently of injustice? Is it possible for justice to be static or stationary? For justice to be itself and to maintain itself—and justice must always be maintained—it must be in motion.[66] However, it is one thing to say that justice must remain in motion as a consequence of the centripetal and centrifugal forces of the centered city, fixed in and as a "fantastic hegemonic imagination"; it is another thing to say that justice must remain in motion because the universe and cosmos, our understandings of life and heat themselves, assume motion.[67] Motion—and the motion of justice—must be qualified. So, although Long is not concerned with justice in the first instance, he is implicitly concerned with justice insofar as he is tracking the primordial and secondary instantiations of the creation of people of African descent as noetic, agentive subjects. This tracking and the subjects of his tracking are acts, processors, and producers of justice.

Still, an initial clue to the complexity of theorizing justice can be found in the very examples that Long provides for "empirical others." Long not only explains the ways "the wild man" European trope models an epistemological foundation, formulation, cultivation, and proliferation for "empirical others," but he also begins with a description of Ilza Veith's history of the disease of hysteria.[68] Long reminds his readers that the word *hysteria* is derived from the Greek word for uterus. He writes:

> The symptom of this disease is a marked emotional tension expressing itself in fainting spells or violent pathological behavior. Through the history of this disease, various diagnoses are made, many defining the uterus as an animal that tends to wander through the body out of its place. A standard remedy prescribed for this disease throughout its history is heightened heterosexual activity. . . . It is especially interesting to note that in the Kahun Papyrus of the Egyptian Middle Kingdom, aromatic agents were to be incorporated in the shape of the ibis. The aroma from this wax upon entering the womb is supposed to pacify the womb. The ibis, a bird, is the symbol of Thoth. Thoth is a male deity personified by the moon and related to the sun. He is also the inventor of writing and the scribe of all the other gods.[69]

Long quotes Veith: "The employment of the image of a powerful male deity to lure a wandering female organ is highly suggestive of the nature of the underlying ideas concerning hysteria even if it is nowhere spelled out in detail."[70] Clearly, Long joins Veith in critiquing the heteropatriarchal empirical othering of women spuriously diagnosed with hysteria. However, he does so in the context of a much larger argument about the fetishization of ancient Vedic philosophy and culture as a foundation of a colonizing, Eurocentric approach to the study of religion; he helpfully exposes the perennial, heterosexually oriented othering of women while glossing over Egypt. In this instance, the Kahun Papyrus of the Egyptian Middle Kingdom is simultaneously implicitly regarded as a philosophical source (through Long's secondary source, Ilza Veith) and critiqued for its problematic, othering philosophical and cultural conclusions.

This rhetorical work that Long does invites theorists of justice to reconsider several debates. One of these debates has to do with the "isness/ontology" of Blackness.[71] Is there such a thing as ontological Blackness—or must we join the press of Victor Anderson and others beyond ontological Blackness and its attending presumptions?[72] Another of these debates begs the question of how competing claims to justice are prioritized and equitably—if not equally—addressed. The handling of distribution and experience remain live questions. And with Long, especially, one must take seriously the value, significance, and priority of epistemic and materialistic (re)centering. Upon this closer glance at Egypt (even through Long and Veith), another critical question is: What really constitutes reparations?

Contemporary discourses on Afropessimism also haunt *Black, Quare, and Then to Where*—entering through the door of "the wild man" that Long opens. The problem to which Afropessimism responds is this: "Black people embody (which is different from saying are always willing or allowed to express) a meta-aporia for political thought and action."[73] Frank Wilderson III explains: "If, as Afropessimism argues, Blacks are not Human subjects, but are instead structurally inert props, implements for the execution of White and non-Black fantasies and sadomasochistic pleasures, then this also means that, at a higher level of abstraction, the claims of universal humanity that the above theories all subscribe to are hobbled by a meta-aporia: a contradiction that manifests whenever one looks seriously at the structure of Black suffering in comparison to the presumed universal structure of all sentient beings."[74] Wilderson laments ways that Black people become the ultimate metaphor for suffering. However, the most concerning condition to which Afropessimism responds is that every liberation struggle—even for those who are Black—is articulated in terms of escaping Blackness.

To the extent that African American religions had been studied in terms of (1) descriptions of suffering and Black responses to suffering, (2) liberation like the Exodus, (3) survival and thriving like Hagar, and/or (4) the Blackness of Jesus and the opacity of a G*d and people, scholars of Black religion could believe it is possible to escape the deleterious impacts of racism and social oppression by transforming the oppression of Black people (read victimhood of Black people and Blackness) into an inherent redemptive possibility for Black people and Blackness. Read: we can be saved because (and only because or primarily because) we are oppressed. Victor Anderson's *Beyond Ontological Blackness*, anticipating the Afropessimist problem, makes it plain that there is no real, true escape. There is no liberation—at least not for Black people. Being Black is not enough to save us or for our redemption. It may be enough for the saving and redemption of others—as we people of African descent provide metaphor and analogy for the suffering of others. However, a being—an ontological status—that is based on suffering and the grotesque does not automatically open itself into redemptive possibility for the/its subject. In fact, being Black disqualifies Black subjects from redemption. Consequently, Victor Anderson argues:

> What is warranted is a healthy pessimism about the fragility of our efforts to transcend absolutely cultural activities that threaten cultural fulfillment and a pragmatic hope that discerns and supports those activities that bring about more fulfillment of basic human needs and subjective goods.
>
> By operationalizing these iconoclastic and Utopian critical dispositions, African American theology (like African American literary and cultural criticism) will be freed up from ontological blackness to play in the grotesquery of both postmodern blackness and postmodern North American life.[75]

For Anderson, "cultural fulfillment" happens through pragmatic engagement in the public sphere: not Afrocentric xenophobia. For Afropessimists, there may not be much hope to speak of—and there may be no angst about anarchic choices to opt out of any formal political democratic process. Instead for such Afropessimists, the best futures may be in the cultivation and expansion of archives.[76] Or in "countermemory" and "counter-normalizing" possibilities.[77] If Long's "opaque," "the wild man," persists—and persists as essentially Black—quare may be a destination of sorts, but not a space-time, a place, a mattering of liberation for people of African descent. There is no final destination. There is only perpetual movement, vibration, and multiplicity. There are justices. And there are fluid spaces of evolving Black gender identities, sexual orientations, and experiences of sexualities—spaces that demand a complementary flexibility with respect to sexual ethics. Quare evokes the multiplicities of justices, genders, and sexualities at work (and play) in Black culture and experience. Conceptually, quare is the destination that invites us to keep moving toward liberating futures and new destinations. The quintessential weaponry of the "opaque" is not only our opacity but (how our opacity facilitates) our mobility. We are destined to move.[78]

A final debate to which Long invites us through his rhetorical flourish on hysteria is the more specific question of the relationship between gender, sexual, and racial justice. And it is within this debate that I throw my anchor. In some ways it might seem unusual to talk about sexuality at such a time as this in the lives of Afrodiasporic people in and beyond the United States. In so many ways, the first twenty years of the twenty-first century have been a continuation of the systemic violence against and destruction of people of African descent that has characterized the previous five hundred years. When the roots, circumstances, legacies, conditions, and proliferations of racial injustice targeting people of African descent are identified, traced, analyzed, and evaluated, the constellation of it all is enormous. So this book considers some appropriate responses to one question that might stabilize this constellation of "dark matter": What do ethical options with respect to sexual orientation and gender identity for people of African descent have to do with broad visions and understandings of justices?[79]

At such a time as this, there is no relevant discourse that fails to acknowledge the injustices facing people of African descent in and beyond the United States—along with countless people and communities whose class, race, gender identity, and sexual orientation locate them outside of a Euro-heteropatriarchal elite minority. For this reason, I believe that the contemporary ethicist must wrestle with the topics of injustice and justices, carefully discerning what these are as living, breathing concepts and providing a well-lighted path toward justices. And, even if it is moving and changing, justices remain the target.

Justices are elusive targets for pursuit though—and still justice has most often been the demand and target. There has been a definitive enough, if debated, sense of what justice is such that appeals continue to be made to it in its singular form. Theorists have wrestled with the matter of whether or not justice can be achieved, whether or not justice can be attained, whether or not justice is an objective toward which individuals and/or communities can work. Reinhold Niebuhr has contended that justice is a pursuit and an objective that is right and possible for individuals in ways that it is not accessible for collectives.[80] Postmodernists and deconstructionists have defended the impossibility of revolution, real reorientation, (the) real, (the) just, justice, or any essentialist or teleological project. Liberationists have given way to a similar nihilism, or a conviction that the end of justice is so elusive, its environs so rapidly changing, and its content so variable for and within individuals and communities—in specific and generalized terms—that, at best, the pursuit of it is eternal. However, this latter possibility among liberationists and other justice seekers informs an explicitly different approach that this project takes. *Black, Quare, and Then to Where* speaks of justices—not (just) justice.

Meeting Maât

In evaluating theories of justice (i.e., justices) as they relate to Black sexuality, this book contemplates justice as an agentive actor that does things—and justices as agentive actors that do things. Specifically, I argue that justice does things—in a personified way—and that the things justice does are different than we might imagine. Justice/s may surprise us as (an) actor/s. Nevertheless, justice performs. However, given the power of the gerundive form, we can simultaneously consider justice as an actor and as an object acted upon in the ways -*ing* specifies.[81]

Maât assists in the personification of justice. She is just that, after all. She has wings with which she might fly—and yet she is still as she weighs the souls of those who have died against a single feather.[82] She acts and she is acted upon. She encounters and is encountered. Maât is flying, jumping, turning, coding, shouting. And, in some senses, Maât is flown, jumped/entangled, puzzled/turned, been/coded, and danced/shouted. Maât bears the marks of immortality and everlasting life, standing at the threshold of those unsure of their mortality at the day of judgment. How does Maât evolve in her timelessness? How does she attain "forever" forever?

In *The Complete Gods and Goddesses of Ancient Egypt*, Richard H. Wilkinson notes that Maât as "goddess" "personified the concepts of truth, justice, and cosmic order" and that she is at least as old as the Old Kingdom (as she is mentioned in the Pyramid Texts found in Saqqara). However, Wilkinson also notes that in the Pyramid Texts, she is "said to stand behind the sun god Re"; by the New Kingdom there is evidence of her being called "daughter of Re"; she was "associated with Osiris—who is said to be 'lord of *maat*' at an early date," though, Wilkinson notes, "in later times she was subsumed to some extent by Isis."[83] Wilkinson continues to describe Maât in this way: "As the daughter of Re Maat was also the sister of the reigning king who was the 'son of Re,' and the relationship of the goddess with the king was a vital one. Both the monarch's legitimation and the efficacy of his reign were ultimately based upon the degree to which he upheld *maat* and it was common therefore for kings to style themselves 'beloved of Maat.'"[84] He goes on to state:

> Her role was multifaceted but embraced two major aspects. On the one hand, Maat represented the universal order or balance—including concepts such as truth and right—which was established at the time of creation. This aspect is the basis of her relationship with Re—for she is the

order imposed upon the cosmos created by the solar demiurge and as such is the guiding principle who accompanied the sun god at all times. The order represented by Maat must be renewed or preserved constantly. . . . As a natural corollary of her identity with right balance and harmony Maat also represented the concept of judgement. In the Pyramid Texts the goddess appears in this role in dual form, as "the two Maats" judging the deceased king's right to the thrones of Geb (PT 317). And in the later funerary literature it is in the "Hall of the two Truths" (the dual form of Maat) that the judgement of the deceased occurs. The gods themselves acting as the judges of the divine tribunal, are called the "council of Maat."[85]

And in sorting through the significance of Maât as a model for, personification/embodiment of, and modern corrective for justice, it is also interesting to consider another of Maât's relationships within the *nṯrw*, or *netcherw*.[86] Wilkinson notes, "The husband of Maat was usually said to be the scribal god, Thoth."[87] This last finding is particularly outstanding because Thoth is the ibis, the scribe, and so critically important for knowledge and its categories, learning, and writing. In other words, there is something about justice and the truth that goes hand in hand with learning and teaching, reading and writing, knowing and wisdom (though another goddess covers more of the wisdom territory).

This returns us to the one reference to Thoth in Long's *Significations*. There Long points out the ways that Thoth has an important role in treating women's "hysteria." In fact, the long beak of the ibis is part of the treatment for this condition. Vaginal penetration by some phallic object seems to be one of the important physical treatments for this condition diagnosed according to various, and at times indefinite, symptoms. Penetration was not the only treatment when this condition was diagnosed in ancient Egypt, but Thoth was the one to whom appeals for healing were made. It is interesting to consider what justice, order, and/or balance is being brought about here—and how and why. Does justice direct Thoth in his effectiveness for this condition? Is Maât honored to support this responsibility of Thoth's? Is Maât ashamed of Thoth's participation in this role—or that he has been assigned it? Does Maât balance Thoth in this, as some inauspicious and/or shameful responsibility? If it is somehow a shameful responsibility, wherein lies the shame—that Thoth is a participant or that the woman's need or "hysterical condition" presents itself? How does shame manifest or not within ancient Egyptian culture and/or religion? How is this evolving over time? How are these roles of Thoth, Maât, and women evolving over time—especially nearly five thousand years—since the attempted (and soon after successful) unification of Upper and Lower Egypt?

Even beyond the possibilities of meaning in the relationship between Maât and Thoth, it is interesting to consider the ways that Maât changes over time. Her relationships change, her importance in religious and social narratives changes. She remains, but the beliefs around who she is related to and how change in the various generational iterations of Maât. This is one of the most attractive elements of Maât as an embodiment of justice and a conversation partner for this quare-womanist-vindicationist project. Like the characters in Alice Walker's *Temple of My Familiar*, we can imagine and, at times, even trace the ways that Maât is shifting not only in meaning and belief but also in sexuality (i.e., sexual practices), form, species, gender, and relationships.[88] Maât is dynamic. We can imagine Maât flying transexually. We can imagine Maât jumping[89] into the sexual aspects of marriage. We can imagine Maât dancing[90] in the freedoms of homosexalities. We can imagine Maât puzzling[91] pieces of interracial intimacies and hybrid identities. We can imagine Maât, an emergent terraspheric being,[92] beyond simulation and simulacra.

In a sense, the isness/ontology of Maât is being herself fully—and she invites those who are mindful of her and her significance into such becoming and belonging. Maât is, however, more than this as she does particular things, performing in particular ways. Maât flying invites we who follow her lead not to be limited to ground travel, to think about movement in ways that move quickly through space-time, to think about journeying through and beyond the atmosphere. Justices are on the move, but not necessarily slow, progressive, or gradualist. Maât jumping invites we who follow her lead to remember that sometimes we must cover hurdles on our course—and (even when) gravity prevails; we may leave the ground only momentarily to accomplish a discrete task. Justices are not always as deep or wide reaching as we would hope; sometimes the best we can do is to establish a better condition of fairness and equity for one, a few, a short period of time, of a specific circumstance. Maât dancing invites us into the centripetal/centrifugal shout, purposeful rhythms, the erotic play, and the social significances of what Imani e Wilson terms "songdance."[93] Justices dancing move in space in creative ways, reorienting power, people, and positions; with rhythm, play, significance, and community too dissonant for evil to prevail, justices are dancing. Maât puzzling is the turning of ideas, thoughts, peoples, and pieces; the working (out) of formula and spelling (out) of logics. Justices puzzling accept that there is mental, psychological, and emotional work involved in any pursuits of justices and that the maintenance of justice is ongoing, eternal work. Justices are solved for—and then solved for again (and again). Maât *being* invites us into complex connections between earthenness and coding; the being individual and communal agents is curated and maintained—just as justice is. Justices *being* are individuals and communities becoming their own better angels with intention—and at pace.

Justices

Part II

Flying Justice 3

Sun Ra's ~~Sexuality~~ and Other Afrofutures

And when I was traveling, I always found that I could . . . pick up a girl because I told her I was playing music. I never got over the feeling of knowing whether I'm . . . some girl would like me because of me just being a person—and not just a performer. And so, after having been married and having a kid I was thinking about eliminating any sexual feeling I could have in my body. So, I was told that was called castration. . . . I realized that our being physical or sexual has nothing to do with what you think or believe. It has more to do with who you think you're affecting—and what you think you're affecting. . . . And so, . . . from that day to this day I have decided there's two kinds of human beings: one female and one male and one man and one woman. So, I decided I would join what I thought the categories would be: I would rather be a man than a male.
—**Ornette Coleman in** *Ornette: Made in America*

So I found myself talking on street corners to black people—I felt they needed it. No white people—I was talking about spaceships, I was talking about flying into outer space. I was talking about everything—satellites!—to black people. A black minister told me, "Hey, well, you know, it ain't in the Bible." I'd say, "They're going to the moon, they're going to go further, I don't care what it says in the Bible—that's what's going to happen." And it happened.
—**Sun Ra quoted in John F. Szwed,** *Space Is the Place*

Can justices fly? Do justices do anything outside of flying? When, where, how, and why might justices fly? These are among the questions that arise when attempting to retheorize justices according to less familiar points of origin. In some ways it might seem unusual to talk about sexuality at such a time as this in the lives of Afrodiasporic people in and beyond the United States. The first twenty years of the twenty-first century, in so many ways, have been a continuation of systemic violence against and destruction of people of African descent that characterized the past five hundred years. When the roots, circumstances, legacies, conditions, and proliferations of racial injustice targeting people of African descent are identified, traced, analyzed, and evaluated, the constellation of it all is enormous. So, *Black, Quare, and Then to Where* considers some appropriate responses to one question that might stabilize this constellation of dark matter: what do the ethical options with respect to sexual orientation and gender identity for people of African descent have to do with broad visions and understandings of justices? This chapter especially considers (1) more familiar theorizations of justice(s); (2) black holes, dark matter, and dark energy; (3) unfamiliar theorizations of justice(s); (4) flying as a theory of justice; (5) Sun Ra as a prophet of flying justice; (6) ~~sexuality~~ as a context through which Sun Ra explored flying justice; and (7) space as the place of Black sexual justice.

Creating as Our Souls Must Have: Religious Afrofutures

This chapter follows a path inspired by what Bev Harrison described as the "dance of redemption" and from which Katie Geneva Cannon extrapolated her distinctive womanist pedagogical method of teaching what Cannon called "liberation ethics."[1] The "dance of redemption" consists of seven parts: Conscientization, Emancipatory Historiography, Theological Resources, Norm Clarification, Strategic Options, Annunciation/Celebration, and Re-reflection and Strategic Action. Cannon describes "liberation ethics" as follows:

> *Liberation ethics is debunking, unmasking, and disentangling the ideologies, theologies, and systems of value operative in a particular society.*

How is it done?

> *By analyzing the established power relationships that determine cultural, political, and economic presuppositions and by evaluating the legitimating myths that sanction the enforcement of such values.*

Why is it worth doing?

> *In order that we may become responsible decision-makers who envision structural and systemic alternatives that embrace the well-being of us all.*[2]

For Cannon, "liberation ethics" informed a course concept of three concentric circles or wheels that addressed (1) "the intellectual predisposition of traditional male thinkers," (2) "the specificity of Afro-Christian culture," and (3) "experiential dimensions of women's texts and interpretations"—"women of the African Diaspora" respectively in each course. As a religious ethicist and womanist, I attempt to follow the wisdom of Cannon's liberation ethics, echoing the rhythms and geometries of wheels turning in the middle of wheels, in the middle of the air, in a dance of redemption.[3]

Building on Cannon's liberation ethics model, Black sexual ethics can be expressed as *"debunking, unmasking, and disentangling the"* racist, sexist, and heterosexist *"ideologies, theologies, and systems of value operative in a particular society."* It is done *"by analyzing the established power relationships that determine cultural, political, and economic presuppositions"* about Blackness, gender identity, and sexual orientation *"and by evaluating the legitimating myths that sanction the enforcement of such values."* It is worth doing so *"that we may become responsible decision-makers who envision structural and systemic alternatives that embrace the"* sexual *"well-being of us all"* and especially people of African descent. I believe that this is also work worth doing for the sake of the everyday, sacred development and release of erons. Cannon explains: *"Erons* is a word coined by Wynn Legerton in May 1989 to describe the erotic particles emitted into the air whenever we are doing the work our souls must have." Cannon charges us to find and cultivate the places in our communities that are "alive with the hum of erons."[4]

Conscientization: Familiar Justice(s)

At such a time as this, there is no relevant discourse that fails to acknowledge the injustices facing people of African descent in and beyond the United States—along with countless people and communities whose class, race, gender identity, and sexual orientation locate them outside of a Euro-heteropatriarchal elite minority. For this reason, I believe that the contemporary ethicist must wrestle with the topics of injustice and justices, carefully discerning what these are as living, breathing concepts—and providing a well-lit path toward justices. And, even if they are moving and changing and multiple, justices remain the targets.

Implicitly and explicitly modern one-third-world approaches to moral reasoning begin and end with variations of Michael Sandel's summary: our moral reasoning comes down to matters of "maximizing welfare, respecting freedom, and promoting virtue."[5] As awkward as it is for most of us to evaluate when, where, and how we are applying any or all of these moral reasoning frameworks at any given moment, when we do reflect on our thoughts, words, and deeds, we can often locate ourselves in one of the following moral reasoning categories presented in the introduction: consequentialist moral reasoning, nonconsequentialist moral reasoning, and virtue-based moral reasoning. In more or less sophisticated ways, these familiar approaches to moral reasoning inform expressions of justice.

Though it seems increasingly rare for individuals to give or take account of the appropriateness, goodness, and/or rightness of their thoughts, words, and deeds on the basis of an evaluation of their applied moral reasoning, the value of such an evaluation remains. Why we do what we do does matter. I argue that this observation about the frequency with which we give or take an account of the virtue of our applied moral reasoning (i.e., actions) may be a reflection of (1) a modern triumph of a consequentialist pragmatism, or (2) a hybridization of moral reasoning, the virtue of which is only ever evaluated at the convenience of primary moral agents and/or the community/ies to which primary moral agents choose to make themselves accountable; a hybridization of moral reasoning that puts a relatively low value on consistency of moral reasoning between diverse circumstances and between diverse people and/or communities with whom moral interactions take place. Whether or not this observation and analysis holds, on the basis of some moral reasoning, possibilities of justices become an aspiration. After all, justices are what sound, applied moral reasoning produces. Justices are that which is morally defensible. While not all moral reasoning is justly applied, not all moral reasoning results in just conclusions, outcomes, and/or actions, and, thus, not all moral reasoning is (rightly) moral, the notion of doing justice begins with an idea or with ideas about what is right and wrong and what makes right right and wrong wrong.

Once there is some sense of what is right and what is wrong (i.e., what is just) in a particular or generalized sense, familiar conceptualizations of how to realize justice(s) come into play. As presented in the introduction, these might include the following: distributive justice, procedural justice, restorative justice, and retributive justice.

As dynamic, layered, continuous, dimensionally varied, and temporally complicated as human existence is; as united and diverse, one and many as human beings are: this is how complex demands for and approaches to justice can be. The theories and praxes that appeal to justice can feel and can be arbitrary. Communitarian senses of common good are often disconnected from the communities whose interests they strive to represent; Martha Nussbaum's central human functional capabilities approach is, on the surface, oblivious to the transtemporality of human existence, diversely measured quanta of time, energy, and matter, and how these impact an equitably realized affirmation of human capacities.[6]

Emancipatory Historiography: Black Holes, Dark Matter, and Dark Energy

The master narratives with respect to justice(s) are familiar parts of our everyday language, even if attending to the demands of justice(s) in balanced and responsible ways eludes us. As familiar as these narratives, moral reasonings, forms of justice, and implicit appeals to (human) rights (i.e., the capabilities approach) are, in many ways, this account raises more questions than answers. However, this reconscientizing work is an important reminder of the ways that master narratives invite the balance of countermemory through emancipatory historiographies. Emancipatory historiographies disrupt what Townes identifies as fantastic hegemonic imagination.[7] Recognizing "the subjective nature of history and memory," Townes notes that understanding "structural evil is to recognize, from the outset, that the story *can* be told in another way."[8] Accordingly, collective memory can be dangerously constructive, reifying, dissociative, and disruptive. Townes explains, "Collective memory endures and draws strength from individuals as group members who are drawing on the cultural and sociopolitical contexts of the group to remember. Collective memory is held together by the confidence found in association and is a constructive and reconstructive process through such cultural forms as music, dance, fiction, poetry, historical scholarship, and theoethical musings."[9] Collective memory offensively manifests as fantastic hegemonic imagination, understood as follows:

> The fantastic is the hesitation experienced by a person who knows only the laws of nature confronting an apparently supernatural event—it is defined in relation to the real and the imaginary.... Essentially, hegemony is the set of ideas that dominant groups employ in a society to secure the consent of subordinates to abide by their rule. The notion of consent is key, because hegemony is created through coercion that is gained by using the church, family, media, political parties, schools, unions, and other voluntary associations—the civil society and all its organizations.... This imagination conjures up worlds and their social structures that are not based on supernatural events and phantasms, but on the ordinariness of evil.[10]

Townes explains that, considering the role of the "very construction of history and memory in shaping and maintaining structural forms of evil," we can see the ways that "when memory and imagination impersonate history they are fruits of the fantastic hegemonic imagination."[11] Townes argues that the fantastic hegemonic imagination is not only the fodder of a flawed collective memory, but that it is draped with clothes that make it real. However, there is countermemory that exists on the exterior of the real-izations and unnatural embodiments of the fantastic hegemonic imagination—countermemory that is often silent and silenced. And this countermemory is real: realer than fantastic hegemonic imagination—and more abundant than that which is imagined, perceived, and named.

It turns out, justices—especially those that sound as countermemory—are elusive targets for pursuit. An ear for the sound of silence is essential for this pursuit—like "the sound of the genuine."[12] Interpreting silence—a task that must always be qualified with an acknowledgment of its imprecision and an admission of its subjectivity—is a tall order. However, particularly for people of African descent, people who have been signified signifiers, Charles Long contends that there is a unique relationship with silence.[13] And not just a distinctive relationship with silence, but also a specific connection with opacity and as opaque. Long is not alone. Contemporary Afrodiasporic theorists of race and difference have long contemplated the best ways to describe the otherness of people of African descent, people of color, and oppressed communities. Wimbush invites the practice of "reading darkly"; Butler clarifies "abject others"; Spillers speaks of "interstices" and the interstitial; Crenshaw describes "intersectionality"; Cohen writes of margins and secondary marginalization; Townes writes of "limbo" and liminal spaces; and Hammonds writes of Black w(h)oles.[14] All of these, in their own ways, attempt to handle holy differences that have suffered profane oppressions—and have, consequently, necessitated active demands for justices.

Long observes the disappearing act of "High God," the ways that master narratives of religion have invoked and silenced a supreme being and, thus, given way to gods of "fertility and creativity."[15] Long explains that these gods were, finally, "present not as voices speaking but as the silence which is necessary to all speech."[16] What is silence for? What is silence about? Whatever it is for, whatever it is about, the silence that evolves through the creative and fertile spaces of divinity is, in Long's analysis, associated with the opaque, empirical others, two-thirds of the world. Though silent, this is space, these are people, whose voices must be heard.

On this point, the physical world is instructive. A black hole is defined as "a place in space where gravity pulls so much that even light cannot get out."[17] While there are some black holes that may be part of what composes dark matter, this is no longer believed to be the case. At the event horizon of a black hole, space-time is stretched. The only substance known to withstand the gravitational pull of black holes is dark energy. Stephen Hawking discovered that there is a radiation emitted from black holes, but as this radiation is emitted, the black hole loses mass and shrinks; there is an information loss; black holes are characterized by contraction.[18] According to NASA, "roughly 68% of the universe is dark energy. Dark matter makes up about 27%. The rest—everything on Earth, everything ever observed with all of our instruments, all normal matter—adds up to less than 5% of the universe."[19] The Chandra X-Ray Observatory explains that "dark matter" is a "term used to describe matter that can be inferred to exist from its gravitational effects, but does not emit or absorb detectable amounts of light."[20] Though dark matter may be composed of baryonic matter, most astronomers believe that it is a particle or particles composed of an unidentified element or elements. Though only about 27 percent of the known universe, the actual content, the composition, of dark matter is unknown. "First discovered about 20 years ago by measuring the distances to exploding stars called supernovas," it is reported, "dark energy is a proposed type of force, or energy, that permeates all space and causes the expansion of the Universe to accelerate. It accounts for about 70 percent of the composition of the Universe. In the 'concordance model,' currently used in most studies of the history and structure of the Universe, dark energy is interpreted as the 'cosmological constant.' That means it is energy associated with empty space, and is constant throughout space and time." Though dark energy was thought to be a constant, this January 2019 report notes that "astronomers have found evidence that an invisible force called dark energy, widely thought to be constant, may be getting stronger with time. If confirmed, this result could force astronomers to re-examine their fundamental understanding of the history and structure of the Universe."[21] This discovery with respect to dark energy is instructive: expansively moving, dark energy is (in a way opposite to black holes) flying into the future through space-time. What the majority of the universe is doing by nature (without discernible causalities) is expanding, exhaling, stretching out—even while it contains black holes, dark matter, and other forms of matter (less than 5 percent of the universe) that are pulling, contracting, and shrinking.

There is more unknown about black holes, dark matter, and dark energy than what is known. For the most part, these seem to be silent aspects of our reality. What we do know or understand we only know and understand on our own terms. None of us really knows the language that black holes, dark matter, and dark energy respectively speak. Nevertheless, black holes, dark matter, and dark energy—appearing opaque and silent to most of us and relatively unknown in content—are still more than two-thirds of the universe that we know. Yet we know that black holes, dark matter, and dark energy have ways of being, tendencies, and rules. Too, we know that black holes, dark matter, and dark energy constitute the connective space-time between the observable, phenomenal matter of stars, planets, and other masses.

Here I introduce the work of Cheikh Anta Diop (1923–86) because of the ways he sought a return to ancient Egypt as a place stripped of its Africanness and Blackness—and undervalued as a source of social order. Ancient Egypt has been cast as a black hole. However, Diop recovers it as a place of order. No vindicationist is more central than Cheikh Anta Diop; in some ways, Diop, the Senegalese historian, anthropologist, physicist, and politician is to the academy what Sun Ra is to music. Diop approached his research and writing in ways that incorporated all of these elements and modeled a way that other vindicationists might take up the holistic, integrated, proto-intersectional, and interdisciplinary work of raising a cultural alternative. He was shaped by Aimé Césaire and Négritude—and, indirectly, by the Harlem Renaissance. The period during which J. A. Rogers was publishing overlapped with that of Diop considerably—though Rogers was born four decades earlier. *Stolen Legacy*, George G. M. James's seminal text, was published in 1954, the same year that Diop's *Nations Nègres et Culture* was published in France; *Nations* included ideas developed toward Diop's thesis on predynastic Egypt for which he could not find a jury of examiners.

In *Civilization or Barbarism: An Authentic Anthropology* (1981 in French; 1991 English translation), Diop offers a comprehensive argument for the Nubian connection with ancient Egypt as well as for the likelihood of Africans with darker pigmentation being the first *Homo sapiens sapiens*.[22] He also disputes any claims of lesser intelligence waged against people of African descent.[23] Diop presents African clans as matrilineal—and as a system that values women and their rights.[24] However, Diop tends to moralize with respect to gender—essentializing gender and gender roles and providing the grounds on which much more misogynist and heterosexist claims are made. Diop's arguments with respect to the long histories of organized African societies and the values of Afrodiasporic cultures provide the foundation for his interdisciplinary intellectual interventions that address political organization, scientific knowledge, and moral instruction as integral coconstitutive elements of human existence.

With respect to political organization, Diop helpfully presents different types of states (sociopolitical, government organizations). Among these, he first presents the "Asian or African mode of production" (AMP).[25] Diop argues that Alexander and the Greeks (and later the Romans) adopted the AMP because, after Egypt (the "Osirian" Egyptian revolution of the Sixth Dynasty, 2100 BCE) and China (An Lu-Shan's ninth-century CE revolt against the T'ang Dynasty) endured early revolutions, they reorganized and established a state structure that was more immune to revolutionary efforts. Diop writes, "By creating state machinery (that of the AMP) allowing the coordination of social, military, and political action on a large scale over a vast territory including several cities, the people had unwittingly forged chains that could be broken only by the progress of modern times, which made possible the education, instruction, information, and coordination of the struggle of working classes on an equally large scale."[26] He explains that had the Egyptian revolution had the benefit of modern "direction and coordination," it would have been even more effective than it was.[27] He argues that a key to successful revolution is a reduction of the empire to the size of a city. "The episodes of this struggle show perfectly that if the empire had been reduced to the size of a Greek city, the revolution would have succeeded, because the capital had been taken and became a desert; this revolution from the bottom up would not have been a mere reinstatement of the old order."[28] Diop also notes that successful revolutions have democratizing—and then (as a byproduct), republic-making—effects.[29] Diop not only specifies that AMP states, and Egypt in particular, charted sociopolitical courses after which other nation-states can and do model themselves but also clarifies the features of effective revolution—and the dangers to be avoided. More than that, he offers blueprints with respect to an effective social order—that revolutionaries might try to pursue if they can overcome the safeguards that contemporary nation-states have put in place to thwart revolution:

- Direction
- Organization
- "The coordination of social, military, and political action on a large scale over a vast territory including several cities"
- The irreducibility of the new social order to a single, conquerable city
- A strong democratic principle and opportunity for democratic exercise
- Protections against the establishment of a republic (or reestablishment of royalty)

Diop's *Civilization or Barbarism* not only provides a clear picture of how sociopolitical organization is a matter of global, historic, transcultural proportions but also asserts that (1) contemporary nation-states are as strong as they are because they are built on ancient Egyptian principles of social organization, and (2) contemporary Pan-African communities on the continent of Africa and in diaspora should be actively pursuing revolution to dismantle the nation-states of which they are a part and to supplant these nation-states with systems of social order and organization that reflect the blueprint elements specified above.

The extent of ancient Egyptian scientific knowledge—especially of physics (and metaphysics) is not (exhaustively) chartable. However, there is an "Egyptian 'cosmogony' attested by texts of the pyramids (2600 B.C.)." Diop writes, "One can distinguish three great systems of thought in Egypt that tried to explain the origin of the universe and the appearance of all that is: the *Hemopolitan* system, the *Heliopolitan* system, the *Memphite* system, and to this can be added the *Theban* system."[30] Between these systems, a concept of creation, scientific principles, and moral codes are crafted. Diop tells the story:

- "The universe was not created *ex nihilo*, on a given day; but there has always existed an uncreated matter, without a beginning or an end.

- "Primitive matter also contained the law of transformation, the principle of the evolution of matter through time, equally considered as a divinity: *Khepera.*"
- "Carried by its own evolutionary movement, eternal matter, uncreated, by dint of going through the stages of organization, ends up by becoming self-aware. The first consciousness thus emerges from the primordial *Nun*; it is God, Ra, the demiurge (Plato) who is going to complete creation."
- "Ra achieves creation through the word"; "Ra's word" is "the *Ka*— or the universal reason that is present everywhere in the universe, and in every thing."
- "Ra creates the four divine pairs, according to Heliopolitan cosmogony: 1. *Shu* and *Tefnut* = air (space) and humidity (water). 2. *Geb* and *Nut* = earth and heaven (light, fire)." Note "the four elements that make up the universe of the Pre-Socratic Greek philosophers. . . . 3. *Osiris* and *Isis:* the fertile human couple that will beget humanity (Adam, Eve). 4. *Seth* and *Nephthys:* the sterile couple that will introduce evil into human history."
- "According to Egyptian thought, the being is composed of three principles (Plato, Aristotle), to which a fourth can be added: the shadow. 1. The *Zed* or *Khet*, which decomposes after death. 2. The *Ba*, which is the body's corporeal soul (the 'double' of the body throughout Black Africa). 3. The being's shadow. 4. The *Ka* = immortal principle that rejoins the divinity in heaven after death. Thus was founded, on the ontological level, the being's immortality (three thousand years before the birth of the revealed religions). Each person possesses a portion of the divinity that fills the cosmos and renders it intelligible to the spirit. Perhaps it is on these grounds that the Egyptian cosmogony makes God say 'that he made man in his own image.'"
- "The Hermopolitan ogdoad is specifically composed of four divine pairs representing the opposing principles of nature that are supposed to be at the origin of things:

  - "*Kuk* and *Kuket* = the primordial darkness and its opposite: darkness and light.
  - "*Nun* and *Nunet* = the primordial waters and their opposite: matter and nothingness.

- "*Heh* and *Hehet* = spatial infinity and its opposite: the infinite and the finite, the unlimited and the limited.
- "*Amon* and *Amonet* = the hidden and the visible, the noumenon and the phenomenon.
- "*Niaou* and *Niaouet* = emptiness and its opposite: the void and the replete, matter (later)."[31]

I quote aspects of Diop's account of ancient Egyptian cosmogony at length because it demonstrates the inextricability of Egyptian beliefs, morality, philosophy, account of creation and faith from Egyptian science, physics, biology, and so on. As with (later) aspects of Greek mythology, the gods (or deities) directly correspond with natural phenomena. Diop provides these critical markers by which a neophyte might begin study of the science of ancient Egypt. Principles of darkness and light, matter and nothingness, the infinite and the finite, the hidden and the visible, the void and the replete become the foundation for modern physics. Most significantly, Diop makes a critical connection between modern physics, moral philosophy, and everyday life experience:

> Thus, modern physics has created the right situation to teach us that classical logic is nothing but the sum of mental habits, of provisional rules that can change when sovereign experience requires it. Reason lapses, but it does not get caught in a vicious circle; it progresses; it is accomplishing under our eyes the most formidable qualitative leap that it has ever made since the origin of the exact sciences.
>
> The reasoning reason, supported by the experience of microphysics and astrophysics, is going to give birth to a super-logic that will no longer be hampered by the archeological materials of thought, inherited from the previous phases of the evolution of the scientific mind.
>
> A new philosophical concept has to be forged, that of the "logical availability" of the mind. Tomorrow, sovereign experience will be able to transform into rational fact what seems to us logically absurd or impossible today. The absolute absurd no longer exists with regard to reason.[32]

"Sovereign experience" can, will, should, and does change physics on the basis of "logical availability." I would be remiss not to acknowledge Diop's agenda. He asks, intimating that the answers are to be found in this critical recovery of ancient Egyptian knowledge, "Could Africa, with the warmth of her social fabric, save Western man from his pessimism and individualistic solitude?"[33]

Even scientific knowledge has been—and, perhaps in more noble ways, should better be—put to social tasks. For Diop, a truer reconciliation between philosophical (i.e., moral) and physical (i.e., scientific) principles—sensitive to sovereign experience—is a hope for civilization in all of its aspects.

With respect to moral instruction, Diop does gesture toward what he associates with a Black way, a philosophical and moral posture that has historic roots in African clanic structure: having an "optimistic cosmogony"; having "no notion of original sin"; having a "pacifist morality"; having a "highly developed" "sense of community" in which "solitude is prohibited"; and where "the notion of private property is marginal, but it is far from being ignored."[34] Morality (in terms of cultural traits) is historic and inherited, but it is not fixed and definite; morality (in terms of cultural traits) has a dynamic and malleable future. Diop writes, "Until now, the cultural traits that we inherited from the past are the very ones that we analyzed in *L'Unité Culturelle de l'Afrique Noire:* goodness, gaiety, optimism, social sense, etc., and this brief account show[s] that there is nothing fixed or permanent about them, but they change with conditions."[35] With respect to moral and philosophical instruction, Diop's project is to affirm and empower his Black readers to cultivate themselves and their spiritual strength. This metaethical work is part and parcel of Diop's intellectual process; this is fundamentally cultural work. He writes of culture in this way:

> For every individual his or her own cultural identity is a function of that of his or her people. Consequently, one must define the cultural identity of a people. This means, to a great extent, one must analyze the components of the collective personality. We know that three factors contribute to its formation:
>
> 1. An historical factor
> 2. A linguistic factor
> 3. A psychological factor[36]

And of Black culture and what he perceives (empirically and normatively) on the horizon, Diop writes, "Today, with the explosion everywhere in the world of these structures inherited from the past, we are witnessing a new moral and spiritual birth among peoples: a new African moral consciousness and a new national temperament are developing before our eyes, and unless the structures resist—and how could they?—this phenomenon of spiritual transformation of the people will become greater."[37] And in this spirit of this "new African moral consciousness" and "spiritual birth," Diop continues, "And the Black of the diaspora? The linguistic bond is broken, but the historic bond remains stronger than ever, perpetuated by memory; just as the cultural heritage of Africa, which is evident in the three Americas, attests to the continuity of cultural customs: it has even been said, I believe, that the difference between the White American and his English, or in any event European, ancestor is the Negro laugh, so pleasant, inherited from the household slave who raised his children."[38] And what does "the Negro laugh" betray? It betrays humanity; it betrays the injustice of oppression; it betrays the possibility and proof of those who survive and thrive notwithstanding oppression; it betrays awareness of the injustice of forced servitude and other forms of oppression; it betrays the long- and short-term strategies of those who rock the cradle. The Black diaspora in the "three Americas" and the Caribbean share a cultural bond and unity with respect to history, (null) linguistics, and psychology that are confirmed in and through sovereign experience.

Diop's emancipatory historiography only takes us so far. Sun Ra complements this historiography with his own sovereign experience. Through Ra's sovereign experience, there are two fundamental rejoinders to Diop's approach that are worth considering. First, Ra is unmoved by the emphasis on fertility and reproduction that sits at the core of Diop's gender and gendered analysis. Second, Ra is unconvinced of race and its relevance—especially to the future of social organization. For Ra, the ultimate response to both of these matters is that he is a child of Saturn. He is the creation of, the offspring of, another planet. He does not, therefore, participate in reproductive patterns or social organizational patterns in the same way that others are prone to engage. His ~~sexuality~~ leads him to out-of-this-world possibilities. Thus, when Ra reclaims ancient Egypt, he is reclaiming the order of more literal black holes, planetary and extraterrestrial possibilities. He is not interested in the revolution that takes place here on earth, but the revolution that draws us into the broader cosmos, causing us to fly. Still, the details of moral, scientific, and social organizational order that Diop specifies are important even to Ra's extraterrestrial visions. Diop's retrieval of ancient Egyptian moral, scientific, and social order through emancipatory historiography are elements to be engaged in the cosmic futures Ra imagines. Diop envisions Wakanda on earth; Ra takes flight to Wakanda in the cosmic pluriverse.[39] As a child of Saturn, Sun Ra has a distinctive sovereign experience at his back as he flies.

In his seminal text *Two Thousand Seasons*, Ayi Kwei Armah delineates "the way" of people of African descent as he details what the beginnings of the transatlantic slave trade felt like for those on the continent of Africa in the form of a novel. The way is reciprocal; the way knows purpose; the way is a way of remembrance; the way maintains community; the way forgives those who go astray and return; the way turns from those who know better but do not do better; the way recognizes the power of dance; the way is worth dying for; the way honors names and naming—and their power. He writes from Dar es Salaam while Julius Nyerere is still alive and Idi Amin is ravishing Uganda. He writes as one born in Ghana who attended boarding school in the United States—followed by Ivy League schools for his undergraduate and graduate training. He writes as one who has seen the world and Black people in the aftermath of the transatlantic slave trade. He returns—and returns his readers—to "the way." It is true, Armah's vision in *Two Thousand Seasons* reeks of homophobia, heterosexism, and sexism. However, for many—including women and LGBTQ people throughout the African diaspora—his words have been like some other vindicationists: water of thirst.[40] Théophile Obenga extends Armah's work to a prior point of origin. Obenga's work asks: from whence this way? And Obenga's work answers: look to the Khemet, fertile with the contributions of Kushite people and culture. Together, Armah and Obenga pick up the work of Diop and direct the reader toward a way where space is the place.

Theological Resources: Unfamiliar Justice(s)

While acknowledging a modern western standard for moral inquiry and reasoning, and theories of justice, *Black, Quare, and Then to Where* centers Maât, as an epistemological point of origin—the one with whom we can fly into these cosmic futures with Sun Ra directing the material way with the help of sovereign experience and intellects like Diop directing the logic of that way. Notwithstanding Katie G. Cannon's interest in Christian theoethical resources that support the work of countermemory and emancipatory historiography that contravenes the hegemonic content about which we must be conscientized, Cannon and others have observed the value of religious and cultural resources beyond any recognizably Christian theoethical toolkit. It is to such theoethical resources beyond Christianity that this book first appeals. A research interest in Maât is consistent with traditional academic discourse insofar as it offers "an interpretation" of a "primitive and prehistoric religious" culture and may contribute to the problem of a "continuing and inordinate concern for the data of primitive religions and methods growing from their interpretations."[41] However, this approach is distinct insofar as it does not reify the inferiority of what Charles Long calls "empirical others"; moreover, this emphasis on Maât disrupts the "cultural phenomenon in which the extraordinariness and uniqueness of a person or culture is first recognized negatively" by which "empirical others" are created.[42] The emphasis on Maât acknowledges an oft-ignored primordial source—real, relevant, and valuable. Evidence of an ancient Egyptian (i.e., khemetic) ethical system dates back as far as the 2500s and 2400s BCE. Given the ways that Europe systematically underdeveloped Africa, the location of a primordial conceptualization of what we might term *justice* in Egypt—and the assertion of Egypt as part of ancient and modern Africa—is a significant historical, geographic, and cultural claim.[43] Such a claim disrupts epistemological patterns that condescend to Africa and erase the modern-day continent of Africa as a first home of human intellect, biological matter, and darker skin pigmentations.[44]

Maât, personified, exceeds the categories of consequentialism, nonconsequentialism, and virtue. Inasmuch as Maât stands for an individual and/or an individual who is part of a constellation of deities, she is different from and more than any contemporary image of justice. She is neither Dike with scales, nor Dike with eyes covered (as of the sixteenth century). Significantly, Maât is hieroglyphic marking and appears consistently with wings—ready to fly or otherwise guide the soul of the righteous to eternity and with her single feather used to determine the merit of the soul of one who is deceased. Anthony Browder identifies the feather of Maât on the Judgment Day scale as that of an ostrich (i.e., a bird that does not fly).[45] However, Maât with wings outstretched is ready to take flight.[46] Moreover, what Maât is determining at the weighing of the soul, as it emerges from the *Book of the Coming Forth by Day* (i.e., *The Book of the Dead*), is the future of the Ba, one of "two primary aspects of the soul."[47] Browder explains:

> The *Ba* was represented by the beaded head of a man on the body of a hawk. It symbolized the "world-soul," which existed within man and the universe. The bird's body represented the soul's ability to move between heaven and Earth. It is the life-giving power of the Netcherw, and death comes to the body when the breath (Ba) exits.
>
> The *Ka* is represented by two arms . . . symbolizing the animating forces within the body. The Ka is also seen as containing all of the powers of creation and is an activator of cosmic forces. . . . On a higher level, the Ka represented spiritual free will, on a lower level it represented the fetters

that bind one's physical being to Earth. A soul becomes enlightened when it is liberated by both the Ba and the Ka.[48]

The question is not simply whether or not justice can fly, but also whether or not the souls that Maât weighs are able to take flight upon final judgment. Are the souls Maât weighs filled with enough Maât? Did the physical vessels of those souls direct enough thought, word, and deed in a way of Maât for those souls to make safe flight into and through eternity? The question of justice flying is not simply its own disembodied or *ntrt*-embodied flight, but also our flight in a cosmic sense.

Norm Clarification: Flying as a Theory of Justice

How does a focused consideration of Black sexual experience and the applied ethics that inform gender identities and sexual orientations among people of African descent impact traditional theories of justice? This is the primary question that invites a dialogue between theories of justice and Black sexual ethics. While the approaches of Michael Sandel, Martha Nussbaum, and Iris Marion Young correct for many of the shortcomings that characterize the Rawlsian tradition that builds upon a contractarian Kantian ethic, these do not fully account for the wheels within their wheel.[49] The wheels within their wheel contain a Maâtian heart of ethics and justice that must be remembered, reclaimed, and reimagined. We can remember Maât through the research of Black twentieth-century vindicationists. We can reclaim Maât as a feminine deity, a *ntrt* such that she cannot be easily appropriated by heteropatriachal Black nationalist ideologies. We can reimagine Maât, highlighting the frameworks and languages for sexual discourse that predate contemporary terms of sexual orientation and gender identity debates while yet remaining relevant to the navigation of complex sexual orientation and gender identity experiences. Here, defiantly shadowing Karenga's categorical lead, I propose more creative readings of "*a way of rightness* defined especially by the practice of the Seven Cardinal Virtues of truth, justice, propriety, harmony, balance, reciprocity and order."[50] Remembered, reclaimed, and reimagined, Maât takes flight. We who dare to be carried are flying justice; justice flies us; and/or we bear witness to justice in flight. And justice should always be moving and in flight.

In *Race and the Cosmos*, Barbara Holmes clarifies the norm of flight as a capacity that is natural to human beings—and especially people of African descent. She invites her readers to reconsider the true possibility of flying, of human beings flying, of flying justice. While referencing the prevalence of flying African stories within African American folklore, she focuses her attention on Toni Cade Bambara's *The Sea Birds Are Still Alive*. Holmes quotes Bambara:

> I say when we came to Africa, we could fly. You heard me. We could fly. . . . But we ate too much salt. Can't mess with too much salt cause it throws things out of proper balance. If you scientific, you know that. . . . And when the forces were all in balance, we were at the center of the field. The electro mag-net-ic [*sic*] field. . . . Gravity? Don't be tellin me about no somesuch gravity. That aint nuthin. We could fly. I'm tellin you something and I hope you listening. We could fly.[51]

Evaluating Fess Newton, one of the main characters in Bambara's *Sea Birds*, Holmes continues:

> Fess Newton is one who has forgotten how to soar. He is now an initiate in the school of reason and logic and is attempting the impossible task of explaining why it is scientifically impossible for human beings to fly. . . . Newton starts off reasonably enough with rhetoric about the properties of salt and about positive and negative poles. To support his point he offers a convoluted explanation of the laws of gravity. But there is a wiser one present, Ma Hudson, who says,
>
>> If you can't dance it . . . And if you can't sing it . . . leastaways tell it right. Tell it in terms of fire, water, air, earth and bond. It's the spirits that—
>> Same thing, Fess Newton hollering. Forces is forces. We just using different names.

With the help of Bambara, Holmes reminds her readers that flying is normal, the norm, and normative (i.e., as it should be and constructively reorienting). Even if flight goes by a different name, still there is a way that human beings ought to be taking to the air. Moreover, there is something in this ought and this possibility that redefines justice. As Holmes clarifies this conclusion, she also draws attention to the work of the Native Research and Scholarship Committee, noting the values to which they commit in their research: "the human family is connected to the Spirit"; "reality is relational"; "human beings are 'partners with the source of life'"; "research goals are subject to community oversight."[52] Honoring these values, Holmes notes the diverse and tangible ways that those who have fought for justice in terms of freedom from slavery and other faces of oppression have flown. One such tangible flight (on the wings) of justice that Holmes presents is the following of the drinking gourd, enslaved Africans' reading the path of the North Star in the sky. Holmes concludes:

> Every culture, no matter where it currently stands, emerged from basic and primal human organizations. It is in the remembrance that we reconnect to our relationship to the universe. Maybe if we can remember, we'll be able to fly. As Ma Hudson says in Bambara's short story, "I was saying that we could fly, but we got messed around with all that salt. Salt treks, salt trails, all those mother's tears, all those bones bleaching in the briny deep, all that sweat." To be certain, salt is the historical reality for many in the two-thirds world. But soaring is the future.[53]

And for those of us who cannot imagine another way, at the very least we can follow the flight patterns of Maât.

Strategic Options: Sun Ra as a Prophet of Flying Justice

Sun Ra uniquely embodied and orchestrated for himself the eronic—or the everyday, sacred development and release of erons. Ironically—and perhaps eronically—Sun Ra, the man who is said to have been born on May 22, 1914, in Birmingham, Alabama, and named Herman Poole Blount was different when it came to sexuality; I describe this difference as ~~sexual~~. Though the historical record on Sun Ra and the contemporaneous account of his life were written prior to the sexual revolutions that would insist on definitions of sexual orientation and gender identity that still have a strange ring to those of us who take up such categories, the life of Sun Ra, the extraordinarily prolific, innovative keyboardist, visionary composer, and legendary performer who would come to know himself as a child of Saturn in 1936 when he was a student at Alabama State Agricultural and Mechanical Institute for Negroes in Huntsville, Alabama, is a bottom-up story of emancipatory historiography.[54]

The chapters of this book have wheels within wheels, like the Hebrew scripture's Ezekiel and Cannon's canon. These wheels include (1) intersections of Black sexual lives and experiences; (2) vindicationist (and adjacent) voices (and their metaphysics); (3) just sex politics; (4) physics; and (5) thinkings-doings-(sayings)-beings of Maât (i.e., justice/s). Inside the wheel of vindicationist voices turn wheels of (a) experiences and (b) justices; these wheels also turn within individuals and communities including, but not limited to, Afrodiasporic people. The turnings of these wheels of experiences and justices may, however, have commonalities among Afrodiasporic people whose experiences of social (and sexual) life, justices, and injustices share commonalities. The wheel of experiences revolves around this question: What happens at crossroads of sexual orientations, gender identities, and sexual practices—especially as they manifest through the lives and perspectives of vindicationists, but also as they manifest in adjacent others? The wheel of justices revolves around these questions: What are the logics of justices for vindicationists? What virtuous formulations of justice do those who have reached back to the African continent (and, in this case, especially Egypt) discern? As these three wheels turn together, they reveal new ways of thinking about, framing, and articulating Black sexual ethics as a byproduct of a critical engagement between vindicationists' theories of justice and their sexual orientations, gender identities, and sexual practices. This same turning, working centripetally and centrifugally, manifests both experience-informed justices that apply to the center of sexual ethics and sexual ethics that apply to outward expressions of justicing experiences. These triadic wheels—voices-justices-experiences—spin throughout the cosmos aligning with and realigning pluriversal wheels of wave-particle-gravitational physical engagements and terra-storial politics.

This first chapter of part II focuses on Sun Ra because he, unique among most others of his day, recognized that he was not of this planet. He saw and understood himself as of another world.[55] This could not simply be attributed to his metanoiac experience at Alabama State; this was also a clarity that the ways of this world, the justices of this world, had no place for him—and could not honor and respect his dignity and equality. As a result, Ra embraced himself as of another planet, not earth; of another species, not human; of another source, not God; and other another mode of travel, flight.

The flight of justice was familiar to Sun Ra. The voice of justice carries on the wind beneath Ra's words:

EVERYTIME A BIRD GOES BY

Everytime a bird goes by
I, too, want to fly.
I have always been fascinated
By things of the sky. . . . .
Life here is some charm-spell-dream . . .

> The people rich and poor are prisoners all
>   Chained by the limits of earth's boundaries . . .
>   Chained by the limits of earth's seven seas. . . . . .
>   Chained by the limits
>   Of earth's ironies
> I take the risk to rebel
>   Even if earth is heaven or maybe hell
>   I am sure as either it would do quite well. . . . . .
>   There was war in heaven. . . . .
>   No doubt it spread to earth
>   Which resembles descriptions of hell . . .
> What care I. . . . .
>   I do defy
>   The monotony earth's sameness constant strife
>   The helplessness of earth's futile death-life . . .
> I do defy
>   Don't dare ask me further why . . .
>   I do not speak of what I think
>   I feel. . . . .
>   I feel. . . . .
>   This earth's whole scene is cruel
>   And crude. . . . .
>   Cut off from communication
>   With everything
>   That is Cosmo-Real.[56]

Though he knew the Bible and claimed, at some points, to be Christian, Sun Ra was committed to a Cosmic-Universal with a keen sense of order—this was an order he had learned through reading books at the Masonic Temple in Birmingham and nearly all the books in the libraries he visited through his undergraduate schooling. When held at Passport Control upon his arrival in Egypt because his name was Sun Ra (Szwed writes, "to be named after the sun god twice was really a bit too much"), Sun Ra suggested that "the guard call the curator of the National Museum of Antiquities with whom he was ready to discuss Egyptology."[57] He was a vindicationist, but he was beyond that too.[58] Ra was in direct dialogue with the Creator, knowing firsthand that G*d was seeking a "pure-hearted person on this planet. Just one. Someone with no ulterior motives, just simple, natural, pure of heart."[59] Dressed and

3.1: In this screenshot of a scene in Sun Ra's 1974 film *Space Is the Place*, the falcon-headed figure to the left of Sun Ra represents the god (*neter*) Ra, and the ibis-headed figure to the right of Sun Ra represents the god (*neter*) Thoth. Both these figures are of great significance to Sun Ra. He has twice named himself for the sun (and Ra), Ra meaning sun. Thoth is associated with written, mathematical, and sometimes musical inspiration; he is invoked as a treatment for the questionable diagnosis of hysteria in women; he is sometimes recognized as the husband of Maât. Sun Ra dons his own space-appropriate attire that evokes his fascination with ancient Egyptian culture. In this scene, he gambles for the futuristic extraterrestrial fate of people of African descent on earth. *Source:* Sun Ra, "Space Is the Place (1974) Sun Ra's Film," video posted on YouTube by Icy10K, October 21, 2020, https://youtu.be/LyMAu1goIMU?t=2739.

writing often as the ibis scribe Thoth, Ra flew with the precise measure of justice known only to the wings and feather of Maât. And so he wrote:

INVISIBILITY

Rise lightly from the earth
And try your wings
Try them now
While I make the darkness invisible

The visibility of the day
Is the invisibility of the night
The invisibility of the day
Is the visibility of the night
So rise lightly from the earth
And try your wings
Try them now
While the darkness is invisible[60]

And, with unseen sight, Sun Ra tried his wings.

Annunciation/Celebration: ~~Sexuality~~ as Context

For a book about Black sexuality, it may seem strange to begin with the annunciation/celebration of ~~sexuality~~ as a context through which theories of justice and Black sexual ethics might be better understood. However, there are good reasons to begin with ~~sexuality~~. The fantastic hegemonic imagination that has relentlessly read Black men as Mandingoes and Black bucks, that has read Black women as Jezebels and welfare queens, is a reason we might recall a different tradition within Black culture and community.[61] I describe this tradition as ~~sexuality~~. On one hand, ~~sexuality~~ implies cultural erasures and (denial or lack of) access with respect to sexuality; on the other hand, sexuality as a chosen context and form of sociality implies transcendent and transversing movement.

In contemplating the context of ~~sexuality~~, we recall the myth of Aunt Jemima and the complexity of Rebecca Cox Jackson.[62] While Aunt Jemima and Rebecca Cox Jackson might be identified as asexual and celibate respectively, there is a way that Sun Ra's gray asexuality or gray-sexuality (i.e., oriented on a spectrum between sexuality and asexuality) does not fit the descriptions of demisexuality, semisexuality, or asexuality. If nothing else, Sun Ra is transcendent. I do not generally defend Afropessimist positions. However, Sun Ra is a powerful example of a vindicationist who not only refused a terrestrial humanity but also refused an ordinary relationship with sexuality. While he pursued otherworldly possibilities with respect to his own ontological value and that of other people of African descent, he had no hope in a terrestrial humanity. As Afropessimist orthographic strategy is the strikethrough feature applied to humanity (i.e., ~~humanity~~), so too there is helpful linguistic significance in ~~sexuality~~. Sun Ra is ~~sexual~~ in the sense that he is past sex. Ra's approach to the social, political, and cosmic all affirm his transcendence: "With all the churches you got, all the governments you got, all the schools you got, you supposed to have a better plan than this. Worldly man has failed: spiritually, educationally, governmentally, he's failed. Worldly, he should be a good sport and say, 'I give up; I need help.' Well I'm right here as a bridge for them to get help."[63] Ra is not just past sex, he is past this world and its brand of humanity.

Sun Ra explored flying justice with a radically different approach to his own sexuality and that of those within his community. With the brief introduction to Sun Ra provided thus far, consider what it might mean to say that he was ~~sexual~~. Here I use the term ~~sexual~~ in an unconventional way. Some might characterize Sun Ra's ~~sexuality~~ as asexual because of the ways he set sexuality aside as something that did not particularly interest him. However, given the ways he was exposed to his mother's sexuality, he managed a physical condition impacting his sexual organ, and he encouraged the community around him to set sexuality aside as he had, I believe it is appropriate to say that he was mindful of sexuality. He was aware and he situated himself beyond it, past it, or even through it. Sexuality would not ground or control him. In this way, there is a crossing over/away from the concern of sexuality that I describe going forward as ~~sexual~~. Note that Sun Ra did not use the term ~~sexual~~ or asexual to describe himself, but, I argue, the former is the identifier that best approximates his sexual orientation in terms of his everyday life and living. Importantly, the fact that he did not use any terminology for this sexual orientation is, in and of itself, instructive; it clarifies the challenges of culture and temporal anachronicity that can attend to such identifiers. Naming Sun Ra's sexual orientation (or gender identity) is a questionable act. Through Rebecca Cox Jackson, Alice Walker teaches her readers a multilayered lesson with respect to social markers of identification.[64] First, do not ascribe to others an identifier they did not adopt themselves. Second, womanism is an identification a womanist must adopt for herself—it cannot be assigned. Third, (and here is where this gets a bit complicated, but) we who understand womanism can say this or that behavior looks womanist; we can say that one is acting womanish/womanist. The distinction may be a fine one, but it is nonetheless important: one can act like a womanist (and do what a womanist might do) without being a womanist; one can be a womanist (having self-identified as a womanist) yet may not always act in ways that are worthy of such identification. There is, nevertheless, value in being precise: Sun Ra was not ~~sexual~~ (i.e., he did not self-identify as ~~sexual~~);

Sun Ra's way of being was ~~sexual~~—flying past the constraints of sex and its categories (even the transcendent ones).

Sociologists have defined asexuality as "a lack of sexual attraction to either sex." The Asexual Visibility and Education Network holds that "an asexual is someone who does not experience sexual attraction."[65] According to Crooks and Baur, the network, "founded in 2001, has 35,000 members worldwide, about 60% of whom are women in their teens through 30s. A national probability study of 18,000 people in Britain found that 1% of those surveyed said they were asexual (Bogaert, 2004)."[66] As a point of reference, in contrast with asexuality, Crooks and Baur state that "a physically mature person who does not engage in sexual behavior is said to be celibate. In complete celibacy a person neither masturbates nor has sexual contact with another person. In partial celibacy an individual masturbates but does not have interpersonal sexual contact. Celibacy is not commonly thought of as a form of sexual expression. However, when it represents a conscious decision not to engage in sexual behavior, this decision in itself is an expression of one's sexuality, and it may manifest a person's sexual intelligence."[67] Asexuality and celibacy are also important to understanding contemporary Black life and culture, as the latter, in particular, is often presented as the only option for sexual purity and respectability for Black women in particular.[68] Like asexuality, celibacy also has its limitations as it pertains to Sun Ra.

For Sun Ra, ~~sexuality~~—and a consequent celibacy—were not so much about sexual purity or respectability, but ultimately about holistic availability to "do the work his soul must have."[69] In letters pleading that the military recognize him as a religious objector, Sun Ra explains that he has a hernia associated with problems of his left testicle. He also confesses, "I have never been able to think of sex as a part of my life though I have tried to but just wasn't interested.... If it were possible to be in civilian life and be of help I would appreciate greatly this consideration. It seems too much to ask for or hope for, however being a Christian, I have never hesitated to ask for the things which I felt were mine. I do not think I ask too much, being as I am through no fault of my own."[70] Of Sun Ra's ~~sexuality~~, John Szwed writes, "When asked directly about why he had never married, Sun Ra answered, 'They neither marry nor are given in marriage but are like angels that shine forth like the sun' (an elaborated paraphrase of Matthew 22:30, where Jesus also says that God is God of the living, not the dead)."[71] Sun Ra was also abstinent and celibate as a course of discipline; he was no incel. Ra's ~~sexuality~~ was part of how he understood his faithful response to his Creator.[72]

Beyond the physical conditions that may have contributed to his celibacy and his own responses to early childhood experiences and ways of processing his mother's presence and absence, Sun Ra made conscious and (seemingly) unconscious decisions to remain celibate. He was both deeply invested in male community and culture and deeply critical of sexual relationships because of the ways he perceived that they took away from the work of others. With respect to his own sexuality, there was no sexuality to speak of: there are no accounts or indications of his sexual attraction to anyone, male, female, or other; there are no indications that Sun Ra had any sexual liaisons or affairs.

Sun Ra did the work his soul had to have—inviting universal participation, emitting erons though free of the wants, needs, or acts of sex. In round-the-clock rehearsals, during which he encouraged men to be gathered together with the singular purpose of creating music; in seasons of practice, performances, and tours that he knew would challenge the health of his band members' sexual relationships; in his film *Space Is the Place* that explicitly challenged the hypersexualization of US and earthly culture: the unique hum of erons was abuzz about him. The buzz created through his music, he believed, he imagined, and he realized was strong enough to transport him and others who were ready to be free.

The work of Sun Ra—that finds virtue and no lack in ~~sexuality~~—along with the recovery of a primordial Maât as an alternative point of origin from which justice might take flight—presents an underdeveloped approach to Black sexual ethics that defies anticipated categories and is necessarily grounded, tested, and relaunched from academic, ecclesial, and every other social space. Sexual discourses within Black religious institutions, society, and the academy are simply a miner's canary for much more significant social challenges of justices. As Mark Jordan notes, "Responding to ideological discourse requires a rule, not just of suspicion, but of inversion: we should attend not to what the discourse says, but to how it operates."[73] Such a discursive approach to Black sexual ethics must operate on the plane of what Katie Cannon terms "metalogues: highly organized or specialized forms of logic, designating new but related disciplines that can deal critically with the nature, structure, or behavior of the original discourse, talk, performance, or recital."[74] This is what Sun Ra is doing when he explains, "I'm talkin' about equations that are in their books. Books from way back in Ancient Egypt, in Greece, and Rome—and their philosophers have been talking a touch of everything I'm talkin'."[75] And Sun Ra is not just flying past sexuality with his intentional ~~sexuality~~, but he is also reframing justice. He explains his theory of justice in this way:

I'm sittin' in the front of the White House, lookin' over an' across the street but I don't see the black house. That's where it oughta be because you can't have a white house if you don't have a black house. In fact you can't have anything unless you have a comparison. You can't have a good government unless you have an evil government. You can't have righteousness unless you've got the wicked with you. You can't have anything without its parallel and its opposite. This is something that the people of planet earth aren't aware of. You can't have a Justice Department that goes out lookin' for only criminals and never go out lookin' for people who are doin' good. You can't have justice if you penalize people for doin' wrong, and don't do anything to help them when they tryna do right.[76]

A ~~sexual~~ space for flight lessons might be a place to begin the discursive metalogues about and beyond Black sexual justices—that cosmic alignment of Black sexual ethics and theories of justice.

Re-reflection and Strategic Action:
Space as the Place of Black Sexual Justice

I attended the Tatnall School in Wilmington, Delaware, for fourth, fifth, and sixth grades. In fifth or sixth grade I would get to school early enough that there was time to spare before the work of the day began. There was a recreational gathering space inside with a stage that had no steps or boundaries on three sides. I do not recall how it began, but at some point I began to ascend the stage, run as fast as I could, and jump off the stage. Soon after I began doing this, I invited others to "learn" how to "fly" with me and began offering "lessons." While I do not believe that any of us—my classmates and I—ever defied gravity, we did try.

Within the past few years, I had my first experience with iFLY: a wind tunnel that simulates the experience of skydiving and, in a way, the sensation of flying. I imagine that one of these days I might be willing to try the leap from a plane. However, the wind tunnel has been satisfying enough. On one occasion I went to iFLY with a young friend. This experience changed my understanding of bodily human flight altogether. While I and others of our party who could see spread our arms and our legs to lie prostrate on the wind—trying our best to be free of the human guide who kept our bodies aligned—my young friend who could not see held tightly to the human guide, who seemed to carry him as a mother carries her child. When my young friend described the experience afterward, he was overwhelmed. He described feeling a sensation he had never felt before. He flew.

Flying justice is not what it seems, not what it appears, not what we believe or think we know it to be. Flying justice is, at the very least, a new form of leaning and depending upon a power we cannot see. In part, this power can be understood in terms of solidarity and effort. Townes writes, "As Topsy and her kinfolk and friends pull up their *own* chairs to the postmodern welcome table and begin to speculate on what it takes to grow, notions of solidarity and difference must be met face-to-face. The womanist dancing mind stares down the fantastic hegemonic imagination to stop it *and* to defeat it in these strategy sessions. The challenges of forging a tough solidarity demands all of our creativity and intellect as we step toward a more just and whole society."[77] Those of whom the story is written in *The People Could Fly: American Black Folktales Told by Virginia Hamilton* also understood solidarity. Hamilton tells the story about flying Africans in this way: "There was a great outcryin. The bent backs straightened up. Old and young who were called slaves and could fly joined hands. Say like they would ring-sing. But they didn't shuffle in a circle. They didn't sing. They rose on the air. They flew in a flock that was black against the heavenly blue. Black crows or black shadows. It didn't matter, they went so high. Way above the plantation, way over the slavery land. Say they flew away to *Free-dom.*"[78] Townes puts it this way:

> no i am not here for the killers
> >   when it comes to solidarity
> > >   which i assume is another way to say justice
> i am not interested in them
> >   except for how to decrease their numbers
> >   and their power[79]

This is the work our souls must have. This is how we learn to fly even without wings. It is the work of solidarity, leaning on a power we cannot see, knowing that flying justice is nothing we can do (just) on our own. Maât has wings!

The most memorable advice that Dr. Cannon ever gave me was to know and be very clear about why I study what I study—why my project is my project. As a quare Christian woman, my own experience helps to make sense of the incongruities and potentialities of Black sexual ethics as a scholarly interest; in a limited way, my lived positionality and the perspective it affords me qualifies me for scholarship that addresses positionalities, perspectives, and subjectivities like my own; the value of self-determination is part of what makes this so (again, in a limited way). On one hand, such unapologetic attention to particularity as a method has been anathema to elite academic traditions; still, objectivity is implicitly and explicitly privileged—as is an aspiration to it, even if such aspiration is deemed impossible to realize. On the other hand, the content of my particularity is a maligned, vulnerable, and dangerous subjectivity within my communities of origin and belonging outside of the academy. Accordingly, I contemplate justices as they relate to Black sexual ethics from an awkward vantage point. Still, notwithstanding the strangeness and difficulty of method or content, justices in the nest prepare to fly, flying from our subjective contexts to contexts yet unfamiliar—joined with other flyers, dependent on an unseen power beyond that flies out in expansion and occasionally contracts, sometimes setting sex aside, and always willing to make the effort.

Before us is an invitation to participate in the eronic exercise of creating as our souls must have, so that our souls, our Ba—lighter than an ostrich feather—might fly like a hawk. A common Afrofuturistic journey unites all of us who are able to hear the call. Perhaps solidarity in Maât will carry us where wings are no more.

BIRDS WITHOUT WINGS

Birds without wings
Birds without wings
Poised, tense———
Are they unaware
There are no wings
Where wings should be?

Birds without wings
Poised and tense
Take off
Sailing . . . sailing . . .
Alas!
They drop to earth.

Are they hurt?
Bruised, bewildered
Angry
They rush to the take-off place

Again.
Poised, tense
Ready, Go!
Birds without wings.[80]

~ * ~

A Black Sexual Ethic

Purpose precedes sex.

A Maâtian Code of Justice

Maât takes grounded flight, reaching the revolutionary climes of Saturn and beyond with more than one feather. Her feathers blanket her wings, enabling them to pass through dark w(h)oles with the confidence of common, unfettered connection.

Heterexpectations   4

Jumping the Broom, Marriage, Democracy, and Entanglement Theory

On this we all agree: Marriage is an institution in serious need of repair, but we can't fix it by fiat or decree. Change, to be healthy, must be preceded by a time of tasting and testing—of trying things on for size. . . .

It occurred to us, from observation and from reasoning, that extramarital sex was not what really destroyed marriages, but rather the lies and deception that invariably accompanied it—that was the culprit. So we decided to give ourselves permission to sleep with other partners if we wished—as long as what we did was honest as well as private, and that neither of us exposed the family to scandal or disease. We had to be discreet and, if the word can be apt, honorable in our behavior, both to ourselves, to whomever else might be involved, and most of all, to the family. And for the most part we were. . . .

OSSIE: Looking back, I'd say no matter what did or did not happen, we freed each other. And in doing that, we also freed ourselves. We turned each other loose and set great wheels in motion once again. . . . Sex is fine, but love is better. That's the most important part of being free.

—Ossie Davis and Ruby Dee, *With Ossie and Ruby*

"A reason, a season, or a lifetime." These are the ways, my mother suggested, that one could be in relationship with others in life. She offered this advice to help me and my siblings understand our acquaintances, our friends, and whatever other relationships were in our lives. She explained that it was important to know and to accept whichever of these ways people were a part of our lives. She spoke this as one who had been married to my father for a long time already at that point; they were together for at least five years before they married. (Married since 1978, they have spent far more years of their lives together in marriage than the years they lived before marriage.) In so many ways, the relationship that they share seems precious and unusual—albeit far from perfect. It is a relationship I have often envied. It is also a relationship I have often critiqued. Notwithstanding the ethical challenges of envy and critique, this intraracial, Black marital relationship that spans the last quarter of the twentieth century well into the first quarter of the twenty-first century prompts this reconsideration of the ways that we are connected with one another and why such connection matters—for reasons, seasons, and lifetimes. Not this marriage, but Black marriage and the wisdom of preparing for and discerning "reason, season, or lifetime" is a tributary through which Black sexual ethics might flow. However, intraracial Black marriages—long or short term, ending in separations, divorces, or deaths—are far from straightforward: they involve comings together and comings apart. Through this chapter I argue that there are cultural expectations that define and constrain marriages, but that the entanglements of intimate relationship are beyond the definitions and constraints of such cultural expectations—and lead to looser, tighter, and different bonds than culture anticipates.

In part two of her 1983 definition, Alice Walker defines a womanist as one who is "committed to survival and wholeness of entire people, male and female. Not a separatist, except periodically, for health."[1] Through this chapter, it is my hope to clarify ways of choosing—and what it is to choose—connection and separation from one another. Among the ethical principles that emerge in this process are the following:

- Every person has the moral agency to choose connection with another/others.
- Every person has the moral agency to separate from another/others—especially for health.
- Separation cannot be absolute—whether chosen, forced, or implied.

- Self-differentiation impacts but cannot dissolve entanglement.
- Health should be discerned and sought as carefully as possible.
- It behooves us to choose to nurture just connections for our health.

In order to reach these precepts, it is helpful to consider what marriage is now and has been among people of African descent in the United States from slavery to the present. Among Afrodiasporic people, far too often, a lifetime marriage has been an aberration; by intentional social design, marriage has been an unattainable, unachievable, and/or unsustainable expectation.

Making Sense of Heterexpectations

Heterexpectation is an expectation that attends to and promotes heterosexuality as normal (i.e., what usually is) and normative (i.e., what should be and what governs cultural norms). Perhaps the most obvious heterexpectation is marriage. A more complex heterexpectation is a specific coupling of (a) particular sexual orientation and gender identity. The heterexpectation evokes both the notion of fixed gender identity (i.e., that one is born with a single gender identity that corresponds with a clear and singular anatomical sex) and the notion of male and female as the only two gender identities. Moreover, these dual gender identities are cast as fundamentally related to each other as compatible, complementary, mutually dependent, and unequal. This gender identity logic provides the foundation for marriage as a consummate—or the quintessential—heterexpectation. To be clear, especially as LGBTQ rights activists centered their aspirations to marriage equality and the rights of LGBTQ people to marry, LGBTQ adopted heterexpectations and chose to participate in a form of heterexpectation.

And expectations are important for theories of justice—especially those that undergird nation-state governance. This is true in the broadest and the narrowest senses. Broad expectations might include the expectation that there is consent to a social contract, that there are rights accorded to individuals, and that a measure of fairness—or an accepted order and fairness according to that order—attend to all levels of governance. Narrow expectations might include the pursuit of education, property ownership, patterns of consumption, patterns of institutional affiliation, and relational patterns. Theories of justice assume that justice is of interest and/or of concern to related actors. Theories of justice also assume that theoretical or hypothetical conditions could have value or significance to the experience, practice, discernment, and/or enforcement of justice. On the flip side, theories of justice confess the limitations of applied justice: because theories are theoretical or based on hypothetical conditions, they are not necessarily practicable.[2] Theories of justice expect that justice matters to the scholars who read and write about justice, the disciplines that include justice within their discourse, and the communities and societies that appeal to justice and/or justices as ideal objectives. Discourses of justice presume rights and wrongs—and that these matter to social organization.[3] Consequently, nation-states (and other greater and lesser organized bodies) operate and function, in whatever extensive and limited ways that they do, on the basis of individual and collective actors operating in ways that can be anticipated, encouraged/discouraged, and/or enforced to some extent. Organized bodies depend on common senses of justice among those they organize. Individual bio-actors—and institutional or communal bio-actors—are expected to participate in their social contexts and to do so in ways that support and nurture both the common senses of justice and the reproductive infrastructures of those social contexts.

Importantly, such expectations on bio-actors—and institutional or communal bio-actors—regulate (i.e., determine in the senses of predicting, controlling, and moderating) bio-action and interactions. Expectation draws out particular action. The value of propaganda, recognizance methods, and polls depends upon reliable predictors of how bio-actors respond (or tend to respond) under certain circumstances.[4] In turn, bio-actors have expectations of other bio-actors, governing bodies, and social institutions including, but not limited to, the nation-state (i.e., given particular bio-actions, other bio-actors, governing bodies, and/or social institutions are expected to act in a particular way or provide particular goods). Action gives way to (expected) (re)action/s. This diurnal process, of course, obfuscates any discursive interest in origins. That is, because this process is so automated, actors and institutions rarely stop to ask themselves, "when, where, how, and why did I agree to participate in this social order?"

Heterosexuality is often a universalized expectation when it comes to the bodies and social experiences of human bio-actors. Marriage (i.e., faithfully monogamous marriage) presents itself as the consummate civil (and civic) expression of heterosexuality. Human reproduction presents itself as the consummate biosocial expression of heterosexuality. Importantly, for Black human bio-actors, the biosocial expression of heterosexuality is expected (even as it is targeted through stereotypes of Black hypersexuality), while the civil and civic expressions of heterosexuality are discouraged or prohibited. This becomes an important distinction as Black human bio-actors are constrained as biosocial but not civic subjects. And because or when biosocial heterosexual expectations are met outside of the civic institutional possibilities, this becomes the grounds for a new stereotype and accusation: Black human bio-actors are immoral. Ironically, Black human bio-actors are (read) immoral because they do not realize heterosexual expectations within a civic context to which they (we) have been refused full access.

This distinction of Black experience is best explained in Achille Mbembe's notion of necropolitics that redacts Michel Foucault's biopolitics, arguing that there are no appreciable "bios" or "life" and "living" futures for Afrodiasporic people and other vulnerable communities throughout the world.[5] Mbembe describes a class of people defined by their disposability. This class of people is fodder. The people who constitute this set are like Marx's reserve army of laborers ready for the extermination, genocide, depletion, or retirement of low-wage, low-income workers but are distinct in that they are not readily available to repeople an anemic labor force. The people of Mbembe's necropolis and necropolitical nation-states are those who can be killed and will die without recourse, without individual or collective notice, acknowledgment, accountability, responsibility, or remorse. The people of Mbembe's necropolis and necropolitical nation-states and global order are part of a death-dealing economy: these people are the feast of the bloodthirsty.

It is the necropolitical foil of biopolitics that makes justice impossible. More precisely, the necropolitical ass of biopolitics exposes the impossibility of a Gramscian common sense of justice.[6] The problem of racial justice in the United States best exemplifies this challenge. The repetition of Black men, women, children, people, and other people of color murdered at the hands of law enforcement officers and vigilante actors does not have the same impact on the whole population of the United States. For white people, there is a desensitization to this as a repeated injustice. It is as if the more it happens, the more normal and acceptable it becomes for some. On the other hand, for Afrodiasporic people and other people of color, these repeated incidents of murder for no cause (other than perpetrators' defense of white supremacy and fear of Blackness) highlight the precarious nature of life for Black people and other people of color. These incidents also highlight that justice—and expectations of justice as a certain kind of fairness—for Black people and other people of color are not and cannot be the same as they are for white people in the US context (and, dare I say, globally).

Less than a month after the murder of George Floyd on May 25, 2020, the rapper Lil Donald, a native of Decatur, Georgia, whose birth name is Donald Brooks, officially released the song "Black Is Beautiful" on June 19, 2020.[7] The rap begins with audio of a reporter's account of Floyd's murder in Minneapolis, Minnesota. The closing words of "Black Is Beautiful" make the difference between the Black and white experiences of justice painfully clear. He writes:

> Close your eyes
> I want you to envision this
> White 17-year-old boy getting pulled over,
> by a black cop
> He pulls him out the car
> Never reads him his rights, never tell him
> what he did wrong
> The white kid fights back
> Breaks away and takes off running
> The black officer shoots him five times in
> the back
> How you feel about that?[8]

No one reads these lyrics—Black or white—and defends this as a just scenario. It is unimaginable to think that "a black cop" could or would enact the scenario described above and much less that, if they did, there would be no appreciable penalty, consequence, cost in pay, jail time, and/or loss of life or limb. And, importantly, although one could substitute white for Black and Black for white in Lil Donald's lyrics to describe the reality of what far too many Black people are experiencing in everyday life in the United States, the opposite is not what most Black people seek as a justice, a reparative justice, in the face of this reality. Calls for justice among Afrodiasporic people are not: "This is a just scenario; it should just go both ways; white people should be subjected to the same treatment by (empowered) Black people that Black people are subjected to by white people." The calls for justice can often be reduced to a call for freedom from harassment and, sometimes, imprisonment and/or death for the perpetrators of such deadly violence against Black people. And there is no justification for the de facto criminalization of Black people—and men in particular—except the ongoing dehumanization strategy of the transatlantic slave trade and cultivations of conditions of poverty that drive individuals to acts of desperation in order to survive and thrive. There is no essential difference between the Black seventeen-year-old and the white seventeen-year-old other than this: the de facto criminalization of Blackness. Justice, however, for the white seventeen-year-old is that Lil Donald's scenario will never play out for him; justice for the Black seventeen-year-old, at best in the current climate, is that when Lil Donald's scenario plays out with the racial script flipped, the victim is remembered well, the family is paid well, the perpetrator is convicted and punished with imprisonment or death, and the systemic violence of racism is more effectively (and finally fully) dismantled. Such justice never comes for Black people. Yet there is always an appeal to and for justice. Black people and white people are not suffering under the same injustices and, consequently, are not calling for a common justice. In biopolitical logic, according to Mbembe, the necropolitical and its abject victims are part of the social economy; there is no injustice in the double standard because the double standard is baked into the system. For the specific context of this chapter, Black people are not supposed to live up to and into heterexpectations; we are expected to be the erotic, exotic foil that perpetually reaches for a manifestation of the heterexpectation that is eternally impossible for us. The successful intraracial Black marriage is the one that does not figuratively end in a deadly traffic stop or encounter with law enforcement officers or vigilante white supremacists—the kind of stop or encounter for which individuals within the Black community must prepare upon waking each morning and going to sleep each night. Black people are living under everyday conditions of terror—and, ironically, contemporary submission to certain heterexpectations may be no more than an acquiescence to such terror. The work of vindicationist Frances Cress Welsing helps to sort through the connection between the terrors exacted upon Black people individually and in relationship as a result of white supremacy and the role of intraracial relationships.

Unified Field Theory

In her collection of essays *The Isis Papers: The Keys to the Colors*, Frances Cress Welsing offers an integrated theory of race (including color and racism), sex (including family theory, gender, and sexuality), religion (including ancient Egyptian religion and Christianity), what she terms science, and justice. While Welsing's training as a psychiatrist has informed her perspective, it is evident that she has drawn from a variety of interdisciplinary sources in order to inform her claims. Welsing simultaneously makes six critical ideological claims that must be read singularly (for understanding) and (again) together for their significance: (1) racism is white supremacy; (2) racism evolves from conscious and unconscious responses to the presence and absence of melanin—and, specifically, a desire for melanin and its production; (3) racism (and those who exercise it) are consciously and/or unconsciously aware of the ways that sex, sexuality, and gender can produce and/or inhibit the production of melanin; (4) nonwhite resistance to racism is the work of justice (and, thus, defines justice); (5) the work of justice can be helpfully articulated through the myths and symbols of ancient Egypt; and (6) the work of justice is multivalent.

At the heart of her work is a definition of racism that informs every objective that follows. The simple definition of racism for Welsing is "white supremacy." The extended definition of racism is as follows:

the local and global power system structured and maintained by persons who classify themselves as white, whether consciously or subconsciously determined; this system consists of patterns of perception, logic, symbol formation, thought, speech, action, and emotional response, as conducted simultaneously in all areas of people activity (economics, education, entertainment, labor, law, politics, religion, sex and war). The ultimate purpose of the system is to prevent white genetic annihilation on Earth—a planet in which the overwhelming majority of people are classified as non-white (black, brown, red and yellow) by white-skinned people. All of the non-white people are genetically dominant (in terms of skin coloration) compared to the genetically recessive white-skinned people.[9]

More forceful than definitions of racism that skirt the issue of who manipulates (or holds) systemic (and often individualized) domination power, the point of origin for Welsing's definition of racism refuses a generalization or universalization that ignores the function of white-identified racial coloration. This definition insists that racism is a white system of social domination.

Explicating racism as white supremacy, in her earliest of the essays included in the *Isis Papers*, which were written over nineteen years beginning in 1970, Welsing published "The Cress Theory of Color-Confrontation and Racism (White Supremacy): A Psychogenetic Theory and World Outlook." Building upon the definitions of racism that Neely Fuller presents, Welsing explains that, "impressed that the concept of a 'system' of white domination over the world's 'non-white' people could explain the seeming predicament and dilemma of 'non-white' social reality," she considers "what possible motivational force, operative at both the individual and group levels, could account for the evolution of these patterns of social behavioral practice that apparently function in all areas of human activity."[10] Her assessment is that the premise upon which racism thrives is that "the quality of whiteness is indeed a genetic inadequacy or a relative genetic deficiency state, based upon the genetic inability to produce the skin pigments of melanin (which is responsible for all skin color)."[11] Welsing continues, "The vast majority of the world's people are not so afflicted, which suggests that color is normal for human beings and color absence is abnormal."[12] This is an uncomfortable theory for those who have worked to deny the biological grounds of racism. Specifically, racists have been cited for making false biological claims about the inferiority of people of African descent; the response of antiracists has been to deny biological difference between people of African descent and people of European descent, between people of differing melanin expressions—and a leveling insistency on the biological sameness and equality of people of different colors. An important strategy that characterizes this discursive resistance to racism is, moreover, a rejection of hierarchy and an insistence on sameness, equality, and equity as values. Not only does Welsing disrupt this discursive pattern through her embrace of a biological truth and explanation of race, but she also redeploys a biologically based racial epistemology to invoke, defend, and promote a "black" racial superiority. Thus, Welsing disrupts familiar modern and postmodern moves to deny biological meaning and rank. She maintains that "the white or color-deficient Europeans responded psychologically, with a profound sense of numerical inadequacy and color inferiority, in their confrontations with the majority of the world's people—all of whom possessed varying degrees of color-producing capacity. This psychological response, whether conscious or unconscious, revealed an inadequacy based on the most obvious and fundamental part of their being, their external appearance."[13] The psychological sense of inferiority, Welsing claims, accounts for every expression of racial animus directed from white people toward nonwhite people. Moreover, this sense of melanin deficiency is, in its ultimate and final expression, melanin envy.

In this framework, Welsing presents a theory of justice that is fundamentally about the dismantling of white supremacy. She writes that "there are serious problems posed for the vast majority of humankind by the specific dynamic of Western (white supremacy) culture." Her objective is to "assist Blacks and all other people—who have as their cosmic responsibility the resolution of the problem of injustice in the world—in identifying the problem of that specific injustice more clearly than ever before." Ultimately, for Welsing, the work of justice is summarized in this way: "Those who *will* to work for justice and who understand that work as their conscious responsibility will be found in all places and in all walks of life, at all levels of formal education and at all income levels. There are no class divisions nor language barriers for those who do this cosmic work. It is time to solve this problem once and for all. It is time for justice on the planet Earth."[14] This work of justice, for Welsing, is broad enough to include all people and even that which ostensibly exceeds the specificity of race. However, in no uncertain terms, the work of justice still begins and ends with addressing the biological problem of whiteness that has achieved psychological and sociological expressions.

Inasmuch as this study of justice draws on vindicationist methods of recalling Black and/or African genealogies of thought and symbolism to state and affirm the humanity, dignity, and strength of people of African descent, it is necessary to acknowledge the personage, symbol, and form of African descent to which Welsing appeals for justice. Welsing explains:

> Isis was the most important goddess of ancient Africa (specifically, Egypt). She was the sister/wife of the most important Egyptian god, Osiris ("Lord of the Perfect Black"), and the mother of Horus. In the astral interpretation of the Egyptian gods, Isis was equated with the dog star Sirius (Sothis). According to the ancient African story, after the murder and dismemberment of Osiris by his evil brother Set (Seth), Isis discovered the crime, recovered the pieces of the body of Osiris, and put them together again, restoring his existence and his power. According to legend, Isis admired truth and justice and made justice stronger than gold and silver.
>
> In the present era, truth and justice have been crushed by the global power system of white supremacy, making the existence of peace on the planet impossible under this reign of terror. The attempt in this work to reveal some aspects of the in-depth truth about the white supremacy power system for the ultimate purpose of establishing justice and peace in the world is in the tradition of the great African goddess, Isis.[15]

Interestingly, the appeal to Isis narrows in on Maât, but is not Maât. As Welsing puts it, "Isis admired truth and justice." She was not, herself, the personification of truth and justice. Instead, Isis would have, herself, referenced Maât. Thus, Isis appeals to a more robust form of truth and justice. However, she does not quite succeed as a symbol of these.

The sexual aspects of Welsing's theory are as intriguing as her choices of symbolism. Two aspects are most noteworthy. First, the complexity of the sexuality of Isis does not satisfy the standard for Black sexuality Welsing promotes. One could conveniently attribute this to the mythological aspects of Isis as a feminine deity. However, this raises the question of how one adjudicates between the literal and the figurative aspects of Isis as prototype for Blackness: Isis—the sister/wife, the one who reassembles and buries Osiris's dead, dismembered body that it might rise again. Notwithstanding Plutarch's claim that Osiris's penis was missing—an account not confirmed in other Egyptian sources—Welsing emphasizes the importance of Black women not coddling (their) male children, especially into and through adulthood. Thus, the reparative role of Isis as a female figure leaves questions about the consistency of Isis with the rest of Welsing's Black family model. Second, Welsing maintains that white orgies, homosexualities, asexualities, white male sexual desire for Black women, and white male projections and interceptions of Black male and white female intimacies are all manifestations of the self-alienation, anxiety, and narcissism that surface as a result of white supremacy qua melanin envy. There is, of course, much to dissect and critique here. While there is much to critique in terms of how Welsing reaches and defends her heteropatriarchal framework, of interest is the fact that she defends a racial difference between whites and nonwhites when it comes to sexual ethics, and, for Welsing, the difference between Black and white sexual ethics has to do with an Afrocentric natural law, on one hand, and white supremacy, on the other hand.

    The irony of Welsing's theory cannot be overstated. At once, Welsing is making a claim about the biological superiority of people with more melanin and the superiority of the people who constitute the majority of the earth's population because they are the majority. According to natural selection, among other principles of evolution, Welsing makes the claim that those with more melanin are dominant; the recessive gene of melanin deficiency is subordinate. This is ironic both because Darwinian principles of natural selection were used to explain the inferiority of people with more melanin— associating more melanin with a closer proximity to nonhuman primates— and because of the ways this claim has been used to undergird the secondary claim that evolutionary dominance is reflected in an emerging or ascending minority characteristic (instead of the majority characteristic). If Welsing's theory is correct, and racism is a matter of melanin envy and the survival of whiteness (as a recessive gene), theories of race and racism that have been defended as categorically different are not all that different from one another after all. Whether the claim is made that racial diversity should be defended in a melting pot mixture or a tossed salad matters not. The everyday defenses of difference as such and the defense of white superiority in less uncertain, more direct, and specific terms are two sides of the same coin if what racism is really about is defending the existence and survival of genetic traits that would be classified as white. And of course, diversity arguments would not only benefit people of European descent, but, in the halls of predominantly white institutional spaces, diversity arguments would benefit those (melanin-rich) who have been cast as intellectually inferior; diversity arguments would not only benefit people who carry recessive genetic traits reflected in skin color, but also people who carry recessive genetic traits that are often perceived and categorized in terms of physical abilities; and, if Welsing were persuaded that diversities of sexual orientation (and gender identity) were genetic—which she is not—those in the minority categories of orientation and gender identity, too, would be among the defended minorities. In this way, Welsing might claim that whiteness is variously defended both by discriminatory practices of excluding those who are melanin rich(er) and by inclusive practices of including those who are melanin rich(er)—the latter, insofar as inclusive practices convey and solidify a cultural, ideological perspective that would (or could) defend whiteness if and/or when and/or as whiteness (i.e., melanin deficiency) becomes an increasingly minoritized genetic trait.

Engaging Welsing's theory is more than a thought experiment. It challenges how we sociologically and theoethically engage science and how we think about race and diversity theories in critically important ways. What should be done if even critical theories of race and diversity are fundamentally defenses of whiteness and white supremacy—or can easily be recast for this work? This is a fundamental question that must be answered. And surely, there are as many theoethically defensible purist and/or naturally selective Judeo-Christianities as there are hybrid and/or ethnically diverse Judeo-Christianities. Ultimately, Welsing's critique must be seriously engaged. However, the ease with which Welsing caves in to the power-over, domination-power models she perceives and rejects within white (i.e., melanin-deficient) culture is an irony and hypocrisy that cannot be affirmed. At once, it must be possible to defend diversity and the value of both dominant/majority and minority/recessive traits without affirming the nefarious, insidious, and "natural" human tendency (according to Adam Smith) toward self-interest expressed in prejudiced, genocidal, and/or discriminatory practices. It must be possible to reject power-over and domination power perspectives, claims, and ideologies for more right or justifiable reasons. In other words, a distinguishing factor between theories of race and diversity that simply reify or easily turn toward a reification of white supremacy and theories of race and diversity that disrupt white supremacy and are not easily turned toward promulgating white supremacy (including white survivalism qua exceptionalism) may come down to a question of motivations. And how might we measure motivations? Who rightly discerns motivations? The strongest I can make here is a rejection of hierarchical power-over or domination power, an appeal to critical applications of science, a regard for how easily theories can be appropriated for aims outside of their original and explicit concerns, and a genuine interest in the dignity of people of African descent and people of color.

Still, the central scientific point of reference within Welsing's approach is of great interest. She refers to her theory—the Cress Theory of Color-Confrontation and Racism (White Supremacy)—as a "unified field theory." For Welsing (whose maiden name is Cress), this approach is drawn from Einstein's comments on "unified field" in *The Meaning of Relativity* (1922). In that text he writes (as quoted in Welsing), "The object of all sciences, whether natural science or psychology, is to co-ordinate our experiences and to bring them into a logical system—the only justification for our concepts and system of concepts is that they serve to represent the complex of our experiences; beyond this they have no legitimacy."[16] In many ways, this is the essence of scientific method: the validity or (scientifically, objective) truth of a claim depends upon whether that claim is always true under every condition. For Welsing, this means testing a claim under every condition she can imagine. In a sense, this limits how true her claims could be to her own imagination and/or to the imagination of those who engage her work or claims. In another sense, it may be impossible to test or try any claims that are rooted in a suspicion of motivation or even motivation itself. How could one know—through testing, trying, and proving—that an appeal to diversity is not simply a firewall for white supremacy? Still, until there is definitive proof to the contrary, Welsing's claims can no more be disproven than they can be proven. What is most intriguing about Welsing's application of the unified field theory is that it also lays the foundation for a social principle of entanglement theory. Indeed, Einstein's unified field theory is at the heart of entanglement theory—even as it allows for multiple realities to be true at once, it also insists on relativity, insists on relationship, and insists on specific relationship (even though the nature of relationship can and does evolve). Put differently, entanglement theory as an expansion of the unified field theory simultaneously demands a verification of specific relationship and makes infinitely more relational possibilities true at once. Fully extended, this theory can destabilize the location of heterexpectations in marriage—if not in gender specificities (in Cress Welsing's case).

The deleterious impact of white supremacy on intraracial Black marriage and relationship is by no means lost on Cress Welsing. In her essay "The Crisis in Black Male/Black Female Relationships: Is It a False Problem? (July 1985)," Welsing begins:

> Disenchantment with the institution of marriage . . . hardly any Black persons knowing five happy Black couples.
>
> Given these dynamics as ever-present realities in the Black community, it would seem that there is a crisis of immense and serious proportions in the Black male/Black female relationship in the final decades of the 20th century.[17]

Cress Welsing argues, however, that this is a "'false' problem": Black male/Black female alienation is not the problem that must be addressed; the source of that alienation is the problem that must be addressed. Cress Welsing writes, "Failure to analyze the white supremacy dynamic deeply is a tragedy because this dynamic is the fundamental cause of the failed relationships between Black males and Black females."[18] There are two aspects of Cress Welsing's approach to Black intraracial intimate relationships that are important to note here in conjunction with her unified field theory. First, the conditions and experiences of white supremacy directed toward Black men and Black women by gender and individually are key to understanding the breakdown in their relationship with one another. Cress Welsing argues that the "excessive and disproportionate pressure on the Black male by the global white supremacy system produces a grave imbalance between the Black male and the Black female, even though both are victimized by white supremacy."[19] This claim is important because it underscores the ways that a divide-and-conquer technique not only mitigates against a common theory of justice among white and Afrodiasporic people in the United States, as highlighted in Lil Donald's lyrics, but also how the potential of a common theory of justice is compromised even among Afrodiasporic people differentiated by gender identities and experiences of gender. Second, Cress Welsing argues that purposeful connection against white supremacy, not marriage, is the telos of intimate intraracial Black relationships.[20] This is a different way of thinking of entanglement that is not about the establishment of the nation-state. Cress Welsing writes, "If we understood white supremacy, the number one priority for *each* Black male and Black female would *not* be to reach out for one another with designs of dependency, love, lust or marriage. Instead, we would seek to master specific patterns of perception, logic, thought, speech, action and emotional response that would counter the white supremacy dynamic scientifically."[21] Cress Welsing commends "a continuous exchange of information, knowledge, and understanding (like true team members) about how to counter white supremacy more effectively."[22] Cress Welsing's approach here is key. She is unimpressed with the institution of marriage or "designs of dependency, love, lust." Intimate Black intraracial relationship, for Cress Welsing, is about the dismantling of white supremacy. It is the singular purpose for Black individual and relational existence. For Cress Welsing, the intimate entanglement of Black people with one another is and should be a given. However, this entanglement is not for the purpose of any kind of romantic drama, but for the defeat of the injustices of white supremacy and all its institutions. Black people in more or less proximate and intimate relationship are definitively entangled in this purpose.

Marriage in Black Community

The significance of marriage for cultures and societies in modern civilization is beyond question. In the context of the United States, marriage has been a hallmark for Victorian conceptualizations of womanhood and for American aspirants to that model. It has been an ironic religious and civic institution in a country founded on a separation between church and state. It has been a false division of the secular and the sacred—that has consistently yielded to the fervor of evangelical Christian, populist revivalism. However, marriage has also been a racialized institution. Historically, it has not always been accessible for Black people in the United States, and contemporary socioeconomic challenges complicate this even further.

In their 2019 article "Incarceration, Unemployment, and the Black-White Marriage Gap in the US," Nezih Guner, Christopher Rauh, and Elizabeth Caucutt write, "In 2006, 67% of white women between ages 25 and 54 were married, while only 34% of black women were—a gap of 33 percentage points." They go on to explain that this matters because "marital structure has important implications for the living arrangements and well-being of children. In 2015, about 54% of black children lived with a single mother, while the share of white children living with a single mother was about 22%. Differences in family structure are a contributing factor to differences in economic resources. In 2006, 33% of black children were living below the poverty line, while only 14% of white children were." To explain what might account for the racial disparity, the authors of this article turn to William Julius Wilson's book

The Truly Disadvantaged (1987). Guner et al. write that Wilson "suggests that characteristics of the black male population, and in particular the lack of marriageable black men due to high rates of unemployment and incarceration, are an important factor contributing to the black-white differences in marital status. This is usually referred to as the 'Wilson hypothesis.'" Guner et al. find that "the sex ratio accounts for 21.2% of the [racial] gap" (i.e., there are more Black women than Black men) and "the effect of employment is larger 38.4%, while the effect of prison is smaller 10.4%. Next, we consider the different factors together. If black men face the employment and prison dynamics of white men, the racial marriage gap is reduced by more than 50%. Finally, putting together all three pieces of the Wilson hypothesis (eliminating black-white differences in the sex ratio, incarceration transitions, and unemployment transitions) closes more than 80% of the racial marriage gap." Beyond these statistics demonstrating how marriage is functioning in contemporary terms (in and beyond the lives of people of African descent), there is a deeper question about what marriage means in the context of the modern nation-state. Marriage is not neutral to the existence, formation, evolution, and continuation of the nation-state, society, governance/government, and community. That marriage is a point of contention for people of African descent is no surprise when the role of marriage as a social institution is clear. Marriage in the antebellum context—and especially the marriage of people of African descent—functioned as the impossible and denied aspiration for enslaved people of African descent held to standards like those described in the Willie Lynch letter and by like-minded slaveholders.[23] Marriage in the postbellum and early modern context—and especially the marriage of people of African descent—functioned as the difficult (and sometimes impossible) requirement imposed on persons formerly enslaved (i.e., heterosexual monogamous marriage) specified in the Moynihan Report and among those who protested both the infrequency of legal Black marriage and the relative inaccessibility of marriage for people of African descent. As far as sexuality goes, marriage is the hallmark, the gold standard from the vantage point of civilized Western society. And this is no accident. In fact, according to Georg W. F. Hegel, the centrality of marriage as the consummate context for sexual expression and the foundational relationship for civil society and the nation-state is by design; in fact, marriage comes as close to being a matter of natural law and order as Hegel gets with respect to any matter.[24]

Why might we consider Hegel and marriage when addressing theories of justice and Black sexual ethics in terms of heterexpectations? There are two primary reasons for this theoretical jaunt. First (to reiterate) Hegel definitely understands marriage—and the heteronuclear family—as a nascent form of the nation-state. Second, key thinkers among Black theoethicists have critically engaged the work of Hegel. Most prominently, these theoethicists include W. E. B. Du Bois, Martin Luther King Jr., Charles Long, and Cornel West. Though they have focused on the master-slave dialectic, for King especially, it is clear that Hegel's work has been of interest and import beyond an application of the master-slave dialectic and that the master-slave dialectic has not emerged ex nihilo. The master-slave dialectic is at the root of other philosophical handlings of injustice and helps qualify the call for nation-state formation that has not completely crushed the spirit of its subjects.

Importantly, the key feature of marriage for Hegel is not sexual attachment but "the free consent of the persons . . . to make themselves one person, to renounce their natural and individual personality to this unity of one with the other. From this point of view, their union is a self-restriction, but in fact it is their liberation, because in it they attain their substantive self-consciousness."[25] Thus, while sexual intimacy may be a part of the marital relationship and/or contract, it is first and foremost a matter of personhood and the agency of the partners in the relationship as freely consenting persons. Marriage is both self-restriction, insofar as each partner renounces "natural and individual personality," and liberation, insofar as each partner attains "substantive self-consciousness." This serves as a reminder of the ways in which freedom is always limited, contingent, or somehow qualified. This also serves as a reminder of the ways that limitations, contingencies, and qualifications can be chosen and/or selected. (Think of how liberation happens in the master-slave dialectic.) Still, marriage is the quintessential gesture that presages an assumption of the "free consent" of subjects to the nation-state.

In the same way that Long must remain suspicious—only cautiously optimistic—about the prospects of the slaves in the master-slave dialectic attaining a true liberation whereby their full humanity is confirmed and affirmed, in the same way that Cress Welsing appeals to purposeful relationship as opposed to formalized marriage, so too it is important to question the freedom of consent—and both the freedom of consent to marriage and the freedom of consent to be governed within the nation-state context. Moreover, when some gesture of consent is made, some willingness to participate in the formalities or informalities of entangling marital or quasi-marital intimate boundaries remains. The consent to be called *spouse* is not consent to the violation of rape within marriage. The consent of casting a democratic vote is not consent to be treated with Jim Crow justice. And the consent of participation in democratic processes is no more consent to the nation-state in which those processes take place than marriage between two enslaved people signaled their joint and mutual freedom, full humanity, and rights in the antebellum context.

And there is some intuition of these observations: that marriage does not carry the same meaning for all people (i.e., it does not mean the same thing for Afrodiasporic people historically or in contemporary terms), that marriage is not equally accessible to all people, that marriage is more constraining than liberating in terms of private and public significance, and that marriage signals consent in dangerously ambiguous and implicit and explicit ways.

For many Afrodiasporic people—both historically and in contemporary contexts—marriage is a deception. The rights and privileges it confers on others are not necessarily conferred on married Afrodiasporic people. And even the traditions that are said to accompany it are vague, obfuscating, and sometimes just false. With respect to the tradition of "jumping the broom," Dianne M. Stewart explains that

> the stark truth is we still don't know enough about enslaved couples' matrimonial rites, and many have incorrectly presumed a generic African heritage as the source of the one ritual most have come to associate with enslaved weddings—"jumping the broom." Since the airing of the 1977 television miniseries Roots, which featured Kunta Kinte and Belle's broomstick wedding in episode two, African Americans have attached sentimental value to the ritual, considering it a dignifying African tradition that their ancestors preserved to sanctify their nuptials.
>
> A good number of enslaved persons, when permitted to marry, did indeed submit to jumping the broom with pledges of everlasting love until slave owner–induced separation would tear them asunder. In doing so, however, they were upholding European rather than African customs. Pre-Christian Roma and Celtic communities in the British Isles were notorious for jumping the broom to seal their wedding vows. Accounts from the 1880s describe multiple instances among these groups in which jumping over a broomstick was the central legitimating act in the marriage ceremony. Rural Anglo-Saxons were known to embrace the practice as well. The Welsh, in particular, sustained the ritual at least until the 1840s and likely carried the tradition to the American South, where so many of them settled throughout the slave period. In fact, the United States is the only region beyond the British Isles with a preponderance of analogous broomstick marriage customs.[26]

Alan Dundes also takes up the quasi-vindicationist longing for this to be an African-derived tradition. However, his research does not bear this out, and he explains, "while one can surely deplore the strong Eurocentric bias in the historical beginnings of African American folklore scholarship, one can hardly accept the assertions of Afro-centric writers who make unsubstantiated claims of African origins while providing little or no hard evidence."[27] He goes so far as to say "replacing one form of racist bias with another would not appear to represent a step forward."[28] Nevertheless, the impulse to reach back and find what is redemptively free of the master and the cultural traditions of the master is understandable. It is such an impulse that sits at the heart of this book. However, as with jumping the broom, we can reach back and retrieve some elements that are part of a liberative hidden transcript, but not everything historic (or historically African—which jumping the broom is not—or historic for Afrodiasporic people) is liberative.[29] At best, jumping the broom might be categorized as African American, hybrid, an artifact of the transatlantic slave trade on territory now called the United States. Justices entangle and are entangling. Entangling justices describe the fancy footwork required of intraracial Black intimacies confused with democratic nation-state building interests from which such intimacies and the people involved in them never fully benefit.

Jumping the Broom?

Still, beyond the question of current socioeconomic circumstances that impact the viability of marriage among Afrodiasporic people in the United States, there is a history with respect to marriage (and the denial of marriage) as part of a socioeconomic strategy to disempower people of African descent that is worth a deeper dive. In the section titled "The Negro Marriage" in the Willie Lynch letter regarding the making of a slave, the writer explains:

> We breed two nigger males with two nigger females. Then, we take the nigger male away from them and keep them moving and working. Say one nigger female bears a nigger female and the other bears a nigger male; both nigger females—being without influence of the nigger male image, frozen with a[n] independent psychology—will raise their offspring into reverse positions. The one with the female offspring will teach her to be like herself, independent and negotiable (we negotiate with her, through her, by her, negotiates her at will). The one with the nigger male offspring, she being frozen subconscious [with] fear for his

life, will raise him to be mentally dependent and weak, but physically strong; in other words, body over mind. Now, in a few years when these two offsprings become fertile for early reproduction, we will mate and breed them and continue the cycle. That is good, sound and long range comprehensive planning.[30]

Notwithstanding words like these, enslaved people of African descent discerned ways to be connected to one another that exceeded visions like those reflected in the Lynch letter.[31] I will share some stories from the *Slave Narratives* of the Federal Writers' Project that reflect this—stories that recall broom jumping as part of the way such connections were made.

First, consider the narrative of Donaville Broussard of Beaumont, Texas. Broussard was "a polished gentleman of his race, was the son of a mulatto slave of Emilier Caramouche. He was born in 1850, but appears vigorous. Light skinned, with blue eyes and a genial expression, he gave the story of his life in the French patois spoken by Louisiana French Negroes, which has been translated into English." He recalls a wedding and explains:

> My aunt got married. M'sieur Caramouche killed a big pig. The white folks ate in the house. The slaves sat under the trees and ate in the yard. At four o'clock the justice of the peace came. He was the friend of M'sieur Caramouche. He made my aunt and the man hold hands and jump over the broom handle. When the priest came he made M'sieur sign some papers. A slave always had to ask M'sieur to marry. He always let the women slaves marry who they wanted. He didn't loose [*sic*] by that. He was so good the men would come to his plantation.[32]

4.1 (opposite): This photograph of Minerva and Edgar Bendy was taken in Woodville, Texas, in 1937; it is included in Lot 13262 (226) of *Born in Slavery: Slave Narratives from the Federal Writers' Project, 1936 to 1938 (603)*, Library of Congress, https://www.loc.gov/item/99615235/. In an interview for the related Federal Writers' Project, *Slave Narrative Project*, Edgar Bendy celebrates aspects of his life after slavery with Minerva: "My wife, Minerva, she used to go huntin' with me." Minerva Bendy is quoted explaining their relationship: "I's a June bride 59 year ago when I git married. De old white Baptist preacher name Blacksheer put me a dat nigger over dere, Edgar Bendy, togedder and us been togedder ever since. Us never have chick or chile. I's such a good nuss I guess de Lawd didn't want me to have none of my own, so's I could nuss all de others and I 'spect I's nussed most de white chillen and cullud too here in Woodville." Federal Writers' Project, *Slave Narrative Project*, vol. 16, *Texas, Part 1, Adams-Duhon* (Washington, DC: Library of Congress), accessed April 22, 2023, https://www.loc.gov/item/mesn161/.

For Broussard's aunt, marriage was—to an extent—an act of agency, though jumping the broom was something that became a part of this experience at the invitation of the justice of the peace.

Tempie Herndon of Durham, 103 years old when her experiences of enslavement were recorded in the Federal Writers' Project, was thirty-one years old when "de surrender" of the Confederate Army came. She tells of her wedding day:

> When I growed up I married Exter Durham. He belonged to Marse' Snipes Durham who had de plantation 'cross de county line in Orange County. We had a big weddin. We was married on de front porch of de big house. Marse George killed a shoat an' Mis' Betsy had Georgianna, de cook, to bake a big weddin cake all iced up white as snow wid a bride an' groom standin' in de middle holdin han's. . . . After uncle Edmond said de las words ever me an' Exter, Marse George got to have his little fun: He say, Come on, Exter, you an' Tempie got to Jump over de broom stick backwards; you got to do dat to see which one gwine be boss of your househol. Everybody come Stan' 'roun to watch. Marse George hold de broom bout a foot high off de floor. De one dat jump over it backwards an' never touch de handle, gwine boss de house, an' if bof of dem jump over widout touchin it, dey won't gwine be no bossin, dey jus' gwine be 'genial. I jumped fus', an' you ought to seed me. I sailed right over dat broom stick same as a cricket, but when Exter jump he done had a big dram an' his feets was so big an' clumsy dat dey got all tangled up in dat broom and he fell head long. Marse George he laugh an laugh, an' tole Exter he gwine be bossed 'twell he skeered to speak less'n I tole him to speak.[33]

For Durham, jumping the broom was not a dignity, but rather it was just another occasion for her master to degrade those whom he enslaved and to make an amusement of them.

Hamp Kennedy of Mahned, Mississippi, explained, "We had 'bout 60 slaves on our place, an' if a nigger man on one plantation fall in love wid a slave girl on 'nother place, dey jus' come to her plantation an' jump ober de broom an' den dey is mar'ied. De slabes never had preachers lak dey do at weddin's dese days. If de girl didn't love de boy an' he jumped ober de broom an' she didn't, den dey wa'nt mar'ied."[34] For Kennedy, jumping the broom was a matter of agency.

Again, historian Tyler D. Parry explains that broom jumping is transnational and multicultural. Beyond the fact that "the earliest references to jumping a matrimonial broom stem from groups throughout the British

Isles, including Romani, Celts, and English laborers,"[35] Parry notes that there was ambivalence (at best) among the enslaved about whether or not jumping the broom was the most official way to get married, was their self-selected way to get married, or was even about getting married—as opposed to just "shacking up." Analyzing George P. Rawick's *The American Slave: A Composite Autobiography*, Parry notes that only 28 percent of the 548 references to "slave weddings" mentioned broomstick ceremonies; 38 percent mentioned "other" ceremonies and 34 percent did not mention ceremonies.[36] Moreover, tying the knot shares Celtic roots with jumping the broom. Thus, what has been presented as a difference (i.e., tying the knot versus jumping the broom) is, in fact, not different in the ways that have been historically suggested. There is no racial distinction to be made between the origins of these terms. Perhaps their eras were different—or the communities among whom each respective marriage phraseology became popular. It is not, however, that one marriage phraseology was somehow explicitly rooted in Africa. Even here, it is important to acknowledge that the reasons a phrase may gain more traction, feel more familiar, or be most easily appropriated very well may have to do with experiences of access (that follow imposed lines of racial difference) and/or conscious and unconscious connections to contexts of ethnic origin. While Parry notes the European roots of "jumping the broom," he also clarifies that jumping the broom has consistently gained the most traction among marginalized groups and that African Americans appropriated the practice in distinct ways.[37]

And there remains more to be said for how people of African descent took up the ritual of "jumping the broom" and what people of African descent made of it. Parry quotes an anonymous woman's account of an antebellum broomstick wedding on a southern plantation:

> When the colored folks got married, the man would lay the broom down on the floor with the bushy end to the north, then he would take the girl by the hand, then they step over the broom, then backward again. Then the girl picked up the broom, laying it down again with the bushy end facing the south, then the girl took the man by the hand and they step over it and backward again, to keep evil away and bad spirits through their life.... [M]other said many a night she would steal down and watch when she heard some of the colored folks were going to get married.[38]

In this account, Parry reads "a process of equality and balance." In this account, Parry reads the couple ensuring "they fulfilled both directional pulls by jumping forward *and* backward in a unilateral motion, from east to west and vice versa." In this account, Parry reads a potential re-creation of "a Kalunga line, which serves as a threshold separating the terrestrial realm from the ancestral." In this account, Parry reads freedom from slaveowners' influence; a safeguarding "from evil spirits"; mutual assistance and an acceptance of "one another's partnership."[39] Parry identifies African cosmologies and moral constellations in this broomstick wedding account. Not every broomstick wedding was like the ones this woman recounted. However, the geographical, geometrical, and directional awareness implied in her description reflect a physical consciousness within the communal psyche of the enslaved that might both have provided some inspiration for Cress Welsing's relational diagrams and provide a contemporary redrawing of these social maps.

Democracy, Marriage, and (Better) Uses of the Erotic

Alongside the complexities of broom jumping as opportunity and imposition, rarely a true and unambiguous sign of agency and freedom, we are invited to think about our own attitudes toward democracy. I attempt to model a personal contemplation about democracy in this section—beginning with two confessions. First, I did not remember that I was a believer in democracy until recently; second, I only remembered that I was a true believer in democracy when I was convinced that (soon enough) we (i.e., people of color) will be the numerical majority. I might even say, I became a born-again believer after hearing the Brookings Institute report—more than once: "that the nation will become 'minority white' in 2045" and that "during that year, whites will comprise 49.7 percent of the population in contrast to 24.6 percent for Hispanics, 13.1 percent for blacks, 7.9 percent for Asians, and 3.8 percent for multiracial populations."[40] And I became a born-again believer when I encountered the white nationalist "illiberal" confession and confessors. It was a kind of Sartrean bad-faith default to democracy. For there is no evidence of any democracy in ambiguous broom jumping—and there is no evidence that literal and figurative broom jumping is a thing of the past.

Before this point, my doubts had effectively compromised my convictions. These doubts stemmed from the obvious: what has passed for democracy has never benefited people of African descent in a singular and unequivocal way; whenever what has passed for democracy in what we now call the United States has ostensibly benefited people of African descent, this benefit has always been entangled with other complementary, competing, contingent, or otherwise coalescing interests. Then, there are the most tangible present measures of the failure of democracy: the uptick in hate crimes—especially against persons as opposed to property—in recent years, new forms of gerrymandering, purges of the electorate, countless micro and macro forms of voter suppression, election interference in physical and cyber forms, disorienting recounts, and gleeful reliance on the Electoral College.[41]

I will testify regarding the day that the illiberal face of contemporary white nationalism reconvinced me of democracy. On December 6, 2019, in a segment titled "The Dead Consensus" on the radio show *On the Media*, Brooke Gladstone introduced Matthew Sitman, the associate editor of *Commonweal* magazine and cohost of the *Know Your Enemy* podcast, explaining, "The GOP's appeal to respect the people's will is hollower even than it sounds because its leadership no longer is interested in majority rule." Sitman describes a process of conservatives aligning with nationalism—and these aligning with "illiberalism." Sitman offers the following explanation of illiberalism as it relates to democracy: "When you take aim at human equality that we're all equal individuals who possess certain rights. That's also the basis not just of, say, a liberal judicial order, but the foundation of democracy. One person, one vote. That's rooted in individual equality. That is what they're rejecting. They're saying that actually they know better that the key is to implement the highest good the order they think is true and just."[42] Like me, perhaps you hear "highest good" and think "common good." You will recall the "common good" discourses that so many ethicists have touted as their raison d'être, their *raison d'étudier*. Such ethicists insist that their commitment to Western models of rationality and appeals to reason, their appeals to Kant's imperatives and personally interpreted, clandestine jaunts behind veils of ignorance were simply an expression of their interest in the common good, the highest good, the order they think and know is true and just.

The hallmark of contemporary white nationalism—as illiberalism—is a rejection of democracy, characterized by a distinctive ethical posture in which:

- "The ends justify the means. It's what you give yourself permission to abide by. It's what you're willing to overlook," to quote Sitman again.[43]
- Racial dog whistles prevail: Sitman quotes Amy Vox, a University of Pennsylvania law professor and mouthpiece for the illiberals who argued at a conservative conference: "There has to be a return to national tradition. Anglo American traditions of constitutionalism, the common law, the English language and the Christian religion."[44]

- There is no clear commitment to civility, niceness, or the notion that other people with differing views also/still have rights; traditional conservative religious liberty arguments, like those of David French, do not obtain.
- There is a willingness to wage war on those who are different and/or believe differently. This is live and do not let live.

"Against the Dead Consensus"—the manifesto of the illiberal movement published in *First Things* on March 21, 2019, holds an old conservativism responsible for the advances of progressive agendas. The authors write, "Yes, the old conservative consensus paid lip service to traditional values. But it failed to retard, much less reverse, the eclipse of permanent truths, family stability, communal solidarity, and much else. It surrendered to the pornographization of daily life, to the culture of death, to the cult of competitiveness. It too often bowed to a poisonous and censorious multiculturism."[45] They continue to explain their central claims under the following categories: "We oppose the soulless society of individual affluence.... We stand with the American citizen.... We reject attempts to compromise on human dignity.... We resist a tyrannical liberalism.... We want a country that works for workers.... We believe home matters."[46] The explications of these relatively innocuous headings expose an (ironic) hybridization of ideas strategically and variously invoking rhetoric from liberal and progressive discourse. The stolen rhetoric and jargon are either reappropriated or misdeployed for the agendas of white supremacy.

Even more concerning, the claims expressed in "Against the Dead Consensus" are distorted perspectives on sexuality and society. The authors write, "Our society must not prioritize the needs of the childless, the healthy, and the intellectually competitive. Our policy must accommodate the messy demands of authentic human attachments: family, faith, and the political community. We welcome allies who oppose dehumanizing attempts at 'liberation' such as pornography, 'designer babies,' wombs for rent, and the severing of the link between sex and gender." And they continue, "We affirm the nonnegotiable dignity of every unborn life and oppose the transhumanist project of radical self-identification." Importantly, this does not negate the danger of more traditional conservativisms—including those that reject Donald Trump. These conservativisms still maintain "live and let live": "You let me practice my religious faith the way I want. I don't have to bake that cake."[47] Still, these who have gone the way of David French are no more true defenders of democracy than Sohrab Ahmari, the conservative first-listed author of "Against the Dead Consensus," and can no longer keep up the jig of democracy they once danced.

In fact, it is an offense that these would claim democracy as their preferred form of governance—or identify themselves with the term; and, these days, many conservatives would not. Most are content with the notion of a republic and are no longer interested in a democracy. The regard for a democratic republic or a republican democracy has withered in the face of populist possibility in the form of white nationalism and democratic development in the form of flourishing diversities. Interestingly, the language that undergirds the concept of a republic and a democracy portend this outcome. Remember: *republic* comes from the Latin composite word *respublica*, combining *res*, meaning "entity, concern," with *publicus*, meaning "of the people, public."[48] And remember: *democracy* comes from the Greek composite word *demokratia*, combining *demos*, meaning "the people," and *kratia*, meaning "power, rule."[49] When remembered in this way, the difference between *republic* and *democracy* is evident. Republic is a matter of concern, or even identity in the sense of an entity; democracy is a matter of power, or even action in the active senses of *rule*. N.b. The *re* in *republic* is not the *re* of *return*, *repeat*, or *again* (i.e., making anything "great again"); it is the *res* of concern.

Still, as an ethicist—and one who still believes in living and strives to live as ethically as I possibly can—the compromise of convictions in the face of doubt presents moral and practical dilemmas. In the moment of my democratic rebirth upon hearing Matthew Sitman's explanations of illiberalism, I immediately wondered, "*Why* do I suddenly feel 100 percent better about democracy?" In fact, my born-again moment was all too consistent with our contemporary cultural context. According to our contemporary cultural context, the merit of a system of governance is judged according to whether or not it works for an individual, and namely, the person asked to judge the system's merit. Worse, according to our hegemonic common sense, the merit of a system of governance is determined neither with regard to a rational (read: an impossible, but attempted objectively discerned), holistic, or comprehensive national good nor with regard to a rational, holistic, or comprehensive sense of personal good. Rather, the system's merit is often measured on the basis of fleeting and fickle desires, common capitalist consumptions, and unexamined and unassessed interests. So, while this particular political moment may lead me to democracy, the fact of its recent advent suggests that the motivations behind my rededication to democracy are all too similar to those of contemporary white nationalists, so-called US patriots, who have turned their backs on democracy in this same hour. Such compromise of convictions exposes crises of courage, commitment, and creativity. Moreover, the motivation behind my re-membered hope in democracy causes me to question the politics of conversion and sanctification, birth and rebirth—"O, I know I've been changed," but does it matter—and how does it matter—what motivated my change? Is this change enough change?

Just as some of us are reclaiming our time, others of us may need to reclaim a democratic political agenda. (Here, I assure you that I do not speak of the party, but of the form of governance.) As Frederick Douglass justified his harsh critique of pseudo-Christians, we now must continue, publish, and justify our critique of pseudo-democrats. Douglass wrote in the appendix to *Life of an American Slave*, "I love the pure, peaceable, and impartial Christianity of Christ: I therefore hate the corrupt, slaveholding, women-whipping, cradle-plundering, partial and hypocritical Christianity of this land. Indeed, I can see no reason, but the most deceitful one, for calling the religion of this land Christianity. I look upon it as the climax of all misnomers, the boldest of all frauds, and the grossest of all libels." We must repeatedly recalibrate and—where appropriate, when possible—reaffirm our convictions. Contemplating my democratic rebirth, I stumbled afresh on fierce and once more familiar voices. These voices declared:

> Because of these young people, I think for the first time we have the chance to make democracy a reality in the United States.[50]

We thank Fannie Lou Hamer for her voice.

> "America, you must be born again." . . . The birth pangs have already begun, my son. Let's sing together. The children are waiting. I think they really want to be born again. . . . Let the Spirit guide your steps. We all get a chance to be born again. And tell the girls (as if they don't already know) that we all get a chance to be midwives.[51]

We thank Vincent Harding for his voice speaking through Martin Luther King Jr. and to Barack Obama—their mothers and their mothers' mothers.

> Pragmatic theology regards faith and hope as genuine possibilities against the powers that threaten democratic cultural norms. The test of theological adequacy is whether the internal languages of theology identify the signs of grace in those moments of cultural transcendence in which

persons become open to others and freed from totalizing preoccupations with their own selfish interests.[52]

We thank Victor Anderson.

No, life is tragic in the Du Boisian sense because U.S. slavery and segregation created a social fabric that did not render recognition of black people as human beings.... The question is where we, as individuals or as a collective, have confronted the spiritual isolation that antiblack racism created and still creates in the contemporary world.... By expanding the terrain of public discourse, tragic soul-life seeks to increase the individual burden that moral actors carry in democratic societies.[53]

We thank Terrence Johnson.

Today, the tendency to assume that the only version of democracy available to us is capitalist democracy poses a challenge. We must be able to disentangle our notions of capitalism and democracy so to pursue truly egalitarian models of democracy. Communism—or socialism—can still help us to generate new versions of democracy.[54]

We thank Angela Davis.

What can we retain? What must we discard? Even when we hear these voices, we must still ask the hard questions: When has Christianity been pure, peaceable, or impartial? Can we associate any Christianity with Jesus or with Jesus as Christ? Where do our youth lead us today? Must America ever be born or born again? Do we want America to be America for you and/or me? How do we cultivate the spirituality that honors and heals tragic Black life? And, in our present historic moment, I believe that the culminating question is this: How do we disentangle ourselves and our senses of democracy from the capitalism through which America has been born, the tragic has been perpetuated, and according to which our Black beings have been commodified? At such a time as this, there is a need to know the adversaries against whom we fight, to know the commitments we have and will maintain, and to know the strategies we will deploy in defense.

These voices invite us to make a renewed appeal to democracy—and democratic participation. However, they also expose the specific civic and moral problem of Black bio-human actors denied the particular heterexpectation of marriage if and when marriage is an institutional civic marker. Beyond democracy, there is also the possibility of a different, new, or renewed socialism that might attend to democracy. Some known and revised strategies to which I appeal are that we might be more like intentional democrats in waiting, democrats united in uses of the erotic, and self-assured democrats. What do these possibilities mean or look like?

What are democrats in waiting? Democrats in waiting are actively strategizing and anticipating the best opportunities and strategies for interventions. Democrats in waiting apply ethics of biding one's time—not to be confused with pacifism or progressivism. Vincent Harding contends, "When it comes to creating a multiracial, multiethnic, multireligious, democratic society, we are still a developing nation."[55] We must recognize that we are in a time of formation. We do not give in to the eternal (and paralyzing) promise of coming democracy (in Derrida's terms), but we do recognize that on some matters we must bide our time as we explicitly fight on other fronts.

What possibilities are there for democrats to unite in using the erotic in new ways? There are ethics of eros—not to be confused with the pornographic or pornographizations of our bodies and cultures. This is an opportunity to expand on Audre Lorde's invitation to explore and apply the erotic in the expected and unexpected places its power reaches.[56] For those to whom such rights are not so necessary and fundamental because of dominant identity, it is tempting to give up on defending reproductive choice, non-heterosexualities, and other forms of sexual justice and bodily integrity. Now is not the time to release these commitments. If we are able to unite around these commitments, we will find the power of the erotic giving force to our commitments—as this power relates to its subjects in terms of form and function.

What possibilities are there for democrats to walk in a different kind of self-assurance? There are ethics of confidence—not to be confused with arrogance or narcissism. After G*d's Holy Spirit is said to have performed an IVF procedure on Mary, it is said that she declared that what is impossible for human beings is possible for G*d. Thus, she carried a self-assurance that in her circumstances she was living out the embodiment of G*d. This was a quare confidence—not arrogance, not the narcissism of the executive branch and its defensive mob.

Might we, resocialized in this way, take up the words of Douglass again? "There is a prophet within us, forever whispering that behind the seen lies the immeasurable unseen."[57] When we discern and draw out the prophet within, we are not consenting to a nation-state, not pledging allegiance to a party, but we are attempting a just and peaceable way of belonging in community with others. We are doing the best we can with an entanglement we cannot undo. Perhaps such democratic participation is more about better and best uses of the erotic (more than the heterexpectative marriage).

Baldwin appeals to a political hope in *The Fire Next Time*. It might include democracy, but it is doubtless more. Baldwin's political hope is the impossible work of love. For Baldwin, whites must be raised up, become equal to Blacks. However, this is not a matter of Black superiority (or white inferiority). This is a matter of human capacities—and the demonstration of human capacities to love. Black people are differently practiced in love because of the conditions that circumscribe love and loving in so much of Black experience and, for Baldwin, the ways white people come to Black people looking for love. However, white Americans are not only looking for love but also avoiding love. Baldwin writes:

> Therefore, a vast amount of the energy that goes into what we call the Negro problem is produced by the white man's profound desire not to be judged by those who are not white, not to be seen as he is, and at the same time a vast amount of the white anguish is rooted in the white man's equally profound need to be seen as he is, to be released from the tyranny of his mirror. All of us know, whether or not we are able to admit it, that mirrors can only lie, that death by drowning is all that awaits one there. It is for this reason that love is so desperately sought and so cunningly avoided. Love takes off the masks that we fear we cannot live without and know we cannot live within. I use the word "love" here not merely in the personal sense but as a state of being, or a state of grace—not in the infantile American sense of being made happy but in the tough and universal sense of quest and daring and growth.[58]

Baldwin continues to explain that the only way the white American "can be released from the Negro's tyrannical power over him is to consent, in effect, to become black himself." What does it look like "to become black himself" in this way? This looks like love—and specifically the capacity to love even those who hate you, to be able to give and receive love, and to love past the truth of our grotesquerie, acknowledging the ways we have contributed to oppression. What it is for the white American to "become black himself" is not for him to start naming all the ways that all of us—including him too—are oppressed. To "become black himself" is first to recognize that the United States is not white, it is hybrid (read: Black), and everyone who is American (i.e., of the United States) is hybrid (read: Black). This becoming begins with the confession and celebrated affirmation: America is not a white (Western) country. To "become black himself" is also a matter of stepping into the shoes of Black people, trying to see the world from the eyes of those targeted as Black people have been and, having done this, choosing to fight tirelessly against those who would create such conditions of oppression for Black people and anyone else. "Becoming black" is doing the best with entanglements we cannot undo.

How does such a political love relate to the erotic—or an ethics of erotics? In *The Fire Next Time*, James Baldwin teases the reader with notions of sex and sexuality—remarking on his and his peers' sexual "becoming" during his adolescence, the sexualization he endured when police stopped and frisked him as a youth, what it is "to be born, in a white country, an Anglo-Teutonic, antisexual country, black," the "brave and sexless little voices" that issue the singing (and songs) of white Americans, the sexual insecurity of white soldiers, and, finally, "a civilization sexually so pathetic that the white man's masculinity depends on a denial of the masculinity of the blacks."[59] Baldwin is painfully aware that the dysfunction of the United States as it pertains to Black people is broad—and it includes (anti)sexual components. Antisexuality is not acceptable for Baldwin. Love puts sex, sexuality, sex positivity, and diversities of gender identities and sexual orientations back on the table! Sex becomes possible (and ethical and moral) as Baldwin's articulation of love is realized. Sex that is about taking off the masks "that we fear we cannot live without and know we cannot live within" for the sake of "daring and growth," in the beauty of a mutual choosing, is about love. This is a love that sex should not do without. The insidious ways the erotic pales as the potential uses of the erotic become clear. The erotic can be a site for the proliferation of love. This is a love that could drive, inspire, create, and paint an ethical erotic masterpiece. And democracy can only be if it is a site for the proliferation of love.

Emerging Entanglements

In his book *The God Effect: Quantum Entanglement, Science's Strangest Phenomenon*, Brian Clegg explains entanglement in this way: "Once two particles become entangled, it doesn't matter where those particles are; they retain an immediate and powerful connection that can be harnessed to perform seemingly impossible tasks."[60] To expound upon quantum entanglement, Clegg explains quanta (i.e., the plural of quantum) as "tiny packets of energy and matter that are the building blocks of reality. A quantum is usually a very small speck of something, a uniform building block normally found in vast numbers, whether it's a photon of light, an atom of matter, or a subatomic particle like an electron."[61] Key here is that the particles addressed are discrete.

Clegg explains how the German Erwin Schrödinger introduces the term *entanglement*, drawing upon the meanings of the German word *Verschränkung*, the meaning of which has to do with "enfolding, crossing over in an orderly manner."[62] Clegg quotes Schrödinger:

> When two systems, of which we know the states by their respective representatives, enter into temporary physical interaction due to known forces between them, and when after a time of mutual influence the systems separate again, then they can no longer be described in the same way as before, viz. by endowing each of them with a representative of its own. I would not call that one but rather the characteristic trait of quantum mechanics, the one that enforces its entire departure from classical lines of thought. By the interaction the two representatives [the quantum states] have become entangled.[63]

Speaking of twos as a way of thinking about entanglement—and even marriage—I believe, presents us with some familiar challenges of binarism. Even if a couple jumps backward over a broom to signify a divorce, they still jump together.[64] They remain entangled.

Mathematical and statistical mistakes are far more common than most of us care to acknowledge. In an interview with Ira Flatow on Science Friday, Kit Yates, the author of *The Math of Life and Death: Seven Mathematical Principles That Shape Our Lives*, describes one common mistake: "the prosecutor's fallacy." To explain this mistake, he writes, "The idea is that it starts by saying, if the suspect is innocent, seeing a particular piece of evidence is extremely unlikely. But what the argument neglects to take into account is any possible alternative explanations in which the suspect is innocent... and also neglects the possibility that the explanation the prosecution is proposing... is actually just as unlikely, if not more so."[65] At the heart of the problem with "the prosecutor's fallacy" is a binary mathematical system that sees only yes or no, black or white. Yates notes:

> Binary is obviously the system that we use in our computers, and it's great for computers because they work on binary logic. You can run a little current through a transistor, and it can give you a yes or no answer. But actually, when it comes to human affairs, binary answers are not that useful. Humans aren't black or white.... Some of our favorite literary characters are actually morally ambiguous... people who are both good and bad. And everyone has a little bit of that in them. So yeah, trying to characterize

people as good or bad or one thing or the other is not particularly helpful. So binary isn't a particularly good number system for us to use in terms of human affairs.[66]

Despite the capacity of computers to utilize a binary base to perform "incredibly complicated tasks by converting our requests into a series of ones and zeros and applying cold, hard logic to flip these bits back and forth until they provide a lucid answer," as Yates puts it, at times this "most primitive base has let its masters down."[67]

adrienne marie brown describes a less binary approach for describing and participating in patterns of social relationality. brown writes, "Emergence notices the way small actions and connections create complex systems, patterns that become ecosystems and societies. Emergence is our inheritance as a part of this universe; it is how we change. Emergent strategy is how we intentionally change in ways that grow our capacity to embody the just and liberated worlds we long for."[68] Through emergence we can see how Ruby Dee and Ossie Davis became together. Their marital entanglement turned not on the binary question of whether there was fidelity or not, but on the consistent cultivation of love and freedom through relationship. With brown, I believe that a fresh question we might ask ourselves is, How are our entanglements emerging? And with Yates, how might our entanglements press beyond a binary base?

Purposeful Entanglements

Consider the story of Dora Franks of Aberdeen, Mississippi, who estimated that she was about one hundred years old when she shared parts of her biography while enslaved as a youth and young woman with an interviewer for the Federal Writers' Project in 1936. Her story about her Uncle Alf conveys the complexities of entanglement when it comes to marriage as part of a US Black sexual ethic and the bottom line of freedom as the ultimate aim:

> Us never had no big fun'als or weddin's on de place. Didn' have no marryin' o' any kin'. Folks in dem days jus' sorter hitched up together an' call deyse'ves man an' wife. All de cullud folks was buried on what dey called Platnum Hill. Dey didn' have no markers nor nothin' at de graves. Dey was jus' sunk in places. My brother Frank showed me once where my mammy was buried. Us didn' have no preachin', or singin', or nothin', neither. Us didn' even git to have meetin's on Sund'y less us slip off an' go to some

other plantation. Course, I got to go wid de white folks sometime an' set in de back, or on de steps. Dat was whan I was little.

Lots o' Niggers would slip off from one plantation to de other to see some other Niggers. Dey would always manage to git back 'fore daybreak. De wors' thing I ever heard 'bout dat was once when my Uncle Alf run off to 'jump de broom.' Dat was what dey called goin' to see a woman. He didn' come back by daylight, so dey put de Nigger hounds after him. Dey smelled his trail down in de swamp an' foun' where he was hidin'.

Now, he was one of da biggest Niggers on de place an' a powerful fas' worker. But dey took an' give him 100 lashes wid de cat o' ninety-nine tails. His back was somethin' awful, but dey put him in de fiel' to work while de blood was still a-runnin'. He work right hard 'til dey lef'. Den, when he got up to de end o' de row nex' to de swamp, he lit out ag'in.

Dey never foun' 'im dat time. Dey say he foun' a cave an' fix him up a room whar he could live. At nights he would come out on de place an' steal enough t'eat an' cook it in his little dugout. When de war was over an' de slaves was freed, he come out. When I saw him, he look lak a hairy ape, 'thout no clothes on an' hair growin' all over his body.[69]

For Franks—and her Uncle Alf—"jump de broom" was neither just about marriage nor just about sex. It is also not the case that jumping the broom was not about sex or marriage. However, more than marriage or sex, jumping the broom as it is signified here in this story is about freedom and an access to it. The ability to "steal away," to be able to make such a choice and to make such a choice is the beginning and end of the ethical discourse here. It is in stories like that of Uncle Alf and his niece Dora that the important choices to be made around entanglement in Black human bio-activity—intraracial intimacies within and beyond questions of marriage—are evident.

~ * ~

A Black Sexual Ethic

Intraracial Black intimacies should model purposeful entanglements designed for democratic (qua dem-erotic) disruptions of death-dealing dualisms of justice and constructions of life-giving, true-true[70] public and private consent.

A Maâtian Code of Justice

Maât's feather is one of many, layered and connected to her being, body, and substance. Plucking a feather to weigh against human hearts reminds us that the democratic flow of her plumage suffers but is willing to be entangled with us—and to discern if we can remain with her through eternity.

5

Dancing Justice

Just Black HomoSexualities

I'm tired of this church.
—Naszir Ferrell

I had a dream last night that I was dancing. That's all I really remember. Dancing my ass off. No one came to choir rehearsal this morning so I rehearsed by myself. Despite the turn out (or lack thereof) I felt great after rehearsal. On my way out the door I started listening to some music. I started dancing my way down the street and singing at the top of my lungs. I danced my way to the park. Then I danced around the park like 4 times, still singing. I didn't really care whether or not anyone was watching. It was like my dream.
—Joseph Lamar, "SIN Diary [I]"

CHARMAINE: I don't know if I relate our love or sex to justice . . . but our love is political and revolutionary. We are Butch Femme. I only date butch women as my politics. I am invisible (as a femme) without her. She stands out without me, and because of me. We are visible together—in our community and outside of it. . . . [Ez] doesn't trigger what made me a victim, but she is strong and challenges it with her sex. She doesn't wound. We heal each other when we are together.

EZRA (TO CHARMAINE): You allowed me to be myself. And you allowed me to lead. You are a strong woman that many would want to break but it's sexy when you submit.

—Ezra and Charmaine Jackman, a Black lesbian couple. Ezra and Charmaine were each raised Christian but now both identify as "spiritual seeking."

5.1: On December 25, 2018, six-year-old Naszir Ferrell declared to a congregation he was visiting with his grandmother, "I'm tired of this church," after his grandmother would not permit him to give a speech he had not adequately prepared and he went up on stage, taking the microphone. This screenshot of a video that went viral is a reminder of a younger generation's unfettered contempt for institutions like Black churches that do not quite suit the needs and desires of emerging generations. While Ferrell's comment may well have been a simple reflection in the moment about his own broader disappointment about the situation, it also resonates with others who have attended and analyzed Black churches and who have reached a similar sentiment (for similar and different reasons). One reason Black churchgoers have come to resonate with such a sentiment is the ways Black churches have (mis)handled matters of sexuality and failed to attend to the development of Black sexual ethics appropriately and constructively; this is a sentiment that is especially familiar to Black LGBTQ members and former members of Black churches. *Source:* "I'm Tired of This Church (Original Video)," video posted on YouTube by Diinodiin Edits, December 27, 2018, https://www.youtube.com/watch?v=G4mWBKX_T8k&lc=Ugw7h4lnK-6×35YzOW14AaABAg.

What are just Black sexualities? When Black churches attempt to answer this question, far too often, there is an immediate narrowing that begins and ends with an emphasis on a monogamous marital relationship between a Black cisgender heterosexual man and a Black cisgender heterosexual woman—both of whom love the Lord, have waited to become sexually intimate until marriage, and will demonstrate affection outwardly on occasion in measured and purposeful ways. With a Black church context as backdrop, this chapter explores the question of what constitutes just Black sexuality from the vantage point of Black-gayness or gay-Blackness. What makes us "tired of this church"?[1] Ultimately, this chapter invites readers to discern what constitutes integrity with respect to sexuality within or on the outskirts of Black churches. For this chapter, the contemplative vindicationist partner is a contemporary artist, Joseph Lamar (i.e., Jojo). Dancing justice glides through this chapter with the double rhythmic purpose of relationship with the divine and exorcism of the funk that attaches itself to contemporary Black life. Notwithstanding a history of "holy dance," contemporary Black churches—and its parachurch spaces—stifle dancing justice. For the sake of Jojo, for the sake of all of us who hear echoes of our stories in his, and for any worthy Black church futures, there must be the freedom of dancing justice.

~Joseph Lamar: Dreaming the Dance~

How do we see dreamers? How do we meet those whose minds dance in the cloak of night and translate dance into thought, into song, and into being for an audience of one, then an audience of One, then an audience of hundreds, and then an audience beyond count? How do we encounter eternal beings? To experience the music of Joseph Lamar and more, to know him as an artist, an acquaintance, or friend, is to engage such a person: a dreamer, a dancer, a translator, and an eternal being. Joseph Lamar describes himself on one of his websites: "In this universe, Joseph Lamar {he_she_they} comes in many forms. A being that creates across numerous mediums, he is a singer, songwriter, and producer—a creator of narratives and paradox. Joseph's work unites the cerebral and the visceral, the secular and the spiritual, the micro and the macro. It emerges from the void—an evolving mystery of complex thoughts and theses."[2] Elsewhere, in a briefer self-description, he writes of himself: "creator + singer + songwriter + producer + storyteller + observer + genre-fucker + truth teller + truth seeker + sacred heathen + . . ." Through these two accounts, a picture may come into focus of an artist who is constantly thinking about his own meaning and existential purpose, but also thinking about the ways he makes meaning in the spaces and worlds through which he passes.

However, there are also other aspects of Joseph Lamar—a Black, gay, gender-nonconforming millennial—who occasionally walks the streets in skirts, for a period donned all in black, every now and then with ass-out pants, some days with flowers appearing to grow from his beard, always stylistically stunning and creatively matching in ways that always work but few others could imagine. My friend, Ona Osirio-Maat, once told Joseph, "*You are too much for Brooklyn!*" This was after seeing him on the day he wore black shorts, a black blouse, and a monarch butterfly cape. As with Sun Ra, his appearance matters and is part of his art and who Joseph is as an artist. The colors matter; the clothes matter; the energy and vibe matter. And, too, Joseph's words and music matter.

Joseph is the primary vindicationist companion (with George G. M. James and Aimé Césaire) for this chapter contemplating just Black sexualities in Black church contexts because he is also a son of the Black church. Growing up in Colorado Springs, his grandfather, who served as the pastor of King Solomon Baptist Church, was one of his primary guardians. Jojo's first introduction to the art of music—singing it and making it—was through the church. However, it was also through his Black church experiences—and the doctrinal scaffolding of the church that pierced his relationships with family and friends connected to and through the church—that Jojo began to understand himself as both different and a problem. Specifically, in implicit and explicit terms—especially once he came out to some of his family—it was clear that his sexuality was a problem. Questions like, "Are you just gay or are you a practicing homosexual?" confirmed a mutual separation for Joseph from church and for church from Joseph. And *church* included church leaders like his grandparents. This separation was not only from church, therefore, but also from family.[3]

Dancing justice with Joseph—holy dancing that presses in, through, and beyond churches—is an unlocking and locking of doors into new dimensions of time and place. Joseph passes between past, present, and future seamlessly. Though Joseph and his work are contemporary, he carries a vindicationist spirit with him. Reflecting on ancient Egypt himself, Joseph writes:

> I've had ancient Egypt on my mind lately. When I saw Pastor Leath the Sunday after she had nothing but good things to say. She told me about a lot of parallels between Egyptian mythology and my work. She pointed

out my key earring and she said "you know the ankh is the [*sic*] sometimes referred to as the 'key of life.'" She gave me an ankh. A tiny one that you put on a necklace. I've been wearing it as well as the one my brother Aaron gave me a few years ago. That key thing is interesting. I've been attracting keys to me for a few years now. I found a skeleton key on the ground. A stranger, an elderly, bisexual white man named Wolf who was walking the earth when I met him, had a ring with about 200 keys on it. Each one was at least 100 years old. The one he gave me was made in 1887. My friend Victoria's son Jeremiah gave me a key for Christmas with the word JOURNEY inscribed on it. I like keys. It's a reminder of our duality. You can access things. You can lock things away. Anyway. Egyptian mythology. And the ankh. On Thursday night, I had trouble sleeping again. While I was lying in bed, I started thinking of the ankh. I started watching videos and reading articles about it. Interestingly, sometimes the ankh was in the place of the words "air" and "water" as well as the word "life." There are some fringe theories that the ancient Egyptians had electricity. The top portion of the ankh looks like an ohm (Ω). Ohms are a unit of measuring electrical resistance. We know now, that the energy of water and air can be harnessed to create electricity. I don't know what that has to do with the album.

Oh. And Ptah. Supposedly, he had the original vision of creation and actualized it. He was also the god of craftsmanship and writing. It made me think of the first two lines of *In The Beginning*,

> *It started with a vision*
> *Then God made a decision*[4]

While Sun Ra flies justice into outer space, Joseph is dancing justice on earth. This is to say, Sun Ra is a transcendent figure who invites those who hear and follow him to explore the possibilities of justice that exist in an eternity that is cosmic, not earth bound, connected at once to Saturn (i.e., the planet that is Sun Ra's mother and home, the place through which he is born again) and to ancient Egypt (wherein emphasis is placed on the eternal life that potentially follows earthly death). To get where Sun Ra is going in terms of his philosophy, work, and sex, one must fly (or transport). One is not dancing into this reality. In contrast, dancing is a grounded, earthbound activity. Through dance, Joseph is connecting material spaces—from his bedroom to the streets to the church to the streets and, eventually, onto the stage. Joseph is dancing justice as he puts together otherwise disjointed rhythms, steps, sounds, and tunes. He is not putting them together for flight, but for dance, for step, for walking into and through—on earth (as it is for Sun Ra in the heavens). The distinction between the flying and dancing of justice might be explained in terms of the difference between a justice that is abstract, postponed, perfect(ed), and ostensibly everlasting, on one hand, and a justice that is concrete/material, now, imperfect(ed), and ostensibly fleeting. These are both ways that justices can do, ways that justicing does. What is just in practical terms is not always just in theoretical terms. What is just in a discrete, immediate, and/or circumscribed sense is not always just in an extended long-term (and future) and/or sprawling sense. Anticipating a kind of "electric slide," Joseph seeks a deeper understanding of the ankh and adds meaning to it, knowing "that the energy of water and air can be harnessed to create electricity."[5] The vindicationist aspects of Joseph's persona come to life in new ways as he seeks to make material sense out of what calls to him from ancient Egypt. Joseph had been introduced to some ancient Egyptian symbols and ideas—and had also perceived value in exploring ancient Egypt before, but as *SIN. [act I]* was becoming, Joseph discerned something ohm (Ω), electric in the ankh—and in the ancient culture within which the ankh was so significant. From Jojo to Joseph, from ankh to ohm, Joseph Lamar dances out vindicationist possibilities, "remembering what we never knew."[6] Where Sun Ra is transcending sexuality flying justice, Joseph is materializing sexuality (i.e., a holistically positive embodiment of sexuality) dancing justice. And, even if dancing has moments of suspension, gravity is sure to ground the expression.

What happens in the space between Joseph discovering himself as gay and knowing himself as {he_she_they}; between Jojo, Justin (a name with which Joseph identified himself to white children with whom he played as a child because of the ways it felt more fitting than his real name), Joseph, and knowing himself as "he who adds"; between Jojo's extraction from Black church and Joseph's return to Black church as an agnostic spiritual leader of worship and arts? What kind of context leaves Jojo—a young person with spiritual, musical, and philosophical gifts—dissociated from himself, his family, his culture, and institutions (like church) that have been instrumental in his very formation? What are the implicit and explicit doctrines that drive Jojo to rethink G*d? What are the resonances and dissonances between theory and praxis that call for a reorientation with respect to religion?

5.2 *(opposite)*: Joseph Lamar in Cairo, Egypt, on August 4, 2021, near the Great Pyramid of Giza. *Source:* Photograph by tour guide using author's phone/camera.

~Checking Black Churches: Unholy Dance~

Too often, Black churches project a perspective on justice as it relates to Black sexuality in terms of very particular commandments. Anecdotally, as a child with questions, I can recall being directed by the most astute in Black culture to the following commands: I Corinthians 6:18: "Shun fornication! Every other sin that a person commits is outside the body; but the fornicator sins against the body itself"; Leviticus 18:22: "You shall not lie with a male as with a woman; it is an abomination"—with a nod, of course, to Leviticus 20:13, which echoes this command with a death sentence specified for those who do not obey. Note that these are not among the Ten Commandments. Also note that these texts are not part of a commonly memorized and quoted canon but exist as part of a hidden transcript.[7]

It is unclear what, exactly, Black churches in the United States need to encounter, engage, or otherwise experience to accept sexual and gender diversity that has always existed within and beyond Black church and community. Having read the works of Emilie M. Townes, Cornel West, Kelly Brown Douglas, Anthony Pinn, Marcia Riggs, E. Patrick Johnson, and Katie Cannon, among others—along with a new generation of scholars, including Tamura Lomax, Monique Moultrie, Ashon Crawley, and Nikki Thelathia Young—there is no doubt that much has already been written about the fact and moral value of diversities of gender and sexual orientation of people of African descent in and beyond the United States. This is a diversity that has yet to be affirmed in and through institutionalized Black churches.

However, the majority of Black churches—and the clergy and laity who compose them—have not committed themselves to a systematic approach with respect to discerning what is right and wrong as it relates to gender identity and sexual orientation. Black churches do, though, have cultures at local, regional, and national levels that convey particular ethical perspectives about gender identity and sexual orientation. While Black churches have not, for the most part, identified or committed to a way of discerning what is right and wrong, implicit and explicit heteropatriarchal biases prevail in most local, regional, and national communities. Hand in hand with the absence of a clear discernment process is a diversity of beliefs and praxes when it comes to gender identity and sexual orientations. With this diversity, variously, comes hurt, confusion, paralysis, permission, and complacency. Decisions, proclamations, and positions are made ad hoc—and often as a manifestation of deeper and questionably connected institutional politics. In some ways, the absence of clear and compassionately discerned positions on gender identity and sexual orientation is not unique; conclusions on these matters are vetted no more or less than other matters in an institutional structure that operates as an oligarchic structure with a democratic veneer. In addition to this political reality, there is also a curricular crisis, insofar as Christian education leadership within the largest Black denominations and conventions has been slow to address the most pressing cultural matters that surface within Black churches. Sometimes, predominantly Black nondenominational churches do better in this respect. Still, identifying a process for discernment with respect to positions and right praxes as they pertain to human sexuality (including, but not limited to, gender identity and sexual orientation) and executing such a process with due diligence are the only ways that Black churches can begin to earn the kind of moral authority that precedes moral leadership on matters of human sexuality and gender. However, Black churches have yet to sense the urgency of identifying and applying such a process—and of doing so with integrity.

With the help of Césaire, we can see that Black churches (and other religious institutions) have lost their moral ground. Césaire notes, "capitalist society, at its present stage, is incapable of establishing a concept of the rights of all men, just as it has proved incapable of establishing a system of individual ethics."[8] To capitalism, Césaire adds "formal humanism" and "philosophic renunciation." And churches have adopted the economic and labor models of capitalism—in some instances more perfectly than professional economists and financiers; in some ways, the philosophic and humanist trends can be observed as well. To the extent that this has happened in Black churches or any institutions, there is danger. For Césaire, the direct outcome is Hitler—and all that Hitler stands for in terms of genocidal autocracy and fascism.

~*SIN. [act I]*: A Review of Joseph's Album and Diaries~

He will add. He will add the dance of justice. This meaning of Joseph's name is clarified to all who open their senses to experience what Joseph offers through *SIN. [act I]*, the album he released in 2020. This album—its lyrics, its melodies, its rhythms, its dream journal annotations, its visuals, its performance—invites us to contemplate isness as addition and addition as isness.[9] Through *SIN. [act I]*, we not only meet versions of Joseph Lamar, but we also meet versions of ourselves. Most importantly, we encounter the complexities and nuances, contradictions and dissonances of belief—and, specifically, what and how those skeptics and targets forged in the fires of

Judeo-Christian, faux-liberal, capitalist, s.o.g.i.racism believe about ourselves and our world.[10] Joseph creates new meanings and interpretations. He invites his audience to receive his account, to join him in believing, and/or to develop their/our own meanings and interpretations. For Joseph, there is no salvation outside of the agency, integrity, and dignity of his person. For Joseph, any theoethical framework must meet a standard of self-love characterized by such agency, integrity, and dignity.

The journey with Jojo is more than a tour of our present and impending dystopias. Through his work, we who are students of the faith that brought us to this point are returned to our old landmarks. We are taken back, taken back, dear Lord, to the place where we first received G*d; taken back, taken back, dear Lord, (to) where we first believed.[11] And even further, we must crawl through the implicit and explicit lessons we were taught at Sunday School, in moments of ritual faith praxis in our homes, in new members' church classes, and in studies of the catechism. In this journey, Jojo insists that we reconsider doctrines of sin and salvation; creation and eschaton; liberation, deliverance, and condemnation; paradise, heaven, and hell; humanity and divinity. To Jojo, these concepts matter, and what we believe with respect to these matters. There are several virtues that characterize an ethical code and new religion for Jojo. These principles come to life through the flow of the album's songs: "In the beginning...."; "fear"; "obedience"; "paradise 1"; "x_tears_in_paradise"; "god is a white guy"; "PARADISE 2"; "paradise (3 + 4)"; "protection"; "GET OUT"; "Inside"; "_"; "Outside"; and "TEENAGE ANGST." The virtues are: (1) believe in the divinity, dignity & integrity of human existence; (2) commit to processes of positive evolution; (3) resist sin—a) sin and righteousness, sacred and profane, are arbitrarily defined, fluid, part of the same source; b) people are not sin/s; sin is a refusal to yield to (positive) human transformation; integrity is normative; (4) procreate—a) sex is an opportunity for integrity—not the essence of sin; b) resistance must be systemically oriented—and race is but a cog. However, a sophisticated doctrine of sin precedes these principles.

~Choreographing Black Church Virtues~

Joseph explicitly and implicitly lays foundations for a dance of faith that can sustain him. He begins to lay out a system of virtues that does him justice. Here, doing Joseph justice demands articulation of a moral constellation that affirms his agency, dignity, and integrity. Consequently, doing Joseph justice also requires a framework that reveals to him and his community that he has agency, dignity, and integrity. Joseph's hopes for religious virtue are not altogether foreign to Black church virtue traditions. The very existence of predominantly Black churches was forged out of a similar concern for justice (i.e., doing justice by people of African descent in the nation-state we know as the United States). Predominantly white religious institutions, religious leaders, and culture were not doing right or justice by/for people of African descent. The agency, dignity, integrity, and general value of people of African descent was not affirmed and, worse, was undermined. Consequently, Black churches became spaces committed to the affirmation of Black culture and community—as well as individual Black people formed in the church community.

And Black churches draw upon a rich heritage of virtues rooted beyond Judeo-Christian and Greco-Roman cultures. George G. M. James contends that "the Egyptian Mystery System contained ten virtues, and from this source Plato copied what have been called the four cardinal virtues, justice, wisdom, temperance, and courage."[12] James goes on to explain: "Temperance meant complete control of the passional nature. Fortitude meant such courage as would not allow adversity to turn us away from our goal. Prudence meant the deep insight that befits the faculty of Seership. Justice meant the unswerving righteousness of thought and action."[13] James writes:

> In the Egyptian Mysteries the Neophyte was required to manifest the following soul attributes:
>
> (1) Control of thought and (2) Control of action, the combination of which, Plato called *Justice* (i.e., the unswerving righteousness of thought and action). (3) Steadfastness of purpose, which was equivalent to *Fortitude*. (4) Identity with spiritual life or the higher ideals, which was equivalent to *Temperance* an attribute attained when the individual had gained conquest over the passional nature. (5) Evidence of having a mission in life and (6) Evidence of a call to spiritual Orders or the Priesthood in the Mysteries: the combination of which was equivalent to *Prudence* or a deep insight and graveness that befitted the faculty of Seership.
>
> Other requirements in the ethical system of the Egyptian Mysteries were:
>
> (7) Freedom from resentment, when under the experience of persecution and wrong. This was known as courage. (8) Confidence in the power of the master (as Teacher), and (9) Confidence in one's own ability to learn;

both attributes being known as Fidelity. (10) Readiness or preparedness for initiation. There has always been this principle of the ancient mysteries of Egypt: "When the pupil is ready, then the master will appear." This was equivalent to a condition of efficiency at all times for less than this pointed to a weakness. It is now quite clear that Plato drew the four Cardinal virtues from the Egyptian ten; also that Greek philosophy is the offspring of the Egyptian Mystery System.[14]

According to this system, justice itself is a virtue. However, justice is not the only virtue. It works in tandem with other virtues. Similarly, for Joseph, justice is but an aspect of a system of virtues.

While James walks through historical Greek scholars, naming them one by one and explaining how we might trace their insights back to Egypt, Césaire is retracing new orbits. Césaire's is a dancing mind, retracing himself and his worlds outside of the parameters of assimilation again and again. He tries out new steps of abstraction and order, weaving in and out of poetry and prose.

VIRTUE 1: BELIEVE IN THE DIVINITY, DIGNITY & INTEGRITY OF HUMAN EXISTENCE. Joseph believes in his divinity. Of his creative process and the evolution of *SIN*, he writes:

> When you try to be better in any way, physically, mentally, spiritually, artistically, whatever, what you're presuming is "there's more to me than the person I am at the present moment." If it's true no one's perfect, then no matter how much better you get there's always gonna be more to you than who you are right now. The divine self, the true form, is endless. I AM ENDLESS. In my physical form I am fundamentally limited. But every act of betterment gets me closer to freedom. The void is the divine self. To seek self-discovery, self-actualization is to step into the void. It's a leap of faith. An act of trust. You have to trust yourself. How else can you weather the onslaught of doubts and fears and insecurities and despair and character flaws that arise when you seek enlightenment? You have to trust that evolution is not an event but a process.[15]

What Joseph believes matters. And what we (i.e., human beings) believe matters because of how it impacts what, how, and who we can be to ourselves, to (and with) others in community and society, and to, with, and as divinities and Divinity. What we believe, in no small sense, determines how we show up in the world. Jojo implicitly and explicitly believes in his own value. He believes that he is precious, that his life has value and meaning.

Jojo can (and does) point to moments in his journey of creating *SIN. [act I]* when he believed or acted in ways that did not honor his full value. However, the creation of this album demanded self-actualization—an actualization that could take place only through an honoring of self. Joseph's relentless belief in his intrinsic value births this album. Every day he sets himself to the task of musical creation. Joseph says "yes" to himself and refuses to give up to anything within him that might be tempted to quit, anything within him that felt or feels inadequate or unable, anything within him that says he can't, he won't, or he shouldn't, anything outside of him that would try to shut him up. On September 29, 2018, Joseph writes, "Self-actualization. Freedom. Personal growth. Progress. Evolution. That's what *SIN.* is about. But *SIN.* is more than just an album. It's an era in my life. I'm living these songs. I'm defying my limitations. I'm undergoing a self-imposed evolution. I'm discovering my intrinsic nature. I'm challenged everyday." Though he does not name it as such, Joseph believes in *imago dei*—that he is, that human beings reflect the image of G*d and that, because human beings reflect a divine image, human beings have value. Importantly, Jojo frames his value as simultaneously actual and potential. It is not that Joseph must prove his value, but Joseph does believe that he must live up and into his value. His life and what he does—his praxis—must confirm the value he knows he has. He writes:

> I really want to be recording all the time. But thankfully, I'm using my time fairly well. Trying to stay on top of my health, practicing and doing some emotional and spiritual work. Everyone around me is in some sort of romantic relationship. Sometimes I get a little lonely and that's hard. Doing what I'm doing is hard. It's hard to pursue self-actualization. It's hard to become truly independent. I understand the reasons why some people quit. I also understand the reasons why I could never do that. The biggest reason is, I'm not *some people*.[16]

Joseph knows that he is exceptional. He does not believe himself to be better than anyone else, but he does know that he cannot live by the same standards and rules by which it may appear that others are living. Joseph believes in the divinity of his human existence. The more Joseph believes this, the more he can testify: "Lately, I'm starting to feel less like I'm playing a video game called 'Joseph's Experience' and more like I'm actually *Joseph*."[17] Joseph becomes his divine self. The discipline with which he puts his beliefs into confirming action corresponds with the extent to which he appreciates his divinity.

While *SIN. [act I]* has distinct songs—each of which carries a unique message—the ideal way to receive the gift of this album is through uninterrupted listening from beginning to end. Perfectly mastered, the songs seamlessly flow into one another, fading glorious style into glorious style, guiding the contemplative spirit in a journey of awakening, self-discovery, and self-recovery, exposing the erotic aspects of spirituality—as well as the spiritual aspects of eroticism. Throughout this personal, spiritual musical journey, Jojo asks, "What is the purpose of my existence?" Joseph answers, "Live with dignity and integrity." What is living with dignity? It is living with one's head held high, with confidence, with pride (without being proud). What is living with integrity? It is living in tried-and-true honesty and transparency, such that beliefs/thoughts and actions are all aligned and consistent. This means: when you have a gift, use it for good; when you know your truth, tell and live it; when you sense the divine, honor it; when compassion moves you, help; when you doubt, explore until you discern; when you know yourself, be and love yourself; when you know your strength, apply it to be a blessing; do not grieve your muses, ancestors, or the divine; do not shirk from responsibility—especially the responsibility to be your best, actualized, and ever-improving self; do not resist the process that the cultivation of such integrity requires.

VIRTUE 2: COMMIT TO PROCESSES OF POSITIVE EVOLUTION. Surely *SIN. [act I]* stands on its own. However, a fuller understanding comes in reading Jojo's diary, written as he was creating this album. *SIN. [act I]* did not simply happen. Joseph did not just wake up one day and compose, record, and master the album—all at once. Jojo marks countless moments on the journey to complete this musico-theoethical treasure. Most striking is the repeated theme of anticipated completion—often followed promptly by an acknowledgment that the lyrics, songs, mastering, album, personal formation that had been finalized was not finished after all. There is a constant push and pull between completion and process. There is a reluctant acceptance that steady progress is being made, but the finished product is often intangible or imperceptible. There is something mysterious and slippery about the end.

In many ways, process becomes a foundational theoethical virtue for Jojo/Joseph. Jojo's/Joseph's acceptance and articulation of his intrinsic value is not to be taken for granted. This is a process. He is writing the "inner revolution" that makes "GET OUT" and "Outside" possible. Joseph also knows that there is no true finish:

> You can get free without discipline but you won't stay free. If you don't master yourself you'll always be a slave. As hard as it is to get free it's even harder to stay free. You can't rest once you cross the finish line. You have to stay in shape. You'll have to run longer races. You'll have to climb higher mountains. You'll have to fight greater battles. You'll have to solve more complicated problems. You'll have to slay bigger monsters. You'll have to learn and relearn and unlearn. You'll have to [sic][18]

There is always more to the process of personal formation. This is unending and, as such, is perpetually demanding. Joseph discerns an effective approach: discipline.

The completion of the album cannot be taken for granted. This, too, is a process. In fact, this is the most painful of processes to read—with over twenty references in Joseph's diaries to being done and having completed the project—only for him to realize and remark upon something more there is to do. Still: the process is paradise. Paradise is not an antithesis to change. How does the overmind relate to paradise and change? How does any aspect of Joseph's discerned and constructed reality relate to change? All of these aspects of existence are opportunities for a process toward positive evolution. And in this, there is something better than paradise. It is not even the paradise of paradises. What exists is something better than the category of paradise—or paradise is no longer the linguistic sign for a perpetual and static utopian state.

VIRTUE 3: RESIST SIN. Sin and righteousness, sacred and profane, are arbitrarily defined, part of the same source. However, they are not the same. Joseph explains the fluidity of his experience and voice as he has imagined SIN. [act I]. Joseph can see himself in the various characters he has created and the system that he has constructed and discerned as the reality through which his life's process must take him. Even as he understands and sees himself in the overmind, the snake, god, masquerades as god, and the targeted protagonist who is variously the good guy and the bad guy, Joseph is still clear about his own sense of right and wrong. He is not content to be a puppet, a product, or a progenitor of a colonizing system.

The sin of systems must be resisted. Resistance must be systemically oriented—and "Race is But a Cog." However, Joseph comes to this realization.

At some points he knows exactly where and how to locate race; he is unapologetically Black. However, at other points it is clear that he is enamored with, interested in, and even sympathetic toward whiteness. He seems to believe that there is something less dysfunctional about whiteness. He is permissive when it comes to his friend and musical collaborator Kendall. However, Joseph gets clearer and clearer that colonizing systems, institutions, and concepts—like race, gender, and sexuality—are the vehicles through which sin loves to come alive. And a truer liberation comes in this revelation. Even still, this revelation is a gift to Black churches that are still interested in a meaningful and relevant existence post-Joseph—and those of us who can relate to his process and points of disappointment and disillusionment.

"People are Not Sin/s." It is sinful to cast others as sin or to try to change others. As such, people should not be resisted—nor should anyone attempt to change people against their will. Stasis is sin. However, this is where sin becomes slippery again: people should be open to their own change and transformation through their own process of discernment and positive evolution. None of us is free of external influence. However, each of us has an opportunity to balance this with independent thought—and each of us has the capacity to cultivate our sense of independence and independent thought in ways that have integrity. We can make ourselves and our ideas available to challenges and questioning and critique—without compromising our integrity and dignity. We can be open to growth and development without losing ourselves. Sin is a refusal to yield to (positive) human transformation. Resisting change, resisting destiny, refusing to yield: these are sin.

VIRTUE 4: PRO-CREATE. Pro-creation is not a matter of reproductive sex. Pro-creation is adding. It is allowing everything that we do—including, but not limited to, sex—to add. It is a matter of adding value, integrity, dignity, and a sense of divinity. Pro-creation adds belief (i.e., faith), commitment to process, and resistance to sin. Pro-creation also adds sex as an opportunity for integrity—not the essence of sin. Joseph clarifies the problematic association of sin with sexuality, through both the album and his journal entries. He describes the ways that he comes into an awareness of his homosexuality: he becomes aware of attraction; he begins to view diurnal experiences, like watching everyday television sitcoms, through a lens of sexual attraction—and he is conscious of this lens; he follows a graffitied advertisement for porn in a school bathroom to view predominantly white, gay, male pornography that confirms and strengthens the attraction of which he has become aware.

His awareness of his homosexuality is coupled with an awareness that this is not an approved sexuality.

Joseph knows that his attraction is taboo. This is key: it is not necessarily that he associates his sexuality or his sexual attraction with sin—though he recognizes that others do. However, it seems to be the common sense of Black church culture that an awareness that a sexuality, sexual expression, or sexual attraction is nontraditional, not consistent with a heterosexual, patriarchal, cisgender, monogamous, maritally oriented norm, is a de facto awareness and acknowledgment of its sinfulness. This distinction is important to any analysis of what follows. Is Joseph's homosexuality merely different (in its deviance/deviation) from dominant cultural sexualities, is it sinful (in its deviance/deviation) from dominant cultural sexualities, or both? Does Joseph know that his attraction is merely different and not sinful, is he unsure of whether his sexual attraction is merely different or is sinful, or does he know that his sexual attraction is different and sinful? If his homosexuality is sinful, what makes sin sin? If his homosexuality is not sinful, what makes sin sin? What makes sin something to avoid? If at all, to what extent do Joseph's awareness and beliefs about his sexuality impact the objective and/or subjective sinfulness of his sexuality? Are there axioms that hold, as one thinks sin, so it is? As cultures construct sin, so they are? Sin is to be resisted?

Consequently, Joseph hides both his same-sex attraction and the ways that he is discovering affirmation in and of his same-sex attraction through pornography. What is sin in Black churches and among individuals and families acculturated in implicit and explicit Black church sexual ethics: homosexuality is sin; and, too, secrets—anything that must be kept secret, especially sexual secrets—are sin; enjoyment of pornography is sin. Refusing to accept these notions of sin, Joseph makes it clear that an inconsistency with one's thoughts and actions, with what one believes and what one does, is the road that leads to sin. He writes:

> Your choices reveal what you value. Today I had my infusion at the hospital, then I had two back to back meetings regarding music videos. I scrolled through Grindr a little bit and I got messages from a few guys. I could have had sex but I opted out in favor of taking a late night run to the grocery store. Now, I won't have to leave the house for food for the rest of the week. Tomorrow, I can have a full day of recording. I just finished doing some more work regarding the videos and the album. I feel like my values are changing. I value my health. I value my work. I value my vision.

I value my intuition. I value my growth. I'm glad I chose not to get laid. I might masterbate [sic] before bed though.[19]

Ultimately, for Joseph the question is: are we doing (and making choices) according to what we truly, normatively, should and do value? If our actions and choices are not lining up with what we think or say we value, then what we think and say we value is not what we value after all. In fact, our choices in action are the true measure of our values.[20] Valuing or prioritizing sex is not sin. Saying, believing, or thinking that we do not value or prioritize sex, but allowing it to drive all of our choices in action, is a hypocrisy, a deceit, and (in this way) sin. Righteousness is valuing the right things to an extent but is mostly acting with integrity upon what we value. Joseph does not give up on satisfying his sexual desire altogether; his sexual desire is not sin. Joseph simply prioritizes it in a way that is consistent with other desires and values.

From Joseph's perspective—from the vantage point of his upbringing—sexuality is the (presumptive) sin of the fall from paradise. It is important to note that, for Joseph, the paradise of the Garden of Eden that marks the inception of earthly and human existence in Judeo-Christian traditions is variously synonymous with and distinct from the paradise that marks the end of the world and is known elsewhere as heaven. In this way, the concept of paradise can best be understood as a matter of proximity to the divine. However, because of a perversion of what constitutes goodness and "Godness," the divine does not exist uninterrogated for Joseph. More precisely: because of his sexuality, race, and gender identity—and the ways that these have meant that religion has rejected him and he has rejected religion—Joseph has had to articulate a new theoethics, a personal theoethics. Joseph has had to add. He adds for his dignity, his integrity, his divinity. He adds for his survival. He adds for his liberation.

~Broken ♥'d Believers: Homosexualities and Church Exoduses~

SIN. [act I] was not considered for a Grammy for best gospel album for 2020. However, it delves deeper into theological contradictions, contradistinctions, and contraindications than most gospel records ever will. Through this audiovisual masterpiece, Joseph Lamar leads us in the paths of suspicion for his name's sake, leads us beside critical waters, and helps us see how flocks of the disaffected could leave Black churches in search of an unrecognizable "house of the Lord" for green(er) pastures. Still there is faith. *SIN. [act I]* appeals to the soul and defends its integrity. "god is a white guy" and "inner revolution" provide the recessional marching music for those of us who are done, tired of (this) church, and ready to go. This musical exodus appears to be the psalm of the hopeless and the dirge of the faithless, but is the vetted hope and resilient faith of one who cannot be crushed. *SIN. [act I]* will be read and misread again and again through the final generations of human existence, just as Jordan Peele's horror film *Get Out* was evaluated as a comedy. It might be considered antifaith or cast as antibelief. However, at its core, it is the crooning of one who has sought love—and whose heart has been broken. It is not simply that Joseph has sought but not yet found a love—a lasting, committed sexual and/or relational intimacy—in another person. Joseph's album reveals that he also sought love from family and community deeply rooted in Black church. He writes of the former love interest here, but I believe it also applies to the latter:

> My ♥ is broken. That occurred to me tonight, though there wasn't anything that happened tonight that broke my ♥. My ♥ has been broken for a while. Maybe my whole life. I realized only broken ♥'d people think and act like I do. I guess what I feel now is an awareness that my ♥ is broken. In a way, it's nice to know. I guess I spent most of my life with a broken ♥ and thinking it wasn't broken. When you operate that way, the adage "follow your ♥" can be deadly. Think about it. Imagine all the damage you can drag yourself and others through when you let a broken ♥ lead you.[21]

Where were the models of love for a beautiful gay Black boy growing up in Black church community in Colorado Springs, Colorado—too close to South Park, Colorado, USA? Where were the examples of healthy love in intimate relationships—especially LGBTQ ones? Where were the examples of theoethics rooted in authenticity—and not pious hypocrisy?

Joseph and a gospelized layered chorus sings in "Outside": "Let me out right now" / "I'm a virgin to sin, I'm a virgin to sin." The chorus that sings with Joseph could consist of so many of us—the disaffected Black LGBTQ believers, the ♥broken, the millennials who cannot stomach or make sense of "don't ask, don't tell," who know that our silence will not protect us, who know that a denial of our identities and realities will not save us.[22] The story has been told too many times now. Black LGBTQ people have left Black churches in droves.[23] Who cares where we have gone and what we are doing? Who cares where our spiritual care is coming from? Who cares how we are having to build our faith up from the ashes of burned phoenixes? Thankfully Joseph does:

> My heart is broken. Just being able to say that is liberating. It's not me. I'm not stupid or unworthy or anything like that. And neither is my heart. My heart did what hearts do. It tried it's [*sic*] best to keep pumping no matter what went wrong. So I could survive. I've just reached a point where I wanna do more than survive. I'm beginning to understand the concept of Wabi Sabi. They would paste broken vases or cups or plates back together with liquid gold. I used to think that was to illustrate how something actually becomes more beautiful when it's been broken. Now I'm thinking of it differently. It's not the brokenness that makes it beautiful. It's healing from the brokenness. It's the fact that even though it was once broken it's now whole. It's about utilizing your pain in service of your evolution. That's kinda how I felt on the dance floor tonight. A group of us went out dancing for Jake's birthday. When we got out there on the floor I felt a lot of my old psychological baggage show up. And I realized I was broken. But my being broken didn't mean I couldn't dance. Dancing was like saying "I'm broken but slowly but surely, I'm gonna put myself back together." I'm already doing it. I'm already better off. Everytime I choose life in spite of my brokenness I take a step toward wholeness. I will myself to evolve.[24]

Justice dances itself into wholeness. It is a process. In process, we accept being enough and not enough, done and not done, okay and improving all at once. We know process is not procrastination; process is not being lax in achievement. Process is for healing. And this healing work is theological, philosophical, and deep.

Joseph puts to art the familiar contemplation of escape from life, community contexts, closets, and soul-crushing conceptions for so many Black LGBTQ people. He evokes difficult questions that are common to us: What does it mean to run away (especially on/with wax wings)? What does it mean not to come back? What exactly are we running from/to? Is church the place in which one can't stay, is it the people and the theologies and the constructed and reconstructed realities that compose church, or are these two aspects indistinguishable? Is leaving real or really possible? What does leaving fix? Joseph seems to reply: in or out, here or there, wherever I am, I will find G*d in deviance as resistance.[25] In the midst of brokenheartedness, Joseph dares to dance. This is deviant. This is a daring joy in the midst of sorrow and heartache. The deviant dance of the broken ♥'d is a healing salve of self-love. It is a return to Joseph's catechismic virtues. Dance remains: when the love of intimate companionship is absent and forbidden, when dysfunctional believers and systems have obfuscated divine love.

~Club of Refuge~

The spiritual needs of Black LGBTQ people do not go unmet. The documentation of spaces and places that fill the gaps Black churches have left grows and grows. Most notably, Cathy Cohen, E. Patrick Johnson, Alexis Pauline Gumbs, Thelathia Nikki Young, and Ashon Crawley have captured the stories of those who have forged spiritual community in chosen family, choirs, in clubs, in academic space, in television fandom, in activist community building, in music, and in other pop culture outlets. Anthologies have been written documenting the ways that Black LGBTQ people have been finding spaces of refuge outside traditional church and institutional settings. The Pulse Nightclub massacre is but another proof of this.[26]

José Esteban Muñoz offers one of the most eloquent theorizations of this alter-space and the ways that LGBTQ people of color who find spiritual, philosophical, and healing homes outside of institutional strictures build a future. Transforming the concept of a stage (i.e., a phase that passes) into a stage (i.e., an honorable place of performance), Muñoz weaves a tapestry of hope that is essential to the unique pro-creative futurity of LGBTQ people of color. He writes:

> I dwell on hope because I wish to think about futurity; and hope, I argue, is the emotional modality that permits us to access futurity, par excellence. Queers, for example, especially those who do not choose to be biologically reproductive, a people without children, are, within the dominant culture, people without a future. They are cast as people who are developmentally stalled, forsaken, who do not have the complete life promised by heterosexual temporality. This reminds one of the way in which worried parents deal with wild queer children, how they sometimes protect themselves from the fact of queerness by making it a "stage," a developmental hiccup, a moment of misalignment that will, hopefully, correct itself or be corrected by savage pseudoscience and coercive religion, sometimes masquerading as psychology.... I consider the idea of queerness as a "stage" in a way that rescues that term from delusional parents and others who

attempt to manage and contain the potentiality that is queer youth.... I enact a utopian performative change in the signification of the phrase "it is only a 'stage,'" deployed in the name of the queer child—in this case, the queer wild child of punk subculture.[27]

And it is not just stages that Muñoz queers but also clubs and venues of cruising for sex in the abstract and material. The club—and other such spaces of queer refuge—are for such a time as this. They are in this right time and place: then and there. They do not let the present off the hook. They do not give churches opportunities to condemn, dismiss, or otherwise oppress. And there is a hermeneutic that accompanies this space, a hermeneutic that methodologically presses beyond suspicion:

> A queer utopian hermeneutic would thus be queer in its aim to look for queer relational formations within the social. It is also about this temporal project that I align with queerness, a work shaped by its idealist trajectory; indeed it is the work of not settling for the present, of asking and looking beyond the here and now. Such a hermeneutic would then be epistemologically and ontologically humble in that it would not claim the epistemological certitude of a queerness that we simply "know" but, instead, strain to activate the no-longer-conscious and to extend a glance toward that which is forward-dawning, anticipatory illuminations of the not-yet-conscious. The purpose of such temporal maneuvers is to wrest ourselves from the present's stultifying hold, to know our queerness as a belonging in particularity that is not dictated or organized around the spirit of political impasse that characterizes the present.[28]

For in the present, it is true that as much as many people within Black churches would be glad to escape the discourses of sex and gender wars, there is an economy that relies on the subjugation of Black LGBTQ people within Black churches. "The spirit of political impasse that characterizes the present" is not only about the ways that "reproductive majoritarian heterosexuality" functions to maintain modern nation-states but is also about the ways that "reproductive majoritarian heterosexuality" maintains the institutional pillars of modern nation-states—pillars like Black churches.[29] The financial support and the worshipful spirituality of Black LGBTQ members silences those concerned about the sin of homosexuality with respect to salvation. However, these and others who are simply intoxicated with power still find ways to silence the gayness and stunt the political aspirations of those Black

LGBTQ members who dare to stay in Black churches with varying degrees of transparency about their gender and sexuality.

A queer utopian hermeneutic displaces paradise—and sin. And this becomes a refuge for those pawns of Black church politics. More importantly, however, a queer utopian hermeneutic changes time. It literally changes the rhythm of dance within the ecclesial space—and wonders which dance partners can show up, keep up, and dress up for the occasion.

~Shouting Justice: Holy Dance and Beyond~

In "SIN Diary [I]," Joseph writes:

> Between the album and church stuff I haven't been writing as often as I want. So many things have happened. I hardly even know where to begin. I think, in a nutshell, I'm starting to see my growth in action and I'm becoming more aware of the places in me that still need attention. I'm starting to put names to the things I feel. I'm becoming more familiar with myself and I'm feeling closer to God. My birthday was chill. Even though I'd talked with some friends about going away for awhile and taking mushrooms I didn't end up doing that. There was a two day revival at church that I ended up playing/singing for. The revivalist, a deep complected woman with a heavy voice that seemed to carry with it the fear of God, prophesied over everyone. On the first night (Wednesday June 5th) she said to me "You have a gift and you're meant to do great things but the weight you carry keeps you here," (she indicated with her hands a sort of plateau.) Then she said "I'm seeing 6-6 . . . does that mean something to you?" I didn't answer. It wasn't until later that I thought June 6, the day I was born. She told me "God says that you were given three songs that you have not released." I had to think about that one too. Then it hit me. The night before, I had a vivid dream in three parts. There was a different song in each dream and in between each dream I woke up, with the song still fresh in my brain. And even though I keep a notebook and staff paper at my bedside for the purpose of writing those things down, I didn't. Each time, I woke up feeling drowsy and I'd go back to sleep saying to myself "that song wasn't all that good anyway" (or something to that effect.) She also told me there are some relationships of mine that aren't serving me. That they're part of the weight I carry and that I need to "snip them." After the service was over I asked her to elaborate. There were five people in the church at

that moment, the revivalist and her assistant, Pastor Leath, Sister Berry and me. I admit, I was both intrigued and intimidated by the revivalist's presence... She told me that there are people I know who don't honor the person I'm becoming. They want me to be the person I was. She said "Does that make it more clear?" I said "yes" but truth be told I was hoping God would tell her a name or at least a good hint but whatever. She went on, "It's not an accident that your name is Joseph. It's not an accident that you dream of music." She asked if she could touch me and I consented. She asked me to remove my coat so I slid my arms out of the sleeves and let the coat drop to the ground. "Never do that!" she said "Everything that belongs to you is sacred. You don't drop sacred things on the ground. Put it on the pew." I did as she said. Then she started to pray over me. I closed my eyes and as I stood there in front of the altar I just got this urge to move but I didn't really feel like I was doing the moving. I almost felt like a puppet. Like there were invisible strings attached to me. My elbows slowly pointed toward the ceiling. My heels lifted until I was standing on my tiptoes. My head started to move back and forth. The whole time, I felt like I was watching myself move. Every now and then I'd think "what am I doing?" "What's going on?" Then I silenced my mind and I just surrendered. Then my foot started to move around the floor. My arms and fingers stretched out. I started to do these organic movements. Then I started to stomp and clap. At first it was arrhythmic but the clumsy sounds and movements quickly evolved into a complex amalgamation of West African, gullah geechee and afro-brazilian rhythms. I started to hear faint melodies in my head. But I couldn't hear the words. It was just gibberish... deh doh fee no no... deh doh fee no no... I listened more intently and words started to come... speak to me oh Lord... speak to me oh Lord... I must have danced and sang for about 15 minutes, moving around in front of the altar with my eyes closed. By the time I was finished, I'd sung three distinct songs with these rhythmic segues in between. Slowly, my body went back to neutral and I opened my eyes and the prophetess, her assistant and Sister Berry were just standing there staring at me. Pastor Leath was sort of bent forward in a trance. Earlier Sister Berry had offered me a ride home. But as everyone stood there staring at me I said to her "I think I'd like to walk home after all." I collected my things and I got out of there quick. I wasn't embarrassed or anything. I just needed to keep moving. It was sorta damp outside. The streets and the sidewalk were kinda glistening. I felt incredibly light. I just felt a sense of joy and peace I couldn't explain. As I walked down the street I was still singing and clapping and dancing. I probably looked crazy but I felt great. I passed by some yuppie bar where there were about a dozen people standing outside. I almost hopped over the fence to talk to each and every one of them. I didn't know what I was gonna say. I just had to tell someone about what I was feeling. In retrospect, I'm really, really glad I didn't do that.[30]

Dancing justice. Joseph is dancing justice in the church. Joseph is dancing justice down the street. Justice is dancing. Justice is dancing through Joseph. Justice can be danced; justice can dance. The steps of dancing justice are clarified through Joseph's account:

1. Joseph is connected with himself.
2. Joseph is connected with the divine in himself.
3. Joseph is connected with something greater outside of himself (the divine).
4. Rev. Burns is a vessel for the Holy Spirit—it dances in her.
    a. (She does not ask—and is not hindered with the questions of whether or not Joseph is gay and/or whether or not he is a practicing homosexual.)
    b. She is able to hear from the Holy Spirit on behalf of Joseph without invoking sexuality (in any way—either to condemn or affirm).
5. The Spirit, moving through Rev. Burns:
    a. speaks to Joseph,
    b. sees and calls forth his gifts,
    c. touches Joseph in a way that causes him to dance, and
    d. connects him that much more with himself,
    e. the divine in himself,
    f. something greater outside of himself,
    g. with her, and
    h. with others around her (i.e., community and church that have remained present through this moment).
6. Joseph goes out in the power of the dance and reconnection— inspired to share it with others.

And this is a dance that he carries with him on the inside and through the outside world he encounters. However, this conversion experience is also a process. Almost a year later, Joseph is still learning the freedom of dancing justice he received in June 2019. He writes:

Tonight when I got home I listened to snippets from my album while dancing. That in and of itself seemed like a sign. That was the first time I'd ever sang [sic] and danced along to my music instead of scrutinizing it or looking for things to fix ... And I've been realizing that I have this deep fear and it's not a fear that my dreams won't come true. It's a fear that even if they did come true I wouldn't deserve it. I have no problem projecting myself into that space. And in a way the sort of questions I ask myself about what I'd be like if these songs were massively, publicly successful seem to presume that I'm capable of achieving that sort of success. So on one hand I want it and on the other hand I don't feel it belongs to me. I think the worst case scenarios I sometimes play out in my mind have been my way of scaring myself into submission. Maybe I've been afraid to identify with this more actualized version of myself. I've been playing small. Walking down the street tonight I found myself thinking about how joy has always been this private thing for me. Like I was afraid to share it openly for fear someone would piss all over it. Like I didn't have a right to it. That's why I started dancing in my room. Cause I'd been walking down the street listening to music and imagining myself dancing but I wanted to *actually* dance. I wanted to move in all the ways I know that only I can move. I've spent most of my life in my head, imagining myself doing the things I wanted to do. I coded this mental simulation where I got to be who I truly was. I guess what I'm saying is, I don't wanna live in my head anymore.[31]

In evaluating theories of justice as they relate to Black sexuality, this book contemplates justice as an agentive actor that does things. Specifically, I argue that justice does things—in a personified way—and that the things justice does are different than we might imagine. With Jojo, Joseph, He Will Add, justice dances. He dances inside and outside of subjects and institutions. Joseph "comin' alive" no longer polices his dance—closeting it with his joy in his room.

~From Black to Quare~

Are there churches of the future? Are there Black churches in the future? Sadly, Black churches have opted for a path of judgment. The Jojos of Black churches are judged for their unconventional sexual relationships and/or behaviors. Then we ascribe the same judgmentalism to G*d and call it justice. We imagine that G*d judges as we do. Instead, justice with respect to (Black) sexuality in (predominantly) Black churches should look like a cultivation of the full actualization of individuals and of their communities. Individuals like Joseph, me, and so many others should be encouraged to live out the fullness of ourselves and be able (and be helped) to discern our spiritual gifts. We should be encouraged to act in the power of our spiritual gifts.

If there are churches—and Black churches—in the future, they are quare.[32] There is a Black queerness, a Blackqueerness. Muñoz explains queerness in his introduction to *Cruising Utopia: The Then and There of Queer Futurity:*

> QUEERNESS IS NOT yet here. Queerness is an ideality. Put another way, we are not yet queer. We may never touch queerness, but we can feel it as the warm illumination of a horizon imbued with potentiality. . . . The future is queerness's domain. Queerness is a structuring and educated mode of desiring that allows us to see and feel beyond the quagmire of the present. The here and now is a prison house. We must strive, in the face of the here and now's totalizing rendering of reality, to think and feel a *then and there.*[33]

Muñoz offers ideas and reflections on the spaces and places that aspire to queerness. These are spaces of hope—and potentiality. These are spaces of dancing. These are spaces of better sex: better conversations about sex, better teaching about sex, better approaches to sex, better ways of handling sex. These are not spaces of policing, but of pleasure; these are not churches of abuse, misconduct, and oppression, but of awe, genuine care, and liberation. In fact, Muñoz begins to construct a scaffolding for utopia—like paradise on earth. Above all, such a place consists of queer futurity. Muñoz writes, "Queer futurity does not underplay desire. In fact it is all about desire, desire for both larger semiabstractions such as a better world or freedom but also, more immediately, better relations within the social that include better sex and more pleasure."[34] Quare churches no longer traffic in subtleties. Thoughtful, relevant, diversely informed theological formation is what Black churches should be providing on matters of sexuality and other doctrinal matters. This kind of religious education should include, but not be limited to, information about Black Judeo-Christian traditions; this information should include topics and philosophies of the continent of Africa and African diaspora. Such support with discernment, encouragement, and empowerment is what Black churches should be doing with respect to other aspects of the diverse identities, gifts, and graces of their members.

One of the ways we might understand the work that Black churches must do is through the relationship between classical and quantum mechanics. Where a focal question for classical mechanics is the position of a particle, a focal question for quantum mechanics is the wave function of a particle.[35] When considering Black sexualities and sexual ethics with respect to Black churches especially, we must ask ourselves: are we asking the right questions? When we focus on doctrines—and especially the doctrine of sin—are we focused on the right questions? When we focus on intrainstitutional politics, interests, powers, and categories, are we focused on the right questions? In some sense, the shift away from a classical unequivocal defense of monogamous heteropatriarchal marriage as the only context appropriate for sexual expression (and there, only certain sexual expressions) and toward a quantum concern with the sovereign experience of individuals—some of whom, communities of whom meet G*d, their sexualized, and their whole selves through other sexualities, sites of sexual expression, and homosexualities—is comparable to the shift between classical and quantum mechanics.

An important detail of quantum mechanics is the function of measurement. David Griffiths writes of the Schrödinger's cat paradox:

> The measurement process plays a mischievous role in quantum mechanics: It is here that indeterminacy, nonlocality, the collapse of the wave function, and all the attendant conceptual difficulties arise. Absent measurement, the wave function evolves in a leisurely and deterministic way. . . . It is the bizarre role of the measurement process that gives quantum mechanics its extraordinary richness and subtlety. . . . The Schrödinger cat paradox forces us to confront the question "What constitutes a 'measurement,' in quantum mechanics"? Does the "measurement" really occur when we peek in the keyhole? Or did it happen much earlier, when the atom did (or did not) decay? Or was it when the Geiger counter registered (or did not) the decay, or when the hammer did (or did not) hit the vial of cyanide? . . . Most physicists would say that the measurement occurred (and the cat became either alive or dead) well before we looked in the window, but there is no real consensus as to when or why.[36]

Barbara Holmes contemplates the metaphysical challenges brought to bear through the cat paradox of quantum physics. She considers the possibility that the "cats" in the box whose fate is uncertain before measurement in Schrödinger's hypothetical experiment are often "the poor and the oppressed." She writes, "They often live in closed environments where there is the potential or actual release of deleterious elements (i.e., drugs, crime, economic impoverishment, and inferior educational systems). Like Schrödinger's cat, they are both dead and alive. One wonders if anyone is interested enough to lift the lid and find out."[37] She continues with an evaluation of quantum mechanics:

> Quantum theories present aspects of reality that overturn our previous assumptions. We really can't say what reality is or how it works. To date, we can say that the quantum world exists but its contours are elusive and potential rather than actual. With all of this potential emerging, something is missing. It is the potential of the two-thirds world. Yet even with its exclusion, dominance and victimization are only one aspect of reality, an aspect that is not insurmountable. No one can fill the categories of victimizer or oppressor permanently and totally. The potential exists to embody many aspects of reality simultaneously and to dissolve the myths of static categories of ontology.[38]

For Holmes, the fate of the "cats" matters, and our measurement of that fate should not be delayed on account of our uncertainties regarding what we will find.[39] Even if measurement is questionable, it is essential to attend to and cultivate the potential of those who have been discarded and/or marginalized. In the case of Black churches, this means that a new, delicate, holy dance must be learned. The new rhythms of dancing justice demand that LGBTQ people—and others whose sexual expressions are rightly consensual but fall outside of traditional norms—are seen.[40] Our potential should be recognized and honored in Black ecclesial spaces. And where our fate in the closet/box is rendered invisible—as we exist in the imagination, stereotypes, falsehoods, and gossip of powers that be in the liminal space of alive/dead—new forms of measurement must be considered and utilized to see what's in the closet/box without destroying what's in the closet/box, while trying to save, cultivate, and revive the good of what's in the closet/box and its potential.

Beyond and including sexuality, Black churches should not shy away from difficult conversations. Honoring that sexuality is a part of life for all people (as aspects of sexuality factor into conception processes)—and honoring that for some people sexuality is a part of their calling and vocation—is a gift that Black churches can choose to offer. In fact, sexuality can be a primary or important way that individuals will come to understand G*d, themselves, and their role in this world more fully. This is the case for many of us who have felt the rods of judgment and condemnation in Black churches.

The post-COVID-19—and postclosing—litmus test for belonging includes subscription to familiar and expanded virtues: justice, courage, fortitude, and prudence—with qualified belief in dignity, integrity, and divinity; commitment to process; resistance to sin; and pro-creation. Quare churches hear the teachings that "make ways out of no ways" and accept that G*d is change.[41] Quare churches—along with other Black social institutions—can affirm the visibility and participate in the healing and wholeness of couples like Ezra and Charmaine Jackman. What can Black churches do? Black churches can repent and find ways to celebrate and recover people who have left—and the spiritual gifts and fortitude of Jojo and people like him who have left churches, carrying their gifts with them, unsure of whether or not there is a G*d, knowing there is no G*d, or knowing that the G*d of Black churches has nothing to do with them. Black churches can identify the Jojos in congregations and receive the prophecy of their (and our) quare futures together with gladness. Black churches can invest in the Jojos of the congregation—ensuring that they are able to face the void and come forth whole, baptized in the waters of justice, cleansing the atmosphere with holy dance. Black churches can choose to be(come) quare churches.

Dancing justices may not have churches, but any congregation daring to call itself "church" must have dancing justices.

~ * ~

A Black Sexual Ethic

The diversities of Black sexualities—including homosexualities—are divine gifts that give way to holy dances of mind, body, and spirit altogether, at once.

A Maâtian Code of Justice

Maât's feather weighing our integrity rests on an open scale, with an open measure according to her precepts, open to the ancestors. We do not hide our sexualities as she honors her fluidities and utopically reimagined fertilities.

Ancient Mixologies

6

Joel Augustus Rogers and
Puzzling Interracial Intimacies

[Sexual ethics] could mean consent and all kinds of things. It could mean mutual pleasure, caring, etc. [It could mean] [m]utual commitment to sheltering queer and gender nonconforming young people and creating a space of rest for them, . . . [b]ut creating those kinds of care networks has actually been one of our challenges and has meant our own erotic energy has been in service to the world and not to each other. . . . [W]e are interested in care and undoing patriarchal ideas of human connection: [v]isioning and being Lorde's erotic where each person's creative life-force energy has its autonomy, is not forced . . . into capitalism or imperialism; [n]urturing rebellions against patriarchal logics which say you have to be married and a caretaker and have to be servicing somebody else.
—A queer Black woman and her partner, a queer white woman

The asserter of race purity is either a psychopathic, or a hopeless ass.
—Joel Augustus Rogers, *Sex and Race*, vol. 1

Phones are up, video is running, pictures are snapping. I can see some of this from the corners of my eyes at first. This white man has his knee pressing down on my neck. We talk in Black community about the white man's foot on our neck, but now it's literal; now it's my neck. I am already restrained! Handcuffs hold my arms behind my back! I am pleading for my life, pleading for mercy, pleading for my mother, pleading for an end to my suffocation (if not his restraint). I do not know the safe word. I do not know the safe word that will end my suffering, the violation, this tragic end to my life. There is no safe word. Even if there were a safe word, I doubt he would believe my proximity to death—or care if he believed. This "dom" would not believe me: that I need mercy, that I need relief.[1] What sick fantasy of his am I? (And, since I am Black: can I [even] feel pain—as far as he and all the people watching are concerned?) Did I agree to be a "sub"?[2] I did not. Would I, could I agree and consent to be a sub? It does not matter: I did not. I did not agree and consent to being a sub just by virtue of being a Black man in this territory called the United States. I can feel pain. I do feel pain. I am not without pain by virtue of being a Black man. And still: the absence of the feeling of pain would not qualify me to be a perpetual sub; it would not justify my subjugation to this position. And what does it mean that this white man knew me before he kneeled on my neck for nine minutes and twenty-nine seconds (nine minutes and twenty-nine seconds)—before I was dead? Seventeen years this white man worked outside of a club as its off-duty police while I, a Black man, worked inside of the club—also providing security. Is there a "Blacks Only" entry to safety? Is "Whites Only" the only safe space?[3]

This framing of the fatal subjugation of George Floyd under the knee of Derek Chauvin suggests that the offense of Chauvin's murderous so-called law enforcement was limited neither to its generalized callous disregard for human life nor to its specific expression by a white man toward a Black man.[4] Implied in the particular position of man over man was a domination power ripe with sexual innuendo—especially to an eye that can see sexuality as a space for expressions of power and power as a vehicle through which sexuality is expressed, and power as a container that far too often holds sexual fetishes along with countless other charms. Is this a perverted view of the perversion of power already in effect? Is this a corrupt sexualization of what is already sullied as an abuse of power? (How dirty is sex anyway?) Or is this merely an observation of what is already so? How do we know when sex is present—when sex or sexuality are impacting and/or are relevant to any given circumstance, situation, entanglement, or relationship? If we discern the presence of sex or sexuality as a factor, how, then, can we determine its impact on any given relationship or circumstance?

This chapter takes up these latter questions regarding sexuality and power within the unique context of interracial sexual relations in domestic US territory—with an emphasis on the specific intimacies between people of European and African descent. The familiarity of George Floyd's fate and the contemporary carceral state provide bookends for this chapter that travels through major landmarks of racialized sexuality and sexualized race on the journey from the transatlantic slave trade to the present day. The chapter's narrative begins with a reflection on interracial sexual intimacies over the centuries with Joel Augustus Rogers as the guide. It takes up the ubiquity of interracial sexual intimacies—while laying the groundwork for how these intimacies have been problematized in different eras and regions in different ways. While Rogers traces interracial tensions and complexities in the evolution of different modern nation-states, he identifies the culture of slavery especially as manifested in the Southern region of the domestic US territory and "perfected" in Nazi Germany as temporal and material sites of the fomentation of what moderns recognize as racism and racialism—and the concepts of antimiscegenation that attend to these. This section plays with interracial imagination—taking up the relationship between those who claim interracial identity but do not identify as biracial; those who are in interracial relationships that they or others recognize as such, especially between those who identify or are identified as white and those who identify or are identified as Black; and those who recognize themselves as biracial and/or the offspring of interracial relationships.

Toward the end of the chapter, I also reflect on how Frantz Fanon might become a piece of this puzzle. Parts of Fanon's biography make him an interesting interlocutor in this chapter. He is a Martinican who enlists and fights for the French in World War II; he studies in France; he goes to Algeria with his training as a psychiatrist. Along the way, he marries his wife, Josie, who is French. There he finds his voice articulating the psychological and social conditions of Algeria and decries the immoral French colonialist presence. Integration into a democratic society is not the outcome Fanon anticipates, and Fanon marries someone who is not Black. As far as colonized peoples, Fanon sees violence and bloodshed on the horizon.[5]

In contrast with Rogers, Frantz Fanon is not seeking to demonstrate how intermixing has been the human "true-true."[6] Fanon is focused on the rage that results from the denial of Black humanity. The fact of hybridity is a given. Fanon sees no hope in convincing white people that they are Black, they are mixed, and/or that intermixing is a given. Fanon recognizes that even if hybridity is true and accepted, European colonizers have neither shame nor inhibitions about the rape culture that undergirded the transatlantic slave trade and colonization.

The chapter continues with a more careful look at interracial sexual intimacies in terms of exploitations. Notwithstanding the fact of interracial sexual intimacies throughout recorded human history, the transatlantic slave trade and the racist ideologies that underpin it disrupt celebratory, affirming, and/or normative readings of racial hybridities and the sexual intimacies that enable them. Historically, too much of the story of sex has been conquest. This truth cannot be overstated in the context of people of African descent and their European conquerors. The story Rogers tells—the moral of which affirms more intentional and conscientious interracial sexual intimacies (and consequent racial hybridities)—is difficult to reconcile with interracial sexually based terrorism. This terrorism has been well documented. Its reach into the contemporary context of the carceral state is evident.

What kind of contemporary politics can contend with such a legacy? Beyond the question of specific body politics, do we overcome through comprehensive desegregation efforts, as Rogers seems to suggest? Or is the political future closer to what Fanon prophesies? What kind of political system, what kind of community framework or organization aptly responds to and corrects such a history of sexual terror? I contemplate the possibilities of anarchism as a rejoinder to personal and political acts of racialized sexual terror (i.e., the backside of antimiscegenation laws and traditions). I take up political and bodily anarchies.[7] I assess anarchies that build on and that build away from democratic principles. I wrestle with the ways that protest spaces give birth to anarchism, and with the similarities and differences at the extremes of Black and white nationalisms I argue that there are productive anarchies—with respect to sex, sexualities, and politics—that can inform alternative ways of handling old puzzles.

I continue with a comparative analysis of the ethical frameworks of Marie Fortune and Kelly Brown Douglas as they pertain to human sexuality. The cultural particularities of these perspectives are exposed; the prospects of an interracial sexual ethic are contemplated. Finally, the relationship between these individual and integrated accounts of sexual ethics are reconciled with implicit and explicit conceptualizations of justice at work for these ethicists. Considering whatever constitutes just interracial sexual intimacies and whatever constitutes exploitative sexual intimacies, I offer a constructive word with respect to justice (generally).

I conclude with a reflection on puzzling justice. The hybridities of interracial sexual intimacies appear as unsolvable puzzles in the matrices of racism—along with sexism, classism, heterosexism, and ability. The ubiquity of interraciality informs a reasonable intuition: interracial sexual intimacies are not the puzzle requiring extraordinary logic to solve; racism and other ideologies of hegemonic power together constitute the puzzle needing a new logic. However, the intersection of interracial intimacies is fraught. Beyond questions about what particular ethical responsibilities attend to conscientiously interracial, consensual sexually intimate relationships, there are questions about how to establish, maintain, and cultivate justice in response to interracial people who had no choice in their interracial existences, those who have born interracial children by force, and those who have forced the proliferation of interracial people and communities without conscience and/or through violent force.

Sex is not (just) about sex (and/or whatever other romantic or experientially informed ideas we may have about sex) but is also always about power. Power is neutral but bends to the matter of justice. Sex is about justice: sexual intimacies—and what precedes and follows these intimacies—in relationship invite participants to be just actors, moral agents. That sex is about power and justice does not require the mindfulness of those who participate. Sex participates in economies of power and justice with or without knowing it. Ultimately, this chapter maintains that interracial relationships and its offspring are ubiquitous. Everyone is interracial; thus, everyone is in an interracial relationship. Notwithstanding these facts, appearance (i.e., color), language, and acculturation all contribute to the extent to which one identifies with or is identified in terms of a particular racial category—even as an interracial person or not; in turn, this dictates whether or not intimately connected individuals are perceived as part of an interracial relationship or not. When self-identified—or externally perceived—interracial intimate relationships attempt egalitarian, mutual, equal, and equitable expression, they are often frowned upon by white supremacists as well as those who identify with a particular racial, ethnic, or cultural group and are interested in maintaining the identity, existence, or sociocultural integrity of that group. Then there are coercive and/or exploitative interracial intimacies that explicitly weaponize race in order to deny any egalitarian possibilities. When the interracial subjectivity of an individual and/or the interraciality of relationships of intimate partners are subjectively defined as such—whether according to a self-determination or a discernment of this in the eyes of some public—a racially based power differential can be assumed in addition to any other power differentials at play because of gender or any other identifying factors. Within a person who identifies as interracial—or is identified as interracial—there can be both an internal power struggle associated with race and an external experience of race-based power differentials within the context of relationship.

I take up the ways that magnetism—and principles of attraction and repulsion—can be an important way of navigating the puzzle of interracial intimacies. While there are ways that one can logically learn and/or memorize steps to solve certain types of puzzles—like the puzzle of a Rubik's cube— there are also affective, tactile, and tangible ways of feeling and leaning into answers to the 3-D, multidimensional, cubic puzzle. Where does one feel tension as one holds and twists the elements of the Rubik's cube? Where does one (physically or otherwise) feel the pull and tension like an attractive magnetism? Where does one (physically or otherwise) feel the looseness and release like a repelling magnetism? Both of these are natural physical sensations important to the organic flows of terrestrial life.

There is no simplistic normative claim to be made with respect to Black sexual ethics as it pertains to interracial sexual intimacies and racial hybridity. Interracial sexual intimacies must be acknowledged for what they are—neither universally positive nor negative, neither perfectly corrective nor the quintessential danger to a normative Blackness or white supremacy. The terror of interracial sexual intimacies—in terms of both present and historic realities—remains a private and public moral burden even in contexts of resistance, appropriation, consent, and love through interracial sexual intimacies. How we choose to see racial hybridity (everywhere) can be a tool for dismantling racism as easily as it can be a tool for reifying racism and its deleterious effects (e.g., colorblindness). This chapter offers ethical ways to navigate—if not solve—this puzzling set of circumstances.

Interracial Sexual Possibilities:
Mixed-Race Relations and People

In the foreword to the first volume of his three-volume *Sex and Race* series, the first of which, *Negro-Caucasian Mixing in All Ages and All Lands*, first published in 1941, at the height of World War II iterations of Nazism and fascism, Joel Augustus Rogers writes, "We shall see that mankind began as a single family; that the family circle widened and widened until it broke into segments, and with that came the illusion that the segments were no longer parts of the circle. But thanks to mechanical progress and the spread of knowledge the segments are coming together again; the various ends are being united; the cycle is being completed; and a single understanding family is once more being formed."[8] While it can be hard to imagine normativity—much less deviance from the normative or the normative deviance toward which this chapter points—Rogers's words drip with purpose. Specifically, Rogers is committed to the purpose of demonstrating that we are, finally, all "one (albeit mixed) blood." However, in order to make this claim, Rogers must pass through a threshold of origins that equally challenge human belief (or faith) and ontology (the study and/or constitution of being) even into the present. In the second chapter of volume 1, he asks, "Which Is the Oldest Race?" It is here that Rogers most directly reminds us of a fundamental double question that haunts the study of religion, broadly, and a question that embodies different, but no less significant, specters in Afrodiasporic and sexuality studies: Where do we begin—and what is the importance of (our) origins? If nothing else, Rogers's volumes *Sex and Race* demonstrate that even when the points of origin we choose are the most ancient of spaces, places, and times, they betray racial and ethnic hybridities. And as he makes this claim, he also asserts that origins are important—and the ancient spaces, places, and times about which we know most are in Africa. For Rogers, the importance of origins is intrinsically connected to the importance of patterns—specifically, patterns of human behavior. Hybridity, thus, is an ancient pattern of human behavior. Notwithstanding the clarity of Rogers and others about the ubiquity of interracial sexual intimacies and human identity—and the fallacy of any pretention of past, present, or future racial purity—interracial sexual intimacies have consistently been criminalized and punished or weaponized as a quintessential feature of social control and domination through racial logics.

One of the modes of attack against antimiscegenation for Rogers is psychological. He writes, "The doctrine of racial superiority as it now exists in Germany and the United States is the insanity of the many for the gain of a few."[9] However, there are much broader psychological questions at play in Rogers's work than the matter of sanity. How does the psychology of being in a mixed-race relationship (that one recognizes as such) relate to the psychology of being the offspring of a mixed-race relationship? And how do the psychological challenges that these two conditions pose relate to the psychological perspective that begins with an acknowledgment that we are all (already) interracial? For those persuaded of the interraciality of all (already), how is this reconciled with the cultural dissonance of perspectives that insist that racial difference is real, racial purity is possible, there are Black and white people and cultures, and there are people and cultures racially coded beyond even these? I pose these questions especially as they relate to the relationship between people who identify as Black and whose ancestors were enslaved Africans, and people of European descent who identify as white in the territory identified as the United States. In a sense, Rogers provides points of origin from a modern perspective for us to begin wrestling with these challenges of the mind and intellect as they pertain to race and racial hybridity.[10]

As Joel Augustus Rogers aptly points out, there is no such thing as racial purity; he quotes Albert Einstein: "All modern people are the conglomeration of so many ethnic mixtures that no pure race remains. . . . It is impossible for any individual to trace every drop of blood in his constitution. . . . After we go back a few generations our ancestors increased so prodigiously that it is practically impossible to determine exactly the various elements which constitute our being."[11] Still, the subject of interracial sexual intimacies and relationships was still relevant and important enough for Rogers to write about in the mid-twentieth century. After all, for the sake of maintaining, establishing, or cultivating racial purity and socioeconomic segregation, the allegation of interracial sexual attraction alone was grounds for countless lynchings—bolstered by antimiscegenation laws. In 1776, when the independence of the United States as a sovereign territory was declared, seven of the thirteen colonies had antimiscegenation laws. These laws were repealed and reenacted through the mid-twentieth century. As many as thirty states had such laws at one point in the history of the domestic US territory. (It would not be until 1967, a year after Rogers's death, that the Supreme Court would discern the unconstitutionality of all state antimiscegenation laws through its decision in *Loving v. Virginia*.) As Rogers explains in the first volume of *Race and Sex*, it is astounding to think that racial purity remains a goal when there is little to no record of a sustained racial purity. Rogers describes the purpose of the first volume of *Race and Sex* as showing "from the most authentic facts available what and what and what have entered into the family trees of the 'superior' and the 'super-superior' race; whether in the case of Aryans it may not be a case of the pot calling the kettle black."[12] Thus, Rogers takes up the cause of proving what Einstein and others had already observed.

More fundamental than the psychological question for Rogers, however, is the moral questions that attend to racial hybridity. For some, Rogers's objective—especially given the proof of interracial mixing already in plain view—seems strange. The problem for the Aryan, ultimately, is not one of misinformation or ignorance. The problem, as Rogers perceives, is moral: "And what was the moral calibre of all these millions of ancestors? The race purist never stops to ask. All he knows is that it was glorious. . . . What a sight that would be! Cannibals, phallic worshippers, wretched Egyptian peasants, chiefs, kings, pharaohs, philosophers, prostitutes, thieves, thugs, poets, physicians, pirates, convicts, counterfeiters, horse-thieves, a Pope or Tome or two, rogues of the deepest dye, and saints of the most finical honesty."[13]

The question of the "moral calibre" of one's ancestors—with a recognition that there is surely as much moral diversity as there is ethnic or racial diversity among one's ancestors—is just the tip of the iceberg. Rogers is clear: if anything should be of concern with respect to one's ancestry, it is the matter of who one's ancestors have been as moral agents, as spiritual conductors. Then there is another moral matter of concern for Rogers—"the real issue in the matter of race-mixing": "The problem is not anthropological. It is ethical. Races have always mixed and will continue to mix; if not in accordance with man-made laws, then against them. The real question is whether the Anglo-Saxon, the Nazi, the Fascist shall continue to maintain their fake position on 'the purity of race,' whether they shall continue to eat their cake and have it, too."[14] There is the ethical trouble of dishonesty—regarding the general facts of racial mixing, regarding the specific and personal facts of racial mixing, expressed in the ambivalence and paradox of hatred for and intrigue with ethnic others, expressed in being part of what is deemed inferior and maintaining a superior separateness. Differently put, Rogers not only insists that ancestors of Africa and its diaspora are moral agents, are authors of moral philosophies, and, thus, have moral gravitas, but also implies through this unfatigued insistence that social belief matters and that it can and should be realigned with research and evidence that affirms the dignity of people of African descent. Though critical of religion, Rogers's work maintains there is virtue in believing, belief, and faith in—and, ultimately, there is virtue in knowing—the value of the lives of Black people on earth.

Joel Augustus Rogers was born on September 6, 1880, in Westmoreland Parish, Jamaica. Rogers was the son of Samuel John Rogers, a Methodist minister and schoolteacher, and Emily Johnstone Rogers; he had ten siblings. Unable to acquire a scholarship for further study after high school, Rogers enlisted in the "British Royal Army and served with the Royal Garrison Artillery at Port Royal for four years."[15] After emigrating to the United States and living in Chicago from 1908 to 1921, where he had enrolled at the Chicago Institute of Arts in 1909 with hopes of becoming an interior decorator,

Rogers worked as a Pullman porter for over a decade in order to support this and his other professional objectives. After his years in Chicago, Rogers primarily lived in Harlem until his death in 1966. His widow, Helga Rogers-Andrews, was chiefly responsible for the republication of his works. Several aspects of Rogers's biography make him a particularly interesting subject of inquiry and point of origin for discourse on the intersection of race, religion, and sexuality. Rogers was not only transnational and well traveled but also maintained a significant local presence in the Afrodiasporic community of New York developing through the Harlem Renaissance. Moreover, his autodidactic methods of historiography and anthropology won him the acclaim of such notable figures as Hubert Harrison, Marcus Garvey, and W. E. B. Du Bois. Rogers is introduced for consideration as a quare figure—having met the *Sidewalk* literary standards of which Mitchell Duneier writes, but having slipped through the cracks of the affirmed institutional canons.[16]

One of his biographers explains that once Rogers had relocated to Harlem in 1921 from Chicago, "Rogers was active amongst a network of 'Street Historians' such as Carter G. Woodson, John Edwards Bruce, Arthur A. Schomburg, Marcus Garvey, and Pauline Hopkins who were responsible for the dissemination of culturally and historically empowering information for 'African-Americans.'"[17] For some, it is difficult to reclaim a figure like J. A. Rogers because he had no interest in objectivity and was unapologetic about it; of course, his unequivocal rejection of objectivity in his own methodological approach was also a critique of objectivity altogether. Historian Thabiti Asukile writes, "J. A. Rogers's journalistic and historical writings are considered part of the tradition that social scientist St. Clair Drake referred to as 'vindicationist history.' Rogers dedicated his life to advancing the view that people of African descent were throughout world history extremely influential in the building of ancient and modern civilizations which made significant contributions to human progress."[18] Asukile further explains that "vindicationist" was an appropriate descriptor not just for Rogers's approach to history, but also for Rogers's approach to journalism, through which he also "sought to vindicate the lives and experiences of Africans and people of African descent throughout the African Diaspora." Such vindicationist work evokes a kind of moral dilemma. Surely the personhood of Black individuals—and Black community as part of the sociological tapestry of humanity—is and ought to be such a given that it demands no vindication. Moreover, the idea that there is some process of attaining or recovering personhood and humanity is horrifying.[19] However, historically and throughout the present day, the personhood of Black individuals—and Black community as part of the sociological tapestry of humanity—has not been a given. And even when the moral agency, personhood, and humanity of Black individuals and communities are externally ascribed to individual and collective Black bodies, an idea of Black inferiority pollutes the air.

Thus, vindication is essential—if only as a matter of setting records straight. Still, there is a strange irony in the simultaneous urgency and necessity of denying the prospect of objectivity and insisting on the categorical "isness/ontology," existential value, dignity, and equality of people of African descent.[20] Too, the vindicationist project does not stop with an insistence upon Black and African worth but must also disrupt the dishonesty of Western philosophy about its roots. The validity of a system of justice, in some measure, must be evaluated on the means by which the system was discerned (if such information is available). Contemporary Western philosophers, theorists of justice, and religious ethicists have insidiously selected Greco-Roman sources as their points of origin without regard for the khemetic educational systems, if not named teachers, to whom they are completely indebted. Beyond a cursory acknowledgment of its unknown khemetic sources, the contemporary Western academy is responsible for transforming the language and systems of teaching within its epistemic fields to at least rescind the attribution of classical moral thought to Greco-Roman empires and their representatives. In many ways, the metaethics of vindicationist work, such as that of J. A. Rogers, clarifies an a priori value, a deontological principle—which also functions as a virtue—which some have derived from research on ancient khemetic moral beliefs and practices for modern Black individuals and communities: there is a dignity of all creation; specifically, race, color, and ethnicity have nothing to do with human or moral worth.

J. A. Rogers addresses matters of race and sexuality head on, directly. In his magnum opus, the three volumes of *Sex and Race* published in the 1940s in the wake of Nazism and fascism, Rogers is bold enough to declare the ubiquity and normalcy of racial mixing and homosexuality and deft enough to prune the bittersweet fruit of poets like his Brussels-born US transnational contemporary Adolf Wolff, who exemplified the distortions of Black sexuality in white minds in his poem "To a Negro Belle."[21] He even goes so far as to provide images to support his claims—ambiguous in their pornographic intention and effect. In the face of hybridity's ubiquity, Rogers names the intermarriage of antimiscegenation and political expediency. Rogers quotes Hitler regarding race: "I know perfectly well just as all these tremendously clever intellectuals, that in the scientific sense there is no such thing as a race. . . . But I, as a politician, need a conception which enables the order which has hitherto existed on historic bases to be abolished . . . and for this purpose the conception of race serves me well."[22] In the face of hybridity's ubiquity, Rogers names the intermarriage of antimiscegenation and ego. Rogers maintains that "your asserter of race purity . . . is gnawed by a vast inferiority complex that can be satisfied only when he is looking down on someone else. When there is none such, he becomes a nobody even in his own estimation."[23] In the face of hybridity's ubiquity, Rogers names the intermarriage of antimiscegenation and classism. Rogers quotes the British historian Arnold Toynbee: "Our modern Western racialists have rationalized their Calvinism by substituting White and Black skins for damnation and grace and expurgated it by omitting the divine cause. The result is not science but fetishism."[24] In his own words, Rogers writes, "mankind is thundering with avalanche speed back to the Dark Ages, and it is not race-mixing that is the cause; it is the doctrine of race purity, underneath which is the fight for money and markets."[25] Antimiscegenation is unnatural to human existence, yet it becomes an ever ready and willing partner to other prevalent forms of social oppression.

Interracial Sexual Exploitations:
From Slavocracy to the Carceral State

To understand the insidious and pervasive nature of racism in the United States, one must acknowledge the ubiquity of interracial sexual violence. In fact, interracial sexual violence is as ubiquitous as racial hybridity. Ironically, even racial hybridities (and interracial sexual intimacies) that spring from authentic love and consent cannot escape the stain, the suspicion, and the burden of racialized sexual violence and sexualized racial violence. Racialized and sexualized violences are the foundational pillars of the United States as a nation-state. The quintessential proof of this is slavery—and the particular socioeconomic demands of slavery on the entire economy of the United States as a burgeoning nation-state. The focus of this chapter thus far has been on the challenges of interracial intimacies, where intimacies are neutral. Intimacies include the discomforts of unwanted proximity as well as the comforts of desirable proximity. In this section, I emphasize two distinct forms of explicitly violent sexual intimacies. The first of these is the violent sexual intimacy of European American people—women and men—who have directly participated in the sexual exploitation of people of African descent through personal, shared involvement in the sexual lives of people of African descent. This first aspect of discourse begins with white slavers (i.e., kidnappers, transporters, owners, and overseers of enslaved Africans) and extends to include contemporary sexual relationships—"consensual" (i.e., consensual, but not attending to the persistent problems of race) and nonconsensual between European American people and people of African descent. The second form of explicitly violent sexual intimacies with respect to the relationship between European American people and Afrodiasporic people in the US nation-state is what I term *systematic sexual surveillance*. It can include individual and collective forms of cuckolding. It also includes implicit and explicit interests in strategic breeding, genocide, and any form of concern with the reproductive patterns of people of African descent from the vantage point of those who do not identify and are not identified as people of African descent. In its broadest sense, systematic sexual surveillance is about white people's awareness of Black people as sexual and sexualized subjects. Reflecting this awareness of gender identities and sexual orientations, systemic sexual surveillance expresses itself in conscious and unconscious, implicit and explicit forms of policing of Black people's bodies. Systemic sexual surveillance is about how white supremacy exploits Black sexuality even in presumably intraracial—quasi-racially pure contexts.[26]

Through this section I demonstrate the ways that this two-strand twist of Black sexual subjectivity within discourses on interracial sexual intimacies—where Black people are the direct objects of European American sexual desire and systemic sexual surveillance—has developed from the arrival of the first enslaved Africans in 1526 on what would become "American" soil and in Virginia in 1619 to the present as citizens of the United States and, disproportionately, as carceral subjects. I will point to ways that violent sexual intimacies and racism complicate any personal or collective interest in positive engagement in the discourses and praxes of race, gender, sex, and justice. The facts of this legacy will become a foreground to a more robust comparative and constructive approach to Black sexual ethics and theories of justice.

Of the notion of African beauty in the eyes of Europeans, Stephanie M. H. Camp writes, "It was to no slave trader's advantage to insist that Africans were uniformly revolting people. The irony, of course, is that slavery's logic of commodification evacuated beauty of the power it often held. Commodified and enslaved beauty was anything but powerful."[27] European openness to the beauty of Africans, however, shifted in marked ways. Beauty sans power was not destabilizing enough for the economy that was being built on the exploitation of Africans. Camp writes, "When American scientists invented their own concept of race, they did so by defining black bodies as, among other things, singularly ugly."[28] In *The Erotic Life of Racism*, Sharon Patricia Holland attempts to expose and parse the subjectivity of inventions such as Black as ugly and ugly as Black. She points toward the moral import of training desire—or at least acknowledging its corruptibility. She begins her chapter titled "Desire or 'A Bit of the Other'" with the following citations for comparison: "Kwame Anthony Appiah tells us, 'In our private lives, we are morally free to have aesthetic preferences between people, but once our treatment of people raises moral issues, we may not make arbitrary distinctions.' Writing in another time, Emmanuel Levinas asks, 'Is the Desire for the Other (*Autrui*) an appetite or a generosity?'"[29] Appiah's concern seems to hinge on two concerns: the relationship between the public and the private, and the morality of desire as a medium through which one can do justice (or not). Of interest in the Holland's Levinas citation is the question of how organic, natural, or essential desire is. Holland offers several interventions for the navigation of these concerns, but I name only one that I find helpful: Holland's application of Judith Butler. She writes, "Butler worries about the efficacy of desire as an end unto itself. Thinking through our historical location, Butler moves to drag desire through history's gauntlet, reminding us that 'there is no full-scale escape from our historical situation and the legacy of domination that has become ours' (173)."[30] In other words, desire can and must be interrogated even if it cannot be decontextualized.

The training of desire does not mitigate the interracial violences of sexual intimacy that characterized the transatlantic slave trade. Beyond the stereotypes that have been named and rehearsed within and beyond womanist discourses, there are two notable features I will name here.[31] First, the fundamental (un)rapeability of enslaved Black women during (and beyond) slavery cannot be overstated. I purposefully use the term *(un)rapeability* because, on one hand, enslaved Black women could not be raped because they were considered property. On the other hand, enslaved Black women were never true property, and so the sexual use of enslaved Black women's bodies was always rape. "Many enslaved women [were] purchased solely for sexual purposes," Rachel Feinstein explains.[32] These women became objects whereby white men learned to have sex and how to maintain racialized heteropatriarchal domination. Among white women especially, white men were framed as "adulterers opposed to rapists and black women as wanton" when white men were found to have raped enslaved Black women.[33] Ultimately, "raping" enslaved Black women did not exist. Rape (i.e., forcing unconsensual sex) of enslaved Black women was not only legal, but encouraged—and not called rape. This complexity and legal ambiguity betraying questions about the personhood (or property nature) of enslaved Black women becomes a critical foundation for interpreting, understanding, and translating contemporary Black-white interracial sexual intimacies and subsequent racial hybridities.

Second, often overlooked is the prevalence of sexual violence against enslaved Black men. In *Rethinking Rufus: Sexual Violations of Enslaved Men*, Thomas A. Foster exposes violences against enslaved Black men by white men and women that often "included punishments that involved nakedness," involved sexualized depictions of Black men, and sexual harassment and assaults in the life experiences of well-known figures who recorded their experiences while enslaved (i.e., Equiano Olaudah and Frederick Douglass).[34] In discerning a reasonable contemporary interpretation of Derek Chauvin's murder of George Floyd, a critical awareness of this history is essential. White men's assertion of physical and sexual domination over Black men was essential to the logics of African slave economies. This domination simultaneously exposed, celebrated, and undermined Black male virility. Moreover, the perverse particularities of these sexual violences seep beyond rape and into explicit cannibalisms.[35] White men and women who benefited from the slaveholding economy and sociopolitical system not only practiced their sexual desires on Black men (and women) but also nurtured a culture of sexual surveillance.

One of the most horrific manifestations of systemic sexual surveillance was embodied in slave breeding. Not only the visual-sexual pleasure of white slaveholders but also the interest in sustaining and growing the slave population—especially after the discontinuation of new enslaved African imports—drove this sexual surveillance. Sexual surveillance was manifested in the establishment, expansion, and proliferation of Black Codes, anxieties about declining slave populations, and (whether or not the objective was to shame a culture into abolition) the inclusion of breeding stories in slave narratives and abolitionist rhetoric.[36] The very opposite of breeding, however, is also endemic to white supremacy's toolkit. Vincent Woodard writes of the 1934 lynching of Claude Neal in which Neal is made to eat his own penis and testicles and say he likes it.[37] After the domination power analysis of this violence, one must contend with the ways that this act forced a most perverse sexual act on Neal—and involved a community of lynchers who desired to (force and) watch this atrocity. Such systemic sexual surveillance does not easily fit in the category of the gaze alone. The very act of such a forced sexual act and the surveillance thereof is at once an act of domination power and of (unusual?) sexual desire.

In her book *No Mercy Here*, Sarah Haley demonstrates the frequency with which Black women are subjected to convict leasing, chain gangs, and jail on account of charges of infanticide and murder of an (often abusive) male spouse and/or family member in the generations following emancipation. However, she also provides proof of just how often courts refused to honor pleas for reunification with children, spouse, or family; moreover, she exposes the (1) ubiquitous forms of sexual violence (including rape), (2) erased and ignored offspring conceived and born within the penal system to Black women that could only be the outcome of rape, and (3) efforts of white women like Rebecca Latimer Felton to defend the sterilization of Black women presumed to be inherently lascivious, alongside (4) the lynching of Black men presumed to be inherent rapists. At times, the seepages are more like leaks. Haley excavates the life of "queer" that preceded its signifying male effeminacy or homosexuality: "'queer' was most consistently used in Atlanta's mainstream press to describe perverse black bodies, ideas, and behaviors that could only be interpreted and governed through police and judicial action."[38] However, *No Mercy Here* at once exemplifies an affirmation of Audre Lorde's warning that our silences will not protect us and demonstrates the ways that silence did, at times, protect the women about whom she writes and was used as an important tool of resistance.[39] Haley shows that systemic sexual surveillance is a pillar of the earliest days of the prison industrial complex in the lives and experiences of policed and imprisoned Black women in particular. The ways that violent interracial sexual intimacies and racial hybridities led to incarceration and were further exacerbated for those in prisons historically—ways shown in Haley's work and elsewhere—provide clear roots for the contemporary carceral and policing state. Prison and policing continue to traffic in paradigms that that fix the racial, sexual, and social domination of whites and subordination of Blacks and other people of color—even when intraracial intimacies and hybridities are at play.[40]

Do Democracy and Anarchy Mix?

Born into slavery in 1851, Lucy E. Parsons became a leading anarchist figure in the early twentieth century. In Waco, Texas, Lucy met Albert Parsons, a white former Confederate soldier turned radical Republican, whom she later

6.1: In this photograph taken in her Chicago home, Lucy Parsons points to a picture of her late husband, Albert Parsons. On May 1, 1886, police fatally shot six people at Haymarket Square, attempting to disperse protesters advocating for an eight-hour workday. Albert was executed in 1887 following his conviction along with five others for the Haymarket Square bombing that occurred on May 4, 1886, when organizers returned to decry police violence and continue advocating for labor rights. An interracial couple, Lucy and Albert coalesced around a common call to and vision for worker's rights and an anarchistic socialism that could dismantle class inequities. The photograph speaks to their relationship—its power, merit, and significance with respect to various social measures, but also to the devastating demise of their relationship because of Albert's suspect conviction and execution. Ironically, the class struggle appears to be the ultimate catalyst for Albert's death, though this couple fled the South, recognizing that their interracial relationship could not survive the racial struggle as it broiled there. *Source:* Brigid Kennedy, "A Fighter for Workers' Rights," Chicago History Museum, https://www.chicagohistory.org/lucy-parsons/.

married. Together, this interracial couple became powerful labor organizers in Chicago, where they moved in 1873. Ultimately, Albert would be executed for "'speaking in such a way as to inspire the bomber to violence' following the Haymarket Riot" of 1886; Lucy died in a 1942 house fire.[41] Most of her writings have been lost. However, for Lucy, it is clear that democracy and anarchy do not really mix.

Lucy Parsons's version of anarchism was powerful, principled, and consistent with those of other anarchists of her day. In her writings and speeches, Parsons quotes the platform of the International Working Peoples' Association agreed upon at their 1883 congress, calling the association the "representative organization of communistic anarchists": "1. Destruction of the existing class rule, by all means, i.e., by energetic, relentless, revolutionary and international action. 2. Establishment of a free society based upon co-operative organization of production. 3. Free exchange of equivalent; products by and between the productive organizations without commerce and profit-mongery. 4. Organization of education on a secular, scientific and equal basis for both sexes. 5. Equal rights for all without distinction to sex or race."[42] Beyond these constructive points, she was clear about the limits of democracy:

> It was during the great railroad strike of 1877 that I first became interested in what is known as the "Labor Question." I then thought as many thousands of earnest, sincere people think, that the aggregate power, operating in human society, known as government, could be made an instrument in the hands of the oppressed to alleviate their sufferings. . . . I came to understand how organized governments used their concentrated power to retard progress by their ever-ready means of silencing the voice of discontent if raised in vigorous protest against the machinations of the scheming few, who always did, always will and always must rule in the councils of nations where majority rule is recognized as the only means of adjusting the affairs of the people.[43]

Parsons perceived the problems of the tyranny of the majority.[44] She was clear-eyed about the fact that even with a majority, even with enfranchised masses, there were still ways that democracy was prone to corruption. Even if the majority and masses could be educated, empowered, and trusted to act on behalf of their collective self-interest, the organization of government itself tended toward problematic constraints for individuals and groups of workers. Parsons would argue that the scaffolding and mechanisms of government and rapidly industrializing industries corrupted the natural human tendency to enjoy meaningful work and creation.

And for Lucy, peaceable ways of pursuing the kind of human freedoms and actualizations she sought had been depleted. To Parsons's mind, George Floyd's alleged passing of counterfeit bills likely would have registered as passive (and pacifist) resistance to an illegitimate capitalist socioeconomic system. In response to his sadistic suffocation, Parsons's fire-for-fire approach would have burned loud and strong. Lucy wrote, "I despise murder. But when a ball from the revolver of a policeman kills, it is as much murder as when death results from a bomb."[45] Parsons could not justify the impunity of law enforcement officers—or other agents of the state (even if she did, at times, call on them for aid, according to Jones's biographical account). More concerningly, Jones explains of Lucy that "she and Albert lost faith in the power of words to persuade and educate, turning instead to using words to threaten and intimidate, a fatal decision that sent him and his comrades to their deaths."[46] Whether or not Jones would have recommended a more pragmatic approach for Parsons, the outcome of (even principled) vitriol was clear. This is not, finally, an argument for or against violence, for or against pacifism. However, it is necessary to acknowledge that violence begets violence (whether or not it is justified).

Notwithstanding her fierce radicalism, Lucy Parsons's is not the answer to the complexities of racial hybridity, interracial sexual intimacies, and a normative, categorically defensible intervention with respect to the terrors of the US body politic and its systems. Of Lucy, Jones writes, "Her story is a cautionary tale about the challenges of promoting a radical message that would appeal to laborers divided by craft, ethnicity, religion, political affiliation, gender, and ideologies of race."[47] Jones describes Lucy as "a frankly sexual being who presented herself publicly as a traditional wife and mother" who also abandoned her mother and siblings when she left Texas.[48] According to Jones, the dissonance between Lucy's perspectives on and practices of sexuality did not serve her ultimate agenda with respect to anarchism: "Parsons seemed to believe that certain sorts of suspect behavior, such as sexual promiscuity, along with her birth as a slave, would likely discredit her in the eyes of her supporters, while other kinds of behavior, such as her shocking language in the service of anarchy, would invariably please them. At any rate, she was convinced that neither the circumstances of her birth nor her personal life-choices had any relevance to her broader political message."[49] Parsons failed to aptly connect the personal and the political. Jones explains that when the anarchist message turned toward sexual freedom and "varietism," Lucy had no sympathies for these connections: "Parsons lost little time in distancing herself in print from the idea that 'it is not greater restriction that is needed in sexual relations, but greater freedom,' as one writer in the Firebrand put it.... Parsons wrote that women would never freely choose 'variety' in sex: 'We love the names of father, home and children too well for that.' If 'varietism' had anything to do with anarchism, she said, 'then I am not an Anarchist.'"[50] Jones suggests that among the "ironies and contradictions" of Lucy's life that make hers such a cautionary tale were also the ways she obfuscated her ethnic origins: "Though she was of African descent, she did not consider herself black, and went to considerable lengths to deny the circumstances of her birth and her childhood in slavery. And yet she did not attempt to pass for white, either, and certainly a claim of that sort would have been problematic, given her physical appearance. In effect, she rejected a personal historical or ethnic identity in favor of presenting herself as the champion of the laboring classes; that, she thought, was all that people needed to know about her."[51] It is true that US democratic principles and practices do not achieve liberty, justice, equality, or equity and can often reveal the most insidious forms of hypocrisy. However, Parsons's postracial posture with respect to her own race and with respect to her ideological strategies on behalf of labor were both short-sighted and counterproductive. Lucy Parsons's anarchism could scarcely have parsed and treated the sexualized racism and racialized sexism evident in George Floyd's asphyxiation—or the sufferings of others for whom it was not so simple as to slip into an anticlassist relationship with a recovering Confederate soldier. The verity of anarchistic critiques, principles, and claims cannot escape intersectional accountability. And still, there are no easy answers or resolutions to the illegibility of justice in the context of racial hybridities and interracial sexual intimacies.

    The interracial mixology of the Parsons's politics may overshadow alternative anarchist possibilities. Perhaps Parsons's approach would have resonated more with Fanon than with Rogers insofar as she did not eschew violence as a communal strategy to achieve (a) justice and reached for an unqualified way of being human, a way that was not a slave to identity politics (and other legacies of the transatlantic slave trade and colonialism). And maybe there were—and are—other ways to pursue an anarchist model of justicing. Keri Day's work reminds us of this possibility as she notes the ways William Seymour and early Black and multicultural Pentecostal communities eschewed signs, symbols, and accoutrements of wealth, capital, and elitism;

sympathized with anarchists who were actively resisting the exploitation of labor; and chose countercultural ways of being political.[52] Moreover, Day demonstrates how the unique religious space of Azusa reflect anticapitalism, an egalitarian anarchism, interracial eroticism, and spiritual power all at once. She writes: "The practice of the laying on of hands overturns these cultural representations of black subjects and asserts the humanity of such subjects. White participants at Azusa challenged the erotic life of racism through touching, hugging, kissing, and desiring black congregants as human beings with equal dignity and worth. Moreover, the humanity of black people at Azusa becomes the 'home' out of which white members experience intimacy and belonging. Whites could not experience their humanity in all of its fullness when engaging black people as objects, only as subjects."[53] And all of this also constituted a political way of being. I would argue, this is actually a form of political anarchism. As Day clarifies, it is misguided to read the Azusa community and its descendants as apolitical. To take this a step further, I wonder if the community Day describes might more aptly be described as an oasis of spiritpolitical anarchism that provides necessary nutrients to a functioning democratic ecosystem. Day writes:

> The politics of Azusa is about offering *forms of reexistence* by which to challenge disciplinary power and its bio-political order of race in order for individuals to take up practices of freedom toward self-actualization, dignity, and worth. Not every account of politics needs to be singularly material or structural in scope; there are accounts that address questions of freedom and transcendence, who we understand ourselves to be and how we should move about in the world in efforts to challenge disciplinary modes of normalization. Revolution in relation to our subjectivities is an equally important political issue. Azusa embodied a humbler notion of how we shape political futures: through refashioning oneself and the collective life one is part of, which has profound social and political implications.[54]

With Day's description in mind, Azusa's brand of spiritpolitical anarchism manifests as just the kind of symbiotic partner democracy needs to thrive. The relationship between this spiritpolitical anarchy and vitalizing democracy might be described as a matrimonial entanglement.[55]

However, the legibility of anarchy is not only a matter of discerning and executing just structures of social governance and order but also a matter of individuals' and communities' readiness to engage in violent and nonviolent resistance to achieve justices. It is helpful not only to consider this anarchist way of being political that flies under the radar of what registers as political but also to consider ways of being violent that fly under the radar of what registers as violent. Philip Butler completely shifts the dyadic discourse that casts violence and nonviolence as the prototypical protagonistic and antagonistic forces. Instead, he clarifies where there are violences (and nonviolences) happening everywhere, all the time. And, most important, he names a violence we often ignore: the violence of surviving and thriving in the face of genocidal threats. It is violent to *be* when dominant forces threaten erasure. Inviting us to participate in what he calls a "spirituality of revolt," Butler writes: "So, be you in the most indignant way. Engage in the violence of being yourself. I think the late Neighborhood Nipsey Hustle (Nip tha Great) might have described Revolt Spirituality the best. Revolt Spirituality is being 'disrespectful and arrogant, but who gon' stop us.'"[56] The "Revolt Spirituality" that resists oppressive hegemonic powers, that rejects respectability, that refuses anything other than transhumanity is violent in its flourishing because it compromises the vitality of its adversaries. There is no symbiotic relationship here.

Interracial Sexual Ethics in Discourse: Traditional Sexual Ethics

Contemporary scholars of religion and ethics have taken up the task of articulating constructive sexual ethics for some time. For some—scholars of religious ethics, many of whom happen to be white—the tone of these texts generalizes experiences of sexuality, proffering an approach to human sexuality that is relevant and valid for all people, or all gay people. This can happen in explicit and implicit ways. For some scholars of color who work in the field of religious ethics—who also study the ethics of their own racial ethnic group or other nonwhite racial ethnicities—there is often a different underlying assumption. Like the sexual ethics of religious ethicists who happen to be white, sexual intimacies are presumed to be intraracial. To be more precise, what is described in terms of empirical observations of sexual ethics either assumes intraracial intimacies or does not explicitly take up the specificity of how sexual ethics are impacted when the context of these intimacies are interracial (i.e., self-declared and/or culturally perceived). This is fascinating because scholars writing from the perspective of—on behalf of and about—dominant culture (i.e., many scholars of European descent) and scholars of color (with an emphasis on scholars of African descent) are both writing with an underlying presumption of intraracial intimacies. And such a presumption betrays an underlying belief in racial purity—or at least a weak resignation to it.

In Kelly Brown Douglas's seminal text, *Sexuality and the Black Church: A Womanist Perspective*, most of the first half of the book addresses the impact of white culture on Black sexuality. With little exception, she focuses on the exploitative and violent aspects of interracial intimacies—specifically uncovering the sexual violences of white culture, communities, and individuals that have denigrated Black culture, communities, and individuals. Douglas's text speaks directly to Black people, Black churches, Black "churchpeople."[57] Building on the work of Emilie Townes, whose work "notes that the Black community is 'sexually repressed,' that is, unable to speak honestly about matters of sexuality," Douglas offers that Black community is called into "sexual discourse" as a first act of sexual ethics. She writes that "it is mandatory that the Black community initiate a comprehensive form of sexual discourse if it is to repel and disrupt the power of White culture in relation to Black bodies, sensuality, and spirituality."[58] She explains that such "a sexual discourse of resistance has two central goals: to penetrate the sexual politics of the Black community; and second, to cultivate a life-enhancing approach to Black sexuality within the Black community."[59] Differently put, "it is *deconstructive* in that it helps Black people to understand the many forces, especially White culture, that have shaped Black sexuality. It is also *constructive* in that it seeks to provide more life-enhancing views and attitudes concerning Black sexuality."[60] Through this double-functioning discourse, there are ways that Black-white dualistic logics are challenged. However, in another sense they are reified: dismantling "White" cultural impact and cultivating the "Black."

Though Douglas does not speak of this "sexual discourse of resistance" in terms of a Black sexual ethic per se, the constructive agenda she offers for the discourse lays out particular ethical actions that must be taken up as a part of this discourse. She writes that "a sexual discourse of resistance will":

- "Expose the manifold impact White culture has on Black sexuality."[61]
- "Divulge the numerous and insidious ways in which this culture has caricatured and exploited Black sexuality" (69).
- Clarify "that while the Black community and its institutions have not engaged in a studied and comprehensive sexual discourse, sexual rhetoric has been consistently present" (69).
- Lead "toward Black people gaining agency over their own sexuality" (72).

- Empower "Black women and men to celebrate and to love their Black embodied selves" (75).
- "Help Black people to distinguish who they are from what White culture suggests of them" (75).
- "Help . . . name the pain of White culture's racialized sexual humiliation so that they could move on to a place of healing and regard for their body-selves" (75).
- Strengthen "Black people's ability to penetrate the impact of White culture's exploitive sexual politics upon their personal and interpersonal matters" (83).
- Enable "Black men and women to confront their complicity in fostering notions of Black hypersexuality, especially when it comes to Black men" (81).
- Lead "toward helping Black men and women to understand that homophobia threatens Black well-being instead of protecting it" by exposing "how the sexual politics of White culture, with its varied attacks on Black sexuality, has made it appear that homophobia is compatible with Black life and freedom, even though this is not so" (106). This will "disrupt the terrorizing manner in which Black people have used biblical texts in regard to homosexuality" (107).
- "Help Black people understand how they are using the very tools of power that have been used against them to oppress gay and lesbian persons" (107).
- "Stress that Black well-being is *not* fostered by adopting the oppressive, destructive, life-negating tools of White culture" (107).
- (Possibly, as Douglas uses the word *could*) "nurture the kind of discussion that promotes acceptance and appreciation of the rich diversity—even sexual diversity—within the Black community. It would empower, if not compel, Black men and women to disavow and dismantle any structures, systems, or ways of behaving or thinking that in any way foster homophobia" (107).
- "Call Black people back to their African religious heritage, which rightly views human sexuality as divine." Douglas expands this point further:

    Such a discourse will make it abundantly clear that, on the one hand, an African perspective has fostered an understanding of Christianity that supports the quest for Black life and wholeness, while on the other hand, a Euro-American, "flesh-denying" perspective has fostered Black oppression, especially the denigration and exploitation of Black sexuality. A Black sexual discourse of resistance, while clarifying the meaning of God's revelation in Jesus, will basically highlight the life-sustaining and liberative strands of Black faith grounded in a religious tradition, at once African and Christian, that affirms the goodness of human sexuality in all of its complexity. (121)

- Enable "the Black community . . . to break free from the complexity of sin created by the White cultural attack upon Black sexuality" (124).
- Transform the conduct of "Black church community, especially its leaders" with respect to women and gay and lesbian persons (139).
- Clarify "that there is no longer an excuse for the Black church behaving in such a way that compromises the humanity or mocks the sexuality of any individual" (139).
- "In highlighting the sin of homophobia," stress "that sin is any activity that frustrates Black life" (140).

Douglas explains that if this discourse is effective and "truly disruptive," "it not only transforms the way people think, but also significantly affects the way they act" (139). Such discourse gives Black (and even conscientiously racially hybrid) people recourse in the face of systemic interracial sexual violence and consequent racial hybridity.

Marie M. Fortune's *Love Does No Harm: Sexual Ethics for the Rest of Us*, published four years prior to *Sexuality and the Black Church*, stands in contrast with Douglas's work. Defining ethics as "the process of considering a choice between right and wrong, a choice which then shapes behavior" and morals as "the more commonplace term . . . sometimes contrasted with ethics," Fortune describes her work as a discussion of "the process of ethical discernment: the choosing of actions, the consequences of each choice, and the values which one wants to embody in her/his actions."[62] (She defines "moral agency" as that which describes "the fact that persons have the capacity to make ethical decisions and act on them.")[63] Fortune's premises are that "most people live in relationships of varying degrees of intimacy and most would prefer to do this with integrity"; "both women and men are moral agents and both possess the capacity and responsibility for ethical decision making and action"; "no particular gender or relational configuration is assumed"; "healthy intimate relationships are possible only in the open, and in community."[64] Fortune's thesis is "love does no harm to another. If I am seeking to love another person, I can best begin by trying not to do harm to that person. Love your neighbor as yourself. Self-love is necessary if I am to ever love another person. These mandates represent the foundation for any viable sexual ethic."[65] She makes a point of distinguishing between love and harm—noting that their dissonance is not clear to everyone: "Harm is that which inflicts physical pain, damage or injury and/or diminishes the other person's dignity and self-worth. (Harm is not the distress experienced by an abusive partner when he is arrested and held accountable for assaulting his partner.) Love is a passionate, affectionate desire characterized by genuine concern for the well-being of the other."[66] *Love Does No Harm* blossoms with Fortune's "guidelines" that provide "standards by which you can determine your choices and actions":[67]

1. "Is my choice of intimate partner a peer, that is, someone whose power is relatively equal to mine? We must limit our sexual interaction to our peers" and recognize that those who are vulnerable to us, that is, who have less power than we do, "are off limits for our sexual interests" (75).
2. "Are both my partner and I authentically consenting to our sexual interaction? Both of us must have information, awareness, equal power, and the option to say 'no' without being punished, as well as the option to say 'yes'" (85).
3. "Do I take responsibility for protecting myself and my partner against sexually transmitted diseases and to insure reproductive choice? This is a question of stewardship (the wise care for and management of the gift of sexuality) and anticipating the literal consequences of our actions. Taking this responsibility seriously presupposes a relationship: knowing someone over time and sharing a history in which trust can develop" (102).
4. "Am I committed to sharing sexual pleasure and intimacy in my relationship? My concern should be both for my own needs and those of my partner" (114).
5. "Am I faithful to my promises and commitments? Whatever the nature of a commitment to one's partner and whatever the duration of that commitment, fidelity requires honesty and the keeping of promises. Change in an individual may require a change in the commitment which hopefully can be achieved through open and honest communication" (38–39, 128).

To her credit, Fortune foregrounds the discourse of power. While Douglas works through this in Foucauldian terms, Fortune walks through a critique of power using a series of anecdotes, examples, and sentences of wise insight on how power can corrupt sexually intimate relationships. And while Fortune does name the problem of racism, gender and those who provide care (i.e., counselors, religious leaders, teachers, and medical professionals) are privileged as the primary site of abuses of power with respect to relationships involving sexual intimacies. Fortune observes that "some of us, because of our social positioning or circumstance, will never have adequate power and resources to negate our vulnerability and insure against our being victimized."[68] She goes on to name a fundamental ethical challenge that follows: "How should we relate to vulnerability, both others' and our own?"[69] As she names this dilemma and the ethical challenge that follows, with respect to race and power, Fortune notes that "racial minorities in a majority culture have less access to resources (unless steps have been taken to insure equity) and as such are vulnerable."[70] In this way, Fortune locates the discourse on race in a broader discourse on power.

Race surfaces in other indirect ways in Fortune's text. She quotes Audre Lorde with respect to matters of sadomasochism. She provides an example of the prejudice her African American traveling companion in Hong Kong experienced. And, in her chapter on faithfulness, she argues that "lying is about power. Lying is the way that those who have power try to keep it and that those who don't have power try to get it."[71] She grounds her claims with respect to lying on the strength of the work of bell hooks, whom she quotes at length: "The many southern black women who learned to keep a bit of money stashed away somewhere that 'he don't know about' were responding to the reality of domestic cruelty and violence and the need to have means to escape. However, the negative impact of these strategists was that truth-telling, honest and open communication, was less and less seen as necessary to the building of positive love relationships."[72] She goes on to quote Adrienne Rich: "There is a danger run by all powerless people: that we forget we are lying, or that lying becomes a weapon we carry over into relationships with people who do not have power over us."[73] Still, Fortune anticipates that this may not be enough to have adequately addressed the challenge that people of African descent and other people of color—and especially those from other regions—may level against her book on "sexual ethics for the rest of us." She writes, "There are some who will critique this book as the product of white, North American privilege, suggesting that it is a privilege to even be able to reflect on such 'personal' issues when many people don't have enough food to eat or a place to sleep."[74] Anticipating this challenge, she states that she has "found women and men concerned and struggling with these very questions regardless of their race, class, or nationality."[75] Still, Fortune intuits that there is something more that she may have overlooked with respect to power and identity, even in these last few lines of her book.

Is a nod to the problem of racism enough in a book that is concentrated on sexual ethics in general? In a broad sense, a nod to the problem of racism is never enough while racism continues to impact and ravish every aspect of social life. More specifically, a nod to the problem of racism is not enough when the particularity of race—especially as expressed in the exploitative and abusive sexual intimacies that have characterized the assault of people of European descent against people of African descent—directly and definitively impacts dominant perspectives on and practices of gender and sexuality for most people, globally. Recognizing that one might argue the same with respect to class or other social identifiers, the question becomes: Are "integrity, authentic intimacy, and the eroticization of equality" possible without delving deeper into a discourse on race? To what extent do those who (think they) do not have a race problem need to delve into the work of dismantling racism in order to reach and maintain an "eroticization of equality"?

As Martin Luther King Jr. has written, "Injustice anywhere is a threat to justice everywhere."[76] So too, inequity and inequality anywhere is a threat to equity and equality everywhere. And in a strange twist, injustice, inequity, and inequality anywhere *also* become threats to injustice, inequity, and inequality everywhere because of the passion they spark in bodies, minds, and souls of the disinherited. Partial justices, local equities, and limited equalities are like water splashed to extinguish an oil- or gas-fueled fire: these partial approaches usually just make things worse. How do we ever know which fight (or which part of the fight) for justice, equality, and equity must be prioritized or emphasized in any given moment? How do we discern this? When we look at this in terms of coalition politics, movement building, and other quests for systemic change on a macro scale, this is a formidable and consistent challenge—albeit external in key ways. When we look at this in terms of the individual, a micro scale, this is a different kind of challenge: flaws and/or a lack of integrity in one aspect of a person's life implies flaws and/or the lack of integrity in another aspect of a person's life. Yet, similarly, self-improvement is often a slow, daunting battle. Virtues are often cultivated and habituated little by little, even one by one—slowly. How does one prioritize which internal, personal battle is necessary for now? How does one discern what must be handled first, how, and why? Starting wherever one sees fit is not adequate. Starting wherever one can, too, may not be the best way to solve every crisis. There are more questions than answers.

Puzzling Justice

One of the objects I have used to describe this challenge of layered injustices and vices is a Rubik's Cube. The challenge of the traditional Rubik's Cube is that after its cubes have been moved out of sync—such that there is there is no face of the six-sided cube that contains all one color—the cubes must be put back in order, such that all the squares on each face of the cube are the same color. Unless one has a perfect memory of the order according to which squares were disordered and can backtrack each of these steps, another method is necessary. Having never solved a Rubik's Cube, I have for many years been stuck on the perfection of this object as a metaphor for the impossibility of solving for justice (where injustice is the disordered Rubik's Cube and justice is the Rubik's Cube on which each face is one color only). The reason that this is such a great object metaphor is that we often cannot remember all the steps we took to reach conditions of injustice, inequality, inequity, and other forms of oppression. Too, when we are solving for justice with the Rubik's Cube analogy, whether or not we have made the necessary or right step in order to reach the final objective of rightly ordered monochromatic sides of the cube, on the way to that final objective it always appears (and is, in fact, the case) that some other aspect of the cube is pushed out of order. So often, this is exactly what pursuing justice—especially through polyvalent coalition work—looks and feels like. A gain in one direction always shows up as a loss in another direction—even if the loss is temporary, not real, or en route to a later or ultimate gain and order. The challenge is not a rational defense for refusing to solve the cube. (Although an argument could be made that solving the cube should never result in monochromatic sides but rather equally, definitively, or chaotically polychromatic sides.)

Notwithstanding the challenge of monochromatic sides, the Rubik's Cube can be solved. And if the disordered cube is a proper metaphor for injustice, inequality, inequity, and other forms of oppression, then it must and should be solved. As I was working through this metaphor—not content with being stuck in and with the unresolved Rubik's Cube—it occurred to me that even though I have not been able to solve one on my own, others have! In fact, there are even others who have solved Rubik's Cubes, explained, taught, and demonstrated their solutions online—posting them on YouTube and/or other multimedia platforms. As helpfully descriptive as the disordered cube is for conditions of injustice, these explanations, teachings, and demonstrations are for how to solve for justice in the face of injustice. One teacher explains a path whereby a core square on the cube—perhaps the one carrying the cube's logo and one of its base colors—is the center in a face and is made the top; next, the colored squares that match the color of that center square are brought from their location at the bottom of the cube and arranged as a cross out from the centering square; once this has been done the corners can be addressed, and so on. However, we can simply consider the significance of these few steps alone in terms of how to solve for justice in a disarrayed Rubik's Cube of injustice: the core (e.g., Black lives) is centered—at the top; (other) Black folks who are at the bottom are brought to the top with the (core) Black lives that have been centered at the top; these others are organized on cross-intersecting lines with the core.[77] Critically important to this model, however, is that though everything can be altered and brought into order eventually and altogether, only one piece can be moved at a time, and more disorder may precede order. In many ways, the question is: Can we be fast enough to solve the cube at a record pace, while being wise enough not to make errors or unnecessary steps along the way, while being patient enough with the process that is about the function of the cube, that maintains an internal tethering of each of the pieces to one another?[78]

All of these questions might extend even further to another question: What ethical responsibilities do those who are vulnerable have? What ethical responsibilities do those who are vulnerable in some ways, but powerful in other ways, have? When one has endured hardship, trauma, and/or abuse, how does one cope with it, process it, deal with it, and heal from it—and do so without harming others, without replicating the damage that one has experienced in one's own life and context? These questions are of a different nature. In this case, the issue is not the disorder of injustice where unaligned elements must be realigned for the sake of equality and equity—and an absence of oppression. In one sense, inasmuch as one who has been made vulnerable has made another vulnerable, the primary vulnerable-oppressive moral agent is like one of the final squares to be reconciled in a monochromatic side of the cube. These can be the most difficult, the most disruptive, and the easiest to deny (their) justice. In another sense, even when these have been reconciled to the ordered space of the monochromatic side, it is as though their color has been tarnished, compromised, victim to the wear and tear of the process of being brought back into alignment. These are redeemable and redeemed, but never quite the same—in an undeniable perceivable way. In a sense, this is where hooks, Hine, Rich, and Fortune pause, noting the complexity of those who are without power attempting to claim it through dishonesty or dissemblance; this is where they pause to observe the difficulty of containing a survival strategy, vice, or injustice like dishonesty in one aspect of one's life or in one type of relationship. More tragically, this is the plight of those who have been abused emulating—at its worst replicating most precisely—that abuse with respect to someone else they have consciously or unconsciously identified as weaker than they are.

Who is to say that solving the puzzle looks like homogeneity on each side of the cube? The colors on the cube faces are, perhaps, deceptive because the true site of the puzzle is within the cube, where one knows the ties that bind the cube together—ties that are tangled together in degrees of tension (and degrees of connection and separation that feel more or less appropriately attracted and repelled). Within the cube is also a hidden space. The manufacturer knows the quality and content of the sinews that hold the cube of cubes together, but we do not. What if we troubled not only the colored faces of the entire cube or individual cubes—and what constituted a solved Rubik's Cube—but also what was holding the cube together?

Consider electromagnetism as an alternative physical force that could maintain some external order of the Rubik's Cube from an uncharted interior. What if, like the earth, the cube was filled with a magnetically charged metal like iron? What if the cube had within it elements that attract and elements that repel—informing a more tangible sense of what makes a solved or unsolved cube? Magnetism can be defined as "an effect produced by the motion of electric charge, resulting in attractive and repulsive force between objects."[79] If the solving of the Rubik's Cube and its complexity can help us understand the difficulty of working through interracial sexual intimacies and racial hybridities, can help us understand the puzzling of justice as it pertains to these intersections, the interior of the Rubik's Cube is of great interest. If this interior is more like electric charge than material sinews at certain points and in certain ways, then what is the electric current that produces the constellation of attractions and repulsions invoked, evoked, and provoked with respect to racial hybridities and interracial sexual intimacies? What is charging the challenge and tensions of the puzzle? And what kinds of countercharges are possible? How might we shift the charges and reorder the face/s of the Rubik's Cube? Through electromagnetism, we can reimagine the solving of puzzling Rubik's Cubes—charging and recharging the elements of monochromatic and polychromatic options, testing the terms of hybridity and interracial sexual intimacies against the tangles of violence, mixing metaphors of material and energetic connection to comb through terrorizing (con)texts.

Puzzling Power or Desire

Physicist Chanda Prescod-Weinstein, self-identified as a "Black (Caribbean American) Jewish queer woman," writes of her own experience of rape.[80] Prescod-Weinstein writes, "Rape is now part of my story of being a professor of physics."[81] Over ten times in her chapter "Rape Is Part of This Scientific Story," Prescod-Weinstein explicitly specifies how rape is and has become a part of her scientific story. Prescod-Weinstein explains how she was raped—and survives. However, Prescod-Weinstein also acknowledges other ways rape enters her story—and her "scientific story." She writes:

> We know that the majority of Black Americans have some European heritage, mostly due to rape, and certainly this must generally be true across the two American continents. I am what is called light-skinned. People often assume that this lightness is simply because my father is a white man, and indeed, he is a white Ashkenazi Jew. I am light-skinned because of who my dad is, yes, but I am also light-skinned because of who my foremothers' rapists were. My mother is not nearly as light as me, but she is also on the lighter end of the spectrum. Our melanin—and our lack thereof—tells stories about what my ancestors endured.[82]

The story of rape is written on the bodies of people of African descent in the United States even before we experience the physical violences of rape culture as a real-time, material(izing) aspect of contemporary life and living. And the material(izing) of rape culture is not just what we experience in times of personal, physical violation. Prescod-Weinstein notes that science itself participates in rape culture—as do transnational political frameworks:

> There in my email inbox is a thank you for a donation to a Jewish organization that is being attacked for recognizing the humanity of Palestinian people. Underneath all of this lurks rape, I think. The rape that Palestinian women have surely had to deal with. The rape that Jewish

women in the Israel Defense Forces have also had to deal with while they were violently policing the boundaries of the Palestinian women's lives. The rape Black women in academia have to deal with. I am a Black woman in academia. The rape I have to deal with. Forever. Rape is part of my scientific story because I am forever going to be a woman in science who was raped, and we can't and shouldn't stop talking about all of the rape that is everywhere because the rape keeps happening because there are people who . . . well I don't know why the rape keeps happening. Except that, as I said before, anti-rape activists tell me it's about power.[83]

Rape happens. And rape is happening. And while this chapter addresses rape in the context of interracial relationships, rape is clearly not limited to that space. Yet rape shares a logical thread with racism. Rape and race might be two cube colors of the Rubik's Cube.

Prescod-Weinstein connects the puzzl(e)ing pieces of what it means for rape to have become an inextricable aspect of the work that she does as a scientist, how she thinks of rape with respect to the discipline of science and everyday politics, and how she reconciles her own interracial identities. Turning these pieces of rape culture in relation to one another, she offers fresh perspective on the perennial debate about the relationship between power and desire in rape. On one hand, she writes:

> In thinking about this, I've realized that the act of finding someone sexy or not sexy isn't really just about feelings, is it? It's also a power move. A power move where you tell someone whether they are sexually valid or not. Anti-rape activists say that rape is about power, and I guess I've always felt some conflict about this because it seemed very real to me in that moment that the pressure to take back my "no" was about his pleasure, not exerting power over me. But is it because of the power? Did he pressure me to take my "no" back so that he could feel powerful? Are men really so fragile that they can't control themselves? It's in the context of these thoughts that I do science.[84]

On the other hand, Prescod-Weinstein explains:

> How is rape part of my scientific story, or how is science not like rape when both are about power? Both are indeed about power, but this is not manifest to us, which is part of how the power dynamic works. We are told that rape is about desire when really it is about ownership; we are told science is driven by curiosity when really . . . I still can't bring myself to say

it is about control because I'm not sure it always is or has to be. But that's what it has been when we integrate all of the scientific activity in the last five hundred years of the Western world. That's what it is.[85]

As she parses the relationship of power and desire as they relate to rape, however, Prescod-Weinstein is also imagining what justice looks like, what justice means in the wake of rape. How does a person live—and choose to keep living? How does a person survive? How does a person heal? And then somehow, what kind of restitution is desirable—or possible? Prescod-Weinstein turns to physics for a first answer.

> In physics, power has a very specific meaning: it is the rate of changing energy, of doing work. Work has a very specific meaning too: work is when a force causes something to move along the direction of the force. Like say, when a man forces you to be close to him, he is doing work. The object being moved does not do any work. Power is the amount of work that the man does over the time that he is forcing you to be close to him. The object being moved does not have any power associated with it.
>
> I want to have the power to eject this memory: to force it far, far away from me. By that I mean I would like to have the power to eject this memory into the nuclear inferno that is our sun. The sun is, effectively, a series of nuclear explosions, mostly converting hydrogen into helium. Better this memory blow up inside the sun than inside of me. But this memory is written on my body so instead I have to trace the lines of force that are available to me. I look to see what work is possible. For years, I had nightlong knife fights where I was the only person present.[86]

The nefarious work of the rape can be fought back with other positively transforming work. However, this yields many sobering questions. What work should one have to do to prevent rape? What work should one (have to) do to retaliate against rape and/or a rapist? What work should one have to do to heal after being raped? What does it mean to think about the experience of rape not only in terms of being overpowered but also worked on? What compensation is there for the (forced) work that must be done to be restored when we have been overpowered and worked on in such ways? This is but another form of servitude!

Prescod-Weinstein considers a second answer: "Lacy M. Johnson wrote in The Reckonings, 'I want him to spend the rest of his life in service to other people's joy.'" She writes:

I want that too, but I don't have any hope for it. I know he will seek the spotlight and power as he pleases, never holding himself back, never thinking about his responsibility to transform the conditions in which I work. I know the only force I can possibly enact on him is to allow myself to become a nuclear inferno, engulfing him, yes, but also converting myself into something else: no longer a scientist, just that woman who a lot of people think lied about that guy because she hates men and wants attention and well, her science wasn't going well so she decided to do this. Helium is lighter than air; to be a rape victim who publicly accuses her perpetrator is to become unmanageably heavy.[87]

Through "work," the "memory" of the rape could be explosively "converted" into an element "lighter than air," but that might leave Prescod-Weinstein—and others who try this option for justice—"unmanageably heavy." The choice becomes remembering and actively, eternally transforming the memory or allowing the memory to continue the work of rape. The work of justice is not (finally, practically) about what happens to the person who raped her, for Weinstein. The pragmatic work of justice is Prescod-Weinstein living and positively transforming.

We should not dismiss the higher hope for justice that requires different work of those who perpetrate rape. In fact, may all perpetrators of rape be made aware of the harm they have caused, stopped from causing any further harm, and bound to live out the balance of their lives dismantling systems and circumstances of rape and rape culture—and "in service to other people's joy." And still Prescod-Weinstein reminds us that part of what justice is and requires is being light enough to live. We might even describe this as being "light as a feather." As has been said about forgiveness: it is more for the one who forgives than for the one who is forgiven. Justice must first serve the holistic needs of the one who is suffering or has suffered the violences of injustice. To be so light—as a feather—is a matter of physics and justice, a quareing approach to Black sexual ethics.

A Maâtian Puzzle

How does Maât help us solve—or at least handle—the puzzle of interracial sexual intimacies and racially hybrid identities? More specifically, how does Maât live in hybrid realities in ways that do not skirt, erase, or ignore the ongoing explicit and implicit, very real and imagined problems of interracial sexual violence? Is there any aspect of how Maât moves in her worlds that could assist in solving challenges as complex as Rubik's Cube—where choices are still being made about what *solved* looks like for such a puzzle? Is there any aspect of how Maât moves in her worlds that could assist in solving challenges as complex as willful blindness to the interracial intimate (sexual?) violence of George Floyd's murder—and willful blindness to the fact of this incident as injustice, willful blindness to the fact of this incident as murder, willful blindness to the ways that this scenario is consistent with a sexually sadistic imaginary? Does Maât tilt toward Rogers or Fanon? Does Maât, instead, create and maintain balance between the two? When Maât is described in story, in place, in space, in time, how is she described? Interestingly, most texts do not focus on Maât in flight, but Maât in community. Specifically, vindicationists like Maulana Karenga focus on Maât in a community of accountability, a community of judgment. Most interesting for this chapter on ancient mixologies is the fact that Maât is part of a *netcherw* of beings that are themselves fundamentally and essentially hybrid. They are assumed to be primarily human—or gods drawn with at least partially or foundationally human form, but they are winged; they have jackal heads; they are cats; they are serpents; they are crocodiles; they are cows; they are falcon-headed; they are blue, black, green, or a color common to the human community of the time. Maât herself is a hybrid being and exists in a community of hybridity. How this hybridity came about we do not know—whether it was forged in love or in hatred, in peace or in war. It does, however, seem that there is a communal agreement to the way Maât adjudicates. Notwithstanding the diversity of the *netcherw*, the cube turns and is solved on the feather of Maât.

Perhaps the most memorable scenes in which we encounter Maât are upon judgment at the end of life. Here she holds court with a sacred and divine consort. She is in mixed company; her work weighing human hearts mixes company all the more. Depicting a version of this scene, Maulana Karenga writes, "The setting for the Declarations of Innocence is the post-mortem judgment scene found in Chapter 125 of the *Book of Coming Forth By Day* whose central themes are judgment, justification, and immortality."[88] He goes on to describe a scene with multiple actors in the Hall of Judgment (also known as the Great Hall of Maati or the Two Truths). The deceased (1) enters this hall; the deceased (2) asks their heart not to betray them; and the risen one declares themselves innocent of all offenses and asserts having done good. In this declaration, "the deceased makes thirty-six Declarations of Innocence of offense against God, humans and nature and then forty-two more before forty-two divine powers (*ntrw*) who sit in judgement of him."[89] Third, the heart of the deceased is weighed. Karenga writes, "The central focus of this scene is 'that balance of Ra in which he weighs Maat.' ... The Balance or Scales of Maat (Truth, Justice) is handled by Anpu (Anubis), the divine power who presides over the deceased. He is called ... Master of the Balance. Standing behind him is Djehuti (Thoth), the Scribe of Heaven and Lord of Just Measure, with pen and palette in hand, who records and announces the results."[90] Karenga goes on to describe the others who are in the Hall of Judgment:

> Behind Djehuti, in this scene of the proceedings, is a hybrid monster called *'m mwt* (Ammut), the devourer of the dead, who devours the deceased if s/he is found unworthy of eternal life. Also in the Hall of Maati are the divine powers of destiny (Shai), birth (Renenet) and nursing/rearing (Meskhenet), authoritative utterance (Hu) and exceptional insight (Sia). And at the end of the Hall is seated on his throne Osiris, whose resurrection from the dead, symbolized and promised eternal life through righteousness for human beings. ... Behind him stands Isis, his wife, and Nephthys, his sister. And finally along one side of the Hall are seated Ra and other members of the Heliopolitan Ennead (The Great Nine Divine Powers).[91]

If one is not judged justified or vindicated, "maa kheru," Ammut "dispatches" that one "into non-existence." This Judgment Hall host reminds me of the hybrid diversity of the United States—with the most quintessential American being Ammut. This devourer, monstrous hybrid, seeks to consume the "delectable" soul that has not been able to declare innocence with accuracy—nor prove any assertion of care for the most vulnerable. I imagine that Ammut is what Ammut eats. And Ammut eats the unjust into nonexistence. Ammut, perhaps, has the odd electromagnetism of a black hole. Neither hybridity nor its production, per se, seems to be what the scale (and Maât's feather) measure.

Nevertheless, within the thirty-six and forty-two declarations respectively, consider Karenga's translations of those having to do with sex most directly: "20. I have not had illicit sex. 21. I have not been licentious." And "19. I have not committed adultery. 20. I have not committed fornication. ... 27. I have not practiced illicit sex. ... 39. I have not been immodest."[92] Who in the milieu of contemporary "America" could stand at such judgment? This question haunts, in part, because of the truth of thoroughgoing and comprehensive sexualized racial violences and racialized sexual violences manifested in hybrid racial identities and interracial sexual intimacies. This question haunts because, at this point, there is no purity. That truth cannot easily be located in any particular skin. The puzzle is perplexing. The interior and exterior of the cube are uncertain. Ammut, the hybrid monster, is fully charged and ready to attract and consume whatsoever leans and slips into an ancient mixology hegemonically seasoned race-sex mess. Ammut does not, however, hunt the hybrid; Maât's feather is unmoved by such weight. Ammut does hunger for those hearts heavy with the unmitigated cries of the most vulnerable and sexual liaisons without purpose, consideration, and benefit to community; Maât's feather is much lighter than such weight.

~ * ~

A Black Sexual Ethic

We are already hybrid—some by force, some by choice, some by both; Black sexual ethics must begin right where we are with each new day.

A Maâtian Code of Justice

Maât's feather has flown through the erons and errors of so great a cloud of witnesses; its moral weight is preconditioned for the puzzling, embodied contexts of our souls. A Maâtian justice includes a dynamic (re)conditioning for equity.

7
Black Web
Disrupting Transnational Pornographies
for Post(trans)national Humanalities

As for those of us who are African, our salvation (redemption) lies in our ancientness and connectedness; not in a romanticized glorification of the past, but in a return to the center in which all contradictions are resolved and from which the spiral of development can continue with clarity. From the center, ikons can be retrieved in our image that will allow us to tap the energy of the collective conscious will of our people.
—Marimba Ani, *Yurugu*

As a person who lives off the land, in a society that's decomposing every day, and different things are becoming legal. So, I'm really in a place where I'm analyzing how . . . roles are shifting and [there is an] emergence of different feelings and ideas. As things currently stand, the physical assessment of being a man, "biological man" . . . with functioning limbs . . . : I'm built for a certain type of sexual interaction. And in a cishetero dynamic, I am supposed to utilize those things to the service of one person, one woman. . . . What I realize is for a lot of modern day women—you have women out there who post videos that say, "I haven't even been touched in like ten years. . . ." A lot of what I do is . . . I am a mechanism that brings them from the past into the future. In those regards, I consider myself a bit of a

tool of liberation. . . . Well, I had to analyze myself about why. Why was I so open to being with so many types of people and having physical interactions with folk? . . . I gotta go back to the colonial experiences we've had in this country. A part of it is that I was designed for that purpose. So now there's a problem with me taking back the power from that design.
—Black male cisgender queer OnlyFans creator based in the United States

What is an ideal trajectory for a quare-womanist-vindicationist approach to theories of justice and Black sexual ethics? One can imagine the first strand of the web a spider is to weave: it moves from point A to point B in a line that conceals the complexity of what is to follow. One might wonder how a book on Black sexual ethics can begin with transexuality and end with pornographies. Woven with this strand are other strands: the strand from flying justice to being justice, the strand from Cheikh Anta Diop to Maulana Karenga, the strand from (extra)terrestrial revolutionary democratic order to a post(trans)-national possibility for just social organization, and the strand from black holes to tantalizing tensions. If nothing else, this final chapter, along with the others that precede it, reveals how complex Black sexual experiences—and Black sexual ethics—are. This quare-womanist-vindicationist discourse exposes the ways that theories of justice shift and shimmy under the weight of historic and contemporary sovereign experiences of Afrodiasporic people. In many ways, this concluding chapter returns to the question of where (in the world) *Black, Quare, and Then to Where* leaves us. However, if nothing else, this book exposes theories of justice and Black sexual ethics as rhizomatic discursive spaces, as independent and layered subjects. Consequently, it is with a critique of the ways we talk about world order and organization that I begin this final chapter that leads through the coded and coding spaces of the worldwide web.

Transnationalism has been offered up as a foil to globalization/globalism for at least a generation.[1] "Transnational connectivities" were imagined as corrections to globalization discourses. Reconciling the earlier definitions of Anthony Giddens and Roland Robertson, Malcolm Waters defines "globalization" as "a social process in which the constraints of geography on economic, political, social and cultural arrangements recede, in which people become increasingly aware that they are receding and in which people act accordingly."[2] Inderpal Grewal argues that "in contradiction to *Empire*, . . . the 'global' is not and never was quite global, but . . . there certainly was a will to globalization that was both profoundly cosmopolitan as well as imperialist, since 'global' capitalism did not constitute the totality of economic or social relations that were existent or possible."[3] She suggests that "rather than the term globalization, it is more useful to think about the heterogeneous and multiple transnational connectivities that produced various meanings of the term 'global.' Conceiving of globalization as an object of knowledge involved discursive practices emanating from and producing a cosmopolitan will to power in which so many different kinds of subjects participated. Thus rather than use this term, I hope to trace the trajectories and histories of knowledges that produced discourses of the 'global' as that which was believed to be pervasive, all-encompassing."[4] "Transnational connectivities," Grewal argues, "within which subjects, technologies, and ethical practices were created through transnational networks and connections of many different types" were also spaces through which the "'global' and the 'universal' were created as linked and dominant concepts."[5] In this way, transnationalism (and transnational connectivities) destabilize the appropriative ideas and agendas of both globalization and empire. Transnational discursive approaches focus on a critical analysis of the ideas and agendas of inter/cross-national movement; transnational discourse explores the experiences of individuals, communities, subjects, technologies, ethical practices, and, I would add, material artifacts and fetishes. Transnationalism keeps us focused on the ways that nation-states, empire/s, the imperial, and globalization are not democratic, do not empower everyday people, and are dangerous to those who are oppressed.[6]

However, transnational discourse has neither definitively disrupted nor decisively dismantled the "corporations are people" and "nation-states are eternal" logic that has characterized neoliberal capitalism's colonization of the earth. Rather, transnationalism has offered a persistent critical account of globalization and the nation-states and corporations complicit in its most deleterious impacts. The casualties of globalization are legion; those whom theorists seek to expose and defend via transnational connectivities are also legion. Climate change, infertility, pandemics, and perennial jockeying for political and economic power are detriments to the entire *dunia* (i.e., terrasphere).[7] These individual and cumulative challenges inform and fuel the misdirections of prejudice, hatred, bigotry, and xenophobia. The question remains: Can the *dunia* and the majority of its inhabitants who are not among the wealthy elite be spared? And, somehow, at the heart of this terrifying discourse that spells the end of human civilization as we know it, sex remains. People are still showing up as sexual beings. Of course, not all sex is created equal. Moreover, there are ways that sex exacerbates *dunia* crises, and there are ways that sex mitigates *dunia* crises. Through this chapter, I attempt to lay bare some of these exacerbations and mitigations—specifically among people of African descent and our life experiences pertaining to sex and sexuality. As in previous chapters, I demonstrate the ways that Black sexuality implicates and is implicated in sociopolitical organization and theories of justice. But whereas "Heterexpectations" addresses Black sexuality as an entangling aspect of marriage as social pillar of modern nation-states, "Black Web" is concerned with Black sexuality being (i.e., ontologizing, making being out of) justice as it creatively defies containment and denies fetishization, while demanding maintenance. A constructive, normative utopic Black sexuality ontologizing justice not only tra(ns)verses nation-states but also challenges nation-states (and their nationalism) with an alternative, integrated way to embody human sexuality (i.e., postnational humanalities). Offering a critical comparative analysis of the United States and Russia as two distinct models of nation-state globalization with respect to sexuality and race, this chapter simultaneously rejects nationalisms (and their nation-states) and defends democracy.[8] This chapter argues for an ethical path of retaining Black sexual creative freedoms (e.g., gender fluidity, power of the erotic, performativity, intimacies, communalities, and freakiness) without reifying the violences of pornography (and the abuses of sex trafficking, rape, sexual abuse, sexual misconduct, pedophilia, incest, sexual harassment, misogyny, and misogynoir that grow from a common root). How can such creative sexual freedoms be retained? This can be done by holding fast to democracy. This can be done by making sense of the simultaneity of our artificialities and our common terrestrial ecology in ways that are unequivocally committed to the fact and potential of our connection. This can be done by demanding creative, agentive, life-giving, harm-avoiding space-time.

Black Pornotopias?

How is pornography a part of the lives of Black people? What ethical challenges and possibilities attend to pornography in the lives of US-based Afrodiasporic people? Also, how do we acknowledge the multidimensional ethical challenge of Afrodiasporic people who create pornography, Afrodiasporic people who watch (i.e., consume pornography), and Afrodiasporic people who create and consume pornography?[9] How do the ethical expectations for those who create pornography relate to the ethical expectations for those who watch pornography and those who do both? Sadly, these are questions that are rarely asked within religious institutional spaces or in mainstream religious studies scholarship. However, they are critically important, considering the prevalence of pornography in popular culture, in the everyday experiences of people of color, and in transnational politics and economies.

Studies on the prevalence of pornography use among Afrodiasporic people in the United States vary. However, one study, "Race and Trends in Pornography Viewership, 1973–2016: Examining the Moderating Roles of Gender and Religion," tracing pornography viewership utilizing race and religious praxis as comparative variables found that "White Americans have increased in their likelihood of viewing pornography from roughly 22% to just over 30% between 1973 and 2016, an increase of about 8%. Black Americans, by contrast, have increased in their likelihood of viewing pornography by roughly 18% during that time frame, from 28% in 1973 to about 46% in 2016."[10] According to this study, "for White Americans monthly [worship] attendance was negatively associated with viewing pornography across time, but not for Black Americans" and "that Black women showed an increasing rate of pornography viewership over time compared to White women, but religious service attendance did not moderate this relationship significantly."[11] This data is significant in that it demonstrates both that pornography viewership is a relevant issue for Afrodiasporic people in the United States, but that it is not necessarily a moral issue (i.e., it is not an issue of much intraracial moral discourse, contention, debate, or policing; pornography is not deemed categorically abject among the Black study participants)—at least to the extent that religiosity and/or worship are adequate markers of central space for Afrodiasporic moral contemplation and discernment. The authors of this study, Samuel L. Perry and Cyrus Schleifer, suggest that pornography has not been "a key moral issue worth opposing (Wood & Hughes, 1984)" within Black communities out of deference to "more immediate, structural issues (Pattillo-McCoy,1998; Shelton & Emerson, 2012)."[12] Regardless of why Perry and Schleifer conclude that pornography has not been a matter of much moral interest within the Black community, it is still worth considering the moral codes that pertain to pornography viewership and creation among Afrodiasporic people in the United States.

In many ways, the Perry and Schleifer study provokes more questions than it provides answers with respect to pornography in the lives of Afrodiasporic people in the United States. Monique Moultrie's work exposes deep pornophobia among Black churchwomen. In an effort to "revalue the erotic" and reconnect Black church women with a sense of the erotic drawn from Audre

Lorde, where the erotic is understood "as power, a creative energy, a type of sensuality, and a form of wisdom, including being responsible to ourselves," something that "does not have to be tied to sexual or genital expression; it is about feelings," Moultrie writes, "Many black churchwomen associate the erotic with pornography or something that to them is sexually illicit, which makes redefining the erotic necessary."[13] And among those who promulgate pornophobia are iconic Black churchwomen such as Juanita Bynum, Cynthia Hale, and Ty Adams, who link masturbation and pornography—and discourage both. Moultrie delineates the suggestions Heather Lindsey offers single women in a 2013 blog post, "Secret Sins: Masturbation and Pornography," advising "(1) that they guard their hearts by avoiding blog sites that talk about sex or show celebrities naked, (2) that they stop hanging out with people who talk about sex, (3) that they avoid music that discusses sex, and (4) that they spend more daily time with God."[14] An interesting irony of this pornophobia is that it is not, fundamentally, a rejection of Black women's (sexual) commodification. It is a conscious abstinence from (sometimes known) sexual pleasures for the sake of a godly holiness that is often presented as reaching its pinnacle in heterosexual marriage (in general) and as the singular site of sexual expression. The beliefs section of Pinky Promise, an online networking platform Lindsey founded, explains:

- We are committed to Jesus Christ, and we believe He died for our sins, rose again and reconciled us back to God.
- We believe in the power of the Holy Spirit that is given to us when we give our lives to Jesus Christ.
- We refuse to give our bodies to anyone who hasn't paid the price for us, which is marriage.
- We set the standard to keep our hearts pure before God, and not test the sexual boundaries in our relationships.
- We guard our heart by monitoring what we see and hear.
- We believe in the covenant of marriage with one man and one woman.
- We seek godly friendships and surround ourselves with believers and women after God's own heart.
- We believe in building our local community by doing community service and praying for our city.[15]

Most notably, these beliefs admit a religious commodification of women whereby marriage is the price a man pays for a woman's body. In a sense, this casts all (Black) women (subscribers and those subject to this teaching) as sex workers—whose (high?) cost is marriage.[16] The irony here is that a popular primary objection to pornography is the ways that it commodifies women. In the religious and sociopolitical economy that Moultrie describes, commodification is not the primary objection; the ways that enjoyment of pornography devalues Black churchwomen and believers in their relationship with God and for their relationships with their respective husbands is the primary objection.

While Perry, Schleifer, and Moultrie demonstrate that much more thoroughgoing investigations of Black folx's relationship with pornography are in order, their studies are still instructive in various ways. And in addition to considering the relationship between religious views and pornography viewership among Afrodiasporic people, it is also helpful to consider the ways that youth are developing sexual mores and the relevance of pornography in the lives of Afrodiasporic youth in the United States. In a relatively small study conducted in Boston (2015) using a sample size of twenty-three male and female Black and Hispanic youth, the authors concluded that, of those they interviewed, "almost every participant (n = 21) reported learning how to have sex by watching pornography. Specifically, they reported that from pornography they had learned sexual positions, what opposite-sex partners might enjoy sexually, and to learn how to engage in particular sex acts (e.g., oral sex, anal sex). Both males and females reported learning about sex from pornography (i.e., seven males and 14 females), although females offered more concrete examples of things that they learned."[17] While the authors acknowledge that this is a relatively small sample, they make a strong case for why this study is still instructive for those considering the sexual formation of youth—and, specifically, low-income Black and Hispanic youth.

So, what is pornography—and why is it the most appropriate category through which we might dissect interracial sexual intimacies in their explicitly violent manifestations? In 1983, feminist scholars Andrea Dworkin and Catherine MacKinnon wrote a "Model Antipornography Civil-Rights Ordinance" that the Minneapolis City Council adopted twice but was vetoed and never enforced. While it was not adopted, the ordinance provided a legal definition of pornography that is the standard for this chapter. They write:

1. "Pornography" means the graphic sexually explicit subordination of women through pictures and/or words that also includes one or more of the following:

a. women are presented dehumanized as sexual objects, things or commodities; or
b. women are presented as sexual objects who enjoy humiliation or pain; or
c. women are presented as sexual objects experiencing sexual pleasure in rape, incest, or other sexual assault; or
d. women are presented as sexual objects tied up or cut up or mutilated or bruised or physically hurt; or
e. women are presented in postures or positions of sexual submission, servility, or display; or
f. women's body parts—including but not limited to vaginas, breasts, or buttocks—are exhibited such that women are reduced to those parts; or
g. women are presented being penetrated by objects or animals; or
h. women are presented in scenarios of degradation, humiliation, injury, torture, shown as filthy or inferior, bleeding, bruised or hurt in a context that makes these conditions sexual.
2. The use of men, children, or transsexuals in the place of women in (a)-(h) of this definition is also pornography for purposes of this law.[18]

While this thorough definition provides a broad foundation for this chapter's discussion of pornography, it is curious that race is not invoked in this definition at all. Still, race is under the surface in the definition Dworkin and McKinnon provide.

Audre Lorde and Alice Walker perceive the importance of race in discourses of pornography—and pornography in discourses of race—right away. In her essay "Uses of the Erotic," Lorde writes, "The erotic has often been misnamed by men and used against women. It has been made into the confused, the trivial, the psychotic, the plasticized sensation. For this reason, we have often turned away from the exploration and consideration of the erotic as a source of power and information, confusing it with its opposite, the pornographic. But pornography is a direct denial of the power of the erotic, for it represents the suppression of true feeling. Pornography emphasizes sensation without feeling."[19] Lorde further explains, "There are frequent attempts to equate pornography and eroticism, two diametrically opposed uses of the sexual. Because of these attempts, it has become fashionable to separate the spiritual (psychic and emotional) from the political, to see them as contradictory or antithetical."[20] And this separation that Lorde describes has specific racial correlates: "In order to be utilized, our erotic feelings must be recognized. The need for sharing deep feeling is a human need. But within the european-american tradition, this need is satisfied by certain proscribed erotic comings-together. These occasions are almost always characterized by a simultaneous looking away, a pretense of calling them something else, whether a religion, a fit, mob violence, or even playing doctor. And this misnaming of the need and the deed give rise to that distortion which results in pornography and obscenity—the abuse of feeling."[21] This "abuse of feeling" that fuels "european-american tradition" with "proscribed erotic comings-together" and "looking away" has, however, been reconsidered in contemporary discourse.

There is an experience of systematic sexual surveillance that characterizes the lives of Afrodiasporic people.[22] This systematic sexual surveillance is a specific extension of a generalized systemic surveillance. Among the surveilled, there is often a knowing, an awareness: we are being watched. This knowing often comes so early that it is intuited, though parents and guardians pass this awareness on to Afrodiasporic children with ambivalence, longing to protect innocences and freedoms of childhood that many of those parents and guardians barely knew themselves. To varying degrees, most of us Afrodiasporic people are also conscripted to surveil one another, criminalizing and sexualizing one another in our intraracial gazes. Then among whites and others who surveil, the training to see through sexualizing and criminalizing lenses is traditioned, learned so early in stages of childhood development that such surveillance could be ascribed to an inherited nature. Systematic sexual surveillance is about white people's awareness of Black people as sexual and sexualized subjects. Systematic sexual surveillance is also about white people's implicit and explicit impacts on Black people as sexual and sexualized subjects.

Most insidiously, systematic sexual surveillance is about how white supremacy impacts and chooses to be impacted by Black sexuality even in presumably intraracial, quasi-racially pure contexts, even between Afrodiasporic people. In her essay "Coming Apart," Alice Walker offers a precise example of this as she hones in on one of the earliest definitions of womanism she presents; the definition emerges as she narrates the experiences of a Black heterosexual married couple, explaining the impact of the husband's introduction of different types of pornographic material in their shared domestic space. The wife in the couple, Walker's protagonist, experiences the husband's engagement with and consumption of pornography as fundamentally racist, regardless of the race of those objectified in the pornographic content.

However, not all who are opposed to oppression are also opposed to pornography. There are those who have given their lives to the fight against racism, classism, sexism, and heterosexism, among other aspects of a common fight for justice, who do not eschew pornography. In her book *The Color of Kink: Black Women, BDSM, and Pornography*, Ariane Cruz acknowledges that her perspective—along with those of Mireille Miller-Young and Jennifer Nash—contrasts with traditional antipornography Black feminists. Cruz writes that "pornography and black feminism maintain a crucial, if volatile, relationship with one another. Rather than viewing this relationship as inherently incompatible, we need to understand porn and black feminism as pushing, not policing, each other in productive directions that elucidate black female sexuality as 'simultaneously a domain of restriction, repression and danger as well as a domain of exploration, pleasure and agency.'"[23] Offering the "politics of perversion" as a rejoinder to the "false ethics" of "politics of respectability" and "politics of visibility" and, instead, an application of "deviance as resistance," Cruz encourages a "depathologization of both BDSM and black female sexuality"—and pornography, by extension.[24] Cruz explains that "perversion maintains an intimate relationship with the concept of 'normal' as its point of deviation.... The politics of perversion works to queer 'normal,' to unveil its kinks, disclose its ethical foundations, and destabilize its privileged zenith on a hierarchy of sexuality."[25] Building on Robert Stoller's "three central components of perversion"—"hostility" at play with desire, "discipline" separating normal from abnormal, and the common denial of perversion (as those in denial decry and live vicariously through the perversion of others)—Cruz claims perversion as "a technology of power deployed in the discursive production of sexuality."[26] Hostility, discipline, and denial are, for Cruz, neither good nor bad. They are real aspects of human experience. Similarly, Cruz "explores how racialized fantasies of abjection, power, and pleasure are not just essential to BDSM practices and their representation in contemporary American pornography, they are also vital in shaping the experiences of racialized sexuality, particularly black female sexuality."[27] Again: abjection, power, and pleasure are, for Cruz, neither good nor bad. They are real aspects of human experience.

Not only is the realism of human experience compelling for Cruz, but also the experience of individual sexual actors. Cruz writes, "Contextualizing sexual fantasies, desires, and performances from the viewpoint of the 'actors' is critical in gaining both a more cohesive, holistic understanding of sexuality and one that has the potential to temper the moralizing psychoanalytic force behind perversions."[28] It matters what Afrodiasporic women, men, and gender-nonbinary folx feel, think, and say about our own sexuality. It matters how we experience our own sexuality. Notwithstanding the oppressive racist, sexist, and heterosexist contexts that define our life experiences and pornography, we—and individual Afrodiasporic people as moral agents—are free to appropriate for ourselves (not to be confused with imposing on others) or reject even that which others have deemed oppressive, regressive, and antiprogressive. Mireille Miller-Young puts it this way: "Rethinking the meaning of agency in relationship to black women's sexuality, I propose to open up the concept of agency by moving away from readings of its equivalence with resistive (sexual) freedom. We might instead read agency as a facet of complex personhood within larger embedded relations of subordination. Depending on the historical moment, agency emerges differently and operates along divergent nodes of power. Agency then might be seen as a dialectical capacity for pleasure and pain, exploration and denial, or for progressive change as well as everyday survival."[29] To put a finer point on this: agency is the vehicle of moral action. Therefore, we might say "moral agency" wherever Miller-Young is refining her approach to agency. The Black women in the porn industry whom Miller-Young studies are moral agents—whose right and wrong are dialectical, not static. In the context of Black religion, this is critical because of the ways it flies in the face of evangelical, orthodox, literalist, and fundamentalist readings of scripture and approaches to faith. Instead of leaning into a black-and-white absolutism about what is right and wrong, this dialectical approach suggests that there are gray areas—some of which are gray depending on the context.

Presentation, exhibition, and use: these are the operative and most frequently used words in the Dworkin-MacKinnon definition of pornography. These are the terms used to specify what Dworkin and MacKinnon deem problematic in pornography. However, Miller-Young writes of early twentieth-century porn, "Unlike earlier black women who were exhibited without their control or consent at slave markets or in scientific studies, black women in early stag pornography are performers, workers who seem to have an interest or a stake in exhibitionism."[30] For Miller-Young, Black women sex workers participating in porn production are actively negotiating "racialized sexuality within historical conditions of constraint and appropriation"; they are making "self-determined choices about how and when to deploy their sexual labor."[31] She demonstrates, by "showing that slavery was in fact pornography, and that pornography relied on racial ideologies, fantasies, and political economies," that Black women make interventions in and through pornography "however compromised, as cocreators of a powerful and enduring sexual culture."[32] Importantly, Miller-Young approaches the morality of pornography with a certain pragmatism. This pragmatic approach begins with the acknowledgment that we all always and already are operating from, out of, and within preexisting conditions. There is no blank slate! There is no value of theorizing from a tabula rasa because there is no way to establish a tabula rasa; none of us is or can be objective enough for that (including Rawls); even at earlier points of human existence, there was no pure paradise that we can rightly or objectively describe in terms of its form, contents, or empirical or normative moral code. Miller-Young makes it clear: we act and operate as moral agents from our current context/positionality.

Questions remain: Is pornography fundamentally violent? Is violence fundamentally pornographic? In what ways is pornography violent? In what ways is violence pornographic? Once these questions are answered, an equally challenging set of questions surfaces. This set of questions addresses the nature of justice work—especially as predominantly Black civil rights activists of the 1960s understood justice work. To the extent that pornography is violent—and to the extent that violence is pornographic—did civil rights activists of the past decry pornography and/or violence? Did these activists understand pornography on the spectrum of violence or violence on the spectrum of pornography? Among civil rights leaders who espoused nonviolence (e.g., members of the Student Non-violent Coordinating Committee) what, if any, discourse was there regarding just war theory—especially as a religious subject? To what extent was such a theory reckoned relevant?[33]

Violences—and warfares—happen on different grounds: ideological grounds, physical grounds, spiritual grounds, and sexual grounds. Violences and warfares on one battleground often are often triggered, sparked, and inflected by violences and warfares on other battlegrounds—even as they trigger, spark, and inflect violences and warfares. Moreover, violences and warfares are layered; they are interactive. Unfortunately, histories of justice work bear witness that the work to disrupt and dismantle intersecting and interactive violences and warfares at once is difficult and rare. More common are attempts to stop the bleeding and harm at the site of the most excessive hemorrhages. Individual moral agents and institutions are left to discern where the worst hemorrhages are on their own—and have full freedoms and latitude to utilize (personalized) resources to address discerned crises of violences and warfares. However, institutions and individuals do this work imperfectly, irrationally, and often without regard to spiritually grounded intuition rooted in love and a robust vision of justice.

Notwithstanding her critique of "the pornographic seeing of Jezebel" (i.e., "jezebel, 'the African'"), the "pornographic *seeing* of race," "pornotroping," and "pornotropia," Tamura Lomax argues against traditional virtue as the antidote.[34] She writes, "Pivotal to unhinging jezebel from our collective psyche is undoing meaning. Whore/ho/promiscuous language/discourse/epistemes/ideology requires further theorizing and disentangling. Namely because it turns the pornotropic gaze and its preoccupations away from the one 'looking' and imagines black women and girls, not the gazer, as sites of danger, evil, perversion, and mockery, thus framing their sexual experiences and choices as pathological and men's (hetero)sexual experiences and choices as evidence of true masculinity."[35] However, she insists that religious theories of Black sexuality must press beyond an overemphasis on "white ideological bias"; expose "black religio-cultural production ... as an additional site of evil" relative to "the reproduction, maintenance, and projection of cultural images such as jezebel, sapphire, and mammy" (i.e., theories of Black sexuality must show the ways that Black people and communities are complicit in generating and circulating negative stereotypes of Black sexuality); "make room for ugly readings" (i.e. readings that explicitly name and unpack hard truths that press beyond politics of respectability); and relocate "black women's experiences" beyond "suffering, resistance, and survival."[36] Lomax presents "black feminist religious thought" as an alternative to both womanism, which has often neglected a fuller engagement with queer and otherwise deviant sexual discourse, and traditional Black feminism, which has often neglected religious analysis.[37] Part of how she defines this alternative is as "a system of ideas for framing, reading, and theorizing discourses on race, gender, sex, and transsexuality, including the discourse on black womanhood." Inching toward a framework that could accommodate pornography—without ever saying as much—Lomax writes:

> Black feminist religious thought holds that black religion is a primary text and source of meaning making in black women's and girls' lives. It maintains that black women and girls are choice-making agents who make decisions within context. It takes seriously women's right to define identity, pleasure, and pain for themselves. It understands that politics and desire are messy and that black women and girls live beyond and sometimes contradict feminist theorizations. It also understands that beauty

and pleasure are sometimes found in what may be defined as antifeminist spaces. Regardless, it holds cultural critiques in tension with possible pleasure principles. It recognizes that politics that block or limit the satisfaction of goods or ends that humans, especially the most vulnerable, minimally require, are death dealing and unjust, and that the right to live free of structural violence is a human right.[38]

Lomax acknowledges that a more robust theoretical framework than exists with respect to both Black women's and girls' sexuality and religion is necessary. Though Lomax evokes Evelyn Hammonds's call to "a politics of enunciation," she stops short of explicitly making room for Black feminist and/or womanist affirmations of pornography.[39] The moral parameters and ethical codes of Black sex workers and Afrodiasporic women and others who create and consume porn are left to the imagination and articulation of Black feminists not steeped in (religious) ethics—philosophical, biblical, social, or otherwise.

It is, of course, possible and more common to focus on the negative impacts of pornography in the lives of Black women, but alternate approaches are possible. Black feminist porn-positive (or porn-open/discerning) scholars point toward some of these approaches:

- Employing a "politics of respect," "an ethics of power"—not respectability. Working through the possibilities of "naivete," "rage," and qualified "acceptance"—and navigating when to protest, when to accept working conditions, and when to opt out—the sex workers Miller-Young engages build on a "politics of illicit eroticism" toward a "politics of respect."[40] In a "politics of respect," cultivating and protecting a domain of erotic sovereignty is of premium concern. Such a domain is characterized by "recognition in" their work, "control over their work," and "a fair playing field" with and among others in their industry.[41]
- Rethinking ourselves deviantly. There are ways that we can flip the script on those who would attempt to exploit us: utilizing "sexual autonomy" and "erotic sovereignty" to "imagine" ourselves "against the grain, through the tactics of illicit eroticism."[42] We can tap into the strength of our deviance. Deviance is where our lives and experiences naturally diverge from what is widely considered "respectable" (i.e., that which upholds the visions of individual, familial, community, and state civility qua morality). Deviance is not necessarily immoral. Deviance is outside of the hegemonic norms. Deviance is

where we imagine options for reconciling belief and action that are not defined by what others have taught, said, or done. Autonomy and (self)sovereignty are key here.
- Ambivalence with respect to absolute escape. Miller-Young notes that "because performers labor within the demands of pornographic capitalism, their attempts to seize agency in their images and performances are sutured to hegemonic forces that necessarily re-exploit them and others."[43] In other words, even when sex workers are exercising moral agency in their sex work (e.g., making choices about what they will and will not do), they are doing so in an economy that has already rendered them immoral—and their acts of moral agency might still be used against them for further exploitation as long as those morally agentive acts are taking place in the economy of sex work. This creates an awkward context. Full liberation and/or escape are not possible. This is a wall that liberation theologians have been running into since their inception. There is no exodus of Black liberation theology without indigenous liberation theology invoking the prerogative of the Canaanites or womanists identifying with the constraints of an Egyptian Hagar. And what does this mean for more explicitly nonconsensual sex and/or relationships and intimacies? Notwithstanding its apparent impossibility, mustn't escape be imagined and pursued? Yes, in relative terms. Yes and no, in absolute terms. In relative terms, we do seek and pursue release from all that binds us. However, human existence dictates that release from one form of bondage is often a release into another form of bondage. We discern and seek release from any new forms of bondage, but we know that other forms of bondage await us on every occasion of release. This produces a kind of humility whereby we must remain ambivalent with respect to absolute escape.
- Reworking our conditions (beyond flipping the script). Miller-Young writes, "Illicit erotic efforts to return the gaze and to recapture erotic sovereignty from sexual devaluement take place under the imposition of varied and profound exploitation, abuse, and constraint."[44] Though we may not be able to escape all exploitative conditions (especially in an absolute sense), we can rework them.
- Ambivalence about and refusal to specify good or bad. Miller-Young writes of "disidentifying with the expectation that [black women pornographers] represent a monolithic figure—positive or negative—of

black women's eroticism."[45] Porn is an easy target: it is easy to say that porn is bad. It is likewise easy, when trying to claim and redeem some aspects of porn, to begin delineating which porn is good and which is bad. This is often mistaken as the work of ethicists—or theorists of justice. When this is not the work, morality must be built elsewhere. Could it be that we are normatively hybrid and diverse internally and relationally? Could it be that we build morality around resistance to harm or being harmed—even while recognizing that vulnerabilities and suffering inform our identity formations, characters, and the experiences that make us who we are?

- Fantasy. Utilize fantastical spaces to *become*. Jennifer C. Nash asks, "What if the black feminist theoretical archive were to imagine fantasy as a productive space of subject formation, a site where subjects (white and black alike) articulate longings, perform pleasures, and name desires in ways that bother traffic in racial stereotype and transcend stereotype (and sometimes both simultaneously)?"[46] Nash clarifies that imagining ourselves out of and in circumstances helps us to relate better to our everyday real circumstances. A seedling of this concept is found in stoicism.

- Ecstasy. Nash offers ecstasy in lieu of pleasure, explaining that an ecstasy orientation "foregrounds how race acts both to limit our sexual imaginations, and to provide us with powerful vocabularies for naming what we desire; it recognizes that the very structures we critique and seek to dismantle can also thrill."[47] And when we are able to acknowledge the "thrill," how do we honor, accept, tweak, revise, retrain, and/or reconsider our desires?

- Self-determination. Miller-Young advocates increased "access to and control over the means of production" as "the best way to improve the images and experiences of black women workers in porn."[48] This means ownership of the production and products of one's sex work. This means that Black women workers in porn are working in the industry because it is their genuine choice to do so and they are not forced by other socioeconomic pressures to make this choice. This means more control over when, where, how, and why one chooses to engage in sex work. This can be pursued and protected as a right for sex workers and for all.

- Solidarity building. Imani Perry asks her readers to "imagine if . . . everyone who regularly consumed Internet porn actually assumed a political identity that saw the people who do the labor on these pleasure vehicles as a community whose well-being was part of their political concern."⁴⁹ Even further, what if we did this while cultivating and protecting spaces where the people who do this labor can fully exercise their democratic rights?

- Rejection of exploitation—including a rejection of defining all porn as exploitative. While Perry suggests that exploitation is what makes porn pornographic—rejecting imaginations "deployed in ways that diminish humanity rather than [expanding] it," when porn is no longer the straw man and there are ways to affirm pornography, exploitation is left to be rejected.⁵⁰ It is, after all, one of the primary qualities that disqualified pornography as socially acceptable.

Transnational Trouble

In his thorough 2019 article "Virtual Hatred: How Russia Tried to Start a Race War in the United States," William J. Aceves carefully delineates the Russian strategy to infiltrate the American political landscape. While other countries who aspire to or attain the role of empire may be as guilty of such tactics of geopolitical warfare, none have been as exposed and critiqued as Russia and its efforts in recent years.⁵¹ Aceves demonstrates that this effort was not limited to a direct threat on US presidential elections.⁵² This was an effort that seeped into other aspects of American life—deliberately meddling in and interfering with domestic civil rights matters. Specifically, Aceves demonstrates the ways that Russia (through the state-sponsored vehicle of the Internet Research Agency), especially utilizing cyberattacks and cyberwarfare, stirred racial strife and contributed to the start of "a race war." Beyond this, the Internet Research Agency also deployed strategies of personalized attacks that focused on discrediting and slandering individuals on the basis of their sexual affairs.⁵³

Running synchronously with these attacks were other suspicious connections between the executive branches of the United States, in the person of Donald Trump, and Russia, in the person of Vladimir Putin. Throughout and beyond Trump's first campaign for the US presidency, reports were surfacing about illicit sexual liaisons that characterized Trump's most recent visits to Russia.⁵⁴ Then, Trump's nominee for labor secretary, former Miami US attorney Alexander Acosta, drew attention to another personal scandal that connected Trump to Jeffrey Epstein and his notorious sexual abuses. The connection to

Russia—and to a global interest in sexual exploitation fueled by the mutual investment of Russian operatives and the Trump administration—starts to come into clearer focus.[55] By no means were Epstein's reach and the stains of his sexual exploits limited to Russia and Trump. However, that there are connections between Epstein's economy of human sex trafficking, Russia, and Trump is both evident and relevant. Sexual trysts—the creation of occasions for them, the sociopolitical blackmail power that existed because of them—became an invaluable commodity during the Trump administration. The megalomania, narcissism, and global power of Jeffrey Epstein, Donald Trump, and Vladimir Putin not only increased the value of this commodity to epic proportions but also effected an increased disparity of power and wealth between those who buy, sell, and pimp sex work and sex workers. In such a cultural climate, the spectrum of pornography ever expands to include human sex trafficking (i.e., slavery) and minors (i.e., pedophilia). Whether or not Afrodiasporic people participated in the creation or consumption of what these men and this culture were producing directly, these men were creating a global market that impacted (and impacts) those working in other areas and extremities of that market. Most striking is the erasure of all the women and girls used, bought, sold, invited, demanded, and/or employed for sex.

Notwithstanding the similarities between Russia and the United States with respect to the ways these two nation-states (mis)handle sociopolitical dissidents, there are important distinctions to be made.[56] On one hand, Russia's intimations toward democracy are fledgling and perennially under attack. While the Cold War era in the United States marks a period of sexual revolution (and expanding freedoms) complemented by a fiscally and (increasingly) sexually corrupt evangelical religious right, the same period in Russia is characterized by sexual repressions and the rise of the Russian Orthodox Church as a corrupt and complicit partner in a shapeshifting (democracy-lite) totalitarian regime. State-sanctioned sexual repressions, however, do not prevent the emergence of sexual diversities. While Russia maintains laws and sanctions against postheterosexualities, the strength of a pornographic underground economy grows and human sex trafficking flourishes. Moreover, Russia marks its digital territory, claiming the World Wide Web as a critical battleground in an ongoing quest for sociopolitical world domination through the cultivation and publication of *kompromat*, a Cold War Russian strategy of sociopolitical combat Malcolm Nance defines as "the use of 'compromising materials' that were used to impugn the reputation of a target. The materials may have been real or forged but were aimed to attack politicians, officials, media or entertainment personalities, or business targets. The materials came in a variety of types—documents, photographs, or videos."[57] Nance goes on to explain, "In the digital era, the ability to generate stories with no basis in reality went beyond the KGB officers in Service A of the First Chief Directorate, spreading the incredible lie that AIDS was created to kill blacks and gays.... Now you could read about how the Democratic Party had a campaign staffer murdered or how Hillary Clinton and John Podesta ran a child sex trafficking ring from the imaginary basement of a Washington, DC, pizza parlor."[58] Russian operatives interested in this agenda of Russian hegemonic world leadership and the displacement of US power, privilege, prestige, and exceptionalism explicitly disrupt and target virtual spaces because of (and to compensate for) Russia's lack of a strong democratic nation-state. The internet becomes a great equalizer—an egalitarian hope of equity for anyone with a good Wi-Fi connection and reasonable computer skills. This disruption is one of the critical ways that Russia has gained contemporary relevance and political clout in a transnational context—vis-à-vis the United States.

One of the reasons it is so important to consider the relationship between online sexual formation and the development of political theologies is because of the ways that powerful nation-states, such as the United States, Russia, and China, are modeling theopolitical control tactics through the control of internet resources. Awareness of the proliferation of fake news and fears about the impacts of this proliferation are widespread throughout the minority communities within the most powerful nation-states and their colonies. On one hand, there is a growing concern about how news is generated and disseminated—and this concern has a great deal to do with formal and informal expressions of state control; this is mediated/tempered with a skepticism about fake news that results in an increased interest in community control and/or input with respect to media accountability for integrity. On the other hand, there is a problematic growth in the availability of and access to sexually explicit and pornographic materials. Theopoliticians tend to associate the availability of sexually explicit material with a general decline in sexual morality among liberal Western (qua European) cultures; this decline is also proven by the expansion of LGBTQ rights within these cultural contexts. What is not necessarily clear to the general public is how to advocate for honest and responsible reporting while resisting state and/or multinational corporation control of news and information. What is not necessarily clear to the general public is how to defend LGBTQ rights, sexual rights, reproductive rights, and sexual freedom while resisting pornographic exploitations, human trafficking, and the forms of slavery it is sponsored by and it sponsors. And it is not clear how to do this on micro and macro levels to disrupt interpersonal and state forms of sexual violence. Publics and community leaders have not demonstrated their capacity to distinguish between all things rendered sexually immoral: LGBTQ identity and rights are not the same as or in the same category as human (sex) trafficking or pedophilia. And unpaid sex trafficking is not the same as sex work—especially for those who have most effectively advocated for agency with respect to their work and have viable, realistic, comparably paying alternative work options. However, for some moralists, these are not only all matters of sexual immorality, but they are also all equally heinous. Part of what theopolitical power within nation-states enables is a confusion and conflation of issues that should be neither confused nor conflated. Such confusion and conflation results in an incapacity to do rigorous moral discernment and social advocacy within the general public. What is most discouraging with respect to the theopolitical powers at work in imperial government structures is the role of spaces traditionally identified as church, religious, and/or holy. In an ironic twist, the religious/sacred/holy interest of religious leaders is best defended, exemplified, and codified in the political leadership of the most morally abhorrent political icons—individuals who defend and demonstrate the most vitriolic forms of pornographic exploitations, racism, sexism, heterosexism, classism, and xenophobia.[59]

Contemplating the impact of net neutrality or similar laws and policies,[60] the availability of pornography, and the unavailability of reliable news media coverage within an empire from the perspectives of those who inhabit its home base is quite different than contemplating these conditions from the perspectives of those who inhabit the outposts or colonies of an empire. Outposts are often places of neglect, places of testing, places of increased and decreased surveillance. These are the places that are made to suffer without electricity for months upon months following natural disasters exacerbated by unnatural political interests. These are the places that become hubs for human trafficking because they are off the radar. These are the places where failed businesspeople from the mother, home country go in order to try again in an atmosphere of lowered standards and expectations. A sneeze in Russia, the United States, or China is, ultimately, pneumonia in Kazakhstan, Puerto Rico, or South Korea. Moreover, the international relationships that have been built between outposts and other imperial powers that can protect the outposts from their mother empire complicate the economy of empire—at once reifying and challenging it (which, finally, means reifying it).

In addition to the online (or two-way telecommunications) political patterns, policies, and laws that exist within each of the mother empires—and how these compare to the patterns, policies, and laws within the colonies or outposts—it is also critically important to consider the religious contexts of the empires and colonies. (In the midst of this consideration, it would be a mistake to ignore the ways that a global general public was and has been conscientized to believe that our contemporary existence is in a postcolonial reality—an appropriated resistance agenda. It is, similarly, essential to be mindful of the ways that the global general public is currently being reconscientized to understand itself in terms of empire and colony—an appropriation for contemporary resistance.) Within the United States, theocratic impulses are strongest and most obvious as evangelical Christianity and religious right conservative politics continually shape-shift and meld into one another. While the theocratic power in Russia was challenged during the rule of the Soviet Union, it is clear that the Russian Orthodox Church grows and maintains a cache of political power and that there is a mutual blessing between that church and the state.[61]

The relationship between Russia and the United States with respect to *kompromat*, digital/online warfare, race, and sex is not without layers of moral import. There is an obvious question of how Russia as a nation-state defends professions of Christianity with the ways it pursues empire. (And the same question would be critically directed toward the United States as well.) However, the deeper moral concerns in my estimation are these: What kinds of neighbors are Russia and the United States to one another? What kinds of rulers are these imperial powers toward those under their power? How do vulnerable racial and sexual minorities fare under their rule? Concerned with Alain Besançon's critical conclusions regarding Russia, but more sanguine than Besançon's, Janusz Dobieszewski reduces the contemporary plight of Russia to a choice: "Russia faces a choice: to follow the road of continuous imperialistic nationalism based on orthodox messianism, endlessly making territorial claims, or to decide to 'accept in good faith the status of an "average empire."'"[62] Dobieszewski believes the latter choice is realistic for Russia.

While conceding the legitimacy of the US government is a disquieting thought for those of us who have descended from indigenous peoples of Turtle Island and "Africa," who have descended from people who have been looted, beaten, raped, and slaughtered, it can feel like the lesser evil. The US nomenclature of democracy offers possibilities for recognition, for voice, for empowerment, and for justice that do not exist under the rule of other contemporary empires. Such nomenclature—and whatever governmental possibilities it contains—would not be possible in an empire without free and fair elections, peaceful transitions of power, term limits for elected officials (especially in the executive branches of government), free speech and press, and freedom from death-dealing propagandistic lies. Such nomenclature—and whatever governmental possibilities it contains—would not be possible in Russia, China, or under the rule of most nation-states and alliances in the Middle East. Without conceding the legitimacy of the United States, I argue that justice—as it pertains to Afrodiasporic sexuality, in particular, and communities that are vulnerable by virtue of a present lack of political power, non-European descent, gender identity, ability, and/or sexual orientation, in general—and democracy (that can facilitate redistributions of power and wealth often written off as socialism) must be defended. The implicit and explicit attacks on democracy from within and outside of the United States, the implicit and explicit hegemonic tendencies of Russia and the United States, are grossly exacerbated as these powers unify on agendas of democracy disruptions, pledge allegiance to cultures of *kompromat*, and collect the bones of exploited, silenced, and trafficked women and girls.

Democracy, Artifici-Ecology, and Creative Space

Imagine with me: the year is 2030. Human sex trafficking abolitionists and sex workers of color around the terrasphere come together for a conference at which women and girls of all ages—transgender and cisgender—discuss their plight. We, abolitionists and workers gathered, explain our hopes, our dreams, our desires, our passions, and our pleasures. We pledge a commitment not to harm one another, to protect one another, to help and bless one another (and the planet) prior to any other allegiances. We discern equitable ways to share voice, vote, and power that exceeds a simple majority. We recalibrate our democratic impulses with the creativity of spiritpolitical anarchy. We discern equitable ways to pool and share our resources with one another. We do not slut shame one another. We celebrate, express, and explore the philosophical, spiritual, and physical powers of the erotic. We gather virtually; we gather physically; we gather safely. We evaluate sciences and technologies that can strengthen our contributions to the health of the terrasphere and all its inhabitants—including us. We come to one another as real, true-true, authentic beings. And we invite our consumers to our next conference.[63] We take up these questions together:

- How do we read, respond, live, act, work, and be "through layers of domination at work... in pornographic images; in low-wage labor markets and underground economies of drugs, illegal sex work, child sexual abuse and sex trafficking that abut and sometimes overlap with porn; on sets of pornographic films and in the films' ownership and distribution"?
- What do we say "about the expansion of marketized sexuality and why it so often accumulates according to conventional patriarchal logics"?[64]

And maybe it is not a conference we hold, but a family reunion, a homecoming, an exhibition, a celebration, a liturgy, a convocation, a tarrying service. Wherever it is, however it is: we disperse knowing that we did the "eronic" work our souls must have.[65]

In 1981, the French philosopher Jean Baudrillard published his treatise *Simulacra and Simulation*. Baudrillard's text took on the ongoing challenges of classism at a critical time in the history of nation-state-directed communism. Ten years before the fall of the Soviet Union, *Simulacra and Simulation* was published in France one year prior to Ronald Reagan proposing arms reduction talks at a summit in Geneva. Baudrillard's *Simulacra and Simulation* was first published in English in 1994. The sociopolitical timing of *Simulacra and Simulation* is as interesting as its content. Politically speaking, the text is being exported and received as the Cold War is ending. The Berlin Wall falls in Germany in 1989; Mikhail Gorbachev resigns in 1991 as the eighth and final general secretary of the Communist Party of the Soviet Union—giving way to the Russian Federation, structured as a multiparty representative democracy, according to its constitution; and Bill Clinton is elected as the forty-second president of the United States—not insignificantly for this chapter, amid various sex scandals. Socially speaking, the internet, which has been evolving from its nascent stages in the 1950s, is taking off at a pace that seems to be faster than the speed of light. In 1993 the internet was only responsible for the transmission of 1 percent of all two-way telecommunications; by 2000, the internet would be responsible for 51 percent of all two-way telecommunications; more than 97 percent of all two-way telecommunications would be transmitted through the internet by 2007.

Given the unique political and technological contexts in which Baudrillard is writing *Simulacra and Simulation*, it is no surprise that his evaluation of capitalism engages these contexts. These he engages through a careful analysis of real, "the real," reality, and whatever is understood to be their material referents. Having applied a sociopolitical analysis to Jorge Luis Borges's fable "On Exactitude in Science" or "On Rigor in Science," Baudrillard presents the following powerful thesis: "Today abstraction is no longer that of the map, the double the mirror, or the concept. Simulation is no longer that of a territory, a referential being, or a substance. It is the generation by models of a real without origin or reality: a hyperreal. The territory no longer precedes the map, nor does it survive it."[66] He goes on to explain how this thesis is applied to the relationship between "the sign" and "the real": "Such is simulation, insofar as it is opposed to representation. Representation stems from the principle of the equivalence of the sign and of the real (even if this equivalence is utopian, it is a fundamental axiom). Simulation, on the contrary, stems from the utopia of the principle of equivalence, from the negation of the sign as value, from the sign as the reversion and death sentence of every reference (6)." And explains the corresponding "phases of the image" as such:

> it is the reflection of a profound reality;
> it masks and denatures a profound reality;
> it masks the *absence* of a profound reality;
> it has no relation to any reality whatsoever: it is its own pure simulacrum (6).

Baudrillard uses this framework to stage a critical analysis of culture—with an emphasis on American culture. For Baudrillard, the proliferation of simulacra is best exemplified in culture as selective "demuseumification" (i.e., handling of art) (7–11), amusement parks (e.g., Disneyland) and the evolution of strange hyperrealities and imaginaries (12), politics (e.g., Watergate; 14–19), a falsification of criminality (19–20), and need for work (26) through an end to the panopticon by way of role and code switch (27–32). The direction of this proliferation is ultimately an unnatural, unreal end. Presenting his case for the empirical fact and results of simulacra and simulation in a linear vision of historical progress, Baudrillard introduces his *Simulacra and Simulation* with the following conclusion: "The apotheosis of simulation: the nuclear" (32). For Baudrillard the nuclear is upon us and inevitable. He writes, "The nuclear is at once the culminating point of available energy and the maximization of energy control systems. Lockdown and control increase in direct proportion to (and undoubtedly even faster than) liberating potentialities. This was already the aporia of the modern revolution. It is still the absolute paradox of the nuclear. Energies freeze in their own fire, they deter themselves" (40). In light of Baudrillard's apt description of our contemporary reality, prescient even in 1981, it is difficult to imagine that his prediction about the conclusion of earth's story—or at least the story of its human empires—is wrong. However, perhaps there is room for some way of living that contradicts this end even if it does not prevent it.

Around the same time that Baudrillard publishes *Simulacra and Simulation*, the feminist scientist, social theorist, and critic of capitalism Donna Haraway is proposing new ways to think about the human species and the role of the human species as part of earth's inhabitants. In 1985, her formative essay, "A Manifesto for Cyborgs: Science, Technology, and Socialist Feminism in the 1980s," is published in *Socialist Review*. By 1991, Haraway has revised this essay and published it as part of a book of essays titled *Simians, Cyborgs, and Women: The Reinvention of Nature*. Whereas Baudrillard gives singular attention to fabricated simulacra, accepting the demise of that which is real—along with the earth, that which is material, and anything substantive—Haraway focuses on the biological future of the earth and its inhabitants. While she is no more sanguine about the future of the earth or real referents through which earthly existence may achieve immortality, she is uncompromisingly committed to the biological welfare of the earth. She is aware of a simian (i.e., of and/or having to do with monkeys and/or apes) past (present and future), a cyborg (i.e., short for *cybernetic organism*, a being with both organic and biomechatronic body parts, a term coined in 1960) present (recent past and future), and a women-oriented, feminist future (past and present) at earth's best.

In the face of a rapidly digitizing world, Haraway encourages an ethical and practical pathway into the future that takes digitization, technological advances, and the proliferation of simulacra seriously, but refuses to completely succumb to all of the logic of such developments. Instead, she eventually builds a case for thinking of the now in which we live as the "Chthulucene." This is not to be confused with "Anthropocene, Plantationocene, and Capitalocene." Haraway explains the Chthulucene in this way:

> I am calling all this the Chthulucene—past, present, and to come. These real and possible timespaces are not named after SF writer H.P. Lovecraft's misogynist racial-nightmare monster Cthulhu (note spelling difference), but rather after the diverse earth-wide tentacular powers and forces and collected things with names like Naga, Gaia, Tangaroa (burst from water-full Papa), Terra, Haniyasu-hime, Spider Woman, Pachamama,

Oya, Gorgo, Raven, A'akuluujjusi, and many many more. "My" Chthulucene, even burdened with its problematic Greek-ish tendrils, entangles myriad temporalities and spatialities and myriad intra-active entities-in-assemblages—including the more-than-human, other-than-human, inhuman, and human-as-humus. Even rendered in an American English-language text like this one, Naga, Gaia, Tangaroa, Medusa, Spider Woman, and all their kin are some of the many thousand names proper to a vein of SF that Lovecraft could not have imagined or embraced—namely, the webs of speculative fabulation, speculative feminism, science fiction, and scientific fact. It matters which stories tell stories, which concepts think concepts. Mathematically, visually, and narratively, it matters which figures figure figures, which systems systematize systems.[67]

And one of the most interesting ways that Haraway's vision is being expressed is through the work of adrienne maree brown. In her book *Emergent Strategy: Shaping Change, Changing Worlds*, brown identifies as a "Pleasure Activist," "Healer/Doula," "Writer/Artist," "Independent Science/Visionary Fiction Scholar." From each of these identities (and evolving from an inspiring interest in the work of Octavia Butler), brown develops *Emergent Strategy* in community. She defines "emergent Strategy" as "the adaptive and relational leadership model found in the work of Black science fiction writer Octavia Butler (and others)."[68] More than the average leadership model, *emergent strategy* is a guideline for being and action that those of us concerned with a just future for earth and human communities might follow. On one hand, brown emphasizes the importance of Butler's change principle:

> All that you touch
> You Change.
> All that you Change
> Changes you.
> The only lasting truth
> Is Change.
> God Is Change.[69]

On the other hand, brown builds on the work of thinkers like Margaret Wheatley, who published a book called *Leadership and the New Science*, based on her work with organizations and leaders on what is effective, through a lens of quantum physics, biology, and chaos theory in 1992. Her key learnings were that:

1. everything is about relationships, critical connections;
2. chaos is an essential process that we need to engage;
3. the sharing of information is fundamental for organizational success;
4. and vision is an invisible field that binds us together, emerging from relationships and chaos and information.[70]

Ultimately, what comes from a synthesis of ideas like Butler's change mantra and Wheatley's key learnings in *Leadership and the New Science* is the concept and way of life called emergent strategy, the core principles of which are:

1. Small is good, small is all. (The large is a reflection of the small.)
2. Change is constant. (Be like water).
3. There is always enough time for the right work.
4. There is a conversation in the room that only these people at this moment can have. Find it.
5. Never a failure, always a lesson.
6. Trust the People. (If you trust the people, they become trustworthy.)
7. Move at the speed of trust. Focus on critical connections more than critical mass—build the resilience by building the relationships.
8. Less prep, more presence.
9. What you pay attention to grows.[71]

And the elements of which are shown in table 7.1.

brown offers a new way to think about terrastories and *dunia* possibilities through her consideration of the earth and its elements. Table 7.1 shows aspects of the biological workings of earth and its inhabitants. The fractal, adaptative, interdependent and decentralized, nonlinear and iterative, resilient and transformative, and creative aspects of our common ecological context generate questions that humans, posthumans, transhumans, and thinking beings can (and should) be asking ourselves while inviting us into mutually sustaining and complementary ways of being. The elements also inspire possibilities for just quare maâtian discernment and expression as fractals are expressed in pluri-sized pieces of pleasure, adaptations are expressed in the evolutionary, interdependence and decentralization are expressed in centrifugal health, nonlinearity and iterativity are expressed in acting around, resilience and transformative justice are expressed in climactic excess, and the creation of more possibilities is expressed in pro-creative multiplication.

Among the most natural and organic ways of understanding and expressing emergent strategy are brown's invocation and application of the following:

Table 7.1: Natural Elements of Emergent Strategy for Just Quare Maâtian Ethics

Element	Nature of Element	Just Quare Maâtian Expression
Fractal	The Relationship Between Small and Large	*Pluri-sized Pieces of Pleasure:* What parts of pleasure make us singularly and collectively whole?
Adaptative	How We Change	*Evolutionary:* What piques our senses of sacred erotic-spiritual alignment and tweaks our isness accordingly?
Interdependence and Decentralization	Who We Are and How We Share	*Centrifugally Healthy:* What centripetal force and gravitational grounding sanctify our mutual erotic-eronic offerings to one another?
Nonlinear and Iterative	The Pace and Pathways of Change	*Acting Around:* What are the time-space, particle-wave-gravitational characteristics of our orbital seasons?
Resilience and Transformative Justice	How We Recover and Transform	*Climactic Excess:* What is the manifested hope of a spirituality of revolt, resistance, and love?
Creating More Possibilities	How We Move Toward Life	*Pro-Creatively Multiplying:* What carries us through life, death, and life again—and again?

SOURCE: The first two columns of this table were originally printed as "Natural Elements of Emergent Strategy" in adrienne maree brown, *Emergent Strategy: Shaping Change, Changing Worlds*, 52–53.

- Biomimetics or biomimicry is the imitation of the models, systems, and elements of nature for the purpose of solving complex human problems.
- Permaculture is a system of agricultural and social design principles centered around simulating or directly utilizing the patterns and features observed in natural ecosystems.[72]

These two principles finally connect a practicable activism to Haraway's call for earthlings to enter, embrace, survive, and thrive in a kinship-oriented Chthulucene. brown invites us to relentlessly hold on to "real"/"the real," defending it against the threat of simulacra that poses as and erases "real"/"the real."

Understanding Haraway's description of the Chthulucene is essential—as is understanding her invitation to her readers and all who are concerned about the future of the earth and its inhabitants to embrace the Chthulucene in a particular way. Literally, from a translation of the Greek, the Chthulucene is the "new subearth" or the "time of the new subearth." *Khthon*, transliterated and translated, means earth; the Greek *khthonios*, transliterated and translated, means in, of, or underneath the earth; the *-cene* suffix is from the Greek *kaino*, which, transliterated and translated, means new. The chthonic Greek gods, in fact, were known as the gods of agriculture (among whom were Hades and Persephone) or gods of the underworld (ruled by Hades and Persephone). The rich mythology that accompanies Hades and Persephone reminds a student not only of such mythology of the natural processes through which the earth cycles but also of the divine and earthly significance that these processes may have for interactive rational beings. Among the truths revealed through the complex relationship between Hades and Persephone is that there can be portals and passages between life and death, earth and subearth. Notwithstanding this etymological and mythological genealogy of the term Haraway recovers, it is previously uncovered in the science fiction work of H. P. Lovecraft. In his 1928 short story "The Call of Cthulhu," Lovecraft describes a creature similar to the chthonic god identity, but his creature is different in important ways that Haraway names: Lovecraft's is a "misogynist racial-nightmare monster Cthulhu (note spelling difference)." In contrast, Haraway is after the primordial chthonic possibilities—that include death, life, and passages between the two, marked in dying—and the communities that exist in death and dying, and in agriculture. It is to this time of the Chthulucene—the new subearth—to which Haraway calls her readers. And it is in this Chthulucene that Haraway simultaneously sees deep connection to both the biologically real, agricultural earth and a call to create, emphasize, and promote nonbiological kinship as a new real and the only substantive possibility for our shared future as earth and earthlings (humans included).

If the 2030 conference is a success, pornography is possible. Pornography not only presents space to resist sexual exploitations through sexual and otherwise erotic materiality, but pornographic also becomes an active ground for reorganizations of power. However, the exploitations that have come to define pornography are not all possible. There are grounds for consent, mutuality, and respect that have unashamed advocates. Children cannot be stolen or conscripted into pornographic economies. Adults—with an appropriate maturation of their frontal lobes—are permitted to discern, determine, and specify their worth, their bodies' worth, their sex's worth, and their terraspheric membership's worth. Deep fakes, nonfungible tokens (NFTs), and stereotypes (i.e., a precursor to deep fakes) are regulated and bracketed to constrain the nuclear outcomes Baudrillard anticipates.[73] Women and girls, transgender and cisgender, gender-nonconforming people, men, all people, and all organic and inorganic complementary aspects of the terrasphere are appropriately honored and respected in our capacities for self-determination, agency, consent, mutuality, flourishing, fluidity, integration, and segregation (for health). *Pornē* (i.e., the transliterated Greek word for *prostitute*, translated as *sex worker* in contemporary terms) and *graphein* (i.e., the transliterated Greek word for *writing/to write*) are possible together as the *pornē graphein*, her/their own story, narrative, autobiography, destiny, and course, as she/they/he interact with spirit, divine, G*d—or not—on her/their/his own terms. *Pornē graphein* is possible as *pornē* is part of the *dēmos* (i.e., the transliterated Greek word for *people*) with *kratia* (i.e., the transliterated Greek word for *power*) or with whom *kratia* is equitably shared. If the 2030 conference is a success, *pornē* are fully and equitably vested with *kratia*, recognized as full and equal parts of the *dēmos*. If anything, that life's circumstances have led one to choose or to find oneself among the *pornē* makes one more qualified, not less qualified, to have full and equitably em-*kratia*-d (i.e., *kratia*-endowed) voice among the *dēmos*. To be clear, it is not (in this vision) pimps, managers, and exploitative producers and directors who do the *pornē graphein*. It is *pornē* who do their own *graphein* and are endowed with, acknowledged as having, and operating in a fullness of their *kratia*. These connect with screens and digital worlds in new ways; these rework the relationship between their "real" and their work/praxis/experience; these determine the artificial skins and fluids that protect skins and fluids from skins and fluids; these determine what is holy and sacred to themselves as they agree to participate in an economy that resists and rejects harm done unto them or by them; these dissolve all efforts to publicly shame them—especially by those who secretly enjoy their work—these establish their value (with and without respect to sex). And these participate in biological rhythms that are not always monogamous—often reproducing with different partners and with the help of other creatures over a life course; biological patterns that are not always modest—showing glorious large, small, and diverse pistils and stamens. And if the 2030 conference is a success, pornography is then redacted and rewritten again with invited and welcomed, consenting audiences—now participant observers.

Beyond the virtual space of pornography—and the spectrum from online dating and sex toy shopping to sex work and human sex trafficking such space can imply—this chapter also briefly addresses practices of masturbation and attitudes about masturbation among Afrodiasporic people in the United States. In some way, the connection of this chapter's aforementioned online subjects with masturbation materializes the online subjects of the chapter. Still, masturbation (often) maintains a definitive distance from the materiality of an other. In fact, one of the perennial concerns about masturbation for historic churches, traditional Christian ethics, and other Black religious communities has been that masturbation is, typically, disconnected and/or un(re)productive. One might, of course, claim that there are virtually and physically connected ways in which masturbation is practiced (as Moultrie shows that some Black churchwomen do). (Interestingly, these connection claims do not compromise critiques of the un[re]productivity of masturbation because they are linked to a deeper claim about "right" sex only in a committed monogamous heterosexual marriage.)

Baudrillard raises questions about how material anything is in our contemporary context; Haraway and brown raise questions about how material (and in what ways) we can be—to the extent that materiality is normative (i.e., that materiality should be). Masturbation naturally explores these questions given its ambiguity with respect to connection and clarity with respect to (re)productivity: masturbation can sometimes connect one to oneself, to an other, and/or to others; at best, (re)productivity is a by-product of masturbation (e.g., foreplay; as part of the sale of sex and/or pornography). Thus, one might inquire of masturbation: Is it the quintessential example of simulacra with respect to sexuality—having erased the real referent of sex through the physical contact of two or more people? One might further inquire of masturbation: Is it the quintessential example of the Chthulucene (and/or the pleasure principles of which brown writes), insofar as it invites an emphasis on kinship and deemphasizes biological procreation? There are ways that masturbation defies any binary explanations of itself—even as it clarifies the frameworks Baudrillard, Haraway, and brown present for understanding a digitized, online world.

Recognizing the problems and realities of Baudrillard's simulacra, Imani Perry most helpfully clarifies how this must transform approaches to Black feminism.[74] Moreover, she explicitly considers the context of sex workers and the ways that reworkings of real, artificial, and "artifice" demand new ethical approaches:[75]

> More than right or wrong, we have to consider constraint, demands, and how we are all constituted as subjects. The debate that has grown between pro- and anti-porn feminists is illustrative of why such care is essential. Anti-porn feminists appropriately draw attention to the material conditions under which porn is created: how often the choice to enter the industry is produced by limited economic choice and how often coercion becomes force. . . . Pro-porn feminists appropriately recognize the full humanity of those participating in porn: that they are often marked actors making decisions and providing services that are wildly popular, although widely shamed. . . . Both lines of thought often lack something critical in their analyses: Anti-porn activists often replicate the object status of those who act in pornographic film. They treat the actors solely as objects who are being exploited, even as they criticize that status. They fail to distinguish between those who are violently dominated into porn and those who have chosen it as a form of work. However, even the most feminist porn—that which imagines a female consumer and centralizes women's pleasure—is often neoliberal in its orientation. Some pro-porn advocates fail to confront questions about the impact of marketization on human sexuality—one of the most fundamental elements of our humanity, like love, like the need for water.[76]

Expanded ethical frameworks can manifest, can *become*, can come into existence from this kind of balanced perspective.

If justice were anything here, it would be: being justice. Such justice could fantasize, could explore, could imagine, could feel ecstasy over pleasure, could pursue utopia over paradise, but could not change what and where it is/was/will be. Being justice, we each could be—and we could be justice together, but we could not be what we are not. And we, human beings, are fraught. Our isness, our ontic, our ontology is already pornographic. We are written, exhibited, exposed, projected, presented, used for sex work. We are products and producers. We are voyeurs and actors. We are. And our beings are pornographic; and we be/ing (i.e., are) justice. The tensions of imperfect moral codes are not only written into our metaethical workspace. We smell, taste, look, sound, feel, move, gyrate, pulsate, quake, quiver, shake, squeeze, hold, touch, and be these ethical tensions. These ethical tensions are the closest approximations that we have to justice. Even when we can see our way to a normative pornography, we cannot escape the pornography (qua exploitation) of racism. Our justice, like us, be-s imperfect.

Cathy Cohen helpfully considers moral formation and attitudes about sexuality among youth of color as well. While the Boston study on pornography use concentrates on low-income youth, in her book *Democracy Remixed: Black Youth and the Future of American Politics*, Cohen focuses on youth from mixed-income backgrounds. Cohen explores "the politics of values, morals, and norms exhibited by and presented to black youth by their peers, by members of black communities, and by the larger society."[77] She also contemplates the moral perspectives of Black youth from their own perspective. Drawing data from surveys, focus groups, and in-depth interviews, Cohen inquires with "black youth themselves about the moral politics they adhere to and embrace." She details what these young people "say they are doing sexually" and explores "the sexual attitudes of young people and how they talk about and explain their sexual choices." Cohen finds that "in contrast to many of the published reports about black youth, they seem ready and willing to take on the responsibility for making unwise choices in the domain of intimacy." She also notes that the youth who participated in her study often "articulated disapproval of the behavior of other young black people, especially when it came to decisions surrounding sex and relationships." Though she writes that it is "not surprising," perhaps the most significant of Cohen's findings is that "the same young people expressed more conservative attitudes when asked about topics such as abortion and same-sex marriage—attitudes that were at odds not only with those expressed by white and Latino youth but also with their own reported behaviors."[78] This learned, patterned, practiced hypocrisy—already evidenced among youth—is a threat at least equal to the threat of pornography as the primary pedagogical source for youth on sex and sexuality. Cohen writes, "While from the outside it may seem that black youth have walked away from traditional norms and values thought to be critical to success and progress, it may be, instead, that black youth are struggling to reconcile their embrace of idealized dominant norms and values around sex and family with the visible limitations in their lives that prevent implementation of these dominant constructs."[79] Notwithstanding a constant onslaught of intracommunal politics of respectability messaging, Afrodiasporic and Latinx youth are being set up to fail with respect to such politics. Religious institutions are especially implicated in this tragedy mostly because they fail to have authentic conversations about sex at all and specifically fail to have conversations about pornography and sex in ways that suspend judgment. The problem for Afrodiasporic and Latinx youth is not just that paths of respectability do not readily exist for these youth, but also that paths of deviance and/or respect are more appropriate as normative possibilities. Cohen notes the seriousness of this matter: "If we do not address the growing discrepancy between sexual storytelling and true sexual life, we will only exacerbate the negative consequences that result from such silences, including ineffective policies to support the families who actually populate black communities and inappropriate messaging in the fight against HIV/AIDS, all of which threaten the very survival of young black people."[80] Truer stories, explicit enunciations with respect to sex, sexuality, and pornography can make more authentic democrats (i.e., people powers, empowerers of people, power people, and empowered people) and more nuanced, agentive, morally grounded pornographers.[81] Space for creativity (i.e., sexual creativity) and enunciation (i.e., speech acts about and, potentially, of sex and sexuality) are essential for youth and for Afrodiasporic communities of adults whose repressive communicative patterns and practices around sex and pornography are stifling existential possibilities and (racial, gender, and sexual) sin-disruptive discourse. In such space, democracy and artificiecological ways of being can flourish—and can flourish as justice.

Transnational debates on climate change are not concerned with doing the least possible to avoid disaster or redistributing disaster to the most vulnerable to bear the most burden. Transnational debates on climate change are interested in how to transform the inequitable systems that have created unsustainable relationships between people and between people and the earth. Transnational debates on space are not concerned with how to colonize a new frontier or how to make space available to those who have mastered the arts of exploitation and disproportionately benefited from earth's resources so that they can establish the same ways of being elsewhere. Transnational debates on space are interested in how we can cultivate healthier ways of being together—and, specifically, being together on earth so that if or when there are more extensive and widespread travels through other spaces and worlds and new encounters with unfamiliar organisms, we are prepared to engage in a spirit of mutuality, sustained with internalized cultural commitments to equity, and equipped with the humility of those more ready to give according to the needs, interests, and invitations of others and the strength of our resources than we are ready to receive. Black sexual creative freedom begins with an awareness that Black people are organospiritual beings. We are living matter (and neither governed by Foucauldian biopolitical nor Mbembean necropolitical prescriptions). As organospiritual beings, we are alive with the earth and that which lives through it. We are part of a constellation bigger than our minds can articulate. We are alive with all that exceeds what we know about space-time and how it operates. This is one of the ways that we are spiritual. When we embody Black sexual creative freedom, we *axé* (i.e., affirm with the full force of our beings) our own organospiritual beings and other organospiritual beings with which we are alive. We work and rest, we give and take, and separate and connect in sustainable ways. We work within our glocal, transnational locations according to such an ethic. Our creative freedoms are not for exploitation but for organospiritual common becomings. Our Black sexual creative freedom cools the planet. Our Black sexual creative freedom puts down deeper roots in the earth and reaches into space toward the warmth of the sun—and other suns—that beckons to us.

This further complicates justice and freedom debates in Black sexual ethics because it demands deeper intentionality, accountability, and responsibility with respect to our choices with respect to gender identities, sexual orientations, and gendersexuality in general. Woke to the warmth of the planet, we reconsider how we bring new life into being, how we invest in younger generations of Black people, and how we study the pluri/multiverses. We do not stop reproducing and otherwise creating, but we do so as an important part of our strategy for survival. We do not stop teaching and learning, but we do so with unequivocal commitment to indigenous epistemologies and cosmologies.

Tantalizing Tensions

Scientists have been wondering if they have stumbled on a new kind of physics. In this new physics, particles expected to resolve and live out their life span in one way instead resolve in another way.[82] Caroline Delbert explains, "The scientists at the European Organization for Nuclear Research (CERN) call B mesons 'tantalizing tensions,' since the particles break apart into different amounts of electrons and muons than the standard model of physics predicts they should. B mesons are paired quarks that move together and rapidly decay." The researchers who first reported an inconsistency with the principle of lepton universality when they analyzed proton-proton collision data noted that beauty mesons were transforming into strange mesons with emissions of either electrons and positrons, or muons and antimuons. They explain that this matters because "this violation of lepton universality would imply physics beyond the Standard Model, such as a new fundamental interaction between quarks and leptons."[83] There are times when we must ask: What are the forces at work in our physical and metaphysical existences? What are the expected and unexpected consequences of our collisions, interactions, fantasies, and decays? Can the behavior of these forces be reconciled with what we have theorized? If not, how must our theories change? Cheikh Anta Diop reminds us that we cannot ignore sovereign experience. And sovereign experience shows that our ways of moral reasoning and contemplations on justice are inadequate—especially in the face of the complexities of sexual diversities, diversities of sexual experiences, and diversities of moral constitution among consenting, moral, sexual agents.

Dunia Humanalities

In presenting a constructive, normative utopic Black sexuality, this is neither an attempt to essentialize Black(ness) or Black sexuality nor is it an exercise in Black supremacy or Black nationalism (supplanting white supremacist ideologies, practices, and traditions with Black, Afrodiasporic ones).[84] Rather, in representing a maâtian ethic, a khemetic spirituality, a Black diasporic religious tradition, I offer alternative (i.e., Black, indigenous, and Afrodiasporic) points of origin for thought and meaning making, alternative epistemological and hermeneutical centers. These alternatives insist upon a new baseline, different foundational knowledge. Here, to know religious or social ethics—and to do religious or social ethics with a solid foundation—is to know *maât* (and other moral codes among indigenous people subjugated over the past two millennia). Knowledge of ancient Greek, medieval, and Enlightenment European ethics is a specialization, is optional, is marginal. Notwithstanding Greek and European domination of global ideologies and politics over the past two millennia, past domination is no justification for continued domination or epistemic priority. Similarly, global, nationalist, hegemonic, imperialist nation-states—and their predominantly white, male, and cisgender leaders—should not (over)determine *dunia* (i.e., world) futures. Nor should multinational corporations or underground human sex trafficking empires and their leaders determine *dunia* futures.

As with any sacred text adopted from a foreign place, people, or time, translations are numerous and diverse. Each seems to have its own emphasis. In Queen Afua's "42 Laws of Ma'at," drawn from the *Book of Coming Forth by Day from Night* (misnamed *The Egyptian Book of the Dead*), the laws specifically pertaining to sexuality are specified: "I will not abuse my sexuality," "I will not copulate with a man's wife," and "I will not copulate with a woman's husband."[85] Surely, one can ascribe to these a Judeo-Christian conservative sexual ethic. However, we can also decide to dig deeper, to pursue further, to understand the times and the contexts of these notes. Who and what is Maât—and why does she declare forty-two laws, including these? Previous chapters have clarified this in different ways. In this chapter, justice is being; Maât is being. In a close reading of Maât and maâtian texts and ethics in the Amarna period, Maulana Karenga quotes "Ay" ("the divine father"), saying of "Akhenaton": "'he placed Maat in my body.'"[86] For Karenga, this speaks to the ways that *maât* is both "concept *and* practice." However, it also points to a physical exchange that Karenga reads metaphorically and interprets as the "Ay" spoke of pedagogical transmission of "'the cosmic force of harmony, order, stability and security, coming down from the first creation as an organizing quality of created phenomena.'"[87] Maât was truth as "correspondence to reality," but also "righteousness."[88] And Maât was more. Karenga quotes "the nobleman, Tutu," of the Amarna period writing in an autobiographical inscription:

> I did not do what my majesty hates.
> My abomination is falsehood (*grg*) in my body.
> For it is the great abomination of Wanra (Akhenaton).
> To his majesty I presented Maat.
> For I know he lives by it.
> You are Ra who begat Maat.
> You appointed me as a hereditary noble,
> For my voice was not raised in the house of the king.
> My stride was not broad in the palace,
>
> And I did not accept the reward of falsehood
> To repress the righteous person for the sake of the wrongdoer.
> But I did justice (Maat) for the sake of the
> king, doing what he commanded of me.[89]

Here, Maât is not just a way of being, but also a being. Maât not only calls forth a way of being (i.e., a way of being with respect to sex and sexuality and relationship), but (again) is being. Maât is presented both as an other and as one's own self, one's own being. Maât is presented as something received into one's body. Maât is begotten. Ra begets Maât. Yes, Maât can also be done. However, Maât is also a being—and a being who invites the being of others. In contrast with simulacra, Maât invites being something that is both real and refers to something real. Maât's theriocephaly situates her perfectly as a Haraway Chthulucene representative—and brown embodiment of emergent strategy. Within her wings and heart-weighing feathers, Maât is the consummate artifici-ecological defender of being. One brings oneself to her, fully being—and giving account for oneself in one's contexts—and awaits Maât's determinations of truth as accuracy and righteousness. She offers the creative space for us to be and to be just—and, perhaps, to even be justice. I like to believe that the feather with which she weighs our hearts has a supernatural balancing quality within it that adjusts to ensure equality and equity appropriately. Maât disrupts power positions. She invites us to a *dunia* order of created phenomena that include our humanalities (i.e., our humanity plus sexuality, human sexualities, our sexual ways of being human, our human [pornographic, limited, expansive, creative, sacred, and basic] ways of being sexual).

Karenga opens us up to *dunia* terraspheric orientation as he walks us through the halls of Maât. However, the potential eternity that exists in those halls is static and stale. We are left wanting more of Maât. We want her to be more; we want her being more. We want to unlock and understand her code and, coding the world around us with her logic, we want to be ourselves individually and communally with unparalleled ontic force. We want the eternity of the expert masons whose intellect and skill continue to speak through ancient Egyptian sites; we who long for justices do not desire the incestuously autocratic way of the pharaohs. We seek a way that is honest about the unspeakable harm of Enlightenment thought, Christianity, and Islam on people of African descent.[90] With Sylvia Wynter, we can acknowledge the beautiful—and not so beautiful—ways that Black people around the world have adopted and adapted these models. However, we cannot concede to these religio-philosophical models. We cannot deny Black humanity—in the most moral and human senses of humanity. We cannot (and should not) require that religion—or these religious postures—be our portion (or the portion of others). Wynter reminds us that in the fullness of our humanity, we are deeply, fundamentally geographic and biological beings becoming. We are in metamorphosis.

For some, there may seem to be a frightening proximity between problematic empirical Afrodiasporic sexualities (i.e., Five Percenters, Hebrew Israelites, patriarchal polyamorous cults, patriarchal cults/religious institutions that singularly cater to the polyamory of a single [cult leader/pastor] patriarch) and normatively constructive utopic Afrodiasporic sexualities

7.1: Mickalene Thomas, *Sleep: Deux Femmes Noires*, 2012, presents a possibility of Black sexual intimacy—one that might constitute a homosexuality. Piecing together the puzzle of quilted frames and diverse geographic landscapes, Thomas evokes the glocal possibilities of an eco-conscious *dunia* orientation. *Source: Mickalene Thomas: Origin of the Universe*, ed. Lisa Melandri (Santa Monica, CA: Santa Monica Museum of Art, 2012), 65, plate 20.

that celebrate sexual freedoms and creativity.[91] Of course, a decisively paired distinguishing factor between problematic empirical Black sexualities and normatively constructive, utopic Black sexualities is position-power. Problematic empirical Black sexualities bear the signs, symbols, embodiment, content, and character emblematic of hegemonic power positions. What could come out of democratically organized approaches to thinking about, talking about, exploring, and expressing Black sexuality—democratically organized approaches designed to destigmatize consensual adult sexual diversity and explicitly empower those who have been historically marginalized and/or are more vulnerable as a result of intersecting factors of race, class, gender, sexuality, and ability (among other identifiers)? Insofar as such approaches would disrupt and dismantle hegemonic power positions, these approaches would lay solid foundations for normatively constructive utopic Black sexualities that celebrate sexual freedoms and creativity.

Will the Black web of pornography fan flames of racism, sexism, classism, heterosexism, and ableism? Will the Black web of pornography provide necessary space for fantasies that provide an opportunity for virtual exploration while protecting against physical expression? Might the Black web of pornography lead down both or neither of these paths?[92] Each of these creative and created spaces are possible—along with countless others. Where there are simulacra and simulation, organic and inorganic, doing and being justice, pornography as exploitation and pornography as autobiography, democracy as nomenclature and democracy as people power, perhaps we can find ourselves being (with) Maât in utopias of post(trans)national humanalities.

~ * ~

A Black Sexual Ethic

Pornographers recode and be(come) just in writing intimacies (i.e., pornographies) through personal moral agency. The codes of pimps of capitalist commodification, exploitation, trafficking, surveillance, and respectability are secondary to these primary voices.

A Maâtian Code of Justice

Maât flies between space and time—in, through, and beyond halls of justice—she is more than goddess, more than human, more than bird, more than winged creature. Her breadth, span, and distance exceed pluriverses and guide us through the dynamic eternity of post(trans)national humanalities.

conclusion Re-covering Maât

Maâtian justice is stealthy. However, we know some of what Maât does. She flies. She jumps—and entangles. She dances—and shouts. She puzzles. She be's—and codes. She imagines—and we imagine her.

Black sexualities, like the delta of the Nile River, offer a confluence of possibilities. The waters subside and famines come, but the rains fall, the soil is made fertile, and floods come too. Though there is not much evidence of moral affirmation of same-sex intimacies in ancient Egypt, there are accounts of religious and nonreligious sex work and a necropolis section in the Valley of Kings meant for women and some children only.[1] Lise Manniche writes:

> In the period of Egyptian history called the Amarna Period the difference between the sexes appears to be almost obliterated. Men and women of the upper circles imitate the royal couple and wear identical loose garments, so thin and diaphanous that they reveal that the ideal image of the body underneath was virtually the same for men and women. It is the male image adapting to the female. King Akhnaten depicts himself in the image of his wife Nefertiti with small firm breasts, narrow waist and heavily rounded hips and thighs. As Nefertiti sometimes wears diadems and crowns it is often difficult to tell the difference between the two. There was probably a well-defined ideology behind these iconographical

peculiarities. Possibly the king regarded himself as the male and female principles united in his own creative person.[2]

Such gender fluidity is not limited to the Amarna period. Manniche also tells the story of the advent of one of the women pharaohs of Egypt, King Hatshepsut, elsewhere referenced as Queen Hatshepsut. Ruling from 1473 to 1458 BCE, Hatshepsut's title is not the only thing queer about this king/queen. Hatshepsut, like other kings, had to prove her legitimate right to rule. Some pharaohs did this by declaring that the god had come to them in a dream or a statue of the divine had pointed to them; others did this by identifying themselves as a child (the son) of the god. Hatshepsut self-identified as the fruit of a divine sexual liaison between her earthly mother and the god Amun. Manniche shares a translation of this story in which Amun "disguises himself as Tuthmosis I, husband of Queen Ahmosis." The text of this story can be found on one of the walls of the queen's temple at Deir el-Bahari:

> Amun found the queen in the inner rooms of the palace. When smelling the divine scent, she woke up, and she smiled to him. At once he proceeded towards her. He lusted after her, and he gave her his heart. He allowed her to see him in his real god's figure, having come close to her. She rejoiced at his virility, and love for him flowed through her body. The palace became inundated by the scent of god, it smelled like in Put (land of incense).
>
> Thereupon the god did what he wished with her. She made him rejoice over her, and she kissed him. "How splendid it is to see you face to face. Your divine strength engulfs me, your dew is all through my limbs!" The god once more did what he wished with her, and he said, "Truly, Hatshepsut will be the name of the child I have placed in your belly, for this was what you exclaimed." (Urk. IV, 219, 13–220, 6)[3]

Though I traveled to Egypt in 2018 on a quest to find Maât—to see evidence of her presence, her value, her significance, her worth, and her dignity in the visible remnants of ancient Egypt, no surprise was more wonderful than my introduction to King Hatshepsut. At her palace, multiple statuary reliefs of this pharaoh—some seeming like forty feet high or more to me—towered like pillars. They showed her with her arms crossed—fist to shoulder, fist to shoulder—a sign of her life of power, a sign of her resting in power, a sign of her eternal power.

I did encounter Maât in expected and unexpected places. I encountered other female pharaohs. I encountered evidence of Nubian strength, keys of life and signs of fertility, and Akhenaten's gender fluidity and early monotheism. I encountered Nefertiti and Nefertari; I encountered Hathor and Isis. However, Hatshepsut stood tall and strong in a unique way: not god herself, but the child (daughter, son) of god; her very name the exclamation of divine-human erotic passion; a fierce and long-standing leader in her own right.

Around the same time I was beginning to understand my own sexual attraction to people who shared my gender identity, I also entered a Black bookstore for the first time in my memory. Ms. Thalia Harris took me to this bookstore in Wilmington, Delaware, the name of which I do not recall. There are two things I remember from that day. She bought me Alex Haley's *Autobiography of Malcolm X* and a pair of silver earrings that she explained to me were shaped in the image of Nefertiti's head. She told me a bit about Nefertiti, an African queen. I was assured that I, she, we, people of African descent had come from just such a royal lineage. I read *Malcolm X*. I rocked those earrings. I explored the interests of my changing body. I entertained the possibilities of boyfriends and explored those attractions some, but I fell in love with a girl a few years older than me. These things happened all at once for me. A few years into this love and attraction I could not let go, my diary betrayed me to my prying, present parents. I was asked rhetorically: Surely you know it's a sin, your attraction, your love for someone of your same gender? I did not know that, but I did. I did know that, but I did not. What I knew was that for my parents in that moment, there was only one right answer: yes, I know (what you think, what it says in the Bible, what we are supposed to believe). It would take some time before I could hear the voice of the Divine in me assuring me that my attraction to people of my same gender was not a sin, did not render me hell-bound, and would not compromise my fulfilling my Divine call on earth or through eternity. My pride in Blackness, my knowing that Black was beautiful, my acceptance that Blackness was a royal inheritance was soon manifested as a conviction that demanded voice and public proclamation. Similarly, racial equality and equity—along with a call for reparations—became a rallying cry in my spirit. With these, as tensions roiled within me and outside of me, I knew that my gender identity and sexual orientation were also aspects of this life—of my life—that would demand my courage and my voice. Hatshepsut and Maât have helped me find that voice.

Justice is not an option; justices are not optional. Maât is not an option. We live by and on *maât* (i.e., justice/s). In my youth, I needed a justice that could fly, jump, dance, shout, entangle, puzzle, be, and code. I needed a justice more creative than the Clarence Thomas and Anita Hill proceedings. I needed a justice more robust than the Rodney King beatings and unchecked police. I needed a justice that could do more than Spike Lee and John Singleton on the big screen. I needed a justice that could better translate the O. J. Simpson trial and the murders that precipitated it. I needed more of justice. In my maturation, I also recognize that justice needed and needs more of me—and more of us. We fly, jump, dance, shout, entangle, puzzle, be, and code justice. We do justice; we do justices. We are the (prospective) doers of justices.

Far too often we let our differences of conviction and experience stifle our imagination with respect to justice. If I let homophobia stop me from engaging Maât, how much would I have missed of what justice can be? If I let ingrained biases against sexuality or sex work, homosexualities or interracial marriage, heterosexual marriage or pornography drive my inquiry, how might I have been blinded to the moral agency and sexual ethics of those who are living out lives that include these aspects of human sexual existence? What might we all miss about how we can reorganize our personal and collective lives together when we dig our heels into our fundamentalisms, xenophobias, and selective literalisms? What do we miss with our bigotries, prejudices, and biases?

Moving with *maât* (i.e., justice/s) through each chapter, we have integrated an intersection of Black sexual lives and experiences, vindicationist voices, the political implications of this analysis of Black sexual ethics as it reorients justice, a scientific connection that can be made through the study of physics, and a way that these elements altogether might change the thinking-doing-being of *maât* (i.e., justice/s). This journey together has just begun. There is so much more to be written and researched about the lives and beliefs of the humans and *nṯrw* of khemet. We should not assume what we will find—or that all we find will verify what we already believe. However, we can rest assured that it will be a quare journey on which we will keep on discerning and discovering into the horizons of eternity. We can trust that our sovereign experience will remain a relevant pointer in our personal and collective spiritual and moral compasses.

Black sexuality will continue to be contested space. However, this book has provided options for those of us who are unmoved by conservative orthodoxies enslaved to hegemonic, heteropatriarchal political interests within religious and secular institutions, and evident at every level of human governance. When we dare to allow science and sovereign experience to help us hear the voice of G*d, the voice of the Divine within us, the voice of Maât, the voice of those who are not like us, we open ourselves to new possibilities of understanding, connection, and holiness. When we dare to retrieve—to go back and fetch—what we have left behind in ancient khemet, we find that our thinking, being, and doing have new meaning and value. We confirm our own dignity and that of all in this *dunia*, this terrasphere. We become new. We become fertile. We become relevant. We become connected. We become. We are transformed.

In the new world, with a new ethic, that Cheikh Anta Diop imagines,

> Ethics stem from philosophy as the practical behavior comes out of the idea that one has about things. . . .
>
> It is possible to demonstrate the originally "rational" foundation of all moral behavior, for any given mental level. That which is feeling and moral was first conceived as saving knowledge in the natural order.
>
> A new ethics that largely takes into account objective knowledge (in Jacques Monod's sense) and, in short, the interests of the human species is in the process of being built; it is only difficult to internationalize it because of conflicts of national interests.
>
> Ecology, defending the environment, tends to become the foundation of a new ethnic [*sic*] of the species, based on knowledge: the time is not far off when the pollution of nature will become a sacrilege, a criminal act, even and mainly for the atheist, because of the fact that the future of humanity is at stake; what knowledge or the "science of the epoch" decrees as harmful to the whole group thus becomes progressively a moral prohibition. . . .
>
> The end of genocide coincides with the emergence of an international opinion. This fact has brought about a modification of the behavior of the capitalist universe toward the weak; and the phenomenon is irreversible; the result is a forced progress of the world's ethical conscience.[4]

Forty years since these words were first published, will we hear Diop with the ears of Maât? Will we recognize what calls and unites us into necessary ethical unity for the sake of human futures? Will we recognize that justices demand our ongoing fight for the future of the planet and the ecology of which we are a part? Will we recognize that justices demand our tireless resistance to any form of bigotry or prejudice—including gender and sexual bigotries and prejudices—that lead to fatal interpersonal violences and genocide? Will we recognize that giving space for the moral agency of others, for others to work out their souls' salvation (as they deem necessary), is not a betrayal of our faith or any great commission?

Whether we navigate ~~sexually~~, in the heterexpectations of marriage, in homosexualities, in interracialities, or in pornographies, we live, move, and have our beings Black, quare, and elsewhere with Maât.[5] We look back; we go forward.[6] We go back and fetch what we need for our future. In the fullness of our Black sexual beings, in our quareing justices—with Maât, as Maât, the *nṯrt* with wings as a bird—we ready ourselves for new philosophies, new ethics, new calls of truth, right, justice, and new worlds.

And we show up for the creation of quare worlds. Can you see us justicing together?[7]

>Black'n'brown lovers of people—siblings, sisters,
>and brothers—stepped out on mud,
>And we looked around and said,
>We're lonely—we'll make us a quare world.
>
>And as far as our eyes could see
>Misunderstanding covered everything,
>Stranger than "Blacks Only" signs
>Against the rolling stream of freedom riders
>
>Then we smiled,
>And wisdom arrived,
>And ignorance crawled over stone walls,
>And wisdom spoke her truth,
>And we said, "That's good!"
>
>Then we reached out and drew wisdom from
>our ancestors,
>And wisdom danced around in our womanish
>minds
>Until we made ourselves clothes of flesh;
>And we saw our reflection glow with trees
>and sky in the waters;
>And the fabric left from making our flesh
>We quilted it together
>And flung it into all the desolate places
>Comforting those cast from land and

people
Then down within
Others Black'n'brown and queer
We cast a stellar spark
And we said, "That's good!"

Then we walked around—
And our flesh made us (hyper)invisible
And others Black'n'brown and queer or otherwise opaque were before us
The quilt warmed them
But they stood in puddles
And we paused to consult our mothers
They reminded us how to be silent
They taught us when to act up

Then we sat with our elders, listened, and heard:
"Yonder they don't love your flesh."
So we returned to the puddles
And we asked those standing to share their stories
We collected accounts of joys and traumas
Treating the traumas with a healing balm
We stitched these together with a binding of love
Those gathered saw one another,
And, between these sacred texts of flesh, love abounded

Then Black'n'brown queer families were born,
Mothers and brothers from other mothers
and brothers empowering
Sisters and others forging
Communities fortified against battery and abuse teaching
"Deviance" as an "art of resistance"
And we smiled again,
"And the rainbow appeared,"
And curled itself around our shoulders.

Then we raised our arms in praise and waved our flags in worship
In the sanctuaries of ignorance and in the halls of denial
And we said, **"Bring forth! Bring forth!"**
And before the benedictions pronounced or the degrees conferred
Black'n'brown and queer poems and songs
And films and books
Filled Youtube and MetaFriend
Fancified Insta and informed Twitter's alternative
Flew in the face of foul forms of bigotry and xenophobia
And we said, **"That's good!"**

Then we composed,
And we surveyed our past and considered our futures
We looked at all we had made
We looked at our wise flesh
We looked at our covering quilt
We looked at the sacred texts of our stories
We looked at our families
We looked at our socials
We looked in our world
With all its life (and) potential
And we said, "We're lonely still."

Then we walked community onto dry sand
We kept to ourselves for a beat to debrief
muddied feet rinsed in the river we sat on tree branches
The cipher yet moving like a rolling stone
Hand to hand and head-to-head
Till we thought, "We'll make us a quare world!"

Out from the pulpit and the altar
We scooped holy oil, sticky with blood
And into convocations—ticks from Pulse nightclub—we flicked
    some drops
And there—Our Great Power rising
We, the stuff of clay
We, the stuff of stars
We, the stuff of seventh sight
Our Great Power rising,

like mothers of the ballroom meeting aunties who have held our
    secrets in confidence,
We called all our children out into
a global electric slide
Til we all knew love as we danced "the dance electric"[8]

Then into quare world blew exhalations of life,
And living souls flourished quarely.
Amen. Axé. Hotep.

notes

Introduction

1. Johnson, "'Quare' Studies," 1–25.
2. Walker, *In Search of Our Mothers' Gardens*, 80.
3. Crawley, *Lonely Letters*, 4–5 and elsewhere; Johnson, "'Quare' Studies."
4. This term is a feminine singular form of *nṯr/netcher* (masculine singular) and, from this transliteration of ancient Egyptian hieroglyphics, is often translated as *goddess* in English—though the terms *goddess* or *goddesses* do not adequately capture the senses of Egyptian deities, mythological or religious characters, and/or the royalty who adopt aspects of the divine—or to whom aspects of the divine are ascribed. The plural form is *nṯrw/netcherw*. Obenga, *African Philosophy*, 27.
5. Obenga, *African Philosophy*, 187.
6. Obenga, *African Philosophy*, 203.
7. Obenga, *African Philosophy*, 201.
8. Obenga, *African Philosophy*, 202–3.
9. Amun is the "Hidden One," the central deity of Thebes, king of the deities in the Middle Kingdom and nationally worshipped in the New Kingdom; Amun eventually merged with Ra, the sun deity, becoming Amun-Ra.
10. Obenga, *African Philosophy*, 191 (quoting Michel Gitton, "La cosmologie égyptienne"), 606.
11. Djehuty or Djehuti is a *nṯr*, also known as Thoth, associated with the moon, writing, and knowledge. He presided over all scholars and scribes. He is

primarily shown as an ibis-headed chimera; however, the baboon is sometimes used to depict Djehuty instead of this theriocephalic form.
12 Cooney, *Woman Who Would Be King*.
13 Obenga, *African Philosophy*, 191–92.
14 Obenga, *African Philosophy*, 191–92.
15 Consistent with Obenga's explanation of the levels of Maât, Maulana Karenga writes, "*Maat is rightness in the spiritual and moral sense in three realms: the Divine, the natural and the social.* In its expansive sense, *Maat is an interrelated order of rightness which requires and is the result of right relations with and right behavior towards the Divine, nature and other humans.* As moral thought and practice, *Maat is a way of rightness* defined especially by the practice of the Seven Cardinal Virtues of truth, justice, propriety, harmony, balance, reciprocity and order. Finally, as a foundation and framework for the moral ideal and its practice, *Maat is the constantly achieved condition and requirements for the ideal world, society and person*, i.e., the Maatian world, the Maatian society, and the Maatian person." Karenga, *Maat*, 10–11; Obenga, *African Philosophy*, 191–92.
16 Cooney, *Woman Who Would Be King*, 103.
17 Karenga, *Maat*, 9–10, quoting Tobin, "Ma'at and DIKE," 113–14.
18 The Portuguese completed their first transatlantic slave trade voyage to Brazil in 1526. The oldest known depiction of a blindfolded lady justice is found in Bern, Switzerland, and dated 1543; the Gerechtigkeitsbrunnen (fountain of justice), of which the blindfolded lady justice is the feature figure, was sculpted by Hans Gieng. Caviezel, Herzog, and Keller, *Kunstführer durch die Schweiz 3*, 320.
19 Hughes, *Collected Poems*, 31; Perry, *More Beautiful and More Terrible*, 121.
20 Consider Albert Einstein's theory of special relativity and its infamous equation $e = mc^2$ (where energy equals mass multiplied by the speed of light squared) alongside the role of Maât (and Maât's feather) in ancient Egyptian formulations of Judgment Day when the human heart is accounted righteous if it weighs less than Maât's feather. Einstein, *Relativity*.
21 Importantly, as Kara Cooney points out, the Maât of ancient Egypt was largely understood in the hieroglyphic records (primarily accounting for the perspective of the pharaonic elite) as the defender of the monarchy and culturally privileged class. Thus, balance in ancient Egypt was often interpreted as that which established and maintained pharaonic, monarchal order. However, (in theory) the qualities that distinguish the hearts of the righteous are identified according to what individuals have done (i.e., performed) in their earthly lives. Being part of the pharaonic line alone does not accord righteousness to individuals. Complicating the experience of Maât is the fact that many within the ruling elite are consistently claiming Maât, claiming their own righteousness—especially in their funerary designs. Cooney, *Woman Who Would Be King*; Mertz, *Temples, Tombs, and Hieroglyphs*.

22 I make this choice following the lead of Dianne M. Stewart and Tracey E. Hucks, who, in *Obeah: Africans in the White Imagination* and *Orisa: Africana Nations and the Power of Black Sacred Imagination*, volumes I and II of *Obeah, Orisa, and Religious Identity in Trinidad*, explain their orthographic interventions. Stewart notes that an awareness of "Afropessimist analytical interventions in black studies" leads her to "place terms such as 'world' and 'worldmaking' under erasure using the strikethrough feature (~~world~~, ~~worldmaking~~) to signal that [her] use of these words emerges from religious studies frameworks (rather than philosophical theories) concerning the role of sacred poetics (religious ideas, practices, symbols, myths, and invisible powers, deities, and spirits) in orienting Africana communities as they navigate their environments." She continues: "Similarly, mindful of the Afropessimist argument that blacks have no access to the human, when appropriate, I experiment with the terms '~~human~~,' ~~humanity~~, and '~~human being~~'" (*Orisa*, xii). While my use of the strikethrough feature does happen to be applied in a religious studies framework, it is not primarily an indicative of a distinction between philosophy and religion. Rather, I deploy the strikethrough feature to signify erasures and access with respect to sexuality as a fundamental aspect of humanity—as well as transcendent and transversing movement. Consistent with Stewart's response to Afropessimist indictments, I argue that sexuality is not and cannot be the same for ~~humans~~, ~~humanity~~, and ~~human beings~~ as it is for humans, humanity, and human beings; ~~humans~~, ~~humanity~~, and ~~human beings~~ have orientations, identities, and practices that refer to ~~sexuality~~.

23 Hegel, *Elements of the Philosophy of Right*; Žižek, "Hegel on Marriage."

24 Delbert, "Scientists Might Have Just Stumbled." *Dunia* is Kiswhahili for *world*. I use this alongside *terrasphere* to signal difference of place and difference of theoretical and practical approach to thinking about world organization. Here, through the Kiswahili, in concert with many vindicationists before me, I make this linguistic move as part of a nod to Pan-Africanism and its methodologies. I also think there is unique value in utilizing the Kiswahili here because it is a trade language with a Bantu base—having Arabic, English, and German roots. It is part of a protoglobalization narrative. However, in conjuction with the (Latin-rooted) *terrasphere*, *dunia* signals the contemporary, the historic, and the (culturally and otherwise) hybrid all at once.

25 Wesley Kabaila, who self-identifies as "an advocate of Kawaida since 1967, a member of the Us Organization" from 1967 to 1985, serving as its vice chair 1979–85, writes in an open letter:

> It is my opinion, that one of the reasons it remains believable that Dr. Karenga is a police agent in some circles, is because he has been dishonest about his involvement in the torture of two sisters, for which he served 4 years and his current wife, Tiamoyo served a stint also. I wish to state here, unequivocally, that he and his wife not only tortured these two

sisters for a period of over 3 weeks, but also directed two young brothers in the torture also. Prior to this period of torture, he also locked up his first wife, Haiba, in a tiger cage that was housed in the garage of a home he leased in Inglewood, California. Dr. Karenga also hit on wives of some of his closest confidantes and I personally know of one sister, who is writing a book in which she asserts that he attempted to rape her. . . .

My question is, how can Dr. Karenga continue to call himself a High Priest of Maat or Master Teacher, when the very principles he writes about, seemingly do not apply to him.

In sum, I challenge those of us who still consider ourselves Kawaida advocates, to demand from Dr. Karenga an apology for the continued lying, which has affected the credibility of those of us who have defended him. But even more than that, he owes an apology and release to the sister he tortured and to her family which was threatened if she broke silence about her true torturer. If we, who consider ourselves revolutionary, do not check and challenge this kind of behavior, then our revolution is not even worth fighting for. I respect and recognize Dr. Karenga, for his theoretical and practical contributions to our struggle, but that does not excuse his torture tactics of [a] young (18) black woman, lying about it to his followers or the masses, and the continuing cover up of it, although he has already been convicted and served the time.

"On Dr. Maulana Karenga: An Open Letter by Wesley Kabaila." See Griffin, "Op-Ed," for an explanation of another approach to acknowledging both Karenga's contributions and inexcusable faults. Also note two reports regarding Karenga's conviction and sentencing: *New York Times*, "Karenga Arrested on Coast"; Einstoss, "Karenga Sentenced."

26 Spillers, *Black, White, and in Color*; Crenshaw, "Mapping the Margins."
27 Muñoz, *Cruising Utopia*, 29.
28 Moltmann, *Theology of Hope*.
29 I cite lyrics of the Negro national anthem and include these lyrics here in their entirety:

> Lift every voice and sing
> Till earth and heaven ring,
> Ring with the harmonies of Liberty;
> Let our rejoicing rise
> High as the listening skies,
> Let it resound loud as the rolling sea.
> Sing a song full of the faith that the dark past has taught us,
> Sing a song full of the hope that the present has brought us.
> Facing the rising sun of our new day begun,
> Let us march on till victory is won.

Stony the road we trod,
Bitter the chastening rod,
Felt in the days when hope unborn had died;
Yet with a steady beat,
Have not our weary feet
Come to the place for which our fathers sighed?
We have come over a way that with tears has been watered,
We have come, treading our path through the blood of the slaughtered,
Out from the gloomy past,
Till now we stand at last
Where the white gleam of our bright star is cast.

God of our weary years,
God of our silent tears,
Thou who hast brought us thus far on the way;
Thou who hast by Thy might
Led us into the light,
Keep us forever in the path, we pray.
Lest our feet stray from the places, our God, where we met Thee,
Lest, our hearts drunk with the wine of the world, we forget Thee;
Shadowed beneath Thy hand,
May we forever stand.
True to our God,
True to our native land.

Johnson, "Lift Every Voice and Sing"; NAACP, "Lift Every Voice and Sing."
30 Kee, *Cambridge Annotated Study Bible*, Lamentations 3:22–23; Anderson and Henderson, "Great Is Thy Faithfulness," Hymn #84.
31 Crawley, *Lonely Letters*, 4–5 and elsewhere. The phrase "keep on keepin' on" that Carlton Pearson quotes "Mother Sherman" as saying is also common Black church vernacular. Pearson, "Mother Sherman Story."
32 Diop, *Civilization or Barbarism*, 370.
33 In 1960, Frantz Fanon stated in an address to the Accra Positive Action Conference: "Violence in everyday behaviour, violence against the past that is emptied of all substance, violence against the future, for the colonial regime presents itself as necessarily eternal. We see, therefore, that the colonized people, caught in a web of a three-dimensional violence, a meeting point of multiple, diverse, repeated, cumulative violences, are soon logically confronted by the problem of ending the colonial regime by any means necessary" (*Political Writings*, 654). Echoing this sentiment, Malcolm X stated in a 1964 speech in Harlem: "Anytime we know that an unjust condition exists and it is illegal and unjust, we will strike at it by any means necessary. And strike also at whatever and whoever gets in the way"; putting it even plainer: "That's our motto. We want

freedom by any means necessary. We want justice by any means necessary. We want equality by any means necessary" ("Malcolm X's Speech at the Founding Rally"). The writers of the 2017–21 television series *Black Lightning* expand on this concept articulating a central call-and-response mantra at the heart of the character and leadership of Principal Jefferson Pierce (also known as Black Lightning) at Garfield High School (Berlanti, *Black Lightning*):

> JEFFERSON PIERCE: *Where's the future?*
>
> STUDENTS: Right here.
>
> JEFFERSON PIERCE: *And whose life is this?*
>
> STUDENTS: Mine.
>
> JEFFERSON PIERCE: *And what are you gonna do with it?*
>
> STUDENTS: Live it by any means necessary.

One. A Prolegomenon

1   Walker, *In Search of Our Mothers' Gardens*, 80. Also see Cox Jackson, *Gifts of Power*.
2   Walker, *In Search of Our Mothers' Gardens*, 82.
3   Walker, *In Search of Our Mothers' Gardens*, 81–82.
4   Margulies, *Roots*; Dash, *Daughters of the Dust*; Leath, "Revising Jezebel Politics."
5   Young, *Black Queer Ethics*.
6   Higginbotham, *Righteous Discontent*; Cohen, "Deviance as Resistance"; Townes, *Womanist Ethics*.
7   Tinsley, *The Color Pynk*, 5. Consider Tinsley's terminology and definition:

> Black Femme-inist
>
> (with apologies, love, and reverence to Alice Walker and E. Patrick Johnson)
>
> (1) n.—A Black-identified member of the LGBTQIA+ community who embodies resistive femininity. Believes that the dismantling of misogynoir, femmephobia, and transmisogyny are necessary for Black freedom. Knows that Black freedom is necessary for the dismantling of misogynoir, femmephobia, and transmisogyny. Can be cis or trans, binary or nonbinary, AFAB (assigned female at birth) or AMAB (assigned male at birth). Is creative with race, gender, and sexuality, recognizing that creativity is not a luxury for those of us who are Black, queer, feminine, and never meant to thrive.
>
> (2) adj.—Loves other Black femmes, erotically and politically. Practices collaborative solidarity. Recognizes the reality of nonbinary vaginas

and biologically femme penises. Knows love is a bustling highway and not a one-way street.
(3) adj.—Unapologetically Black and beautiful. Enjoys roses while they're still here. Loves stars and STAR. Loves love. Loves themself. Regardless.
(4) Femme-inist is to feminist as pynk is to pink.

8   This is not land grabbing, but storytelling as a way of laying claim to belonging on earth (i.e., terra). I offer "terra-story" as a counternarrative. Specifically, it is a counternarrative to terra nullius. Here I am intentionally evoking the international legal doctrine of *territorium nullius* (Institut de droit international, 1888) (Fitzmaurice, *Sovereignty, Property and Empire*, 289) and terra nullius (introduced as a term with *territorium nullius*). In addition to debates about the first uses of terra nullius, there are also debates about the relationship between this term and the roman legal principle of res nullius (i.e., "nobody's thing") that was part of private Roman law between 753 BCE and 395 CE. Lauren Benton and Benjamin Straumann make a strong case for the claim that terra nullius stems from res nullius directly. Sven Lindqvist, in *Terra Nullius*, exposes just how devastating this legal doctrine has been and continues to be for indigenous populations—and how this doctrine justified genocidal exterminations and colonization throughout the globe. Lindqvist's book begins:

> *Terra nullius*. From the Latin terra, earth, ground, land, and nullius, no one's.
>
> Thus: no one's land, land not belonging to anybody. Or at any rate, not to anybody that counts.
>
> Originally: land not belonging to the Roman Empire.
>
> In the Middle Ages: land not belonging to any Christian ruler.
>
> Later: land to which no European state as yet lays claim. Land that justly falls to the first European state to invade the territory.
>
> Empty land. Uninhabited land. Land that will soon be uninhabited because it is populated by inferior races, condemned by the laws of nature to die out. Land where the original inhabitants are, or can soon be rendered, so few in number as to be negligible.
>
> The legal fictions summed up as terra nullius were used to justify the European occupation of large parts of the global land surface. In Australia this meant legitimizing the British invasion and its accompanying acts of dispossession and the destruction of indigenous society. (3–4)

While Lindqvist includes the Australian Supreme Court's Mabo Decision outlawing the concept of "'*terra nullius*,' thus revising the whole historic and legal basis of Australia as a nation" (226), he also exposes consorts of "attackers" and "revisionists" (109–10) whose scholarship focuses on denying the history, facticity, and/or impact of terra nullius in Australia. *Terra-story* acknowledges the terra nullius while also invoking the sacred landscapes, stories, art, and holistic contributions of the Warlpiri and other aboriginal and indigenous people (182, 197). Benton and Straumann, "Acquiring Empire by Law"; Masuzawa, *In Search of Dreamtime*.

9 Leath, *Is Queer the New Black?*, 63; for "blue notes," see Douglas, "Black and Blues."
10 Gramsci, *Selections from the Prison Notebooks*; Townes, *Womanist Ethics*.
11 Du Bois, *Souls of Black Folk*.
12 Long, *Significations*.
13 Césaire, *Discourse on Colonialism*. First published in 1955, this 2001 edition includes a 1967 interview with Rene Depestre in which Aimé Césaire explains "Antillean Négritude" in this way, having exposed the problematic trend of "assimilation" and "bovarism":

> Our struggle was a struggle against alienation. That struggle gave birth to Negritude. Because Antilleans were ashamed of being Negroes, they searched for all sorts of euphemisms for Negro: they would say a man of color, a dark-complexioned man, and other idiocies like that.... That's when we adopted the word *nègre*, as a term of defiance ... and then I took the liberty of speaking of *négritude*. There was in us a defiant will, and we found a violent affirmation in the words nègre and négritude.... But if someone asks me what my conception of Negritude is, I answer that above all it is a concrete rather than an abstract coming to consciousness. What I have been telling you about—the atmosphere in which we lived, an atmosphere of assimilation in which Negro people were ashamed of themselves—has great importance. We lived in an atmosphere of rejection, and we developed an inferiority complex. I have always thought that the black man was searching for his identity. And it has seemed to me that if what we want is to establish this identity, then we must have a concrete consciousness of what we are—that is, of the first fact of our lives: that we are black; that we were black and have a history, a history that contains certain cultural elements of great value; and that Negroes were not, as you put it, born yesterday, because there have been beautiful and important black civilizations. At the time we began to write people could write a history of world civilization without devoting a single chapter to Africa, as if Africa had made no contributions to the world. Therefore we affirmed that we were Negroes and that we were proud of it, and that we thought that Africa was not some sort of blank page in the history of humanity; in sum, we asserted that our Negro heritage was worthy of respect, and that this heritage was not relegated to the past, that its values were values that could still make an important contribution to the world. (89–92)

14 Imani e Wilson to author, May 15, 2022.

15 Wilson to author, May 15, 2022; Long, *Significations*, 9.
16 Diop, *Civilization or Barbarism*, 211.
17 Kohan, *Orange Is the New Black*; Whitfield et al., "Queer Is the New Black?"; Leath, *Is Queer the New Black?*
18 Johnson, "'Quare' Studies," 2.
19 Walker, *In Search of Our Mothers' Gardens*, xi–xii; Phillips, *Womanist Reader*, 19. In her introduction, Layli Phillips also offers the following definition of *womanism*, which becomes a helpful point of reference for this work as well. "Womanism is a social change perspective rooted in Black women's and other women of color's everyday experiences and everyday methods of problem solving in everyday spaces, extended to the problem of ending all forms of oppression for all people, restoring the balance between people and the environment/nature, and reconciling human life with the spiritual dimension" (xx).
20 Drake, *Black Folk*, 32n18; Paris, *Spirituality of African Peoples*, 16–17.
21 Paris, *Spirituality of African Peoples*, 17.
22 Paris, *Spirituality of African Peoples*, 17.
23 Paris, *Spirituality of African Peoples*, 17.
24 Sylvia Wynter writes:

> In effect, because the systematically induced nature of black self-alienation is itself (like that, correlatively, of homosexual self-alienation) only a function (a map), if an indispensable one, of the enacted institutionalization of our present genre of the human, Man and its governing sociogenic code (the territory), as defined in the ethno-class or Western bourgeois biocentric descriptive statement of the human on the model of a natural organism (a model that enables it to over-represent its ethnic and class-specific descriptive statement of the human as if it were that of the human itself), then, in order to contest one's function in the enacting of this specific genre of the human, one is confronted with a dilemma. As a dilemma, therefore, it is a question not of the essentializing or non-essentializing of one's racial blackness, as Gates argues, but rather of the fact that one cannot revalorize oneself in terms of one's racial blackness and therefore of one's biological characteristics, however inversely so, given that it is precisely the biocentric nature of the sociogenic code of our present genre of being human that imperatively calls for the devalorization of the characteristic of blackness as well as of the Bantu-type physiognomy—in the same way as it calls, dialectically, for the over-valorization of the characteristic of whiteness and of the Indo-European physiognomy.

Here Wynter clarifies that the project of Black studies is not about "the essentializing or non-essentializing" of "blackness," as Henry Louis Gates Jr. has argued. Rather, the dilemma to be addressed through Black studies is about the human potential of Blackness and Black people. Focus on essentialism in Blackness discourse is a nod to the factual potential and relevance of biological race. Wynter suggests that attention to an essential Blackness is a categorical error. Interestingly, Wynter is ultimately sympathetic to many of the scholars and concepts Gates has dismissed through his fixation on the dilemma of essentializing contra nonessentializing. She retrieves scholars and concepts that center (the) (re)valorization (of Blackness). McKittrick, *Sylvia Wynter*, 117.

25 Muñoz, *Cruising Utopia*.
26 Cruse, *Crisis of the Negro Intellectual*. Cruse uses the term "Negro intelligentsia" interchangeably with (and more frequently than) "black intelligentsia."
27 Cruse, *Crisis of the Negro Intellectual*, 178, 180.
28 Marable, *Beyond Black and White*.
29 Armah, *Two Thousand Seasons*, 43 and throughout.
30 Consider "X. Of the Faith of the Fathers," where Du Bois writes:

> It is difficult to explain clearly the present critical stage of Negro religion. First, we must remember that living as the blacks do in close contact with a great modern nation, and sharing, although imperfectly, the soul-life of that nation, they must necessarily be affected more or less directly by all the religious and ethical forces that are to-day moving the United States. These questions and movements are, however, overshadowed and dwarfed by the (to them) all-important question of their civil, political, and economic status. They must perpetually discuss the "Negro Problem,"—must live, move, and have their being in it, and interpret all else in its light or darkness. With this come, too, peculiar problems of their inner life,—of the status of women, the maintenance of Home, the training of children, the accumulation of wealth, and the prevention of crime. All this must mean a time of intense ethical ferment, of religious heart-searching and intellectual unrest. From the double life every American Negro must live, as a Negro and as an American, as swept on by the current of the nineteenth while yet struggling in the eddies of the fifteenth century,—from this must arise a painful self-consciousness, an almost morbid sense of personality and a moral hesitancy which is fatal to self-confidence. The worlds within and without the Veil of Color are changing, and changing rapidly, but not at the same rate, not in the same way; and this must produce a peculiar wrenching of the soul, a peculiar sense of doubt and bewilderment. Such a double life, with double thoughts, double duties, and double social classes, must give rise to double words and double ideals, and tempt the mind to pretence or revolt, to hypocrisy or radicalism.
>
> In some such doubtful words and phrases can one perhaps most clearly picture the peculiar ethical paradox that faces the Negro of to-day and is tingeing and changing his religious life. Feeling that his rights and his

dearest ideals are being trampled upon, that the public conscience is ever more deaf to his righteous appeal, and that all the reactionary forces of prejudice, greed, and revenge are daily gaining new strength and fresh allies, the Negro faces no enviable dilemma. Conscious of his impotence, and pessimistic, he often becomes bitter and vindictive; and his religion, instead of a worship, is a complaint and a curse, a wail rather than a hope, a sneer rather than a faith. On the other hand, another type of mind, shrewder and keener and more tortuous too, sees in the very strength of the anti-Negro movement its patent weaknesses, and with Jesuitic casuistry is deterred by no ethical considerations in the endeavor to turn this weakness to the black man's strength. Thus we have two great and hardly reconcilable streams of thought and ethical strivings; the danger of the one lies in anarchy, that of the other in hypocrisy. The one type of Negro stands almost ready to curse God and die, and the other is too often found a traitor to right and a coward before force; the one is wedded to ideals remote, whimsical, perhaps impossible of realization; the other forgets that life is more than meat and the body more than raiment.

He perceives the presence and dangers of anarchy. And he notes the ways that the religious and political are inextricably linked in the lives of people of African descent. Du Bois, *Souls of Black Folk*, 143–44.

31 Du Bois, "Of the Sons of Master and Man," in *Souls of Black Folk*, 117–33.
32 Johnson, *Tragic Soul-Life*, 6–7.
33 Johnson, *Tragic Soul-Life*, 7.
34 DuBois, "Faith of the Fathers," in *Souls of Black Folk*, 134–46.
35 Long, *Significations*, 78–79.
36 Long, *Significations*, 79–80.
37 Long, *Significations*, 80.
38 Long, *Significations*, 204.
39 Holmes, *Race and the Cosmos*, 123.
40 Holmes, *Race and the Cosmos*, 123.
41 Holmes, *Race and the Cosmos*, 124.
42 *Merriam-Webster*, s.v. "physics," accessed February 22, 2022, https://www.merriam-webster.com/dictionary/physics.
43 Holmes, *Race and the Cosmos*, 10.
44 Holmes, *Race and the Cosmos*, 118–19.
45 Prescod-Weinstein, *Disordered Cosmos*, 20.
46 Prescod-Weinstein, *Disordered Cosmos*, 20–21.
47 Prescod-Weinstein, *Disordered Cosmos*, 47.
48 Prescod-Weinstein, *Disordered Cosmos*, 47–48.
49 Prescod-Weinstein, *Disordered Cosmos*, 48.
50 Prescod-Weinstein, *Disordered Cosmos*, 55.
51 Prescod-Weinstein, *Disordered Cosmos*, 48–49.

Two. Naming (and Transforming) Justice

1 Diop, *Civilization or Barbarism*, 370.
2 Young, *Black Queer Ethics*, 56.
3 Young, *Black Queer Ethics*, 57.
4 Young, *Black Queer Ethics*, 61; italics in original.
5 Cohen, "Deviance as Resistance."
6 Cohen, *Boundaries of Blackness*.
7 The works of Pauli Murray, James Baldwin, Marlon Riggs, André Leon Talley, and Mickalene Thomas—among countless others—come to mind. There is a fine line here between fetishizing and/or overemphasizing the creative gifts of LGBTQ people and acknowledging the creative gifts of LGBTQ people. Moreover, there is the question of what it is about LGBTQ contexts and experiences that they generate irruptive, uniquely creative contributions. The answer to this question might begin with a return to research in Black studies and Holocaust studies that speak to the impact of extreme trauma and oppression on cultural creativity.
8 Williams, "Womanist Theology."
9 Townes, *Womanist Ethics*, 2.
10 Townes, *Womanist Ethics*, 8.
11 Phillips, *Womanist Reader*, 60.
12 Williams, *Sisters in the Wilderness*; Grant, *White Women's Christ*.
13 Day, *Notes of a Native Daughter*, 62–63.
14 I also give some attention to the work of other US-oriented vindicationists as well as students of Négritude in and outside of the United States. However, this book primarily traces a genealogical line from Cheikh Anta Diop through Yosef Ben-Jochannan and John Henrik Clarke, through Joel Augustus Rogers and George G. M. James, through Frances Cress Welsing and Maulana Karenga, through Marimba Ani and Molefi Asante through Gregory Carr and Karen Hunter. However, there are countless scholars who could be included in this genealogical tracing. Moreover, one could trace this lineage in different ways. I allude to one such alternative with the inclusion of Négritude and scholars associated with it. An interesting genealogical path to follow with respect to Négritude would be from Aimé Césaire to Frantz Fanon to Sylvia Wynter, Lewis K. Gordon, and Anthony Bogues. I engage those named as part of this alternative trajectory for several reasons: they interrupt a largely Anglophilic trajectory, disrupt some of the harsher expressions of misogynoir and heterosexism evident in the primary lineage, and offer a broader vision of Pan-African possibilities building on different relationships with the Caribbean and African continent. These genealogies do overlap and intersect in important ways; however, I argue that these are two distinct routes of Black consciousness. And these two routes intersect and overlap with womanist

and Black liberation (Christian) theologies too, but such intersections and overlapping are often muted.

15 Here I am remembering that *ethnic* relates to a subgroup within a culture. Here I am also thinking about culture as multiple and layered.

16 Bernal, *Black Athena*; Lefkowitz and Rogers, *Black Athena Revisited*; Lefkowitz, *Not Out of Africa*.

17 Who wonders what makes this question racist? A Fanonian or Wynterian appeal to personhood is different for sure, related to some philosophic possibility and (yet) a philosophical possibility that does not deny this Egyptian history—or establish distance from it.

18 Holmes, *Race and the Cosmos*; Paris, *Spirituality of African Peoples*.

19 Hood, *Must God Remain Greek?*; Carter, *Race*. The work of Bible scholars of African descent has also addressed this lacuna. See Felder, *Stony the Road We Trod*, and especially Waters, "Who Was Hagar?" in that volume; Smith, Parker, and Dunbar Hill, *Bitter the Chastening Rod*, and especially Williams, "I Am a Human" in that volume.

20 Williams, *Sisters in the Wilderness*, 22. This passage refers to Genesis 16.13–14.

21 Williams, *Sisters in the Wilderness*, 23. Extensive treatment is given to the Egyptian creation myth referenced and to Hagar's Egyptianness on pages 21–27.

22 Tutu, *No Future without Forgiveness*; Stewart, *Three Eyes for the Journey*; Chimakonam, *Ezumezu*; Hucks, *Yoruba Traditions*.

23 Murray and Roscoe, *Boy-Wives and Female Husbands*.

24 Rachel Harding, Queer Theory and Candomblé, conversation via Zoom, March 26, 2021. Also see Beliso-De Jesús, *Electric Santería*; Gill, *Erotic Islands*; Strongman, *Queering Black Atlantic Religions*; Tinsley, *Ezili's Mirrors*; Pérez, "From the Throne to the Kitchen Stove."

25 Rodney, *How Europe Underdeveloped Africa*.

26 Duneier, *Sidewalk*.

27 Duneier, *Sidewalk*, 24.

28 Long, *Significations*, 204.

29 Diop, *Civilization or Barbarism*, 152.

30 Diop, *Precolonial Black Africa*, loc. 3001–2.

31 Thomas, "Erotics of Aryanism/Histories of Empire," 247.

32 Diop, *Civilization or Barbarism*, 370–71.

33 Ben-Jochannan, *Need for a Black Bible*, 104–5.

34 Clarke, "Homosexuality Is Not African."

35 Welsing, *Isis Papers*, 91–92.

36 Welsing, *Isis Papers*, 7–8; Welsing's claim regarding "degrading" sexual acts "not found in non-white cultures" is roundly refuted in Murray and Roscoe, *Boy-Wives and Female Husbands*; Amadiume, *Male Daughters, Female Husbands*. "The Color-Confrontation theory states that the white or color-deficient

Europeans responded psychologically, with a profound sense of numerical inadequacy and color inferiority, in their confrontations with the majority of the world's people—all of whom possessed varying degrees of color-producing capacity.... The experience of numerical inadequacy and genetic color inferiority led whites to implement a number of interesting, although devastating (to non-white peoples), psychological defense mechanisms.... One of the most important of these defense mechanisms was *reaction formation*, a response that converts (at the psychological level) something desired and envied but wholly unattainable, into something discredited and despised." Welsing, *Isis Papers*, 4–5.
37 Welsing, *Isis Papers*, 46.
38 Welsing, *Isis Papers*, 51.
39 Thomas, "Erotics of Aryanism/Histories of Empire," 236–37.
40 Thomas, "Erotics of Aryanism/Histories of Empire," 237.
41 Thomas, "Erotics of Aryanism/Histories of Empire," 251.
42 Thomas, "Erotics of Aryanism/Histories of Empire," 239.
43 Diop, *Civilization or Barbarism*, 370.
44 James, *Stolen Legacy*, 7.
45 James, *Stolen Legacy*, 25.
46 James, *Stolen Legacy*, 43, 54.
47 James, *Stolen Legacy*, 72, 78.
48 Karenga, *Maat*, 374, 380.
49 This is a rendering of patois for "my spirit does not take" or "my spirit takes" a person or thing. When "my spirit does not take" a person or thing, it means that the person or thing does not sit well with me, does not resonate, or does not agree with me. When "my spirit takes" a person or thing, it means that the person or thing does resonate, agree, or sit well with me. Jamaican friends like Charmaine Jackman have confirmed that these colloquialisms are common phrases in Jamaican patois.
50 Sandel, *Justice*, loc. 129. As it happens, Sandel's virtue-oriented approach is the approach that seems most complementary with a vindicationist revival. He writes at loc. 4069: "We've explored three approaches to justice. One says justice means maximizing utility or welfare—the greatest happiness for the greatest number. The second says justice means respecting freedom of choice—either the actual choices people make in a free market (the libertarian view) or the hypothetical choices people would make in an original position of equality (the liberal egalitarian view). The third says justice involves cultivating virtue and reasoning about the common good. As you've probably guessed by now, I favor a version of the third approach."
51 Sandel, *Justice*, loc. 2895.
52 MacIntyre, *After Virtue*; MacIntyre, *Whose Justice?*; Taylor, *Multiculturalism*; Walzer, *Thick and Thin*; Walzer, *Spheres of Justice*.

53 Also consider Terrence L. Johnson's treatment of Threadcraft in Johnson, *We Testify with Our Lives*, 24–25.
54 Threadcraft, *Intimate Justice*, 32.
55 Threadcraft, *Intimate Justice*, 33.
56 Johnson, *Tragic Soul-Life*, 9.
57 "Rendering" here in the sense of a perception, projection, and description of deviance and in the sense of (coercive) impacts of (an) agentive actor/s.
58 Long, *Significations*, 9.
59 Long, *Significations*, 89.
60 Long, *Significations*, 90.
61 Long, *Significations*, 7.
62 Long, *Significations*, 32.
63 Long, *Significations*, 107.
64 Long, *Significations*, 7–8.
65 Long, *Significations*, 204.
66 Townes, *Womanist Ethics*; Holmes, *Race and the Cosmos*.
67 Quote from Townes, *Womanist Ethics*, 18–26. For the "centered city," Long, *Significations*, 79.
68 Long, *Significations*, 91.
69 Long, *Significations*, 91.
70 Long, *Significations*, 91.
71 Townes, *Womanist Ethics*, 31.
72 Anderson, *Beyond Ontological Blackness*.
73 Wilderson, *Afropessimism*, 13.
74 Wilderson, *Afropessimism*, 15.
75 Anderson, *Beyond Ontological Blackness*, 158.
76 Hartman, *Scenes of Subjection*; Marriott, *Lacan Noir*; Jackson, *Becoming Human*; Warren, *Ontological Terror*; Wilderson, *Afropessimism*.
77 Townes, *Womanist Ethics*; Young, *Black Queer Ethics*.
78 I find it fascinating to consider the ways that people of African descent—often by force or socioenvironmental necessity—are established throughout the globe. Interestingly, the proportion of people of African descent outside of Africa exceeds the proportion of Europeans residing in Africa. Further study is necessary to determine the ratio of people of Asian descent living in Africa vis-à-vis people of African descent living in Asia. Notwithstanding the histories of slavery and colonialism that have caused the African diaspora—and the disproportionately poor socioeconomic conditions in which people of African descent often find ourselves outside of Africa, the sustained presence of people of African descent in diaspora speaks to cultural capacities of survival. In a further study, it would be helpful to evaluate the oppressive implications or resistance capacities of African nation-states that can be attributed to the entrenchment of people of European, Euro–North American, and Asian cultures.

79 Prescod-Weinstein, *Disordered Cosmos*. Prescod-Weinstein explains: "Dark matter isn't even necessarily real. 'Dark matter' as a term was coined in French in 1906 by Henri Poincaré, who called it matière obscure. Twenty-two years before, English astronomer Lord Kelvin first proposed in 1884 that 'many of our stars, perhaps a great majority of them, may be dark bodies'" (32). She continues, "Thanks to a variety of astronomical measurements, we—that is to say, most cosmologists and particle physicists—think 80 percent of the matter in the universe is what has come to be known as dark matter. Our current understanding of the universe suggests that the constituents of everything we have ever seen—the very stuff that we are made of—only makes up about 20 percent of the matter in the universe. The rest is dark matter" (33). Most importantly, because of the invisibility of "dark matter," Prescod-Weinstein challenges the contemporary trend among scholars in the humanities to invoke "dark matter" as a way of thinking and talking about contemporary Black life, identity, and experiences. She takes issue with explorations of "dark matter and Black sf writers" as "comparable phenomena" (98). She explains:

> In the case of dark matter, it's not completely clear why we don't understand it. It just hasn't worked out for us so far. This is partly because its very nature makes it fundamentally difficult to interact with. It is distinct in the universe specifically because it is elusive. We know little about it, but that is not for lack of trying. Indeed, we have spent millions of dollars trying to understand its nature, and we have sent some of our best trained and highly prized minds out into the theoretical and experimental world, hoping to learn more about it. By contrast, the hidden nature of Black writers is an entirely manufactured and not at all natural problem. There has traditionally been little effort to directly engage with the work of Black sf writers. The moment she went looking for them, as Thomas chronicles in her introduction, there the writers were, making themselves visible. (98–99)

Prescod-Weinstein variously explains the ways "dark matter" can be especially harmful as a physics concept correlated with Blackness inasmuch as such correlation reifies the stereotypical ideas about the invisibility, mystery, and sometimes even frightful danger of Black people. Also note Hartman, *Scenes of Subjection*; Warren, *Ontological Terror*; Wilderson, *Afropessimism*; Marriott, *Lacan Noir*; Jackson, *Becoming Human*.

80 Niebuhr, *Moral Man and Immoral Society*.

81 This "gerunding" may also be akin to what Townes writes of when she explains, "My use of countermemory throughout this book does not view memory and history as suspect. . . . It is to *begin* the work of dismantl*ing* evil" (italics in the original). The emphasis on the gerunding "-ing" of "dismantling" points toward the present, the ongoing, the active work of dismantling. Townes writes, "These are only parts of systemic evil and the difficulty in

exploring them points to a key reason why I use the present participle 'ing' with dismantle. To eradicate evil is a process, not an event" (5). She also situates "ing" as a part of womanist discourse through the work of Marcia Riggs's "mediating" ethic. We might think of dismantling as an aspect of the work of "justicing" (i.e., doing justice/s, acting justly, manifesting just conditions, enacting justice/s). Townes, *Womanist Ethics*, 27. Too, it is of interest to note that Maât has important significance to the Nubians of ancient Egypt. She has a high place of honor like that of the crocodile-headed god, Sobek—and is at times syncretistically associated with Mandulis, a distinctly Nubian goddess.

82 Traditionally, Maât's feathers are understood to be those of the ostrich—a bird that does not fly. However, the wings suggest an evolution that once included flight, as Nell Greenfieldboyce observes—and, I imagine, could include flight again in a future evolution. Greenfieldboyce, "Big Flightless Birds"; San Diego Zoo Wildlife Alliance, "Ostrich." Of ostriches, Caroline Arnold writes in *Ostriches and Other Flightless Birds*:

> Each feather is formed around a central shaft. The lower bare part of the shaft is called the quill. Beyond the quill, on each side of the shaft, are tiny feathery strands called barbs. Most birds have barbs that are joined together with small hooks called barbules. They make the feathers appear smooth. Ostrich feathers are unusual because they do not have barbules. Instead, their feathers form softly flowing plumes. Another difference between ostrich feathers and those of most birds is their shape. The barbs of the feathers of most birds are shorter on one side of the shaft than on the other. Ostrich feathers have barbs of equal length. Because of its even balance, the ancient Egyptians used the ostrich's wing feather as a symbol of truth and justice. (12)

While visiting ancient Egyptian sites that reflect the importance of Maât, Emad Salama (August 2021) explained that it is believed that the equal number of feathers on each side of the ostrich is what distinguished the feathers of the ostrich as an appropriate symbol for Maât and measure of the just balance of the soul in the Hall of Justice on a person's day of judgment.

83 Wilkinson, *Complete Gods*, 150–52.
84 Wilkinson, *Complete Gods*, 150–52.
85 Wilkinson, *Complete Gods*, 150–52.
86 This term is a masculine plural form of *ntr/netcher* (masculine singular) and signifies the ancient Egyptian pantheon. While the terms *god* and *gods* do not always capture the senses of Egyptian deities, mythological or religious characters, and/or the royalty who adopt aspects of the divine—or to whom aspects of the divine are ascribed—forms of the words *god* and *gods* are the most common English translations of the forms of this word. Obenga, *African Philosophy*, 27.

87 Wilkinson, *Complete Gods*, 150–52.
88 Walker, *Temple of My Familiar*.
89 And entangling.
90 And shouting.
91 And turning.
92 And coding.
93 Imani e Wilson in "James Baldwin and Music."

Three. Flying Justice

1 Cannon, *Katie's Canon*, 138.
2 Cannon, *Katie's Canon*, 140.
3 Cannon, *Katie's Canon*, 138.
4 Cannon and Presbyterian Church, *Womanist Theology Primer*.
5 Sandel, *Justice*, loc. 74. I use this "one-third" phrasing to contrast with references to the "two-thirds" world—a phrasing that disrupts the problematic language of "first world" (i.e., the developed, whiter West) and "third world" geopolitical jargon. The "two-thirds" world phrasing privileges the fact that two-thirds of the world (or more) is not white or primarily European—and rhetorically directs attention to the fact that two-thirds is well over a global numerical majority. "One-third" thus refers to a global numerical minority—that also happens to be more white, oriented in European culture, and Western.
6 Nussbaum, *Sex and Social Justice*, 41–42; Baez, Unruh, and Tifft, "Is Time Quantized?" In *Physics of Blackness*, Michelle M. Wright speaks to this as well:

> In physics, Newton's assertions that linear time provides the "scaffolding" of the universe no longer monopolize all theories of spacetime. Einstein's equations—later demonstrated to be true—revealed that time does not move uniformly but in fact can speed up or slow down. In particle physics, experiments on subatomic matter, most famously Wheeler's 1980 "which path" experiment, demonstrated that subatomic particles travel haphazardly through space and can even exist in two places at the same time. This means that one cannot attempt to track a particle though linear space or time; one can only use the present moment, more specifically, the now, to determine the location of an object. In philosophy, the "now" moment is understood roughly as epiphenomenal time. As noted before, because my own deployment of epiphenomenal time is not tripartite but consists of one moment, it is not based in a linear relation between cause and effect; that is, as in the history of collectives, causalities abound in physics, but it is always impossible to assert convincingly that there is one single reason for any effect. No moment one experiences depends directly on a previous moment in order to come into being. (loc 332–42)

In one sense, she clarifies why a "now" approach to justice is all that is possible, given the impossibility of tracking causality; in another sense, she clarifies that there are multiple causalities and histories that invite constructive response.

7 Townes, *Womanist Ethics*, 18–22.
8 Townes, *Womanist Ethics*, 16.
9 Townes, *Womanist Ethics*, 16.
10 Townes, *Womanist Ethics*, 19, 20, 21.
11 Townes, *Womanist Ethics*, 18.
12 Thurman, "Dr. Howard Thurman's Baccalaureate Address," 14–15.
13 Long, *Significations*, 39.
14 Wimbush, *African Americans and the Bible*; Butler, *Gender Trouble*; Spillers, *Black, White, and in Color*; Crenshaw, "Mapping the Margins"; Cohen, *Boundaries of Blackness*; Townes, *Womanist Ethics*; Hammonds, "Black (W) Holes," 126.
15 Long, *Significations*, 63–64.
16 Long, *Significations*, 65.
17 Wall, "What Is a Black Hole?"
18 Hossenfelder, "10 Things You Should Know."
19 NASA Science, "Dark Energy, Dark Matter."
20 Chandra X-Ray Observatory, "Dark Matter."
21 Chandra X-Ray Observatory, "Dark Matter."
22 Diop, *Civilization or Barbarism*, 33–39, 55.
23 Diop, *Civilization or Barbarism*, 64.
24 Diop, *Civilization or Barbarism*, 112–13.
25 Diop, *Civilization or Barbarism*, 129, 135.
26 Diop, *Civilization or Barbarism*, 143.
27 Diop, *Civilization or Barbarism*, 142.
28 Diop, *Civilization or Barbarism*, 144.
29 Diop, *Civilization or Barbarism*, 142.
30 Diop, *Civilization or Barbarism*, 310.
31 Diop, *Civilization or Barbarism*, 310–13, 353.
32 Diop, *Civilization or Barbarism*, 370–71.
33 Diop, *Civilization or Barbarism*, 361.
34 Diop, *Civilization or Barbarism*, 113.
35 Diop, *Civilization or Barbarism*, 218.
36 Diop, *Civilization or Barbarism*, 211.
37 Diop, *Civilization or Barbarism*, 218.
38 Diop, *Civilization or Barbarism*, 219.
39 Wakanda is the home of the fictional character Black Panther; a Black utopia. Coogler, *Black Panther*, 2:14.
40 hooks, *Teaching to Transgress*.
41 Long, *Significations*, 89.

42 Long, *Significations*, 90.
43 Rodney, *How Europe Underdeveloped Africa*.
44 Bernal, *Black Athena*.
45 Browder, *Nile Valley*, 90.
46 I am intentionally playing with the metaphor of flight in a variety of ways. I am interested in the flight of justice in earth's atmosphere, the flight of justice beyond earth's atmosphere, and the flight of justice as a grounded movement that is at high speed and tantamount to a kind of flight. This latter option is consistent with the connection between Maât and the ostrich. Her feather is often characterized as an ostrich feather. Although ostriches are the highest-speed ground-traveling birds—moving up to seventy miles per hour—they do not (technically) fly. The notion of Maâtian justice as a grounded flight adds meaning as it signals a relevance and connection to the everyday space and place of the average human journey.
47 Browder, *Nile Valley*, 88.
48 Browder, *Nile Valley*, 91.
49 "We've explored three approaches to justice. One says justice means maximizing utility or welfare—the greatest happiness for the greatest number. The second says justice means respecting freedom of choice—either the actual choices people make in a free market (the libertarian view) or the hypothetical choices people would make in an original position of equality (the liberal egalitarian view). The third says justice involves cultivating virtue and reasoning about the common good. As you've probably guessed by now, I favor a version of the third approach." Sandel, *Justice*, loc. 4070–73; Warburton, "Interview."
50 Karenga, *Maat*, 10.
51 Holmes, *Race and the Cosmos*, 68.
52 Holmes, *Race and the Cosmos*, 77–79.
53 Holmes, *Race and the Cosmos*, 88.
54 Szwed, *Space Is the Place*, 83, 26. Ra legally changed his name on October 20, 1952, to Le Sony'r Ra at the encouragement of Alton Abraham in Cook County, Illinois. See Andrychuk, "Sun Ra's Reading List," which includes all the sources first cited in Szwed's work as part of Sun Ra's African-American Studies 198: The Black Man in the Universe course offered in the spring semester at the University of California, Berkeley, in 1971.
55 Keeling, *Queer Times, Black Futures*, 53–65.
56 Ra, *Sun Ra*, 161.
57 Szwed, *Space Is the Place*, 292.
58 Szwed, *Space Is the Place*, 138.
59 Szwed, *Space Is the Place*, 29.
60 Ra, *Sun Ra*, 220.
61 Collins, *Black Sexual Politics*; Douglas, *Sexuality and the Black Church*; Townes, *Womanist Ethics*.

62 Townes, *Womanist Ethics*; Phillips, *Womanist Reader*.
63 Mugge, *Sun Ra*.
64 Walker, "Gifts of Power," in *In Search of Our Mothers' Gardens*; Cox Jackson, *Gifts of Power*. It is also interesting to note a different perspective on this matter. In claiming Caroline Herschel as a scientist and physicist, Prescod-Weinstein notes that "we call Isaac Newton one of the greatest physicists of all time, even when the word 'physicist' didn't exist until 109 years after his death." Prescod-Weinstein, *Disordered Cosmos*, 114.
65 Asexual Visibility and Education Network, "Overview."
66 Crooks and Baur, *Our Sexuality*, 249, 251.
67 Crooks and Baur, *Our Sexuality*, 226.
68 Moultrie, *Passionate and Pious*.
69 Rebecca Cox Jackson also provides a powerful example of this. Walker, "Gifts of Power," 71–82.
70 Szwed, *Space Is the Place*, 41–42.
71 Szwed, *Space Is the Place*, 346–47.
72 Szwed, *Space Is the Place*, 58, 108, 116.
73 Jordan, *Ethics of Sex*, 151.
74 Cannon, *Katie's Canon*, 136.
75 Mugge, *Sun Ra*.
76 Mugge, *Sun Ra*.
77 Townes, *Womanist Ethics*, 150.
78 Hamilton, *People Could Fly*, 171.
79 Townes, *Womanist Ethics*, 154–55.
80 Ra, *Sun Ra*, 78.

Four. Heterexpectations

1 Phillips, *Womanist Reader*, 19; Walker, *In Search of Our Mothers' Gardens*.
2 And, like justice, ethics is a tall order. Often, ethical recommendations are based on theoretical circumstances that imagine what the just (i.e., fair or right) way to think and act is or would be in a particular context.
3 Of course, discourses of justice also assume rights, privileges, and prohibitions, to put this differently and to acknowledge the double entendre of rights language here.
4 Idan, "Show Me Your Friends"; Asmolov, "The Effects of Participatory Propaganda"; Baudrillard, *Simulacra and Simulation*, 141.
5 Mbembe, "Necropolitics."
6 Townes, *Womanist Ethics*.
7 Floyd's murder sparked national and international protests against antiBlack racism that continued en masse through summer 2020 and, in some places, were sustained with considerable intensity through the end of 2020 and

into the following year. Interestingly, June 19, 2021—a year after "Black Is Beautiful" was released—would mark the first year that Juneteenth would be recognized as an official federal holiday in the United States. Juneteenth commemorates the day enslaved people in Galveston, Texas, got the word that their enslavement had been nullified—901 days after the Emancipation Proclamation on January 1, 1863.

8 Lil Donald, *Black Is Beautiful*.
9 Welsing, *Isis Papers*, ii.
10 Welsing, *Isis Papers*, 3–4.
11 Welsing, *Isis Papers*, 4.
12 Welsing, *Isis Papers*, 4.
13 Welsing, *Isis Papers*, 4–5.
14 Welsing, *Isis Papers*, xvi–ii.
15 Welsing, *Isis Papers*, xvii.
16 Welsing, *Isis Papers*, x.
17 Welsing, *Isis Papers*, 275.
18 Welsing, *Isis Papers*, 277.
19 Welsing, *Isis Papers*, 278.
20 Also consider the work of Sobonfu Somé. The Dagara context of Burkina Faso that Somé shares provides an interesting expansion of Cress Welsing's work and is important to consider in relation to ancient Egyptian traditions and resources—especially as some sources maintain that the ancient Dagara people were among those who contributed to the philosophies and symbolisms of ancient Egypt. Somé, *Spirit of Intimacy*.
21 Welsing, *Isis Papers*, 279.
22 Welsing, *Isis Papers*, 280.
23 The historicity of the eponymous "Willie Lynch Letter" purported to have been written in 1712 has not been confirmed. The earliest evidence of the publication of this letter is in 1970 through the Black Liberation Library, according to Frederick Penn, quoted in Adams, "In Search of 'Willie' Lynch." However, Louis Farrakhan quoted from this letter in his 1995 Million Man March speech, and it was distributed at the march in a pamphlet, "Let's Make a Slave Kit." The letter has resonated with contemporary African Americans, seeming to offer a historical account that could explain the ongoing deleterious legacies of slavery on Black families, communities, and individuals. For most scholars, this letter is primarily an artifact of the internet age and hip-hop culture. However, the letter—and 1995 pamphlet—are also part of the margins, perhaps even the palimpsests, of what I have previously referred to as "Black books." Adams, "In Search of 'Willie' Lynch"; *Final Call*, "Willie Lynch Letter"; Shaner, "Searching for Willie Lynch at the Lounge Theatre," 17–18.
24 Hegel, *Elements of the Philosophy of Right*; Žižek, "Hegel on Marriage."
25 Žižek, "Hegel on Marriage."

26 Stewart, *Black Women, Black Love*, 52–53.
27 Dundes, "'Jumping the Broom,'" 324.
28 Dundes, "'Jumping the Broom,'" 324.
29 Scott, *Domination and the Arts of Resistance*.
30 Also see note 23 in this chapter on the Willie Lynch letter. *Final Call*, "Willie Lynch Letter"; Donoghue, *Black Breeding Machines*; Smithers, *Slave Breeding*, 173–74.
31 Tocqueville's *Democracy in America* is the fruit of his 1831 trip to the United States to study its prisons. He observes the young nation's hypocritical and ironic fascination with freedom as the enslavement of Black people persists. His descriptions of how he is observing the making of slaves are as damning as those developed as pseudohistory through documents like the Willie Lynch letter. To explain the impossibility of democracy in the United States and, from an outsider's perspective, explain the sociology of enslavement for Black people forced into the servitude of people of European descent, he writes:

> Seeing what happens in the world, might one not say that the European is to men of other races what man is to the animals? He makes them serve his convenience, and when he cannot bend them to his will he destroys them. . . .
>
> The Negro has no family; for him a woman is no more than the passing companion of his pleasures, and from their birth his sons are his equals.
>
> Should I call it a blessing of God, or a last malediction of His anger, this disposition of the soul that makes men insensible to extreme misery and often even gives them a sort of depraved taste for the cause of their afflictions?
>
> Plunged in this abyss of wretchedness, the Negro hardly notices his ill fortune; he was reduced to slavery by violence, and the habit of servitude has given him the thoughts and ambitions of a slave: he admires his tyrants even more than he hates them and finds his joy and pride in a servile imitation of his oppressors.
>
> His intelligence is degraded to the level of his soul.
>
> The Negro is a slave from birth. What am I saying? He is often sold in his mother's belly and begins, so to say, to be a slave before he is born.

These are not the words of one who is consciously interested in making or sustaining slaves or slavery. These are the words of one who is a firsthand observer of slavery and the enslaved. His harsh language is a reliable account of the acts, intent, impact, and sentiment of what he is observing of slave culture—and the ways "slaves" are being bred. Importantly, part of the critique of this dysfunctional way of growing society for Tocqueville—as for those who cite and/or created the Willie Lynch letter to expose the terror of slavery—is that the development of a heteropatriarchal, monogamous nuclear

family model is inhibited. Tocqueville, *Democracy in America*, 317–18; also see Donoghue, *Black Breeding Machines*, 257.
32 Federal Writers' Project, *Slave Narrative Project*, vol. 16, 151–52.
33 Federal Writers' Project, *Slave Narrative Project*, vol. 11, 285–90.
34 Federal Writers' Project, *Slave Narrative Project*, vol. 9, 84–90.
35 Parry, *Jumping the Broom*, 4; Parry, "Jumping the Broom and the American Cultural Divide."
36 Parry, *Jumping the Broom*, 11.
37 Parry, *Jumping the Broom*, 7, 9.
38 Hyatt, *Folklore from Adams County*, 465, quoted in Parry, *Jumping the Broom*, 1.
39 Parry, *Jumping the Broom*, 2.
40 Frey, "US Will Become 'Minority White' in 2045."
41 Levin and Nakashima, "Report to the Nation."
42 Gladstone and Garfield, "Dead Consensus."
43 Gladstone and Garfield, "Dead Consensus."
44 Gladstone and Garfield, "Dead Consensus."
45 Ahmari et al. "Against the Dead Consensus."
46 Ahmari et al. "Against the Dead Consensus."
47 Ahmari et al. "Against the Dead Consensus."
48 *Oxford Languages*, s.v. "republic," accessed October 31, 2022, https://www.google.com/search?q=republic+etymology.
49 *Oxford Languages*, s.v. "democracy," accessed October 31, 2022, https://www.google.com/search?q=democracy+etymology.
50 Hamer quoted in Harding, *Hope and History*, xv.
51 Harding, *Hope and History*, 202.
52 Anderson, *Pragmatic Theology*, 131.
53 Johnson, *Tragic Soul-Life*, 17–18, 157.
54 Davis, *Abolition Democracy*, 201.
55 Tippett, "Vincent Harding."
56 Lorde, "Uses of the Erotic," in *Sister Outsider*.
57 Blight, *Frederick Douglass*.
58 Baldwin, *Fire Next Time*, 91. Earlier in the text, Baldwin critiques an opposite ideology he observes in the rhetoric of Elijah Muhammad. Describing that ideology, he writes, "There is thus, by definition, no virtue in white people, and since they are another creation entirely and can no more, by breeding, become black than a cat, by breeding, can become a horse, there is no hope for them." This latter invitation to becoming is Baldwin's justice response to both Muhammad's Black nationalist approach and the white supremacist US status quo.
59 Baldwin, *Fire Next Time*, 45, 60, 105.
60 Clegg, *God Effect*, 1.

61 Clegg, *God Effect*, 1.
62 Clegg, *God Effect*, 3.
63 Clegg, *God Effect*, 42.
64 Parry, *Jumping the Broom*, 62–63.
65 Yates, *Math of Life and Death*, 93.
66 Flatow and Yates, "Math behind Big Decision Making."
67 Flatow and Yates, "Math behind Big Decision Making."
68 brown, *Emergent Strategy*, 3.
69 Federal Writers' Project, *Slave Narrative Project*, vol. 9, images 53–55 on pages 49–51.
70 Quoting Patrick Chamoiseau in Townes, *Womanist Ethics*, 161.

Five. Dancing Justice

Third epigraph: Charmaine Jackman and Ezra Jackman, "Black Sexual Ethics & Justice," message to author, March 26, 2023.

1 "I'm Tired of This Church"; Blair, "6-Y-O Boy."
2 Lamar, "Joseph Lamar." As of April 21, 2023, Lamar's bio has been changed and reads in part: "Joseph Lamar is part sage and part space cadet, part cynic and part ingénue, part saint and part heathen. He embodies conflict actively seeking resolution; synthesis giving birth to something uniquely beautiful yet universal. . . . If the "post-apocalyptic gospel" of Sin. [Act I] is any indication, he makes a case for the true meaning of the word "apocalypse." It's not an end but an awakening; it's the collapse of paradise and the possibility of something better." As with his evolving manifestos, his bios change. His current manifesto on this site reads: "1. I am not the subject of my work. I am the starting point. 2. All of my releases will be conceptual. 3. In my life and in my art, I aim to express myself consciously, sincerely, with intention and without regret. 4. I choose to EVOLVE. The alternative is apathy. Inertia. Obsolescence. Extinction._J●S▪P▪"
3 I have chosen not to rehearse the biblical texts used to terrorize gay people. However, the following are helpful resources for those interested in close analysis of these texts: Helminiak, *What the Bible Really Says about Homosexuality*; Guest et al., *Queer Bible Commentary*; Hendricks, *Christians against Christianity*; Lightsey, *Our Lives Matter*. Also consider as a resource for further study: Sorett, *Sexual Politics of Black Churches*.
4 Lamar, "SIN Diary [I]," January 7, 2019.
5 Lamar, "SIN Diary [I]," January 7, 2019. On "electric slide," Townes, *Womanist Justice, Womanist Hope*, 72; Townes, *In a Blaze of Glory*, 20; Townes, *Womanist Ethics*, 177.
6 Cannon and Presbyterian Church, *Womanist Theology Primer*.
7 Scott, *Domination and the Arts of Resistance*.

8   Césaire, *Discourse on Colonialism*.
9   Townes, *Womanist Ethics*.
10 S.o.g.i. abbreviates *sexual orientation and gender identity*. S.o.g.i.racism specifies racism that is fundamentally informed by and rooted in sexism and heterosexism.
11 Crouch and the Disciples, *Take Me Back*.
12 James, *Stolen Legacy*, 8.
13 James, *Stolen Legacy*, 25.
14 James, *Stolen Legacy*, 30.
15 Lamar, "SIN Diary [I]," February 23, 2019.
16 Lamar, "SIN Diary [I]," February 13, 2019.
17 Lamar, "SIN Diary [I]," June 28, 2020.
18 Lamar, "SIN Diary [I]," February 5, 2020.
19 Lamar, "SIN Diary [I]," September 10, 2019.
20 Three Initiates, *Kybalion*. In a later conversation with Joseph, the principle of correspondence—"as above, so below"—came to the surface. This is connected to the relationship between actions/choices and values. Which is above or below? Is there a different valuation between below and above?
21 Lamar, "SIN Diary [I]," December 6, 2019.
22 Lorde, *Sister Outsider*; Lorde, *Zami*.
23 Flunder, *Where the Edge Gathers*; Flunder, "No Doors on Our Huts"; Johnson, *Sweet Tea*; Griffin, *Their Own Receive Them Not*; Townes, *Breaking the Fine Rain of Death*.
24 Lamar, "SIN Diary [I]," December 6, 2019.
25 Cohen, "Deviance as Resistance."
26 Leath, "'By the Glory of G*d.'"
27 Muñoz, *Cruising Utopia*, 97–98.
28 Muñoz, *Cruising Utopia*, 28–29.
29 Muñoz, *Cruising Utopia*, 22.
30 Lamar, "SIN Diary [I]," June 13, 2019.
31 Lamar, "SIN Diary [I]," March 2, 2020.
32 Johnson, "'Quare' Studies," 2.
33 Muñoz, *Cruising Utopia*, 1–2.
34 Muñoz, *Cruising Utopia*, 30.
35 Griffiths, *Introduction to Quantum Mechanics*, 3.
36 Griffiths, *Introduction to Quantum Mechanics*, 461–62.
37 Holmes, *Race and the Cosmos*, 128.
38 Holmes, *Race and the Cosmos*, 131.
39 Holmes writes, "It seems that Schrödinger was inclined toward philosophical pursuits and Eastern religions prior to the publication of his equation. . . . Schrödinger . . . said, 'I am the east and in the west, I am below and above, I am this whole world.'" This echoes one of the first principles

articulated in *The Kybalion*, an anonymously authored text (though it has been attributed to William W. Atkinson, 1862–1932) that draws from the late eighth-century Arabic Hermetic text, the Emerald Tablet. Three Initiates, *Kybalion*. Interestingly, while he was not aware of its hermetic source, Joseph Lamar also has echoed "as above, so below," a rendition of this principle, in conversation in March 2021. Holmes, *Race and the Cosmos*, 127.

40 While this chapter focuses on the work of Joseph Lamar, he is by no means alone in this purposeful artistic, performative, musical theological agenda. He is part of a powerful lineage of artists who have taken the ecclesial contexts that have birthed them, received the truth of their dignity sometimes hidden that theological shell, and transformed the "good news" message into a form others like them (i.e., their tribe) could receive. Lil Nas X does this same work in "Montero (Call Me By Your Name)"—including through his shoe production and his comment in reply to (Black and other) Christian detractors: "i spent my entire teenage years hating myself because of the shit y'all preached would happen to me because i was gay. so i hope u are mad, stay mad, feel the same anger you teach us to have towards ourselves." Lil Nas X, "Nope 🎵 on Twitter"; Abram, "Lil Nas X Is Inviting."

41 Coleman, *Making a Way Out of No Way*; Butler, *Parable of the Sower*.

Six. Ancient Mixologies

First epigraph: Conversation with the author, April 2, 2023.

1 *Dom* is short for *dominant* or *dominatrix* in a sadomasochistic sexual relationship; it is often related or invoked in relation to (a) sub. See note 2 for an explanation of *sub*.

2 *Sub* is short for *submissive* in a sadomasochistic sexual relationship; it is often related or invoked in relation to (a) dom. See note 1 for an explanation of *dom*.

3 Here I take the risk of speaking through and about the suffering death of George Floyd. I acknowledge that I will always do this imperfectly—as any of us do when we attempt the vulnerable work of seeing through another's eyes, walking in another's shoes. Through this passage I challenge the perpetual subordination of Black men and Black people. Without privileging the dom, I want to signal what it is to exist as a conscious sub. I am also suggesting that there is a sexualized and/or sexualizing element in this murder as it is performed—wherein we see one man over another. The murder is not just violent. It is also sexualized insofar as it emphasizes the masculinity of the white man over and against the Black man. Derek Chauvin performed as the alpha male; whatever George Floyd was, he was not the alpha male. To the extent that sexuality has traditionally been overdetermined by heteropatriarchal ideals, the grotesque emphasis on/of the white man's masculinity presents itself not only as an example of gender identity but also as an example of sexual orientation (and,

specifically, an assertion of sexual dominance). This subordination was public. One man was on top of the other. A quare vantage point is distinctly poised to discern and talk about this murder as such.

To my quare I/eye, this is a uniquely troubling rape and death scene. Others may not see sex or sexuality in this homosocial murder; others may only see violence and/or racialized terror. However, quare perspective is not disgusted at the appearance of gender sameness—or difference; quare perspective is also not disgusted at positive and consensual balances of sexual pain and pleasure; quare perspective is simultaneously clear about the unequivocal necessity of consent—especially mindful of and, sometimes, healing from the personal and communal traumas of nonconsensual sexual violation. Consequently, quare perspective perceives sexual possibility between two men who show up as heteromasculine to the public eye; quare perspective appreciates the sexual play and fluidity of gender and power roles; quare perspective does not tolerate nonconsensual violations. When I—as a quare viewer who holds these three concepts together in tension with one another—see the murder of George Floyd, I feel a unique violation that exceeds racialized terror. I also see gender—and because I see gender (and because of the ways gender is performed in this murder), I also see sexuality. The added element of terror, however, is that the gender and sexuality I perceive in the act of murder is the perverse and post-gendersexual form we know of as rape (i.e., that form of violence that masquerades as desire). What Chauvin does is about power, not sex. That does not mean it is not sexual.

4   Note the strange connection between Chauvin's surname and the familiar term *chauvinist*.
5   Fanon, *Wretched of the Earth*.
6   Patrick Chamoiseau, *Texaco*, cited in Townes, *Womanist Ethics*.
7   With respect to bodily anarchies, I develop the idea of bodily anarchies as polyamorous and/as polyracial intimacies.
8   Rogers, *Sex and Race*, vol. 1, x.
9   Rogers, *Sex and Race*, vol. 2, xi.
10 My colleague Katherine Turpin notes the similarity between Rogers's historic agenda and Henry Louis Gates Jr.'s contemporary agenda with respect to exposing the hybrid details of our histories. In an informal correspondence, she noted that the "history of mixedness is being exposed and is experienced as shame and anger and a host of other negatively valanced emotions. Gates is relentless in insisting that all of that is what made up the guest's background.... The guests are almost always wanting not to acknowledge it as 'theirs.' ... This gets particularly direct when he produces the genetic testing pie chart of origins, where it is like 55% Sub-Saharan Africa and 45% European and people sometimes say directly that only one portion of that is what they want to recognize." This not only speaks to the contemporary

relevance of this subject but also to the ongoing moral stickiness of it. Gates, *Finding Your Roots*.
11 Einstein quoted in Rogers, *Sex and Race*, vol. 1, 12.
12 Rogers, *Sex and Race*, vol. 1, 10.
13 Rogers, *Sex and Race*, vol. 1, 13–14.
14 Rogers, *Sex and Race*, vol. 1, 17–18.
15 Asukile, "Joel Augustus Rogers," 323.
16 Duneier, *Sidewalk*.
17 Johnson, *100 Amazing Facts about the Negro*, loc. 163–65.
18 Asukile, "Joel Augustus Rogers," 324.
19 Long, *Significations*; Fanon, *Wretched of the Earth*.
20 Townes, *Womanist Ethics*, 31.
21 Rogers, *Sex and Race*, vol. 1, 218–19, quotes Wolff's "To a Negro Belle":

> You make me dream of distant tropic climes
> Luxurious vegetation; nights serene
> By burning passion made tempestuous,
> The witching scent of rare exotic languorous
> Of music soft and weird, whose savage rhythm
> Compels each fibre of the frame to dance.
>
> I see you as the princess of an isle
> Whose jungles are replete with beasts of prey
> And whose vast forests ever are alive
> With cries and frolickings of birds and apes,
> Whole villages of bamboo huts are full
> Of dusky-hued and happy naked people.
>
> Your simple-hearted subjects pay you homage,
> Prostrated in the dust, they weirdly chant
> Thy praises, even as in my own way
> I sing your praises sweet, exotic princess.
> Oh, let me enter your enchanted realm
> And make of me your happy humble slave.

Also note Rogers, *Sex and Race*, vols. 2 and 3.
22 Hitler quoted in Rogers, *Sex and Race*, vol. 1, 18.
23 Rogers, *Sex and Race*, vol. 1, 14.
24 Toynbee quoted in Rogers, *Sex and Race*, vol. 1, 17.
25 Rogers, *Sex and Race*, vol. 1, 16.
26 See a different formulation of this concept of systemic sexual surveillance in chapter 7. Alice Walker's "Coming Apart" provides a clear example of how white supremacy can be present and/or inserts itself even in Black intraracial sexual intimacies. The "New York Sour" episode in season 4 of *Boardwalk*

Empire shows a cuckolding scene that elucidates this concept from the vantage point of an intraracial white couple (ultimately) interacting with a Black man. While this scene is, in fact, interracial, the implication of the scene is that fetishization of and/or desire for Black masculinity and/or sexuality precedes the physical presence and sexual availability of a Black body—and, in this case, a Black male body for sexual gratification. The idea of systemic sexual surveillance is that Black sexuality haunts white desire even when there are no Black people present. And white supremacist ideas of beauty (as white) haunt Black desire—even when there are no white people present: this too is a manifestation of systemic sexual surveillance. Van Patten, *Boardwalk Empire*.

27 Camp, "Early European Views of African Bodies," 14.
28 Camp, "Early European Views of African Bodies," 29.
29 Holland, *Erotic Life of Racism*, 41.
30 Holland, *Erotic Life of Racism*, 55–56.
31 Townes, *Womanist Ethics*; Douglas, *Sexuality and the Black Church*.
32 Feinstein, *When Rape Was Legal*, 38.
33 Feinstein, *When Rape Was Legal*, 76.
34 Foster, *Rethinking Rufus*, 82, 101, 95, 89–90, 98.
35 For an analysis of Vincent Harding's response to William Styron's *The Confessions of Nat Turner* (1968), see Woodard and McBride, *Delectable Negro*, 180–87.
36 Johnson, *Wicked Flesh*, 127; Donoghue, *Black Breeding Machines*, 328–43; Smithers, *Slave Breeding*, 42.
37 Woodard and McBride, *Delectable Negro*, 171–72.
38 Haley, *No Mercy Here*, 40.
39 Lorde, *Sister Outsider*; Haley, *No Mercy Here*, 210.
40 Fleisher and Krienert, "Culture of Prison Sexual Violence"; Gilmore, *Golden Gulag*.
41 Parsons and Greer, *A Lifelong Anarchist!*, loc. 31.
42 Parsons and Greer, *A Lifelong Anarchist!*, loc. 1802.
43 Parsons and Greer, *A Lifelong Anarchist!*, loc. 122.
44 Tocqueville, *Democracy in America*.
45 Parsons and Greer, *A Lifelong Anarchist!*, loc. 67.
46 Jones, *Goddess of Anarchy*, xi.
47 Jones, *Goddess of Anarchy*, xii.
48 Jones, *Goddess of Anarchy*, xii.
49 Jones, *Goddess of Anarchy*, 247.
50 Jones, *Goddess of Anarchy*, 246. The now antiquated term *varietism* refers to those who sexually engage with several partners.
51 Jones, *Goddess of Anarchy*, xiii.
52 Day, *Azusa Reimagined*, 61, 66–67, 148.
53 Day, *Azusa Reimagined*, 118–19. Also see Crawley, *Blackpentecostal Breath*.

54　Day, *Azusa Reimagined*, 148.
55　I use this term with apologies to August Alsina, Will Smith, Jada Pinkett-Smith, and Chris Rock, whose popularization of the term *entanglement* in Black sexual discourse has given the term new meaning and life—only some of which I invoke through the use of this term in this instance.
56　Butler, *Transhuman*, 134; also see 129–30, where Butler writes: "The spirituality of revolt is embodied by nonconformity, rebellion to indoctrination of docility in all forms, and the insistence of absolute justice. It is dependent upon the action of transhumans for the liberation of transhumans. . . . Revolt spirituality results in a posthuman spawn that acknowledges the convergence of spiritualities, actions, and complexities toward the goal of freedom." And regarding the term *transhuman*, Butler writes: "Very basically, transhumanism is a cultural and philosophical movement. It asserts that any use of technology to augment human intellectual, physical, or psychological capability makes one transhuman" (2).
57　Douglas, *Sexuality and the Black Church*, 121 and elsewhere.
58　Douglas, *Sexuality and the Black Church*, 69.
59　Douglas, *Sexuality and the Black Church*, 69.
60　Douglas, *Sexuality and the Black Church*, 72.
61　Douglas, *Sexuality and the Black Church*, 69. Subsequent page numbers are given parenthetically in the text.
62　Fortune, *Love Does No Harm*, 19.
63　Fortune, *Love Does No Harm*, 19.
64　Fortune, *Love Does No Harm*, 31.
65　Fortune, *Love Does No Harm*, 34–35.
66　Fortune, *Love Does No Harm*, 35.
67　Fortune, *Love Does No Harm*, 38. Subsequent page numbers in this paragraph are given parenthetically in the text.
68　Fortune, *Love Does No Harm*, 43.
69　Fortune, *Love Does No Harm*, 44.
70　Fortune, *Love Does No Harm*, 43.
71　bell hooks quoted in Fortune, *Love Does No Harm*, 129. Also note the similarity of this strategy with dissemblance as described in Hine, "Rape and the Inner Lives."
72　hooks in Fortune, *Love Does No Harm*, 129.
73　Adrienne Rich in Fortune, *Love Does No Harm*, 130.
74　Fortune, *Love Does No Harm*, 141.
75　Fortune, *Love Does No Harm*, 141–42.
76　King, "Letter from Birmingham City Jail (1963)," 290.
77　"Rubik's."
78　For "patient enough," King, "Why We Can't Wait," 518–54.
79　Georgia Public Broadcasting, "Unit 5, Segment J."

80 Prescod-Weinstein, *Disordered Cosmos*, 127.
81 Prescod-Weinstein, *Disordered Cosmos*, 166.
82 Prescod-Weinstein, *Disordered Cosmos*, 94.
83 Prescod-Weinstein, *Disordered Cosmos*, 166–67.
84 Prescod-Weinstein, *Disordered Cosmos*, 161.
85 Prescod-Weinstein, *Disordered Cosmos*, 163.
86 Prescod-Weinstein, *Disordered Cosmos*, 167.
87 Prescod-Weinstein, *Disordered Cosmos*, 167.
88 Karenga, *Maat*, 138.
89 Karenga, *Maat*, 139.
90 Karenga, *Maat*, 139.
91 Karenga, *Maat*, 140.
92 Karenga, *Maat*, 142–47.

Seven. Black Web

Second epigraph: Conversation with the author, April 19, 2023.
1 Grewal and Kaplan, "Global Identities," 663–79.
2 Waters, *Globalization*, 5–6.
3 Grewal, *Transnational America*, loc. 504.
4 Grewal, *Transnational America*, loc. 512.
5 Grewal, *Transnational America*, loc. 149.
6 Transnationalism is a politically charged and complicated concept. The destabilizing critique of nation-states that transnationalism implies (as scholars like Inderpal Grewal articulate it) can give hope to those looking for sharper tools to dismantle the houses of racist, sexist, heterosexist, homophobic, and classist regimes. Moreover, transnationalism can be rendered as the glocal, democratic, rights-based, oppressed masses–driven counternarrative to globalization. Contemporary discourses on empire figure into the transnational equation in interesting ways. On one hand, some approaches to empire have joined in a critique of nation-states—arguing that empire is growing and its growth spells the end of nation-states. On the other hand, while celebrating the demise of nation-states and the softening or erasure of their geographic boundaries, these same approaches to empire proliferate capitalism and do little to destabilize the forms of social oppression that accompany capitalism. The clarity of nation-states as empire building (i.e., imperial) powers is clearer now than ever before. The idea that modern empire subsumes nation-states is false. The United States remains a prototypical modern nation-state as empire; others quickly advance with alternative imperial options. This is clear not only in terms of the ways that the United States extends its imperial reach as a nation-state through outposts and alliances but also in terms of the ways that Russia (e.g., Belarus and Ukraine) and China (e.g., Hong Kong

and Taiwan) are doing likewise. This is to say nothing of the circumstances in Syria, Yemen, Ethiopia, and Eritrea. Clearly, geographical places and spaces have not been rendered irrelevant, land (grabs) still matters, and empire (and the imperial) is still being built out of the aging models of nation-states. Conceptually, transnationalism challenges this trend of empire building—retaining the *nation* nomenclature that remains both imperial debris and imperial foundation. Transnationalism challenges empire and nation-states driving toward cultural disruption and political options that cross borders and boundaries to effectively empower all who are oppressed with the necessary skills and tools to fight their own oppression and the oppression of others. Anderson, *Imagined Communities*; Hardt and Negri, *Empire*; Alexander, *Pedagogies of Crossing*; Grewal, *Transnational America*; Townes, *Womanist Ethics*, 79–110; Stoler, *Imperial Debris*.

7   Spratt and Dunlop, *Existential Climate-Related Security Risk*; Bryant, "Falling Sperm Counts." See note 24 in introduction for further contextualization of the term *dunia*.

8   What about the pharaohs? They and their governmental structures were not very democratic, were they? What kind of political structure gave rise to Maât's forty-two laws? What can and cannot be espoused of various and general frameworks of sexual ethics exhibited over the different periods of khemetic antiquity?

9   What constitutes normative ethics or a defensible moral code or standard is different within each of these categories: creator, consumer, and creator/consumer. However, it is also important to note that defensible moral codes are also particular for people of different races and social contexts. What constitutes ethical behavior as it pertains to porn may be different for those who identify within the parameters of the African diaspora as opposed to those who do not. Historically, so much of ethics—and theories of justice—have been based on the universalizability of moral codes, ethical frameworks, and standards of justice. And this has primarily worked for the benefit of the elite, the empowered, and the least vulnerable. Capehart and Milovanovic note, "Definitions of justice have historically been provided by and/or for the few (elites), with little attention to the needs and desires of the majority (the rest of us)" (*Social Justice*, 2). While there may be some common principles, umbrella codes, or overarching ethical themes that pertain to most people, the ways people execute these principles, codes, and themes (and believe they should) varies widely. Theories of justice are not meant to correct this and to streamline belief and action to promote a singular way of pursuing justice(s). However, as presented in this book, theories of justice are intended to offer readers ways to locate themselves, their beliefs, and their commitments while imagining how to better embody their contexts, beliefs, and commitments (and ultimately putting it all into practice).

10 Perry and Schleifer, "Race and Trends in Pornography Viewership," 68. This study used "nationally representative data from the 1973–2016 General Social Survey (GSS; N = 20,620)" (62). The "outcome measure for this study is pornography viewership from 1973 to 2016. Across the past 43 years, the GSS has asked respondents: 'Have you seen an X-rated movie in the last year?'" The researchers "coded responses such that Yes = 1 and No = 0." And "for religious commitment," they "used a dichotomous measure of religious service attendance, coded 1 = Monthly attendance and 0 = Less than monthly attendance" (65). Among the most serious concerns about this study are its limitation to "Black" and "white," "men" and "women" only.
11 Perry and Schleifer, "Race and Trends in Pornography Viewership," 69–70.
12 Perry and Schleifer, "Race and Trends in Pornography Viewership," 64.
13 Moultrie, *Passionate and Pious*, 134.
14 Moultrie, *Passionate and Pious*, 122–23.
15 Lindsey, "About Us."
16 Presumably, other things a woman could do for a man are permissible outside of marriage; sex is the only definitive boundary between the married and the unmarried. While one might wonder about the price that women are paying for men's bodies, the logic does not quite transfer because Pinky Promise is a women's group—among many such women's groups. Even if there are men's groups focused on male celibacy, these are rare and there is not a culture of such groups.
17 The investigators of this study report the following with respect to the constitution of the sample "of 16- to 18-year-old youth who had viewed pornography in the past year": "A convenience sample of youth was recruited from the pediatric emergency department of a large, urban, Safety Net hospital located in Boston, Massachusetts. The patient population at this hospital is 60% Black, 15% Hispanic, 15% White, 2% Asian, and 8% multiracial or another race; more than 80% are living in poverty. The emergency department setting was used because it was convenient and resource-efficient for the investigators (Rothman, Linden, Baughman, Kaczmarsky, & Thompson, 2013). The participants in this study were 60% female, 47% Black, 43% Hispanic, and 8% multiracial (N = 23) (Table 1)" (737). The questions asked of these youths were the following: "1. What types of pornography do they report watching, where, and for what purpose? 2. Do they feel that pornography exposure has an impact on their own sexual behaviors? 3. What kind of interactions do they have with their parents about pornography?" (737). Rothman et al., "'Without Porn,'" 740.
18 MacKinnon and Dworkin, "Appendix D: The Model Ordinance," 138–39.
19 Lorde, *Sister Outsider*, 44.
20 Lorde, *Sister Outsider*, 45–46.
21 Lorde, *Sister Outsider*, 48–50.

22 Systematic sexual surveillance is related to, but distinct from, Lomax's uses of "pornotroping" or "pornotropic gazing," which she defines as "a way of 'seeing' with both the eyes and the psyche that is simultaneously 'othering'"—building on the work of Hortense Spillers and Anne McClintock. Victor Anderson's "pornotropia," highlighting "the complex multiplicity of the pornotropic gaze and its collective grasp of fantasy, fixation, repulsion, desire, and so on" is explained in Lomax, *Jezebel Unhinged*, 215, 221.
23 Cruz, *Color of Kink*, 19.
24 Warner, *Trouble with Normal*; Higginbotham, *Righteous Discontent*; Cohen, "Deviance as Resistance"; Cruz, *Color of Kink*, 10.
25 Cruz, *Color of Kink*, 16–17.
26 Cruz, *Color of Kink*, 16.
27 Cruz, *Color of Kink*, 27.
28 Cruz, *Color of Kink*, 17.
29 Miller-Young, *A Taste for Brown Sugar*, 17.
30 Miller-Young, *A Taste for Brown Sugar*, 64.
31 Miller-Young, *A Taste for Brown Sugar*, 62.
32 Miller-Young, *A Taste for Brown Sugar*, 65.
33 It is interesting to think about the ways Hugh Hefner is remembered not only for his role in shaping the modern pornography industry but also for his celebrated commitment to civil rights. Can these be written off as insufficient, self-serving, modest even for his time, limited even considering his time? Also, the fact that *Playboy* becomes an important space for Alex Haley to publish and to publish some of the most significant existing interviews with civil rights icons such as Malcolm X and Martin Luther King Jr. is not insignificant to these questions. Bennett, "Hugh Hefner Civil Rights."
34 Lomax, *Jezebel Unhinged*, 44–50, 221–22. Lomax draws from Spillers explaining "pornotroping" as "a way of 'seeing' with both the eyes of the psyche that is simultaneously 'othering.'" Lomax adds that she uses this term to "denote the possibility of representational violence and ultimately material fury—each ignited by 'looking'" (215).
35 Lomax, *Jezebel Unhinged*, 51.
36 Lomax, *Jezebel Unhinged*, 74, 77, 79.
37 Lomax, *Jezebel Unhinged*, provides an extensive comparative analysis of womanism and Black feminism in chapters 3 and 4. From this analysis, she emerges with her call for "black feminist religious thought."
38 Lomax, *Jezebel Unhinged*, 102.
39 Lomax, *Jezebel Unhinged*, 106.
40 Miller-Young, *A Taste for Brown Sugar*, 256, 260–61.
41 Miller-Young, *A Taste for Brown Sugar*, 260.
42 Miller-Young, *A Taste for Brown Sugar*, 280.
43 Miller-Young, *A Taste for Brown Sugar*, 280.

44 Miller-Young, *A Taste for Brown Sugar*, 280.
45 Miller-Young, *A Taste for Brown Sugar*, 281.
46 Nash, *Black Body in Ecstasy*, 150.
47 Nash, *Black Body in Ecstasy*, 150.
48 Miller-Young, *A Taste for Brown Sugar*, 281.
49 Perry, *Vexy Thing*, 147.
50 Perry, *Vexy Thing*, 146.
51 In future work it will be important to develop a comparative analysis of the geopolitical impact, force, and development of several centers of imperial power—especially as they relate to and impact Africa and African and Afrodiasporic people: China, Russia, Arabia, and the United States. For now, I think it is essential to note that—notwithstanding the contemporary culture wars in the US that threaten the publication, distribution, and teaching of books like this one—the other named imperial powers would be more hostile than the US is to research like this.
52 Aceves, "Virtual Hatred"; Mueller and Special Counsel's Office, *Mueller Report*.
53 Mueller and Special Counsel's Office, *Mueller Report*; Maddow, *Blowout*, 228, 338.
54 Swaine and Walker, "Trump in Moscow"; Savage, Goldman, and Kessel, "Analyst Who Reported the Infamous Trump Tape Rumor"; Simpson and Fritsch, *Crime in Progress*.
55 Johnson, "Jeffrey Epstein's East Side Mansion."
56 UN News, "Russia Responsible for Navalny Poisoning"; Potash, *FBI War on Tupac Shakur*; Davis, *Angela Davis*.
57 Nance and Reiner, *Plot to Destroy Democracy*, 106.
58 Nance and Reiner, *Plot to Destroy Democracy*, 121.
59 Dias and Graham, "Christian Conservatives Respond to Trump's Loss"; Dias and Graham, "How White Evangelical Christians Fused."
60 Net neutrality is the idea that internet service providers (ISPs) and government should give equal treatment to all internet data and traffic regardless of content, data, device, platform, or user. Those defending free speech, the free exchange of ideas, and those working in the pornography industry often defend laws that protect the principle of net neutrality. However, this makes for strange bedfellows as there are those who might like to censor hate speech, vehicles for human/sex trafficking, pornography, and sex work but may want to defend uncensored space to combat racism, sexism, classism, ableism, and heterosexism; there are also those who might classify access to pornography and sex work together with crusades against bigotry while eschewing hate speech and human/sex trafficking. Unqualified net neutrality protects access to all of these things—those palatable and those unpalatable to us. Valencia, "What Is Net Neutrality?"

61 At this point, a full reading of China is beyond the scope of this book. However, as Chinese politicians open their doors to religion within China, there is increasing political pressure to ensure that the religious leadership approved externally from power centers such as the Vatican is aligned with the political interests of China's government. Horowitz and Johnson, "China and Vatican Reach Deal."
62 Dobieszewski, "Russian Issues in Alain Besançon's Perspective," 565.
63 "The veil between them must be taken down." Perry, *Vexy Thing*, 146.
64 Perry, *Vexy Thing*, 146.
65 Cannon, The Womanist Theology Primer, 30n49.
66 Baudrillard, *Simulacra*, 1. Further page numbers are given parenthetically in the text.
67 Haraway, *Anthropocene*. Also see Haraway, *Simians*.
68 brown, *Emergent Strategy*, 25.
69 Butler, *Sower*, 3. Also see 79 and 195, where these words also appear but in eight lines; the seventh line is split and the seventh and eighth lines are "God" and "Is Change." brown, *Emergent Strategy*, loc. 389–395. brown's concern with pleasure, queerness, and "real" is a helpful contrast to the Black sexual ethics online. It may also be interesting to assess the ways brown's work is online (i.e., Kindle, her website, and web presence).
70 brown, *Emergent Strategy*, 28.
71 brown, *Emergent Strategy*, 44.
72 brown, *Emergent Strategy*, 25.
73 An interesting intersection with this is Kendrick Lamar's use of deepfakes in his rap video "The Heart Part 5," released on May 8, 2022.
74 In a helpful contrast, S. N. Nyeck reminds us of the importance of Senghorian *présence virtuelle*. Nyeck, *African(a) Queer Presence*, 11.
75 Perry, *Vexy Thing*, 117.
76 Perry, *Vexy Thing*, 145.
77 Cohen, *Democracy Remixed*, loc. 123.
78 Cohen, *Democracy Remixed*, loc. 144.
79 Cohen, *Democracy Remixed*, loc. 1079–82.
80 Cohen, *Democracy Remixed*, loc. 1113–16.
81 Evelyn Hammonds in Lomax, *Jezebel Unhinged*, 106.
82 Delbert, "Scientists Might Have Just Stumbled."
83 Aaij et al., "Test of Lepton Universality," 277.
84 As noted earlier, *dunia* is the Kiswhahili word for *world*. I use this word to signal an appeal to a trade language with a Bantu base that was once the hope for Pan-African linguistic engagement in East Africa (with Julius Nyerere) and among Black Pan-Africanists and Black nationalists in the United States in the 1960s and '70s.
85 Afua, *Sacred Woman*, 12.

86 Karenga, *Maat*, 91.
87 Karenga, *Maat*, 90.
88 Karenga, *Maat*, 91.
89 Karenga, *Maat*, 91.
90 Wynter, "On How We Mistook the Map"; Wynter, "Ceremony Must Be Found"; Wynter, "Unsettling the Coloniality"; Wynter, *Hills of Hebron*; Wynter, "Black Metamorphosis."
91 *Patriarchal* meaning men over women and man over woman; women leaders in a patriarchal community sometimes become the patriarch in this way. Robin Hayes: men who see this and that they are subjected to an "alpha male's" exploits through such a system (may) find themselves more sympathetic to a rejection of toxic masculinity. Robin J. A. Hayes, conversation with the author, March 24, 2021.
92 Hayes, conversation with the author, March 24, 2021.

Conclusion

1 Manniche, *Sexual Life in Ancient Egypt*, 8–17, 22–27.
2 Manniche, *Sexual Life in Ancient Egypt*, 25–27.
3 "'Hatshepsut' may be translated 'the noble best' or the like, a worthy description of the god's performance." Manniche, *Sexual Life in Ancient Egypt*, 59–60.
4 Diop, *Civilization or Barbarism*, 375–76.
5 Adapting Acts 17.28.
6 In the spirit of sankofa, the Twi word of the Akan people of Ghana translated as "to retrieve" or "to go back and get," often symbolized by a bird with its head facing back, its feet facing forward, and an egg in its mouth.
7 I have titled my adaptation of "Creation" from Johnson, *God's Trombones* "Quare Creation."
8 Prince, "God."

bibliography

Aaij, R., C. Abellán Beteta, T. Ackernley, B. Adeva, M. Adinolfi, H. Afsharnia, C. A. Aidala, et al. "Test of Lepton Universality in Beauty-Quark Decays." *Nature Physics* 18, no. 3 (March 2022): 277–82. https://doi.org/10.1038/s41567-021-01478-8.

Abram, Don. "Lil Nas X Is Inviting the Black Church in with 'Montero.'" *Religion News Service* (blog), April 6, 2021. https://religionnews.com/2021/04/06/lil-nas-x-is-inviting-the-black-church-in-with-montero/.

Aceves, William J. "Virtual Hatred: How Russia Tried to Start a Race War in the United States." *Michigan Journal of Race and Law* 24 (2019): 75.

Adams, Mike. "In Search of 'Willie' Lynch: Sometimes the Truth Can Be Found in Myth, Fiction—Even in a Lie." *Baltimore Sun*, February 21, 1998. https://www.baltimoresun.com/news/bs-xpm-1998-02-22-1998053003-story.html.

Afua, Queen. *Sacred Woman: A Guide to Healing the Feminine Body, Mind, and Spirit*. New York: One World, 2001.

Ahmari, Sohrab, Jeffrey Blehar, Patrick Deneen, Rod Dreher, Pascal-Emmanuel Gobry, Darel Paul, C. C. Pecknold, et al. "Against the Dead Consensus." *First Things*, March 21, 2019. https://www.firstthings.com/web-exclusives/2019/03/against-the-dead-consensus.

Alexander, M. Jacqui. *Pedagogies of Crossing: Meditations on Feminism, Sexual Politics, Memory, and the Sacred*. Durham, NC: Duke University Press, 2005.

Allen, Jafari S. *There's a Disco Ball between Us: A Theory of Black Gay Life*. Durham, NC: Duke University Press, 2022.

Amadiume, Ifi. *Male Daughters, Female Husbands: Gender and Sex in an African Society*. Chicago: Zed, 2015.

Anderson, Benedict. *Imagined Communities: Reflections on the Origin and Spread of Nationalism*. New York: Verso, 1991.

Anderson, Victor. *Beyond Ontological Blackness: An Essay on African American Religious and Cultural Criticism*. New York: Continuum, 1995.

Anderson, Victor. *Pragmatic Theology: Negotiating the Intersections of an American Philosophy of Religion and Public Theology*. Albany: State University of New York Press, 1998.

Anderson, Vivienne L., and A. Lee Henderson. "Great Is Thy Faithfulness." In *AMEC Bicentennial Hymnal: African Methodist Episcopal Church*, edited by Robert O. Hoffelt and Vinton Randolph Anderson. Nashville, TN: African Methodist Episcopal Church, 1984.

Andrews, Carol, J. Daniel Gunther, and James Wasserman. *Egyptian Book of the Dead: The Book of Going Forth by Day: The Complete Papyrus of Ani Featuring Integrated Text and Full-Color Images*. Translated by Ogden Goelet and Raymond Faulkner. San Francisco: Chronicle, 2015.

Andrychuk, Sylvia. "Sun Ra's Reading List for African-American Studies 198: The Black Man in the Universe." Sun Ra Studies, Queen's University Library. Accessed November 3, 2022. https://guides.library.queensu.ca/sun_ra_studies/reading_list.

Ani, Marimba. *Yurugu: An African-Centered Critique of European Cultural Thought and Behavior*. Trenton, NJ: Africa World Press, 1994.

Armah, Ayi Kwei. *Two Thousand Seasons*. Popenguine, Senegal: Per Ankh, 2000.

Arnold, Caroline. *Ostriches and Other Flightless Birds*. Minneapolis: Lerner, 1990.

Asexual Visibility and Education Network. "Overview." Accessed June 23, 2022. https://www.asexuality.org/?q=overview.html.

Asmolov, Gregory. "The Effects of Participatory Propaganda: From Socialization to Internalization of Conflicts." *Journal of Design and Science*, no. 6 (August 7, 2019). https://doi.org/10.21428/7808da6b.833c9940.

Assmann, Jan. *Ma'at: Gerechtigkeit und Unsterblichkeit im alten Ägypten*. Munich: C.H. Beck, 1990.

Assmann, Jan. *Maat, l'Egypte pharaonique*. Paris: Maison de Vie, 2000.

Asukile, Thabiti. "Joel Augustus Rogers: Black International Journalism, Archival Research, and Black Print Culture." *Journal of African American History* 95, nos. 3–4 (July 2010): 322–47. https://doi.org/10.5323/jafriamerhist.95.3-4.0322.

Baez, John, William G. Unruh, and William G. Tifft. "Is Time Quantized? In Other Words, Is There a Fundamental Unit of Time That Could Not Be Divided into a Briefer Unit?" *Scientific American*, October 21, 1999. https://www.scientificamerican.com/article/is-time-quantized-in-othe/.

Baldwin, James. *The Fire Next Time*. New York: Dial, 1963.

Baudrillard, Jean. *Simulacra and Simulation*. Translated by Sheila Faria Glaser. Ann Arbor: University of Michigan Press, 1995.

Beliso-De Jesús, Aisha M. *Electric Santería: Racial and Sexual Assemblages of Transnational Religion*. New York: Columbia University Press, 2015.

Ben-Jochannan, Yosef. *The Need for a Black Bible*. New York: Black Classic Press, 1996.

Bennett, Jessica. "Hugh Hefner Civil Rights: Ebony Remembers Hugh Hefner, the Activist." *EBONY*, September 28, 2017. https://www.ebony.com/entertainment/hugh-hefner-civil-rights/.

Benton, Lauren, and Benjamin Straumann. "Acquiring Empire by Law: From Roman Doctrine to Early Modern European Practice." *Law and History Review* 28, no. 1 (February 2010): 1–38. https://doi.org/10.1017/S0738248009990022.

Berlanti, Greg, prod. *Black Lightning*. Berlanti Productions, DC Entertainment, Warner Bros. Television, 2018.

Bernal, Martin. *Black Athena: The Afroasiatic Roots of Classical Civilization*. 3 vols. New Brunswick, NJ: Rutgers University Press, 1987–2006.

Blair, Leonardo. "6-Y-O Boy Who Told Congregation 'I'm Tired of This Church' Goes Viral." *Christian Post*, January 2, 2019. https://www.christianpost.com/news/6-y-o-boy-who-told-congregation-im-tired-of-this-church-goes-viral.html.

Blight, David W. *Frederick Douglass: Prophet of Freedom*. New York: Simon and Schuster, 2018.

Browder, Anthony T. *Nile Valley Contributions to Civilization*. Vol. 1, *Exploding the Myths*. Washington, DC: Institute of Karmic Guidance, 1992.

brown, adrienne maree. *Emergent Strategy: Shaping Change, Changing Worlds*. Chico, CA: AK Press, 2017.

Bryant, Miranda. "Falling Sperm Counts 'Threaten Human Survival,' Expert Warns." *Guardian*, February 26, 2021. http://www.theguardian.com/us-news/2021/feb/26/falling-sperm-counts-human-survival.

Butler, Judith. *Gender Trouble: Feminism and the Subversion of Identity*. New York: Routledge, 1990.

Butler, Octavia. *Parable of the Sower*. New York: Grand Central, 2007.

Butler, Philip. *Black Transhuman Liberation Theology: Technology and Spirituality*. New York: Bloomsbury Academic, 2019.

Camp, Stephanie M. H. "Early European Views of African Bodies: Beauty." In *Sexuality and Slavery: Reclaiming Intimate Histories in the Americas*, edited by Daina Ramey Berry and Leslie M. Harris, 9–32. Athens: University of Georgia Press, 2018.

Cannon, Katie Geneva. *Black Womanist Ethics*. Eugene, OR: Wipf and Stock.

Cannon, Katie Geneva. *Katie's Canon: Womanism and the Soul of the Black Community*. New York: Continuum, 1995.

Cannon, Katie Geneva, and Presbyterian Church (U.S.A.). *The Womanist Theology Primer: Remembering What We Never Knew: The Epistemology of*

Womanist Theology. Louisville: Women's Ministries Program Area, National Ministries Division, Presbyterian Church (U.S.A.), 2001.

Capeheart, Loretta, and Dragan Milovanovic. *Social Justice: Theories, Issues, and Movements*. New Brunswick, NJ: Rutgers University Press, 2020.

Carter, J. Kameron. *Race: A Theological Account*. Oxford: Oxford University Press, 2008.

Caviezel, Zita, Georges Herzog, and Jürg A. Keller. *Kunstführer durch die Schweiz 3: Basel-Landschaft, Basel-Stadt, Bern, Solothurn*. Vol. 3. Bern: Gesellschaft für Schweizerische Kunstgeschichte, 2006.

Césaire, Aimé. *Discourse on Colonialism*. New York: Monthly Review Press, 2001.

Chamoiseau, Patrick. *Texaco*. New York: Pantheon, 1997.

Chandra X-Ray Observatory. "Dark Matter." Accessed September 2, 2019. http://chandra.harvard.edu/xray_astro/dark_matter/index.html.

Chimakonam, Jonathan O. *Ezumezu: A System of Logic for African Philosophy and Studies*. New York: Springer, 2019.

Clarke, John Henrik. "Homosexuality Is Not African. Straight Black Pride." Video posted on YouTube by African Crossroads, January 19, 2020. https://www.youtube.com/watch?v=PvwkvAbyK1U.

Clarke, Shirley, dir. *Ornette: Made in America*. Caravan of Dreams Productions, 1986.

Clegg, Brian. *The God Effect: Quantum Entanglement, Science's Strangest Phenomenon*. New York: St. Martin's Griffin, 2009.

Cohen, Cathy J. *The Boundaries of Blackness: AIDS and the Breakdown of Black Politics*. Chicago: University of Chicago Press, 1999.

Cohen, Cathy J. *Democracy Remixed: Black Youth and the Future of American Politics*. New York: Oxford University Press, 2012.

Cohen, Cathy J. "Deviance as Resistance: A New Research Agenda for the Study of Black Politics." *Du Bois Review: Social Science Research on Race* 1, no. 1 (2004): 27–45. https://doi.org/10.1017/S1742058×04040044.

Coleman, Monica A. *Making a Way Out of No Way: A Womanist Theology*. Minneapolis: Fortress, 2008.

Collins, Patricia Hill. *Black Sexual Politics: African Americans, Gender, and the New Racism*. New York: Routledge, 2004.

Coogler, Ryan, dir. *Black Panther*. Marvel Studios, Walt Disney Pictures, 2018.

Cooney, Kara. *The Woman Who Would Be King: Hatshepsut's Rise to Power in Ancient Egypt*. New York: Crown, 2015.

Cox Jackson, Rebecca. *Gifts of Power: The Writings of Rebecca Jackson, Black Visionary, Shaker Eldress*. Edited by Jean McMahon Humez. Amherst: University of Massachusetts Press, 1987.

Crawley, Ashon T. *Blackpentecostal Breath: The Aesthetics of Possibility*. New York: Fordham University Press, 2016.

Crawley, Ashon T. *The Lonely Letters*. Durham, NC: Duke University Press, 2020.

Crenshaw, Kimberlé. "Mapping the Margins: Intersectionality, Identity Politics, and Violence against Women of Color." In *Critical Race Theory: The Key Writings That Formed the Movement*. New York: New Press, 1995.

Crooks, Robert L., and Karla Baur. *Our Sexuality*. 12th ed. Belmont, CA: Cengage Learning, 2013.

Crouch, Andraé, and the Disciples. *Take Me Back*. Waco, TX: Light Records, 1975.

Cruse, Harold. *The Crisis of the Negro Intellectual*. New York: Morrow/New York Review of Books, 1967.

Cruz, Ariane. *The Color of Kink: Black Women, BDSM, and Pornography*. New York: New York University Press, 2016.

Dash, Julie, dir. *Daughters of the Dust*. Geechee Girls, American Playhouse, WMG Film, 1991.

Davis, Angela Y. *Abolition Democracy: Beyond Empire, Prisons, and Torture*. New York: Seven Stories, 2005.

Davis, Angela Y. *Angela Davis: An Autobiography*. New York: International, 2013.

Davis, Ossie, and Ruby Dee. *With Ossie and Ruby: In This Life Together*. New York: William Morrow, 1998.

Day, Keri. *Azusa Reimagined: A Radical Vision of Religious and Democratic Belonging*. Stanford, CA: Stanford University Press, 2022.

Day, Keri. *Notes of a Native Daughter: Testifying in Theological Education*. Grand Rapids, MI: Eerdmans, 2021.

Delbert, Caroline. "Scientists Might Have Just Stumbled upon a New Kind of Physics." *Popular Mechanics*, March 23, 2021. https://www.popularmechanics.com/science/a35917019/large-hadron-collider-new-physics/.

Dias, Elizabeth, and Ruth Graham. "Christian Conservatives Respond to Trump's Loss and Look Ahead." *New York Times*, November 8, 2020. https://www.nytimes.com/2020/11/08/us/trump-evangelicals-biden.html.

Dias, Elizabeth, and Ruth Graham. "How White Evangelical Christians Fused with Trump Extremism." *New York Times*, January 12, 2021. https://www.nytimes.com/2021/01/11/us/how-white-evangelical-christians-fused-with-trump-extremism.html.

Diop, Cheikh Anta. *Civilization or Barbarism: An Authentic Anthropology*. Translated by Yaa-Lengi Meema Ngemi. New York: Lawrence Hill, 1991.

Diop, Cheikh Anta. *Precolonial Black Africa*. Translated by Harold Salemson. New York: Lawrence Hill, 2012.

Dobieszewski, Janusz. "Russian Issues in Alain Besançon's Perspective." In *Russian Thought in Europe: Reception, Polemics, Developement*, edited by Teresa Obolevitch, Tomasz Homa, and Józef Bremer. Kraków: Akademia Ignatianum Wydawnictwo WAM, 2013.

Donoghue, Edward. *Black Breeding Machines: The Breeding of Negro Slaves in the Diaspora*. Bloomington, IN: AuthorHouse, 2008.

Douglas, Kelly Brown. "Black and Blues: God-Talk/Body-Talk for the Black Church." In *Sexuality and the Sacred: Sources for Theological Reflection*, edited by Marvin Ellison and Kelly Brown Douglas, 2nd ed., 48–66. Louisville: Westminster John Knox, 2010.

Douglas, Kelly Brown. *Sexuality and the Black Church: A Womanist Perspective*. Maryknoll, NY: Orbis, 1999.

Douglass, Frederick. *Life of an American Slave*. Boston: Anti-Slavery Office, 1845. http://utc.iath.virginia.edu/abolitn/dougnarrhp.html.

Drake, St. Clair. *Black Folk Here and There: An Essay in History and Anthropology*. New York: Diasporic Africa Press, 2014.

Drake, St. Clair. *Black Folk Here and There: An Essay in History and Anthropology*, vol. 2. Los Angeles: University of California Center for Afro-American Studies, 1991.

Du Bois, W. E. B. *The Souls of Black Folk*. New York: Barnes and Noble Classics, 2003.

Dundes, Alan. "'Jumping the Broom': On the Origin and Meaning of an African American Wedding Custom." *Journal of American Folklore* 109, no. 433 (summer 1996): 324–29. https://doi.org/10.2307/541535.

Duneier, Mitchell. *Sidewalk*. New York: Farrar, Straus and Giroux, 1999.

Einstein, Albert. *Relativity: The Special and General Theory*. London: Methuen, 1924.

Einstoss, Ron. "Karenga Sentenced." *Los Angeles Times*, September 18, 1971.

Fanon, Frantz. *The Political Writings from Alienation and Freedom*. London: Bloomsbury, 2020.

Fanon, Frantz. *The Wretched of the Earth*. New York: Grove, 1965.

Federal Writers' Project. *Slave Narrative Project*. Vol. 9, *Mississippi, Allen-Young*. Washington, DC: Library of Congress. Accessed June 23, 2022. https://www.loc.gov/item/mesn090/.

Federal Writers' Project. *Slave Narrative Project*. Vol. 11, *North Carolina, Part 1, Adams-Hunter*. Washington, DC: Library of Congress. Accessed June 23, 2022. https://www.loc.gov/resource/mesn.111/?sp=1&st=grid.

Federal Writers' Project. *Slave Narrative Project*. Vol. 16, *Texas, Part 1, Adams-Duhon*. Washington, DC: Library of Congress. Accessed April 22, 2023. https://www.loc.gov/item/mesn161/.

Feinstein, Rachel A. *When Rape Was Legal*. New York: Routledge, 2018.

Felder, Cain. *Stony the Road We Trod: African American Biblical Interpretation*. Minneapolis: Fortress, 1991.

Final Call. "Willie Lynch Letter: The Making of a Slave." May 22, 2009. http://www.finalcall.com/artman/publish/Perspectives_1/Willie_Lynch_letter_The_Making_of_a_Slave.shtml.

Fitzmaurice, Andrew. *Sovereignty, Property and Empire, 1500–2000*. Cambridge: Cambridge University Press, 2014.

Flatow, Ira, and Kit Yates. "The Math behind Big Decision Making" (transcript). *Science Friday*, National Public Radio, January 17, 2020. https://www.sciencefriday.com/segments/math-decision-making/.

Fleisher, Mark S. *The Myth of Prison Rape: Sexual Culture in American Prisons*. Lanham, MD: Rowman and Littlefield, 2009.

Fleisher, Mark S., and Jessie L. Krienert. "The Culture of Prison Sexual Violence." Washington, DC: National Institute of Justice, 2006. https://www.ojp.gov/pdffiles1/nij/grants/216515.pdf.

Flunder, Yvette. "No Doors on Our Huts: Celebrating Community on the Margin." Master's thesis, Pacific School of Religion, 1997.

Flunder, Yvette A. *Where the Edge Gathers: Building a Community of Radical Inclusion*. Cleveland: Pilgrim Press, 2005.

Fortune, Marie. *Love Does No Harm: Sexual Ethics for the Rest of Us*. New York: Continuum, 1998.

Foster, Thomas A. *Rethinking Rufus: Sexual Violations of Enslaved Men*. Athens: University of Georgia Press, 2019.

Frankfort, Henri. *Ancient Egyptian Religion: An Interpretation*. New York: Columbia University Press, 1948.

Frey, William H. "The US Will Become 'Minority White' in 2045, Census Projects." *Brookings* (blog), March 14, 2018. https://www.brookings.edu/blog/the-avenue/2018/03/14/the-us-will-become-minority-white-in-2045-census-projects/.

Gates, Henry Louis, Jr., prod. *Finding Your Roots with Henry Louis Gates, Jr.* Seasons 1–3. Alexandria, VA: PBS Distribution, 2012.

Georgia Public Broadcasting. "Unit 5, Segment J: Magnetism." *Physics in Motion*. PBS Learning Media. Accessed March 29, 2021. https://www.pbslearningmedia.org/resource/d093de49-1201-46d0-905d-4f6a4627e696/unit-5-segment-j-magnetism-physics-in-motion/.

Gill, Lyndon K. *Erotic Islands: Art and Activism in the Queer Caribbean*. Durham, NC: Duke University Press, 2018.

Gilmore, Ruth Wilson. *Golden Gulag: Prisons, Surplus, Crisis, and Opposition in Globalizing California*. Oakland: University of California Press, 2007.

Gilroy, Paul. *Against Race: Imagining Political Culture beyond the Color Line*. Cambridge, MA: Belknap, 2002.

Gilroy, Paul. *The Black Atlantic: Modernity and Double-Consciousness*. Cambridge, MA: Harvard University Press, 1993.

Gladstone, Brooke, and Bob Garfield. "The Dead Consensus." *On the Media*, WNYC Studios, December 6, 2019. https://www.wnycstudios.org/podcasts/otm/episodes/on-the-media-dead-consensus.

Gramsci, Antonio. *Selections from the Prison Notebooks*. Edited by Quintin Hoare and Geoffrey Nowell Smith. New York: International, 1971.

Grant, Jacquelyn. *White Women's Christ and Black Women's Jesus: Feminist Christology and Womanist Response*. Atlanta, GA: Scholars Press, 1989.

Greenfieldboyce, Nell. "Big Flightless Birds Come from High-Flying Ancestors." *All Things Considered*, NPR, May 22, 2014. https://www.npr.org/2014/05/22/314617422/big-flightless-birds-come-from-high-flying-ancestors.

Grewal, Inderpal. *Transnational America: Feminisms, Diasporas, Neoliberalisms*. Durham, NC: Duke University Press, 2005.

Grewal, Inderpal, and Caren Kaplan. "Global Identities: Theorizing Transnational Studies of Sexuality." *GLQ: A Journal of Lesbian and Gay Studies* 7, no. 4 (September 1, 2001): 663–79.

Griffin, Chanté. "Op-Ed: The Dark Side of Kwanzaa's Founder Can't Extinguish the Holiday's Beacon." *Los Angeles Times*, December 23, 2018. https://www.latimes.com/opinion/op-ed/la-oe-griffin-kwanzaa-20181223-story.html.

Griffin, Horace. *Their Own Receive Them Not: African American Lesbians and Gays in Black Churches*. Cleveland: Pilgrim Press, 2006.

Griffiths, David J. *Introduction to Quantum Mechanics*. New York: Cambridge University Press, 2018.

Guest, Deryn, Robert Goss, Mona West, and Thomas Bohache, eds. *The Queer Bible Commentary*. London: SCM Press, 2015.

Gumbs, Alexis Pauline. *Dub: Finding Ceremony*. Durham, NC: Duke University Press, 2020.

Gumbs, Alexis Pauline. *M Archive: After the End of the World*. Durham, NC: Duke University Press, 2018.

Gumbs, Alexis Pauline. *Spill: Scenes of Black Feminist Fugitivity*. Durham, NC: Duke University Press, 2016.

Gumbs, Alexis Pauline, and adrienne maree brown. *Undrowned: Black Feminist Lessons from Marine Mammals*. Chico, CA: AK Press, 2020.

Guner, Nezih, Christopher Rauh, and Elizabeth Caucutt. "Incarceration, Unemployment, and the Black-White Marriage Gap in the US." *VoxEU.Org* (blog), April 6, 2019. https://voxeu.org/article/incarceration-unemployment-and-black-white-marriage-gap-us.

Haley, Sarah. *No Mercy Here: Gender, Punishment, and the Making of Jim Crow Modernity*. Chapel Hill: University of North Carolina Press, 2016.

Hall, Stuart. *Essential Essays*. Edited by David Morley. Durham, NC: Duke University Press Books, 2018.

Hamilton, Virginia. *The People Could Fly: American Black Folktales Told by Virginia Hamilton*. New York: Knopf Books for Young Readers, 1993.

Hammonds, Evelyn. "Black (W)holes and the Geometry of Black Female Sexuality." *differences: A Journal of Feminist Cultural Studies* 6, nos. 2–3 (summer–fall 1994): 126–45.

Haraway, Donna. "Anthropocene, Capitalocene, Plantationocene, Chthulucene: Making Kin." *Environmental Humanities* 6, no. 1 (May 1, 2015): 159–65. https://doi.org/10.1215/22011919-3615934.

Haraway, Donna. *Simians, Cyborgs, and Women: The Reinvention of Nature*. New York: Routledge, 1990.

Harding, Vincent. *Hope and History: Why We Must Share the Story of the Movement*. Maryknoll, NY: Orbis, 2010.

Hardt, Michael, and Antonio Negri. *Empire*. Cambridge, MA: Harvard University Press, 2000.

Harney, Stefano, and Fred Moten. *The Undercommons: Fugitive Planning and Black Study*. New York: Autonomedia, 2013.

Hartman, Saidiya. *Scenes of Subjection: Terror, Slavery, and Self-Making in Nineteenth-Century America*. New York: Oxford University Press, 1997.

Hegel, G. W. F. *Elements of the Philosophy of Right*. Edited by Allen W. Wood. Translated by H. B. Nisbet. New York: Cambridge University Press, 1991.

Helminiak, Daniel. *What the Bible Really Says about Homosexuality*. San Francisco: Alamo Square, 1994.

Hendricks, Obery M. *Christians against Christianity: How Right-Wing Evangelicals Are Destroying Our Nation and Our Faith*. Boston: Beacon, 2021.

Higginbotham, Evelyn Brooks. *Righteous Discontent: The Women's Movement in the Black Baptist Church, 1880–1920*. Cambridge, MA: Harvard University Press, 1993.

Hine, Darlene. "Rape and the Inner Lives of Black Women in the Middle West: Preliminary Thoughts on the Culture of Dissemblance." In *Words of Fire: An Anthology of African-American Feminist Thought*, edited by Beverly Guy-Sheftall, 380–88. New York: New Press, 1995.

Holland, Sharon Patricia. *The Erotic Life of Racism*. Durham, NC: Duke University Press, 2012.

Holmes, Barbara A. *Race and the Cosmos: An Invitation to View the World Differently*. London: Bloomsbury T&T Clark, 2002.

Hood, Robert E. *Must God Remain Greek? Afro Cultures and God-Talk*. Minneapolis: Fortress, 1990.

hooks, bell. *Teaching to Transgress: Education as the Practice of Freedom*. New York: Routledge, 1994.

Horowitz, Jason, and Ian Johnson. "China and Vatican Reach Deal on Appointment of Bishops." *New York Times*, September 22, 2018. https://www.nytimes.com/2018/09/22/world/asia/china-vatican-bishops.html.

Hossenfelder, Sabine. "10 Things You Should Know about Black Holes." *Medium*, August 27, 2015. https://medium.com/starts-with-a-bang/10-things-you-should-know-about-black-holes-7ab9b3a16495.

Hucks, Tracey E. *Obeah, Orisa, and Religious Identity in Trinidad*. Vol. I, *Obeah: Africans in the White Colonial Imagination*. Durham, NC: Duke University Press, 2022.

Hucks, Tracey E. *Yoruba Traditions and African American Religious Nationalism*. Albuquerque: University of New Mexico Press, 2012.

Hughes, Langston. *The Collected Poems of Langston Hughes*. Edited by Arnold Rampersad. New York: Vintage, 1995.

Hyatt, Harry Middleton. *Folklore from Adams County, Illinois*. 2nd ed. New York: Alma Egan Hyatt Foundation, 1965.

Idan, Lihi, and Joan Feigenbaum. "Show Me Your Friends, and I Will Tell You Whom You Vote For: Predicting Voting Behavior in Social Networks." In *2012 IEEE/ACM International Conference on Advances in Social Networks Analysis and Mining*. Istanbul, Turkey: IEEE, 2012.

"I'm Tired of This Church (Original Video)." Video posted on YouTube by Diinodiin Edits, December 27, 2018. https://www.yoube.com/watch?v=G4mWBKX_T8k&lc=Ugw7h4lnK-6×35YzOW14AaABAg.

Jackson, Zakiyyah Iman. *Becoming Human: Matter and Meaning in an Antiblack World*. New York: NYU Press, 2020.

James, George G. M. *Stolen Legacy: The Egyptian Origins of Western Philosophy*. Scotts Valley, CA: CreateSpace, 2014.

"James Baldwin and Music: The Gospel of His Literary Blues." A conversation with Ed Pavlic and Imani e Wilson. Video posted on YouTube by National Jazz Museum in Harlem, September 30, 2021. https://youtu.be/HW9Hev1Fk2o.

Johnson, Axsal. *100 Amazing Facts about the Negro: With Complete Proof: The 2017 Edition Celebrating Black Excellence: A Tribute to J. A. Rogers*. Birmingham, AL: Yusalife, 2017.

Johnson, E. Patrick. *Honeypot: Black Southern Women Who Love Women*. Durham, NC: Duke University Press, 2019.

Johnson, E. Patrick, ed. *No Tea, No Shade: New Writings in Black Queer Studies*. Durham, NC: Duke University Press, 2016.

Johnson, E. Patrick. "'Quare' Studies, or (Almost) Everything I Know about Queer Studies I Learned from My Grandmother." *Text and Performance Quarterly* 21, no. 1 (2001): 1–25. https://doi.org/10.1080/10462930128119.

Johnson, E. Patrick. *Sweet Tea: Black Gay Men of the South*. Chapel Hill: University of North Carolina Press, 2008.

Johnson, E. Patrick, and Mae G. Henderson, eds. *Black Queer Studies: A Critical Anthology*. Durham, NC: Duke University Press, 2005.

Johnson, James Weldon. "Lift Every Voice and Sing." In *Saint Peter Relates an Incident: Selected Poems*. New York: Viking, 1935. https://www.poets.org/poetsorg/poem/lift-every-voice-and-sing.

Johnson, Jessica Marie. *Wicked Flesh: Black Women, Intimacy, and Freedom in the Atlantic World*. Philadelphia: University of Pennsylvania Press, 2020.

Johnson, Richard. "Jeffrey Epstein's East Side Mansion Houses Russian Playmates." *Page Six*, March 8, 2016. https://pagesix.com/2016/03/08/jeffrey-epsteins-east-side-mansion-houses-russian-playmates/.

Johnson, Terrence L. *Tragic Soul-Life: W.E.B. Du Bois and the Moral Crisis Facing American Democracy*. New York: Oxford University Press, 2012.

Johnson, Terrence L. *We Testify with Our Lives: How Religion Transformed Radical Thought from Black Power to Black Lives Matter*. New York: Columbia University Press, 2021.

Jones, Jacqueline. *Goddess of Anarchy: The Life and Times of Lucy Parsons, American Radical*. New York: Basic Books, 2017.

Jordan, Mark D. *The Ethics of Sex*. Hoboken, NJ: Wiley-Blackwell, 2002.

Karenga, Maulana. *Maat: The Moral Ideal in Ancient Egypt*. Los Angeles: University of Sankore Press, 2006.

Kee, Howard. *The Cambridge Annotated Study Bible: New Revised Standard Version*. New York: Cambridge University Press, 1993.

Keeling, Kara. *Queer Times, Black Futures*. New York: New York University Press, 2019.

King, Martin Luther, Jr. "Letter from Birmingham City Jail (1963)." In *A Testament of Hope: The Essential Writings and Speeches of Martin Luther King, Jr.*, edited by James Melvin Washington, 289–302. San Francisco: Harper and Row, 1986.

King, Martin Luther, Jr. "Why We Can't Wait (1964)." In *A Testament of Hope: The Essential Writings and Speeches*, 2nd ed., 518–54. San Francisco: Harper and Row, 2003.

Kohan, Jenji, creator. *Orange Is the New Black*. Tilted Productions, Lionsgate Television, 2013. https://www.netflix.com/search?q=orange%20is%20 the%20new%20black&jbv=70242311.

Lamar, Joseph. "Joseph Lamar." Accessed January 3, 2022. https://www .josephlamar.com.

Lamar, Joseph. *SIN. [act I]*. Digital Album. Denver, 2020. https://josephlamar .bandcamp.com/album/sin-act-i.

Lamar, Joseph. "SIN Diary [I]." Unpublished journal. Denver, 2020.

Lamar, Joseph. "SIN Diary [II]." Unpublished journal. Denver, 2021.

Lamar, Kendrick. "The Heart Part 5." On *Mr. Morale and the Big Steppers*. Los Angeles: pgLang, Top Dawg, Aftermath, Interscope, 2022.

Leath, Jennifer S. "'By the Glory of G*d': From Charleston to Orlando." *A.M.E. Church Review* 132, no. 4 (December 2016): 87–100.

Leath, Jennifer S. "Is Queer the New Black?" *Harvard Divinity Bulletin* 43, nos. 3–4 (summer/autumn 2015). https://bulletin.hds.harvard.edu/in-queer-the -new-black/.

Leath, Jennifer S. "Revising Jezebel Politics: Toward a New Black Sexual Ethic." In *Black Intersectionalities: A Critique for the 21st Century*, edited by Monica Michlin and Jean-Paul Rocchi. Liverpool: Liverpool University Press, 2014.

Lefkowitz, Mary. *Not Out of Africa: How "Afrocentrism" Became an Excuse to Teach Myth as History*. Reprint ed. New York: Basic Books, 1997.

Lefkowitz, Mary R., and Guy MacLean Rogers, eds. *Black Athena Revisited*. 2nd ed. Chapel Hill: University of North Carolina Press, 1996.

Levin, Brian, and Lisa Nakashima. "Report to the Nation: Illustrated Almanac; Decade Summary: Hate and Extremism." San Bernardino: Center for the Study of Hate and Extremism and California State University San Bernardino, December 2019. https://www.csusb.edu/sites/default/files/ALMANAC%20CSHE%20Nov.%202019_11.12.19_1130amPT_final.pdf.

Lightsey, Pamela R. *Our Lives Matter: A Womanist Queer Theology*. Eugene, OR: Pickwick, 2015.

Lil Donald. *Black Is Beautiful*. Ottawa: We Family, 2020.

Lil Nas X. "Montero (Call Me By Your Name) (Official Video)." Video posted on YouTube by Lil Nas X, March 26, 2021. https://www.youtube.com/watch?v=6swmTBVI83k.

Lil Nas X. "Nope 🌿 on Twitter." Twitter, March 27, 2021. https://twitter.com/LilNasX/status/1375857638869585922.

Lindqvist, Sven. *Terra Nullius: A Journey through No One's Land*. New York: New Press, 2007.

Lindsey, Heather. "About Us." Pinky Promise Movement. Accessed April 22, 2023. https://www.pinkypromisemovement.com/about.

Lomax, Tamura. *Jezebel Unhinged: Loosing the Black Female Body in Religion and Culture*. Durham, NC: Duke University Press, 2018.

Long, Charles. *Significations: Signs, Symbols, and Images in the Interpretation of Religion*. Aurora, CO: Davis Group, 1999.

Lorde, Audre. *Sister Outsider: Essays and Speeches*. Trumansburg, NY: Crossing Press, 1984.

Lorde, Audre. *Zami, a New Spelling of My Name*. Trumansburg, NY: Crossing Press, 1982.

MacIntyre, Alasdair. *After Virtue: A Study in Moral Theory*. 3rd ed. Notre Dame, IN: University of Notre Dame Press, 2007.

MacIntyre, Alasdair. *Whose Justice? Which Rationality?* Notre Dame, IN: University of Notre Dame Press, 1988.

MacKinnon, Catharine, and Andrea Dworkin. "Appendix D: The Model Ordinance." In *Pornography and Civil Rights: A New Day for Womens' Equality*, 138–42. Minneapolis: Organizing Against Pornography, 1988.

Maddow, Rachel. *Blowout: Corrupted Democracy, Rogue State Russia, and the Richest, Most Destructive Industry on Earth*. New York: Crown, 2019.

Malcolm X. "(1964) Malcolm X's Speech at the Founding Rally of the Organization of Afro-American Unity." Blackpast, October 16, 2007. https://www.blackpast.org/african-american-history/speeches-african-american-history/1964-malcolm-x-s-speech-founding-rally-organization-afro-american-unity/.

Manniche, Lisa. *Sexual Life in Ancient Egypt*. New York: Routledge, 2016.

Marable, Manning. *Beyond Black and White: Rethinking Race in American Politics and Society*. London: Verso, 1995.

Margulies, Stan, prod. *Roots*. David L. Wolper Productions, Warner Bros. Television, 1977.

Marriott, David S. *Lacan Noir: Lacan and Afro-Pessimism*. London: Palgrave Macmillan, 2021.

Masuzawa, Tomoko. *In Search of Dreamtime: The Quest for the Origin of Religion*. Chicago: University of Chicago Press, 1993.

Mbembe, Joseph-Achille. "Necropolitics." *Public Culture* 15, no. 1 (January 1, 2003): 11–40.

McKittrick, Katherine. *Dear Science and Other Stories*. Durham, NC: Duke University Press, 2020.

McKittrick, Katherine. *Demonic Grounds: Black Women and the Cartographies of Struggle*. Minneapolis: University of Minnesota Press, 2006.

McKittrick, Katherine, ed. *Sylvia Wynter: On Being Human as Praxis*. Durham, NC: Duke University Press, 2014.

Mertz, Barbara. *Temples, Tombs, and Hieroglyphs: A Popular History of Ancient Egypt*. New York: William Morrow, 2009.

Miller-Young, Mireille. *A Taste for Brown Sugar: Black Women in Pornography*. Durham, NC: Duke University Press, 2014.

Moltmann, Jürgen. *Theology of Hope: On the Ground and the Implications of a Christian Eschatology*. Minneapolis: Fortress, 1993.

Moten, Fred. *Black and Blur*. Durham, NC: Duke University Press, 2017.

Moten, Fred. *In the Break: The Aesthetics of the Black Radical Tradition*. Minneapolis: University of Minnesota Press, 2003.

Moten, Fred. *Stolen Life*. Durham, NC: Duke University Press, 2018.

Moten, Fred. *The Universal Machine*. Durham, NC: Duke University Press, 2018.

Moultrie, Monique. *Passionate and Pious: Religious Media and Black Women's Sexuality*. Durham, NC: Duke University Press, 2017.

Mueller, Robert S., III, and Special Counsel's Office, Dept. of Justice. *The Mueller Report: Report on the Investigation into Russian Interference in the 2016 Presidential Election*. New York: Melville House, 2019.

Mugge, Robert, dir. *Sun Ra: A Joyful Noise*. DVD. Winstar, 1999.

Muñoz, Jose Esteban. *Cruising Utopia: The Then and There of Queer Futurity*. New York: NYU Press, 2009.

Murray, Stephen O., and Will Roscoe, eds. *Boy-Wives and Female Husbands: Studies of African Homosexualities*. New York: Palgrave Macmillan, 2001.

NAACP. "Lift Every Voice and Sing." Accessed October 24, 2022. https://naacp.org/find-resources/history-explained/lift-every-voice-and-sing.

Nance, Malcolm W., and Rob Reiner. *The Plot to Destroy Democracy: How Putin and His Spies Are Undermining America and Dismantling the West*. New York: Hachette, 2018.

NASA Science. "Dark Energy, Dark Matter." Accessed September 2, 2019. https://science.nasa.gov/astrophysics/focus-areas/what-is-dark-energy.

Nash, Jennifer C. *The Black Body in Ecstasy: Reading Race, Reading Pornography*. Durham, NC: Duke University Press, 2014.

New York Times. "Karenga Arrested on Coast after Missing Arraignment." October 8, 1970.

Niebuhr, Reinhold. *Moral Man and Immoral Society: A Study in Ethics and Politics*. Louisville, KY: Westminster John Knox Press, 2001.

Nussbaum, Martha. *Sex and Social Justice*. Oxford: Oxford University Press, 2000.

Nyeck, S. N. *African(a) Queer Presence: Ethics and Politics of Negotiation*. New York: Palgrave Macmillan, 2021.

Obenga, Théophile. *African Philosophy: The Pharaonic Period: 2780–330 B.C.* Popenguine, Senegal: Per Ankh, 2004.

Paris, Peter. *The Spirituality of African Peoples: The Search for a Common Moral Discourse*. Minneapolis: Fortress, 1995.

Parry, Tyler D. "Jumping the Broom and the American Cultural Divide." *Black Perspectives* (blog), AAIHS, February 7, 2018. https://www.aaihs.org/jumping-the-broom-and-the-american-cultural-divide/.

Parry, Tyler D. *Jumping the Broom: The Surprising Multicultural Origins of a Black Wedding Ritual*. Illustrated ed. Chapel Hill: University of North Carolina Press, 2020.

Parsons, Lucy, and T. S. Greer. *A Lifelong Anarchist! Selected Words and Writings of Lucy Parsons*. Colorado Springs, CO: Ignacio Hills Press, 2010.

Pearson, Carlton. "Mother Sherman Story." Video posted on YouTube, March 1, 2018. https://www.youtube.com/watch?v=NREG_ZBxzP4.

Pérez, Elizabeth. "From the Throne to the Kitchen Stove: LGBT Lives in Black Atlantic Traditions." Unpublished manuscript, n.d.

Perry, Imani. *More Beautiful and More Terrible: The Embrace and Transcendence of Racial Inequality in the United States*. New York: New York University Press, 2011.

Perry, Imani. *Vexy Thing: On Gender and Liberation*. Durham, NC: Duke University Press, 2018.

Perry, Samuel L., and Cyrus Schleifer. "Race and Trends in Pornography Viewership, 1973–2016: Examining the Moderating Roles of Gender and Religion." *Journal of Sex Research* 56, no. 1 (January 2, 2019): 62–73. https://doi.org/10.1080/00224499.2017.1404959.

Phillips, Layli. *The Womanist Reader*. New York: Routledge, 2006.

Potash, John. *The FBI War on Tupac Shakur and Black Leaders: U.S. Intelligence's Murderous Targeting of Tupac, MLK, Malcolm, Panthers, Hendrix, Marley, Rappers and Linked Ethnic Leftists*. Baltimore, MD: Progressive Left Press, 2008.

Prescod-Weinstein, Chanda. *The Disordered Cosmos: A Journey into Dark Matter, Spacetime, and Dreams Deferred*. New York: Bold Type Books, 2021.

Prince. "God." *Purple Rain: Music from the Motion Picture*. Burbank: Warner, 1984.

Ra, Sun. *Sun Ra: The Immeasurable Equation. The Collected Poetry and Prose*. Edited by Hartmut Geerken. Norderstedt, Germany: Books on Demand, 2006.

Rawick, George P. *The American Slave: A Composite Autobiography*. 41 vols. Westport: Greenwood, 1972.

Riggs, Marlon, dir. *Black Is . . . Black Ain't*. California Newsreel, 1994.

Rodney, Walter. *How Europe Underdeveloped Africa*. Washington, DC: Howard University Press, 1981.

Rogers, Joel Augustus. *Sex and Race*. Vol. 1, *Negro-Caucasian Mixing in All Ages and All Lands: The Old World*. St. Petersburg, FL: Helga M. Rogers, 1968.

Rogers, Joel Augustus. *Sex and Race*. Vol. 2, *A History of White, Negro, and Indian Miscegenation in the Two Americas: The New World*. New York: Helga M. Rogers, 1944.

Rogers, Joel Augustus. *Sex and Race*. Vol. 3, *Why White and Black Mix in Spite of Opposition*. 5th ed. St. Petersburg, FL: Helga M. Rogers, 1972.

Rothman, Emily F., Courtney Kaczmarsky, Nina Burke, Emily Jansen, and Allyson Baughman. "'Without Porn . . . I Wouldn't Know Half the Things I Know Now': A Qualitative Study of Pornography Use among a Sample of Urban, Low-Income, Black and Hispanic Youth." *Journal of Sex Research* 52, no. 7 (September 2015): 736–46. https://doi.org/10.1080/00224499.2014.960908.

"Rubik's." Accessed April 22, 2023. https://rubiks.com/en-US/#.

Sandel, Michael J. *Justice: What's the Right Thing to Do?* New York: Farrar, Straus and Giroux, 2010.

San Diego Zoo Wildlife Alliance. "Ostrich." Accessed February 23, 2022. https://animals.sandiegozoo.org/animals/ostrich.

Savage, Charlie, Adam Goldman, and Jonah M. Kessel. "Analyst Who Reported the Infamous Trump Tape Rumor Wants to Clear His Name." *New York Times*, October 21, 2020. https://www.nytimes.com/2020/10/21/us/politics/igor-danchenko-steele-dossier.html.

Scott, James. *Domination and the Arts of Resistance: Hidden Transcripts*. New Haven, CT: Yale University Press, 1990.

Shakur, Assata. *Assata: An Autobiography*. Chicago: Lawrence Hill, 2001.

Shaner, Madeleine. "Searching for Willie Lynch at the Lounge Theatre." *Back Stage West* 14, no. 21 (May 24, 2007): 17–18.

Sharpe, Christina. *In the Wake: On Blackness and Being*. Durham, NC: Duke University Press, 2016.

Simpson, Glenn, and Peter Fritsch. *Crime in Progress: Inside the Steele Dossier and the Fusion GPS Investigation of Donald Trump*. New York: Random House, 2019.

Smith, Mitzi J., Angela N. Parker, and Ericka S. Dunbar Hill, eds. *Bitter the Chastening Rod: Africana Biblical Interpretation after "Stony the Road We Trod" in the Age of BLM, SayHerName, and MeToo*. Minneapolis: Fortress Academic, 2022.

Smithers, Gregory D. *Slave Breeding: Sex, Violence, and Memory in African American History*. Gainesville: University Press of Florida, 2012.

Somé, Sobonfu. *The Spirit of Intimacy: Ancient African Teachings in the Ways of Relationships*. New York: William Morrow, 2000.

Sorett, Josef, ed. *The Sexual Politics of Black Churches*. New York: Columbia University Press, 2022.

Spillers, Hortense. *Black, White, and in Color: Essays on American Literature and Culture*. Chicago: University of Chicago Press, 2003.

Spratt, David, and Ian Dunlop. *Existential Climate-Related Security Risk: A Scenario Approach*. National Centre for Climate Restoration, 2019. http://archive.org/details/ExistentialClimateRelatedSecurityMay2019.

Stewart, Dianne M. *Black Women, Black Love: America's War on African American Marriage*. Cypress, CA: Seal Press, 2020.

Stewart, Dianne M. *Obeah, Orisa, and Religious Identity in Trinidad*, vol. II, *Orisa: Africana Nations and the Power of Black Sacred Imagination*. Durham, NC: Duke University Press, 2022.

Stewart, Dianne M. *Three Eyes for the Journey: African Dimensions of the Jamaican Religious Experience*. New York: Oxford University Press, 2005.

Stoler, Ann. *Imperial Debris: On Ruins and Ruination*. Durham, NC: Duke University Press, 2013.

Strongman, Roberto. *Queering Black Atlantic Religions: Transcorporeality in Candomblé, Santería, and Vodou*. Durham, NC: Duke University Press Books, 2019.

Swaine, Jon, and Shaun Walker. "Trump in Moscow: What Happened at Miss Universe in 2013." *Guardian*, September 18, 2017. http://www.theguardian.com/us-news/2017/sep/18/trump-in-moscow-what-happened-at-miss-universe-in-2013.

Szwed, John F. *Space Is the Place: The Lives and Times of Sun Ra*. New York: Da Capo, 1998.

Taylor, Charles. *Multiculturalism: Examining the Politics of Recognition*. Princeton, NJ: Princeton University Press, 1994.

Thomas, Greg. "Erotics of Aryanism/Histories of Empire: How 'White Supremacy' and 'Hellenomania' Construct 'Discourses of Sexuality.'" *CR: New*

Centennial Review 3, no. 3 (2003): 235–55. https://doi.org/10.1353/ncr.2004.0013.

Threadcraft, Shatema. *Intimate Justice: The Black Female Body and the Body Politic*. New York: Oxford University Press, 2016.

Three Initiates. *The Kybalion: A Study of the Hermetic Philosophy of Ancient Egypt and Greece*. Hollister, MO: YOGeBooks, 2010. http://www.yogebooks.com/english/atkinson/1908kybalion.pdf.

Thurman, Howard. "Dr. Howard Thurman's Baccalaureate Address at Spelman College, May 4, 1980." Edited by Jo Moore Stewart. *Spelman Messenger* 96, no. 4 (summer 1980): 14–15.

Tinsley, Omise'eke Natasha. *Ezili's Mirrors: Imagining Black Queer Genders*. Durham, NC: Duke University Press, 2018.

Tippett, Krista. "Vincent Harding: Is America Possible?" (transcript). *On Being*. Minneapolis: National Public Radio, February 24, 2011. https://onbeing.org/programs/vincent-harding-is-america-possible/.

Tobin, Vincent Arieh. "Ma'at and δικη: Some Comparative Considerations of Egyptian and Greek Thought." *Journal of the American Research Center in Egypt* 24 (1987): 113–21.

Tocqueville, Alexis de. *Democracy in America*. Translated by J. P. Mayer. Garden City, NY: Doubleday, 1969.

Townes, Emilie M. *Breaking the Fine Rain of Death: African American Health Issues and a Womanist Ethic of Care*. Eugene, OR: Wipf and Stock, 2006.

Townes, Emilie M. *In a Blaze of Glory: Womanist Spirituality as Social Witness*. Nashville, TN: Abingdon, 1995.

Townes, Emilie M. *Womanist Ethics and the Cultural Production of Evil*. New York: Palgrave Macmillan, 2006.

Townes, Emilie M. *Womanist Justice, Womanist Hope*. Atlanta: Scholars Press, 1993.

Tutu, Desmond. *No Future without Forgiveness*. New York: Doubleday, 1999.

UN News. "Russia Responsible for Navalny Poisoning, Rights Experts Say." United Nations, March 1, 2021. https://news.un.org/en/story/2021/03/1086012.

Valencia, Robert. "What Is Net Neutrality? FCC to Roll Back Obama-Era Rule." *Newsweek*, November 21, 2017. https://www.newsweek.com/how-does-net-neutrality-help-porn-and-netflix-understanding-republicans-call-717776.

Van Patten, Tim, dir. *Boardwalk Empire*. Season 4, episode 1, "New York Sour." Aired September 8, 2013, on Home Box Office (HBO).

Walker, Alice. "Coming Apart." In *The Womanist Reader*, edited by Layli Phillips, 3–19. New York: Routledge, 2006.

Walker, Alice. *In Search of Our Mothers' Gardens: Womanist Prose*. San Diego: Harcourt Brace Jovanovich, 1983.

Walker, Alice. *The Temple of My Familiar*. San Diego: Harcourt Brace Jovanovich, 1989.

Wall, Jennifer. "What Is a Black Hole?" NASA, May 21, 2015. http://www.nasa.gov/audience/forstudents/k-4/stories/nasa-knows/what-is-a-black-hole-k4.html.

Walzer, Michael. *Spheres of Justice*. Repr., New York: Basic Books, 1984.

Walzer, Michael. *Thick and Thin: Moral Argument at Home and Abroad*. Notre Dame, IN: University of Notre Dame Press, 2019.

Warburton, Nigel. "Interview: Michael Sandel on Justice." *Prospect*, January 21, 2011. https://www.prospectmagazine.co.uk/magazine/interview-michael-sandel-on-justice-bbc4-justice-citizens-guide.

Warner, Michael. *The Trouble with Normal: Sex, Politics, and the Ethics of Queer Life*. Cambridge, MA: Harvard University Press, 1999.

Warren, Calvin L. *Ontological Terror: Blackness, Nihilism, and Emancipation*. Durham, NC: Duke University Press, 2018.

Waters, John W. "Who Was Hagar?" In *Stony the Road We Trod: African American Biblical Interpretation*, edited by Cain Felder, loc. 2289–557. Minneapolis: Fortress, 1991.

Waters, Malcolm. *Globalization*. New York: Routledge, 2013.

Welsing, Frances Cress. *The Isis Papers: The Keys to the Colors*. Chicago: Third World Press, 1991.

Wheat, David. "Iberian Roots of the Transatlantic Slave Trade, 1440–1640." AP US History Study Guide. Gilder Lehrman Institute of American History, October 18, 2012. http://ap.gilderlehrman.org/history-by-era/origins-slavery/essays/iberian-roots-transatlantic-slave-trade-1440%E2%80%931640.

Whitfield, Darren L., N. Eugene Walls, Lisa Langenderfer-Magruder, and Brad Clark. "Queer Is the New Black? Not So Much: Racial Disparities in Anti-LGBTQ Discrimination." *Journal of Gay and Lesbian Social Services* 26, no. 4 (October 2, 2014): 426–40. https://doi.org/10.1080/10538720.2014.955556.

Wilcox, Melissa M. *Queer Religiosities: An Introduction to Queer and Transgender Studies in Religion*. Lanham, MD: Rowman and Littlefield, 2020.

Wilderson, Frank. *Afropessimism*. New York: Liveright, 2020.

Wilkinson, Richard H. *The Complete Gods and Goddesses of Ancient Egypt*. New York: Thames and Hudson, 2017.

Williams, Delores S. *Sisters in the Wilderness: The Challenge of Womanist God-Talk*. Maryknoll, NY: Orbis, 1993.

Williams, Delores S. "Womanist Theology: Black Women's Voices (1986)." In *The Womanist Reader*, edited by Layli Phillips, 117–25. New York: Routledge, 2006.

Williams, Jeremy L. "'I Am a Human': Racializing Assemblages and Criminalized Egyptianness in Acts 21:31–39." In *Bitter the Chastening Rod: Africana Biblical Interpretation after "Stony the Road We Trod" in the Age of BLM, SayHerName, and MeToo*, edited by Mitzi J. Smith, Angela N. Parker, and Ericka S. Dunbar Hill, 91–108. Minneapolis: Fortress Academic, 2022.

Wimbush, Vincent L. *African Americans and the Bible: Sacred Texts and Social Structures*. New York: Continuum, 2001.

Woodard, Vincent, and Dwight McBride. *The Delectable Negro: Human Consumption and Homoeroticism within US Slave Culture*. Edited by Justin A. Joyce. New York: NYU Press, 2014.

Wright, Michelle M. *Physics of Blackness: Beyond the Middle Passage Epistemology*. Minneapolis: University of Minnesota Press, 2015.

Wynter, Sylvia. "Black Metamorphosis: New Natives in a New World." Unpublished manuscript. New York: Schomburg Center for Research in Black Culture, n.d. https://www.scribd.com/document/493587657/Sylvia-Wynter-Black-Metamorphosis-New-Natives-in-a-New-World.

Wynter, Sylvia. "The Ceremony Must Be Found: After Humanism." *Boundary 2* 12, no. 3–13, no. 1 (1984): 19–70.

Wynter, Sylvia. *The Hills of Hebron*. Harlow, UK: Longman, 1984.

Wynter, Sylvia. "On How We Mistook the Map for the Territory, and Reimprisoned Ourselves in Our Unbearable Wrongness of Being, of Désêtre: Black Studies toward the Human Project." In *Not Only the Master's Tools: African-American Studies in Theory and Practice*, edited by Lewis R. Gordon and Jane Anna Gordon, 107–69. Cultural Politics and the Promise of Democracy. Boulder, CO: Paradigm, 2006.

Wynter, Sylvia. "Unsettling the Coloniality of Being/Power/Truth/Freedom: Towards the Human, After Man, Its Overrepresentation—an Argument." *CR: New Centennial Review* 3, no. 3 (2003): 257–337.

Yates, Kit. *The Math of Life and Death: 7 Mathematical Principles That Shape Our Lives*. New York: Scribner, 2020.

Young, Thelathia Nikki. *Black Queer Ethics, Family, and Philosophical Imagination*. New York: Palgrave Macmillan, 2016.

Žižek, Slavoj. "Hegel on Marriage." *E-Flux Journal*, no. 34 (April 2012). https://www.e-flux.com/journal/34/68365/hegel-on-marriage/.

index

Note: Page locators in italics indicate figures and tables.

accountability, 37, 105, 186, 202, 223, 239
Aceves, William J., 221
Acosta, Alexander, 221
"acting up," 2, 22, 251
Africa, 84–86, 163, 173, 175, 269n78; *Ba* as "double" of the body in, 81; as first home of human intellect, 86, 262n13; homophobic vindicationist accounts, 46; Pan-Africanism, 80, 257n24, 291n84; sexuality in religious heritage of, 190; social warmth of, 82; underdeveloped by Europe, 44, 86; West and South Africa as focus of scholarship, 42–44
African American folklore, 118–19
African descent, as term, 22. *See also* Afrodiasporic people, in United States
African diaspora, in "three Americas and Caribbean," 45, 84, 266n14
Afrodiasporic, as term, 22
Afrodiasporic people, in United States: appeal of khemetic culture to, 39–40; continuity of historic bond, 84; criminalization of, 106–7, 173, 213; as "empirical others," 58, 60, 77, 86; everyday life, improvement of for, 44, 52; evolutionary process of as agentive subjects, 59–60; goodness and value of, 55; as "opaque people," 59, 61–62, 251; as organospiritual beings, 238–39; as signified, 59, 76. *See also* Black churches; Blackness; Black sexual ethics; Black sexuality; enslaved people; feminism, Black; interracial identity; interracial intimacies; interracial sexual violence; intraracial Black relationships; LGBTQ Black people; marriage; quare; slave trade, transatlantic; vindicationism; womanism
Afrodiasporic people, throughout globe, 27, 105, 108, 269n78. *See also* pornography; slave trade, transatlantic; transnational connectivities
Afrofutures, 2, 72–73, 99
Afropessimism, 61–62, 93–94, 257n22
Afua, Queen, 240
"Against the Dead Consensus" manifesto, 126–27

agency: dialectical approach, 215; jumping the broom as, 122; as vehicle of moral action, 215. *See also* moral agency
Ahmosis, Queen, 246
Akhenaton, 241, 245–46, 247
Alexander, 79
Alexander, M. Jacqui, 43
Algeria, 169
alienation, 111, 114, 262n13
Amadiume, Ifi, 46, 48
American Slave: A Composite Autobiography, The (Rawick), 123–24
Amin, Idi, 85
Ammut (deity), 203–4
Amun (deity), 4, 246, 255n9
Amun Ra (deity), *11*
anarchy, 8–9, 25; for Afropessimists, 62; and democracy, 8–9, 25, 170, 184, 234; Du Bois on, 26, 264–65n30; and engagement in violent resistance, *183*, 184, 185, 187–88, 259–60n33; and interracial intimacies, 182–86, *183*; and interracial sexual terrorism, 170; and intracommunal Black religious experience, 25–26; and Pentecostal communities, 186–87; and procedural justice, 54; spiritpolitical anarchism, 187
ancient mixologies. *See* interracial identity; interracial intimacies; interracial sexual violence
Anderson, Victor, 61–62, 129, 217, 289n22
Ani, Marimba, 45, 205
ankh, *11*, 141–42; as ohm, 141, 142
An Lu-Shan, 79
annunciation/celebration, 72
Anpu (Anubis), 203
antimiscegenation, 174, 177–78
Appiah, Kwame Anthony, 180
applied moral reasoning, 74
a priori principles, 36, 39, 53, 85, 177
Aquinas, 40
Aristotle, 25, 28, 40
Armah, Ayi Kwei, 7, 21, 45; *Two Thousand Seasons*, 84–85

Arnold, Caroline, 271n82
artifici-ecology, 226, 242. *See also* Chthulucene; emergent strategy; simulacra
Asante, Molefi, 45
asexuality, 7, 93–95
Asexual Visibility and Education Network, 95
Asian or African mode of production (AMP) states, 79–80
Asukile, Thabiti, 176
Augustine, 40
Aunt Jemima, myth of, 93
Autobiography of Malcolm X (Haley), 247
autocracy, 145
axé (affirmation), 239
Azusa revival, 187

Ba aspect of soul, 81, 86–87, 99
balance, 4–6, 9
Baldwin, James, 131–32, 278n58
Bambara, Toni Cade, 88–89
Baudrillard, Jean, 227–29, 235
becoming, 66, 131–32, 220, 236, 239, 242, 278n58
Behan, Brendan, 22
being justice, 206, 208, 236, 241, 244
belonging, 43, 50, 66, 130, 166, 261n8; and particularity, 99, 158
Bendy, Edgar, *120*, 121
Ben-Jochannan, Yosef, 7, 46
Beyond Ontological Blackness (Anderson), 61–62
binarism/binary mathematical system, 133–34
bio-actors, 104–5, 129
biological difference, denial of, 109
biomimetics/biomimicry, 232
biopolitics, 105
biracial identity, 169
Black, definitions of, 21–22
"black books," 44–45, 276n23
Black churches: absence of clear discernment process, 144–45; broken ♥'d believers, 154–57; capitalist models adopted by, 145; choreographing

314   Index

virtues, 146–54; colonizing systems as vehicles for sin, 152; "holy dance," 139; (mis)handlings of sexualities, 8, 138, 139; and nation-state, 158; path of judgment, 162–63; and politics, 158–59; and pornography, 209–10; quare potential of, 163–66; "tired of this church" feelings, 137–39, *138*; tools of white culture used by, 190; virtue traditions, 147. *See also* homosexualities

Black Codes, 181

Black Folk Here and There (Drake), 23–24

Black-gayness, 139

black holes, 7, 72, 77–78; Ammut as, 203–4. *See also* dark matter

"Black Is Beautiful" (Lil Donald), 106–7, 114, 276n7

Black Is . . . Black Ain't (documentary), 50

Black Lives Matter, 25, 26, 31

Black nationalism, 38, 87, 170, 278n58, 291n84

Blackness, 50, 73, 78; Blackwoman, Blackqueer discursive approach, 18–19; essentialization of, 24, 37, 43, 49–50, 57, 63, 263–64n24; gay-Blackness, 139; Isis as prototype for, 111; "isness/ontology" of, 60–62, 177; liberation in terms of escaping, 61; materiality of, 31–32; power, moral agency, and value of, 21; pride in, 247; as religious subject, 20, 24–25; spectra of, 19; white fear of, 105. *See also* Afrodiasporic people, in United States

Blackqueerness/queerblackness, 2, 4, 10, 18–20, 36, 43, 163. *See also* LGBTQ Black people; quare

Black sexual ethics, 206, 239, 248; approaches to justice, 35–36; for dancing justice, 166; defined, 73; and heterexpectations, 135–36; and hybridity, 204; and interracial sexual intimacies, 172, 179, 189, 201; justice and freedom debates, 239; and marriage, 102, 116–17, 134; particularity of, 38; positionality of scholarship, 98–99; purposeful entanglements, 135; purpose precedes sex, 100; recoding pornography, 244; (re)imagining, 39; sexual discourse of resistance, 189–91; and ~~sexuality~~, 93, 96–97; and theories of justice, 6–7, 19, 24, 34, 35–36, 87; and vindicationism, 7, 24. *See also* sexual ethics

Black sexuality, 12, 50–52, 236; as challenge to nation-state, 208; church perspectives on, 144; creative freedom, 208, 238–39; effect of white supremacy on, 114, 213; hypersexuality, stereotypes of, 104, 190; policing of, 179; problematic empirical, 242–43. *See also* heterexpectations; homosexualities; interracial intimacies; interracial sexual violence; intraracial Black relationships; LGBTQ Black people; marriage; ~~sexuality~~

Black Womanist Ethics (Cannon), 42

B mesons, 239

Book of the Coming Forth by Day from Night (Book of the Dead), 86, 202–4, 240–41

Borges, Jorge Luis, 228

Boswell, John, 48

Brookings Institute report, 124

Broussard, Donaville, 121–22

Browder, Anthony, 86

brown, adrienne marie, 134, 235, 291n69; *Emergent Strategy: Shaping Change, Changing Worlds*, 230–32, *232*

Burks, Kendall, 152

Butler, Octavia, 230

Butler, Philip, 188, 285n56

"Call of Cthulhu, The" (Lovecraft), 233

Camp, Stephanie M. H., 179–80

Candomblé, 43

Cannon, Katie Geneva, 42, 72–73, 85, 89, 96, 98

capitalism, 129, 247, 286n6; Césaire's view, 145; at end of Cold War, 227–28

carceral state, 8, 54, 115–16, 169–70, 182

cardinal virtues, 87, 147–48, 256n15

Index 315

cartouches, 2, 5
Caucutt, Elizabeth, 115–16
celibacy, 93, 95–96, 288n16
centrifugal forces, 28–29, 34, 59, 66, 90, 231, 232
ceremonial center, city as, 27–29, 59
Césaire, Aimé, 8, 45, 78, 140, 145, 148, 262n13
Chandra X-Ray Observatory, 77
change, 230–31, 232
chaos theory, 230–31
Chauvin, Derek, 168, 181, 281–82n3
China, 79, 291n61
Christianity, 59; Douglass on, 128; Du Bois on, 26, 264–65n30; pseudo-Christianity, 128, 129; theoethical resources beyond, 85. *See also* Black churches; religion
chthonic Greek gods, 233
Chthulucene, 229–30, 232–33, 242
cities: centered, 27–29, 59; empires reduced to size of, 79–80
Civilization or Barbarism: An Authentic Anthropology (Diop), 79
civil rights movement, 25, 216, 221, 289n33
clanic structure, African, 83
Clarke, John Henrik, 7, 47
classical physics, 8, 31, 164
class struggle, 183, 184
Clegg, Brian, 132–33
climate change debates, 238
Clinton, Bill, 227
clubs, 158
coding justice, 9, 242, 244, 245, 247
Cohen, Cathy, 237–38
Cold War era, 222, 227–28
Coleman, Ornette, 71
collective memory, 75–76
Collins, Patricia Hill, 38
colonization: and interracial intimacies, 169–70; of knowledge, 41; of religion, 20, 60, 151
Color of Kink: Black Women, BDSM, and Pornography, The (Cruz), 214–15

common good discourses, 75, 125, 268n50, 274n49
common theory of justice, 105, 107, 114
Commonweal magazine, 125
communities: African clanic structure, 83; community of right order, framework of, 3; Maât in, 202; marriage in Black community, 115–19; moral and political judgments shaped by, 55–56; womanist connectedness to, 18, 22–23
Complete Gods and Goddesses of Ancient Egypt, The (Wilkinson), 64–65
concordance model, 77
conquest discourse of sexuality, 170
conscientization, 72, 73–75, 85
consent, 233; freedom of, 117–18; and interracial intimacies, 168
consequentialism, 52, 53, 74, 86
conservatism, illiberal, 124–27
context, sexuality as, 93–97
cosmopolitanism, 206–7
countermemory, 37–38, 62, 75–76, 85, 270n81
counter-normalization, 36–38, 62
courage, 147
Cox Jackson, Rebecca, 93, 94
Crenshaw, Kimberlé, 9
"Cress Theory of Color-Confrontation and Racism (White Supremacy): A Psychogenetic Theory and World Outlook, The" (Welsing), 108–9, 113
criminalization of Black people, 106–7, 173, 213
"Crisis in Black Male/Black Female Relationships: Is It a False Problem?, The" (Welsing), 114
Cruising Utopia: The Then and There of Queer Futurity (Muñoz), 163
Cruse, Harold, 25
Cruz, Ariane, 214–15
Cthulhu, 233
cultural identity, 83
culture, as politics, 21
curvilinear approaches, 33–34

316   Index

dance of redemption, 72–73
dancing justice, 8, 66, 160–62; choreographing of virtues, 146–54; flying justice differentiated from, 141–42; holy dance, 139, 140, 165–66; as process, 156
dark energy, 72, 77–78
dark matter, 63, 72, 75–78, 270n79. *See also* black holes
Davis, Angela, 129
Davis, Ossie, 101, 134
Day, Keri, 39, 186–87
"Dead Consensus, The" (*On the Media*), 125
Declarations of Innocence, 202–3
Dee, Ruby, 101, 134
dehumanization, 169; as strategy, 106–7
Delbert, Caroline, 239
democracy: and anarchy, 8–9, 25, 128, 170, 184, 234; capitalist, disentanglement from, 129; "common good" discourses, 125, 268n50, 274n49; conservative lack of identification with, 127; and creative space, 226; defense of, 208; *dēmos* and *kratia*, 234; etymology of, 127; failure of, 124–25; as heritage of whites, 26; intentional democrats, 130–31, 238; limitations of, 184–85; marriage and (better) uses of the erotic, 124–32; pseudo-democrats, 128; rededication to, 124–25, 127–29; and revolutions, 80; Russia structured as, 227; as site for the proliferation of love, 132; socialist possibilities for, 129–30; transnational critique of, 207; US as better choice than other empires, 225–26; and youth sexuality, 238
Democracy Remixed: Black Youth and the Future of American Politics (Cohen), 237–38
deontological principle, 53, 177
desire, 180, 198–201
deterministic models, 30–31
deviance: normative, 58, 173; as resistance, 37, 156, 214, 251; rethinking, 218–19

dike, concept of, 5, 86
Diop, Cheikh Anta, 7, 45, 46, 78–85, 206, 240, 249; *Civilization or Barbarism: An Authentic Anthropology*, 79–80; *L'Unité Culturelle de l'Afrique Noire*, 83; *Nations Nègres et Culture*, 78–79
discernment, 144–45
discourse: of common good, 75, 125, 268n50, 274n49; egalitarian, 28–29, 171, 187, 223, 268n50, 274n49; of justice, 44, 104, 275n3; metalogues, 96, 97; post(trans)national, 9; sexual, need for, 189–91
disposability, 105
disruption, 36–38
distributive justice, 54–55, 75
diversity arguments, 112–13
divinity, dignity, and integrity of human existence, 148–50
Djehuty (deity), 4, 203, 255–56n11. *See also* Thoth (deity)
Dobieszewski, Janusz, 225
doctrines, religious, 142, 146, 164
domination power, 108, 112, 167–68, 180–82
Douglas, Kelly Brown, 170, 189–91
Douglass, Frederick, 128, 130, 181
Drake, St. Clair, 23–24, 176
Du Bois, W. E. B., 7, 24–27, 264–65n30; on choice between anarchy and hypocrisy, 26, 265n30
Dundes, Alan, 119
Duneier, Mitchell, 44
dunia (terrasphere), 9, 249, 257n24, 291n84; common ecological context, 208, 231; and emergent strategy, 231–32, *232*, 242; globalization's detriments to, 207–8; humanalities, 240–44; sexuality's exacerbations and mitigations, 207–8
Dworkin, Andrea, 211–12, 215

earth: biological future of, 229–30
ecstasy, 220
egalitarian discourses, 28–29, 171, 187, 223, 268n50, 274n49

Index 317

egalitarian traditions, 28–29, 129, 171, 187, 223, 268n50, 274n49
Egypt: Amarna period, 241, 245–46; Dagara context, 276n20; as de facto center of modern research and knowledge, 55; Diop's recovery of, 78–84; Lamar on, 140–41, *143*; Late Period (1085–333 BCE), 2; Nubian connection with, 79; Old Kingdom, 2, 64; "Osirian" revolution of Sixth Dynasty, 79–80; primordial standing of, 45, 86; unification of Upper and Lower, 65. *See also* khemetic (ancient Egyptian) culture; vindicationism
Einstein, Albert, 34, 48, 113, 256n20, 272n6; on "racial purity," 174
electromagnetism, 9, 31, 172, 197–98, 203
Eliade, Mircea, 27
emancipatory historiography, 72, 75–85, 89
emergence, 134
emergent strategy, 230–32, *232*, 242
Emergent Strategy: Shaping Change, Changing Worlds (brown), 230–32, *232*
empire, 206, 286–87n6
empirical others, 58, 60, 77, 86
enslaved people: Black women purchased for sexual purposes, 180; democratic citizenship not possible for, 8; marriage not possible for, 8; sexualized violence of Black men, 181; slave breeding, 181, 277–78n31; (un)rapeability of, 180–81. *See also* slave trade, transatlantic
entanglement theory, 8, 102, 113–14, 132–34, 285n55; *Verschränkung*, 133
enunciation, politics of, 218
Epstein, Jeffrey, 221–22
erons, 73, 93, 96, 204, 227
erotic: democracy marriage and (better) uses of, 124–32; european-american tradition, 213; as source of power and information, 212
Erotic Life of Racism, The (Holland), 180

"Erotics of Aryanism/Histories of Empire: How 'White Supremacy' and 'Hellenomania' Construct 'Discourses of Sexuality'" (Thomas), 46, 48
essentialization of Blackness, 24, 37, 43, 49–50, 263–64n24; of Black women's sexuality, 57, 63
ethics, 247, 275n2; of eros, 130; process of, 191. *See also* Black sexual ethics; sexual ethics
Euclidean geometry, 33
European Organization for Nuclear Research (CERN), 239
evil: structural, 19, 75, 76; work of dismantling, 37, 270–71n81
Exodus model of liberation, 42, 61
expectations, 103–4. *See also* heterexpectations
exploitation: and interracial intimacies, 170, 178–82; and pornography, 219, 221, 233; racism as, 236

fairness, 55, 56, 66, 103, 105
family, 36, 111, 140, 172–73; differences in structure, 115–16
Fanon, Frantz, 8, 45, 169–70, 186, 259n33
fantastic hegemonic imagination, 19, 59, 75–76, 98
fantasy, as space of subject formation, 220
Federal Writers' Project, *120*, 121–22, 134–35
Feinstein, Rachel, 180
Felton, Rebecca Latimer, 182
feminism, as inadequate for addressing racial diversity, 23
feminism, Black, 214, 217–18, 220, 235–36, 260–61n7, 289n37. *See also* womanism
Ferrell, Naszir, 137, *138*
fidelity, 134, 148, 192
Fire Next Time, The (Baldwin), 131–32, 278n58
First Things, 126
Flatow, Ira, 133

flight, as human capacity, 87–88, 98
Floyd, George, 167–69, 181, 185, 186, 202, 275–76n7, 281n3
flying justice, 7–8, 142, 206, 274n46; Afrofutures, 2, 72–73, 99; annunciation/celebration, 72, 93–97; Bird Without Wings, 99–100; conscientization, 72, 73–75, 85; in cosmic sense, 87; dancing justice differentiated from, 141–42; drinking gourd, following, 89; emancipatory historiography, 72, 75–85, 89; flying as theory of justice, 87–89; grounded flight, 100, 274n46; as new form of leaning, 98; norm clarification, 72, 87–89; re-reflection and strategic action, 72, 97–100; and solidarity, 98; strategic options, 72, 89–93; theological resources, 72, 85–87
fortitude, 147
Fortune, Marie M., 170, 191–94
Foster, Thomas A., 181
Foucault, Michel, 105
Franks, Dora, 134–35
freedom, 55, 89, 106, 222, 226, 259–60n33; of consent, 117–18; creative, and Black sexuality, 208, 238–39; and jumping the broom, 124, 135; and naming of experience, 17; quantum physics applied to, 30; sexual, 19, 185–86, 187, 190, 215, 223, 243
Fuller, Neely, 108
future, 10, 58–63; Afrofutures, 2, 72–73, 99; of biological life, 229–30; dark energy flying into, 78; and hope, 157; as quare/queer, 163; and simulacra, 227–29

Gates, Henry Louis, Jr., 263–64n24, 282–83n10
gay-Blackness, 139
gender identities and sexual orientations. *See* LGBTQ Black people
Get Out (film), 155
"Gifts of Power: The Writings of Rebecca Jackson" (Walker), 17–18
Gitton, Michel, 4–5

globalization, 9; casualties of, 207; global white supremacy system, 108–10, 114; transnationalism as foil to, 206–7, 286n6. *See also* nation-state
God Effect: Quantum Entanglement, Science's Strangest Phenomenon, The (Clegg), 132–33
goodness, 53, 55, 74, 83; and "God-ness," 154; of human sexuality, 190–91
Gorbachev, Mikhail, 227
Grant, Jacqueline, 42
gravity, 6, 19, 30, 34, 77, 88, 97, 142
Greco-Roman cultures and philosophy, 5, 18, 233; Egypt as teacher, 45; and Western frameworks, 40, 46, 55, 177
Grewal, Inderpal, 206–7
Griffiths, David, 164
Guner, Nezih, 115–16

Hades and Persephone, 233
Hagar, biblical narrative of, 61, 219
Haley, Alex, 247, 289n33
Haley, Sarah, 182
Hall of Judgment (Hall of the two Truths), *2*, 64, 202–3
Halperin, David, 48
Hamer, Fannie Lou, 128
Hamilton, Virginia, 98
Hammonds, Evelyn, 218
Haraway, Donna, 229–30, 232–33, 235
Harding, Rachel, 43
Harding, Vincent, 128–29, 130
Harlem Renaissance, 78, 176
harm, distinguished from love, 192
Harrison, Bev, 72
Hathor, 42, 247
Hatshepsut (r. 1473 to 1458 BCE), 4–5, 246–47, 292n3
Hawking, Stephen, 77
Haymarket Square bombing, *183*, 184
Hefner, Hugh, 289n33
Hegel, Georg W. F., 116–17
hegemony, 3, 8, 96, 127, 171, 219; dismantling, 23, 243; fantastic hegemonic imagination, 19, 59, 75–76, 98; Russian and US, 223, 226

Heliopolitan system, 80, 81
Hemopolitan system, 80, 81
hermeneutic, queer utopian, 158–59
Herndon, Tempie, 122
Herschel, Caroline, 275n64
heterexpectations, 101–36, 208; biosocial expression of heterosexuality, 104–5; and Black sexual ethic, 135–36; civic context, 104–5, 129–30; defined, 103; entanglements, emerging, 132–34; entanglements, purposeful, 134–35; as foundation of nation-state, 8; gender identity as fixed, 103; LGBTQ adoption of, 103; making sense of, 103–7; and marriage in Black community, 115–19; and masturbation, 210, 235; and unified field theory, 107–15
heteropatriarchal framework, 7–8, 40, 60, 111, 144, 164, 180, 248, 277–78n31, 281n3. *See also* patriarchal logics
hierarchy: "black" racial superiority, promotion of, 109; and city, 28–29; evolutionary dominance, 111
"highest good," 125
Hitler, Adolf, 145, 177–78
Holland, Sharon Patricia, 180
Holmes, Barbara, 7, 30–31, 41, 87–89, 280n39; "cat paradox" of quantum physics, 164–65
homophobia: as sin, 191; as threat to Black well-being, 190; in vindicationist writings, 7, 45–50, 79, 85
Homo sapiens sapiens, 79
homosexualities, 8, 243; and broken ♥'d believers, 154–57; and dancing justice, 161, 164, 166; normalcy of, 177; "sexual deviation" as euphemism for, 47; and sexual discourse of resistance, 190; vindicationist views of, 45–48. *See also* Black churches; LGBTQ Black people
hooks, bell, 193
hope, 131, 157
Horus, 110
Hucks, Tracey, 43, 257n22

Hughes, Langston, 5–6
human functional capabilities approach, 75
~~humanity~~, 93–94, 257n22
Hustle, Nipsey (Nip tha Great), 188
hybridity, racial, 8–9, 44–45; born of oppression, 170; interracial identity, 169, 171–72, 282–83n10; jumping the broom, 119; Maât in *netcherw* of, 202; United States as hybrid, 131–32, 203–4. *See also* interracial intimacies
hypocrisy, 26, 53, 112, 154, 155, 186, 237
hysteria, 60, 62, 65, *92*

ibis, 60, 65, *92*, 256n11
identifiers, ascribing, 94
identity, 262n13; biracial, 169; cultural, 83; interracial, 169, 171–72, 282–83n10; queer, 10
identity politics, 30, 186
Ifá divinations, 43
iFLY wind tunnel, 97–98
illiberalism, 125–27
imago dei, 149
immortality, 64, 81
imperialism, 28, 206–7, 225, 240, 286–87n6; and censorship, 290n51; outposts, 224–25
"Incarceration, Unemployment, and the Black-White Marriage Gap in the US" (Guner, Rauh, and Caucutt), 115–16
indigenous populations, and terra nullius doctrine, 261–62n8
injustice, 4, 56–57, 59, 63, 72–74, 84, 90, 105; Black women's experience of, 56; white desensitization to, 105. *See also* justice
International Working Peoples' Association, 184
internet, 206; fake news concerns, 223; net neutrality, 224, 290n60; Pinky Promise website, 210, 288n16; Russia's attempt to start race war through, 208, 221–27; theopolitical control tactics, 223–25. *See also* pornography
Internet Research Agency (Russia), 221

320   Index

interracial identity, 169, 171–72, 282–83n10; no choice in, 171
interracial intimacies, 8, 284n26; criminalization of, 173; exploitative, 170, 178–82; and Fanon's project, 169–70; intentional and conscientious, 170, 171; interracial sexual ethics in discourse, 188–95; mixed-race relations, possibilities for, 172–78; moral questions for race purists, 174–75; and murder of George Floyd, 167–68; psychological challenges of, 173; and racial hybridity, 171, 172; sexually based terrorism, 170, 172; and transatlantic slave trade, 169, 170; ubiquity of, 169, 171, 173, 177–78, 182; weaponization of, 171, 173. *See also* hybridity, racial
interracial sexual violence, 170, 178–82; against enslaved Black men, 181; Maât and puzzling justice, 201–4; partial approaches as inadequate, 194; sexual discourse to repel white impact on Black sexuality, 189–91; story of rape told on body, 198; systematic sexual surveillance, 179, 181–82, 213, 283–84n26, 289n22; (un)rapeability of Black women, 180–81. *See also* violence
intersectionality, 9, 30, 50, 76, 186
intraracial Black relationships, 102; as connection against white supremacy, 114–15; effect of white supremacy on, 114, 213; threat of violence to, 107. *See also* marriage
intuition, 33, 53, 55, 154, 171, 217
irruption, 36–38, 266n7; disruption-irruption, 37
Isis, 64, 81, 110–11, 203, 247
Isis Papers: The Keys to the Colors, The (Welsing), 107–15
isness/ontology, 60–61, 66, 145, 177, *232*, 236

Jackman, Charmaine, 137–38, 166
Jackman, Ezra, 137–38, 166
James, George G. M., 8, 45, 140; on Egyptian Mysteries, 51, 147–48
Jesus, Blackness of, 61
Johnson, E. Patrick, 1, 7, 17; "'Quare' Studies," 22
Johnson, Lacy M., 200–201
Johnson, Terrence L., 26–27, 129
Jones, Jacqueline, 185–86
Jordan, Mark, 96
Judeo-Christian traditions, 41, 112, 145–46, 154, 163, 241
jumping the broom, 8, 118, 119–32; as European custom, 118–19, 122–23; and freedom, 124, 135; as hybrid, 119; as process of equality and balance, 123–24; used to degrade couples, 122
Juneteenth, 276n7
just Black sexualities, 139–40
justice: as agentive actor, 64, 162; approaches to Black sexual ethics, 6–7, 19, 35–36; being, 206, 236, 244; being and coding, 9; blindfolded "lady justice," 5–6, 256n18; common theory of, 105, 107, 114; contractarian theory of, 57, 87; defined, 50–52; distributive, 54, 75; dominant theories in US, 44; double standard, 105–7; in Egyptian mystery system, 51, 147–48; and fairness, 55, 56, 66, 103, 105; freedom and virtue as starting points, 55; images of, *2*, 5–6; and interracial sexual intimacies, 170; modern Eurocentric/occidental translations of, 52–58; motion of, 59–60, 62–63; normative theories of, 19, 35, 57; "now" approach to, 272–73n6; performance of, 6–7; and planetary survival, 57–58; procedural, 54, 75; quareing, 3–4, 8, 10, 19–20, 24, 201, 250; racial, 56, 62, 105; resistance as work of, 108–9; restorative, 52–55; retributive, 54, 75; shouting, 159–62; in singular form, 63; as a standard, 35–36; as virtue, 51, 148, 268n50. *See also* dancing justice; flying justice; injustice; justices; Maât (deity); *maât* (Maât's moral code, justice/s); puzzling justice; theories of justice

"Justice" (Hughes), 5–6
justices: experience-informed, 90; movement of, 66–67; plural form of, 63; prioritization of, 12–13; solving for, 67, 171–72, 195–98, 202; as targets, 63, 74; understanding, 2. *See also* justice
justice work, 216
justicing, 17, 90, 142, 186, 250–51, 271n81
just war theory, 216

Ka aspect of soul, 81, 86–87
Kabaila, Wesley, 257–58n25
Kahun Papyrus (Egyptian Middle Kingdom), 60
Kantian ethic, 125
Karenga, Maulana, 5, 45, 58, 89, 206, 256n15; *maât* as both concept and practice for, 241; study of Maât, 9, 202–3
Kennedy, Hamp, 122
keys, symbolism of, 141–42
khemetic (ancient Egyptian) culture, 20, 39–44, 56; appeal of to people of African descent in the US, 39–40; Day of Judgment, 51–52, 64, 86, 256n20, 271n82; four divine pairs, 81; and future, 58–63; homophobia and heterosexism in writings about, 45–46, 79; and Kushite people, *11*, 43, 85; losses, 43–44; mystery system, 51, 147–48; quare reading of, 43; Western indebtedness to, 12, 28–29, 40, 46, 177. *See also* Egypt
khthon (earth), 233
King, Martin Luther, Jr., 128, 194
Know Your Enemy podcast, 125
kompromat, 222–23, 225, 226
Kushite people, *11*, 43, 85
Kybalion, 280n20, 281n39

Lamar, Joseph (Jojo), 8, 137, 139–42, *143*; dancing justice, 141–42, 160–62; diary of, 150–51; homosexuality, awareness of, 152–53; self-description, 139–40, 279n2; *SIN. [act I]*, 145–46, 148–55; "SIN Diary [I]," 159–60; virtue 1: divinity, dignity, and integrity of human existence, 148–50; virtue 2: commit to processes of positive evolution, 150–51; virtue 3: resist sin, 151–52; virtue 4: pro-create, 152–54
laying on of hands, 187
Leadership and the New Science (Wheatley), 230–31
leadership models, 230–31
Lefkowitz, Mary, 49, 50
Legerton, Wynn, 73
Lesbos, symbolism of, 18
Levinas, Emmanuel, 180
Lewis, C. S., 30
LGBTQ Black people, 20, 50, 52, 85; belonging of, 50; broken ♥'d believers, 154–57; creativity of, 266n7; refuge, spaces of, 157–59; tools of white culture used by Black church, 190. *See also* homosexualities
liberation: articulated in terms of escaping Blackness, 61; Exodus model of, 42, 61; universal, 39
liberation ethics, 72–73
Life of an American Slave (Douglass), 128
"Lift Every Voice and Sing" (Johnson), 258–59n29
light, and dark matter, 77
Lil Donald, 106–7, 114, 276n7
Lil Nas X, 281n40
Lindqvist, Sven, 261n8
Lindsey, Heather, 210
Lomax, Tamura, 217–18, 289n22, 289n34, 289n37
Long, Charles H., 7, 27–29, 44, 58; "empirical others" defined by, 58, 60, 77, 86; hybridity, view of, 44–45, 59; opaqueness, view of, 29, 45, 59, 62, 76–77; silence, view of, 76–77
Lorde, Audre, 130, 182, 193, 209–10; "Uses of the Erotic," 212–13
love, 131, 191–92
Lovecraft, H. P., 230, 231, 233

Love Does No Harm: Sexual Ethics for the Rest of Us (Fortune), 191–94
Loving v. Virginia, 174
lying, as about power, 193
lynching, 174, 181–82

Maât (deity): as artifici-ecological defender of being, 242; balance established by, 4–6; as being, 67, 241–42; in community, 202; complementarity of, 4–5; and dancing justice, 66; and Day of Judgment, 51–52, 64, 86, 256n20, 271n82; depicted as offering, *11*; as epistemological point of origin, 58, 85; feather of, 2, *2*, 6, 12, 63, 136, 166, 204; feather of as ostrich feather, 86, 271n82, 274n46; forty-two laws of, 202–3, 241, 287n8; as hermeneutic of justice, 6; in hybrid *netcherw*, 202, 242; as individual, 86; Isis referenced by, 111; isness/ontology of, 66; movement of, 66–67; multifaceted role of, 64–66, 86; as *ntrt* of justice and truth, 2, 20, 87, 250, 255n4; Old Kingdom references to, 64; and personification of justice, 63; and puzzling justice, 66–67, 201–4; and right order, 3–6; Thoth as husband of, 65–66, *92*; vindicationist visions of, 39–50; wings of, *11*, 63, 86

maât (Maât's moral code, justice/s), 240, 256n15; and combination of justice and truth, 2–3; and emergent strategy, 232, 242; Maâtian Code of Justice, 100, 136, 166, 204, 244; and monarch's legitimacy, 64; universal, political, and individual levels, 4–5

MacKinnon, Catherine, 211–12, 215
magnetism. *See* electromagnetism
Malcolm X, 13, 259–60n33
"Manifesto for Cyborgs: Science, Technology, and Socialist Feminism in the 1980s, A" (Haraway), 229
Manniche, Lise, 245–46
Marable, Manning, 25
marginalization, 30, 37, 123, 165, 243

marketization, effect on human sexuality, 236
marriage, 8, 101; Black church narrowing of, 139; in Black community, 115–24; and consent, 117–18; as consummate expression of heterosexuality, 104; cultural expectations for, 102; as deception, 118; democracy and (better) uses of the erotic, 124–32; effect of white supremacy on, 114; function in nation-state, 116; inaccessibility of to Black people, 8, 103, 115–16; jumping the broom, 8, 119–24; as racialized institution, 115–16; and religious commodification of women, 210–11; tying the knot, 123; used to disempower people of African descent, 119–21; Wilson hypothesis, 116. *See also* intraracial Black relationships

Mary, biblical, 130
master-slave dialectic, 117
masturbation, 210, 235
material concerns, 29–30
materiality, 233, 235; Black, 31–32
Math of Life and Death: Seven Mathematical Principles That Shape Our Lives, The (Yates), 133–34
matriarchal model, 46, 48, 57, 79
"Maxims of the Prime Minister Ptahhotep" (circa 2450 BCE), 2
Maya people, 33
Mbembe, Achille, 105, 107; necropolitics, 105, 107, 238
Meaning of Relativity, The (Einstein), 113
mechanics. *See* classical physics; quantum physics (quantum mechanics)
melanin envy, 107–9, 111, 267–68n36
memory: collective, 75–76; countermemory, 37–38, 85; transformation of, 201
Memphite system, 80
metalogues, 96, 97
Miller-Young, Mireille, 215–16, 218–21
"Model Antipornography Civil-Rights Ordinance" (Dworkin and MacKinnon), 211–12

moral agency, 5, 171, 177, 248, 250; of ancestors, 175; *Black* as appeal to, 8; and choices of connection and separation, 102–3; de facto, 52, 55; defined, 191; exploitation of, 219; and pornography, 215–16, 219, 244; primary, 74, 196; of sex workers, 219. *See also* agency

moral constellations, 10, 12, 43–44, 63, 73, 124, 238–39; and system of virtues, 146–47

moral reasoning, 35–36, 51–53, 74–75, 240

More Beautiful and More Terrible: The Embrace and Transcendence of Racial Inequality in the United States (Perry), 5–6

motion, 59–60, 62

Moultrie, Monique, 209–10, 235

Moynihan Report, 116

Muñoz, José Esteban, 10, 157–58, 163

mystery system, Egyptian, 51, 147–48

naming, 1, 17–18, 42

Nance, Malcolm, 222–23

Nash, Jennifer C., 220

nationalisms: Black, 38, 87, 170, 278n58, 291n84; imperialistic, 208, 225; rejection of, 208; white, 125, 127, 170. *See also* nation-state

Nations Nègres et Culture (Diop), 78–79

nation-state: and Black churches, 158; Black people not beneficiaries of, 119; Black sexuality as challenge to, 208; built on ancient Egyptian principles, 80; confusion and conflation of issues enabled by, 224; as "eternal," 207; and expectations, 103; "free consent" of subjects, 117; function of marriage in, 116; heterexpectations as foundation of, 8; interracial sexual violence as foundational pillar of, 178; interracial tensions in evolution of, 169; marriage as central to, 116–17; master-slave dialectic, 117; necropolitical, 105, 107; transnationalist critique of, 286–87n6. *See also* globalization; nationalisms; Russia; United States

Native Research and Scholarship Committee, 88

natural law, 111, 116–17

Nazi Germany, 169, 172, 173

Neal, Claude, 181

necropolis, 245

necropolitics, 105, 107, 238

Need for a Black Bible: The Black Man's Religion, Volume III, The (Ben-Jochannan), 46–47

Nefertari, *2*, 247

Nefertiti, 245–46, 247

Négritude, 8–9, 78, 262n13, 266n14; US-oriented expression of, 20

Negro-Caucasian Mixing in All Ages and All Lands (Rogers), 172–78

"Negro laugh," 84

"Negro Marriage, The" (Willie Lynch letter), 119–21

neoliberalism, 207, 236

Newton, Isaac, 272n6, 275n64

Niebuhr, Reinhold, 63

Nile River, 245

No Mercy Here (Haley), 182

nonconsequentialism, 53, 74, 86

normalization, 36–38, 187; queering of, 214

norm clarification, 72, 87–89

n*ṯrw* (deities), 65, 248, 255n4, 271n86

nuclear, the, 228–29

Nussbaum, Martha, 75, 87

Nyerere, Julius, 85, 291n84

Obama, Barack, 128

Obenga, Théophile, 2–5, 7, 45, 85

objectivity, privileging of, 99

one-third-world approaches, 74, 272n5

"On Exactitude in Science" (Borges), 228

On the Media (radio show), 125

ontology, 9, 30–31, 53; isness/ontology, 60–61, 66, 145, 177, *232*, 236; ontological Blackness, 60–62; ontological reasoning, 53; as pornographic, 236

opacity ("the opaque"), 29; of black holes, dark matter, and dark energy, 78; of Black people, 59, 61–62, 251; and silence, 76–78; "theologies opaque," 45

oppression, 59, 61, 84, 131–32, 266n7, 286n6; five categories of, 30. *See also* interracial sexual violence; slave trade, transatlantic; violence

orbits, 29–31, 148, *232*

order, right, 3–4, 6

organospiritual beings, Black people as, 238–39

origins, 80–81, 173

Orisha, as gender-nondiscriminant, 43, 257n22

"Osirian" revolution of Egyptian Sixth Dynasty, 79–80

Osirio-Maat, Ona, 140

Osiris, 64, 81, 110–11, 203

Other: and center/city, 28–29; desire for, 180

Palestinian women, 198–99

Palikurhy people of the Amazon, 33

Pan-Africanism, 80, 257n24, 291n84

"Papa's Maybe" (Spillers), 9

paradise, concepts of, 151, 154, 159; utopia, 163

Paris, Peter, 23, 41

Parry, Tyler D., 122–24

Parsons, Albert, 182–83, *183*

Parsons, Lucy E., 182–86, *183*; failure to connect the personal and the political, 185–86

particle physics, 32, 164, 239–40, 272n6

particles, 32, 164

particularity, 36–39, *37*, 99, 158, 194

patriarchal logics, 167, 227, 242, 292n91. *See also* heteropatriarchal framework

Pedagogies of Crossing (Alexander), 43

Peele, Jordan, 155

Pentecostal communities, 186–87

People Could Fly: American Black Folktales Told by Virginia Hamilton, The (Hamilton), 98

Perry, Imani, 5–6, 220–21, 235–36

Perry, Samuel L., 209, 288n10

personhood, 13, 176–77; antiBlack racist assumptions about, 40; of enslaved Black women, 181; and "free consent" in marriage, 117

perversion, 168, 214–15, 217

pharaohs, 4–5, *5*, 245–47, 287n8; Ahmosis, Queen, 246; Akhenaton, 241, 245–46, 247; female, 246–47; Hatshepsut (r. 1473 to 1458 BCE), 4–5, 246–47, 292n3; Tuthmosis I, 246

Phillips, Layli, 263n19

physics, 6–7, 20; of black holes, 77; and city, 29; classical, 8, 31, 164; electromagnetism, 9, 31, 172, 197–98, 203; and Euclidean geometry, 33; foundations for in Egyptian cosmogony, 82; lepton universality, 239; material concerns, 29–30; Newtonian, 33; particle physics, 32, 164, 239–40, 272n6; power explained by, 200; as science, 21; and sovereign experience, 82–83. *See also* quantum physics (quantum mechanics)

Pinky Promise, 210, 288n16

planetary survival, 57–58

Plato, 28, 40, 81; cardinal virtues, 51, 147–48; charioteer Allegory, 51

pleasure, 163, 167, 230–32, 282n3, 291n69; ecstasy in lieu of, 220, 236; mutual, commitment to, 192; pluri-sized pieces of, 231, *232*; and pornography, 199, 210, 212, 214, 215, 217–18

pluralism, 38, 39

pluri/multiverses, 29, 84, 239, 244

Plutarch, 111

policing, *183*, 184, 185

politics, 6; as "affairs of the city," 25, 27–29; as culture, 21; expanded by religion, 26–27; organizational patterns and governance of people, 25; about sociality, 20

Politics (Aristotle), 25

populism, 127

Index 325

pornography, 9, 152, 206; ambivalence about as strategy, 219–20; Black pornotopias, concept of, 208–21; and creative space, 226–39, *232*; Dworkin-MacKinnon definition of, 211–12, 215; early stag performances, 215; and ethical expectations, 208–9, 287n9; and exploitation, 219, 221, 233; human sex trafficking, 221–24; internet porn, 220–21; in the lives of Afrodiasporic youth, 211, 237–38, 288n17; and moral agency, 215–16, 219, 244; and Pinky Promise ideology, 210, 288n16; *pornē graphein*, 234; pornophobia among Black churchwomen, 209–10; pornotropic gazing, 217, 289n22, 289n34; porn-positive (or porn-open/discerning) approaches, 218–19; pragmatic approach to morality of, 216; race in discourses of, 212–14; and religious attendance, 209; and religious commodification of women, 210–11; as sex instruction, 211; and solidarity building, 220–21; as suppression of feeling, 212–13; and violence, 216; virtual spaces of, 234–35. *See also* internet; sexuality; sex work and sex workers
pornotropic gazing, 217, 289n22, 289n34
positionality, 39, 98, 243
postmodernism, 37, 62–63, 98, 109
poverty, cultivation of conditions of, 106–7
power, 73, 167–204; and African beauty, 179–80; of ceremonial center/city, 27–28; and desire, 199; domination, 167–68; ethics of, 218; perversion as technology of, 214; physics explanation of, 200; and position, 243; science as about, 199–200; sexuality as about, 171–72; sites of abuse, 193; theopolitical control tactics, 223–25
power-over and domination-power perspectives, 112–13
preparedness, 148
Prescod-Weinstein, Chanda, 7, 32–34, 198–201, 270n79, 275n64
prison industrial complex, 182

probability, 32
procedural justice, 54, 75
process, 146, 148, 150–52, 156
pro-creation, 152–54, 231, *232*
prosecutor's fallacy, 133
prostitution. *See* sex work and sex workers
Ptah, 141
Pulse Nightclub massacre, 157
Putin, Vladimir, 221–22
puzzling justice, 9, 171, 195–98; and desire, 198–201; Rubik's cube analogy, 172, 195–99, 202; vulnerability, ethical challenge of, 193, 196–97
pyramid texts (2600 BCE), 80
Pyramid Texts (Saqqara), 64–65
Pythagoras, 51

quantum, defined, 132
quantum physics (quantum mechanics), 30–34, 164, 230–31; and entanglement, 132–34; measurement process, 164; probabilistic nature of, 32; Schrödinger's cat paradox, 164–65
quare: and Black churches, potential of, 163–66; as chosen name, 18; defined, 1, 22; as erased particularity, 36; future as, 163; *maât*/khemetic culture, reading of, 3–4, 43; and opacity, 62; perception of Floyd's murder, 281–82n3; queer distinguished from, 3–4; as space-time discursive, 17; womanism, relationship with, 6–7
quareing justice, 3–4, 8, 10, 19–20, 24, 201, 250
"'Quare' Studies" (Johnson), 22
quare-womanist-vindicationist project, 1–3, 6–7, 19, 24–25, 206
quarks, 239
queer: as futuristic, 10; as inadequate for addressing racial diversity, 23; quare distinguished from, 3–4; spectra of, 19; as term in Atlanta press, 182
queerness, 163
queer theory, erasure of race and empire from, 49

326 Index

Ra, 81, 241; Eye of, 42
Ra, Sun (Le Sony'r Ra), 7–8, 71, 78, 140; as past sex, 93–95; and celibacy, 95–96; as child of Saturn, 7, 84, 89, 141; Cosmic-Universal commitment of, 91; in Egypt, 91; "Everytime a Bird Goes By," 89–90; gray asexuality or gray-sexuality of, 7, 93–95; "Invisibility," 92–93; justice theory of, 96–97; name change, 274n54; as prophet of flying justice, 72, 89–93; sexuality of, 72, 84, 89, 93–95; sovereign experience of, 84; *Space Is the Place* (film), *92*, 96
race: erased from queer theory, 49; pornography in discourses of, 212–14; sexualized, 169
Race and the Cosmos (Holmes), 30, 87–89
"Race and Trends in Pornography Viewership, 1973–2016: Examining the Moderating Roles of Gender and Religion" (Perry and Schleifer), 209, 288n10
racial purity: impossibility of, 174–75; presumption of intraracial sexuality as, 189
racism: antiracist biological sameness strategy, 109; as exploitation, 236; and interracial sexual intimacies, 171; and interracial tensions, 169; melanin, responses to, 107–8; nonwhite resistance to as justice work, 108, 110; s.o.g.i., 146, 280n10; ugliness attributed to Black bodies, 179–80; as white supremacy, 107, 111–12
railroad strike of 1877, 184
rape, 170, 198–201; (un)rapeability of Black women, 180–81
rationality, and city/center, 28–29
Rauh, Christopher, 115–16
Rawick, George P., 123
Rawlsian tradition, 26, 55–56; contractarian theory, 57, 87
Re (sun god), Maât's relationship to, 64–65
Reagan, Ronald, 227

reality, and simulacra, 227–29
reason, 82
Reckonings, The (Johnson), 200–201
Re-Inventing Africa (Amadiume), 46
relationship: ethical choices, 102; for "reason, season, or lifetime," 102; terms for, 20–21. *See also* marriage
relativity, theory of, 113, 256n20
religion: Black feminist religious thought, 217–18, 289n37; Blackness as subject of, 20, 25; as Black subject, 20, 25; colonization of, 20, 60, 151–52; doctrines, 142, 146, 164; formulations of experience, 58–59; grounded in transatlantic slave trade, 25; intracommunal experience, 25–26; as orientation to world, 58; political implications of, 26–27; and political possibility of anarchy, 25–26; and pornography, 209–11. *See also* Black churches; Christianity; Maât (deity)
republic, etymology of, 127
re-reflection and strategic action, 72, 97–100
resistance, 220, 225, 249; and anarchy, *183*, 184, 185, 187–88, 259–60n33; deviance as, 37, 156, 214, 251; sexual discourse of, 189–91; silence as tool of, 182; to sin, 151–52, 166; systemically oriented, 146, 151–52; transformative, 32; as work of justice, 108–9
res nullius, 261n8
respect, politics of, 218
respectability politics, 12, 95, 188, 214, 217–18, 244; politics of deviance as counter to, 19; and youth of color, 237–38
responsibility, 12, 35; and liberation ethics, 73; of Western academy, 12, 177
restorative justice, 52–55
Rethinking Rufus: Sexual Violations of Enslaved Men (Foster), 181
retributive justice, 54, 75
revivalist approach, 45, 268n50
Revolt Spirituality, 188
revolutions, 79–80, 84

Index 327

Rich, Adrienne, 193
Riggs, Marlon, 50
rights, and virtue, 55–57
Rogers, Joel Augustus, 8, 45, 78, 167, 169–70, 186, 282–83n10; early years, 175–76; *Negro-Caucasian Mixing in All Ages and All Lands*, 172–78
Rogers-Andrews, Helga, 176
Roots (television series), 118
Rubik's cube analogy, 172, 195–99, 202
Russia, 208, 221–27; *kompromat*, 222–23, 225, 226; pornographic underground economy, 222; theocratic impulses, 225
Russian Orthodox Church, 222, 225

sadomasochism, 168, 193, 281nn1–2
Sandel, Michael, 55, 74, 87, 268n50, 274n49
Saturn, 7, 84, 89, 100, 141
Schleifer, Cyrus, 209, 288n10
scholarship: antiBlack racism in academia, 40–41, 99; intraracial intimacies presumed, 188–89; religious studies, 40–41, 43, 209, 257n22; white, 24, 40–41, 99
scholarship, Black: dismissal of, 40–42; missed opportunities, 41–43; vindicationist, 23–24, 40. *See also* vindicationism
Schrödinger, Erwin, 133, 280–81n39
Schrödinger's cat paradox, 164–65
science: as about power, 199–200; cosmic myopia, 30; participation in rape culture, 198; in Welsing's theories, 113. *See also* physics; quantum physics (quantum mechanics)
Sea Birds Are Still Alive, The (Bambara), 88–89
"Secret Sins: Masturbation and Pornography" (Lindsey), 210
Seership, faculty of, 147
self-actualization, 148–49, 187
self-assurance, 130
self-determination, 99, 171, 220, 234
Set I, *11*

Sex and Race series (Rogers), 172–78
sexual discourse: languages for, 87; of resistance, 189–91
sexual ethics: interracial, 170; meanings of, 167; traditional, 188–95. *See also* Black sexual ethics
sexual goodness, 55
sexuality: definitions of, 21; discerning presence of, 168; ecstasy, 220; fantasy, 220; goodness of, 190–91; intraracial as presumption, 188–89; and marketization, 236; materializing, 142; as about power, 171–72; socially constructed opposed to biologically essentialized, 49–50; "varietism," 186. *See also* pornography
sexuality, 248, 257n22; annunciation/celebration, 72, 93–97; as context, 93–97; as response to Creator, 95; and Sun Ra, 72, 84, 89, 93–95
Sexuality and the Black Church: A Womanist Perspective (Douglas), 189
sexualized race, 169
sex work and sex workers, 9, 211, 218–20, 222, 233–36; differentiated from sex trafficking, 224; early stag pornography, 215; homosexuality likened to, 47; and politics of respect, 218; summit scenario, 226–27, 233–34. *See also* pornography
Seymour, William, 186
shadow, 81
shame, 12, 65, 282n10
shouting justice, 159–62
Significations (Long), 27–29, 65
silence: interpreting, 76–77; as tool of resistance, 182
Simians, Cyborgs, and Women: The Reinvention of Nature (Haraway), 229–30, 232–33
simulacra, 66, 227–29, 232, 235, 241, 244
Simulacra and Simulation (Baudrillard), 227–29
simulation, 227–29
sin, 164; created by white cultural attack on Black sexuality, 191; nontraditional

sexual attraction as, 153–54; resisting, 151–52, 166; stasis as, 152
SIN. [act I] (Lamar), 145–46, 148–55; "god is a white guy," 155; "inner revolution," 155; "Outside," 155
Sisters in the Wilderness: The Challenge of Womanist God-Talk (Williams), 42
Sitman, Matthew, 125, 127
slavery: and marriage, 116–17; master-slave dialectic, 117; and nation-state, 178; as pornography, 215; Southern US culture of, 169. *See also* enslaved people
slave trade, transatlantic, 169; and "blind justice," 5–6, 256n18; dehumanization strategy, 106–7; and distributive justice, 54; and interracial intimacies, 169, 170; jumping the broom as artifact of, 119; rape culture of, 170; religion grounded in, 25; and "the way," 84–85. *See also* enslaved people
Sleep: Deux Femmes Noires (Thomas), *243*
Smith, Adam, 112
social construction, 49
socialism, 129–30
social modeling, 45–46
sociopolitical organization, 79–80
s.o.g.i.racism, 146, 280n10
solidarity, 220–21
Somé, Sobonfu, 276n20
songdance, 66
soul: *Ba* aspect of, 81, 86–87, 99; *Ka* aspect of, 81, 86–87
Souls of Black Folk (Du Bois), 26
sovereign experience, 7, 36–37, 50, 206, 248; Diop's view, 82–84, 240; and physics, 82–83; subjectivity rooted in, 36; of Sun Ra, 84. *See also* moral agency; moral constellations
sovereignty, erotic, 218
Soviet Union, 227
space: as place, 85; as place of Black sexual justice, 72, 97–100; transnational debates on, 238

Space Is the Place (film), *92*, 96
space-time, 19, 62; as centrifugal haunting, 34; and city, 29; creative, 226–39, *232*; cultural contexts of observation, 33–34; and dark energy, 77–78; and retention of Black sexual freedoms, 208
spectra of meanings, 19
Spillers, Hortense, 9
spiritpolitical anarchism, 187
"spirituality of revolt," 188
stage, concept of, 157–58
state: and sexual violence, 223–24; types of, 79. *See also* carceral state; nation-state
Stewart, Dianne M., 118, 257n22
Stolen Legacy (James), 78–79
Stoller, Robert, 214
strategic options, 72, 89–93
Student Non-violent Coordinating Committee, 216
subearth. *See* Chthulucene
subjectivity: Afropessimist view of, 61; rooted in sovereign experience, 36
suffering: Black people as meta-aporia, 61; and womanism, 38
supernovas, 77
supreme being, silencing of, 77
systematic sexual surveillance, 179, 181–82, 283–84n26, 289n22; and pornography, 213
systemic sin, 151–52
systemic violence, in twenty-first century, 62–63, 71
Szwed, John, 91, 95

"tantalizing tensions," 9, 206, 239–40
temperance, 147
Temple of My Familiar (Walker), 66
Temple of Seti I, *11*
terra nullius, 261–62n8
terrasphere. See *dunia* (terrasphere)
terra-story, 19, 90, 261–62n8
territorium nullius, 261n8
terrorism, interracial sexually based, 170, 172

Theban system, 80
theoethics, 75, 85, 112, 117, 150; personal, 154–55
theological resources, 72, 85–87
theories of justice, 7–10; in "black books," 44–45, 276n23; and Black sexual ethics, 6–7, 19, 24, 34, 35–36, 87; and expectations, 103–4; and womanism, 39. *See also* justice; justices; Maât (deity); *maât* (Maât's moral code, justice/s); vindicationism
Thomas, Greg, 46, 48
Thomas, Mickalene, *243*
Thoth (deity), *92*; as husband of Maât, 65–66, *92*; and "hysteria," 60, 65, *92*; ibis as symbol of, 60, 65, *92*, 256n11; in Long's *Significations*, 65; Sun Ra dressed and writing as, 91–92
Threadcraft, Shatema, 56–57
Timbuktu, destruction of, 46
Tinsley, Natasha, 260n7
"To a Negro Belle" (Wolff), 177, 283n21
Tocqueville, Alexis de, 277–78n31
Townes, Emilie M., 35, 37, 75, 98, 189, 270–71n81
Toynbee, Arnold, 178
transhumanity, 126, 188, 231, 285n56
transnational connectivities, 8–9, 206–7, 286–87n6; climate change and space debates, 238; sex trafficking, 221–24
Truly Disadvantaged, The (Wilson), 115–16
Trump, Donald, 126, 221–22
trust, 148, 192, 231
Tuthmosis I, 246
Two Thousand Seasons (Armah), 84–85
tyranny of the majority, 184

unified field theory, 48, 107–15; and entanglement theory, 113
United States: antimiscegenation laws, 174; (anti)sexual components, 132; as carceral state, 179; doctrine of racial superiority, 173; as empire, 286n6; as hybrid, 131–32, 203–4; interracial sexual violence, 178–82; lynchings, 174, 181–82; move toward minority whiteness, 124–25; repeated murders of people of color, 105; Russia's attempt to start race war, 208, 221–27; sexual dysfunction of, 132; systematic sexual surveillance in, 179, 181–82, 213, 283–84n26, 289n22; theocratic impulses, 225; voter suppression, 125
universal, the, 37, 61
"Uses of the Erotic" (Lorde), 212–13
utilitarianism, 51, 53

Veith, Ilza, 60
vindicationism: "black books," 44–45, 276n23; central claims and contributions of, 45–46; defined, 1; Egyptian contributions, 9; homophobia and heterosexism in claims of, 7, 45–50, 79, 85; homosexuality, views of, 45–48; Maât, visions of, 39–50; Maât as critical aspect of, 7; moral dilemma of, 176–77 (*see also* Rogers, Joel Augustus); Négritude lineage, 8, 266n14; as predominant form of Black scholarship, 23–24; as US-oriented expression of Negritude, 20; Walker's, 38; wheels of experiences and justices, 89–90. *See also* Diop, Cheikh Anta; Lamar, Joseph (Jojo); Ra, Sun; Welsing, Frances Cress
violence: anarchy and engagement in violent resistance, *183*, 184, 185, 187–88, 259–60n33; Fanon on, 259n33; and pornography, 216; of surviving, 188; systemic, in twenty-first century, 62–63, 71; threat of to intraracial Black relationships, 107. *See also* interracial sexual violence
"Virtual Hatred: How Russia Tried to Start a Race War in the United States" (Aceves), 221
virtue: cardinal virtues, 87, 147–48, 256n15; and consequentialism, 52, 53, 86; divinity, dignity, and integrity of human existence, 148–50; expanded, 166; justice as, 51, 148, 268n50; in

Lamar's work, 146–54; new possibilities for, 20–21; and rights, 55–57; as social, 39
virtue-based moral reasoning, 52, 74, 86
Vox, Amy, 125
vulnerability, 218; ethical challenge of, 193, 196–97

Wakanda, 84
Walker, Alice, 1, 7, 17, 22–23, 38, 94, 212; "Coming Apart," 213; "Gifts of Power: The Writings of Rebecca Jackson," 17–18; *Temple of My Familiar*, 66
warfares, 216
Waters, Malcolm, 206
"way, the," 21, 25, 84–85
Welsing, Frances Cress, 7, 8, 45; Black family model of, 111; Color-Confrontation theory, 48, 108–9, 267–68n36; "The Cress Theory of Color-Confrontation and Racism (White Supremacy): A Psychogenetic Theory and World Outlook," 108–9, 113; "The Crisis in Black Male/Black Female Relationships: Is It a False Problem?," 114; ideological claims of, 107; *The Isis Papers: The Keys to the Colors*, 107–15; unified field theory of, 107–15
West Africa and West African traditions, 42–43
Western academy, responsibility of, 12, 177
Wheatley, Margaret, 230–31
wheels within wheels, 73, 87, 89–90
white nationalism, 124–27, 170
whiteness: and Color-Confrontation Theory, 48, 267–68n36; as genetic deficiency, 108–9
white supremacy, 8, 278n58; dismantling of, 109, 114–15; effect on Black marriage, 114, 213; global system of, 108–10, 114; melanin envy, 109, 111; motivations for, 112–13; racism as, 107, 108, 111–12
White Women's Christ, Black Women's Jesus: Feminist Christology and Womanist Response (Grant), 42
Wilderson, Frank, III, 61
"wild man" European trope, 60–62
Williams, Delores S., 38, 42
"Willie Lynch letter," 116, 119–21, 276n23
Wilson, Imani e, 21, 66
Wilson, William Julius, 115–16
Wilson hypothesis, 116
Wolff, Adolf, 177, 283n21
womanism: Black feminist religious thought as alternative to, 217–18; connectedness to the community and world, 18, 22–23; definitions of, 1, 22–23, 213, 263n19; lesbian relative to, 17–18; quare, relationship with, 6–7; quare-womanist-vindicationist project, 1–3, 6–7, 19, 24–25, 206; spectra of, 19; and suffering, 38; and theories of justice, 39; as "whole," 18. *See also* feminism, Black
Womanist Ethics and the Cultural Production of Evil (Townes), 37
Woodard, Vincent, 181
work, as change in "energy," 32
World War II, 172
Wright, Michelle M., 272–73n6
Wynter, Sylvia, 9, 45, 58, 242, 263–64n24
Wynterian project, 1

Yates, Kit, 133–34
Yoruban cultures, 43
Yoruba Traditions and African American Religious Nationalism (Hucks), 43
Young, Iris Marion, 30, 87
Young, Thelathia Nikki, 36–37
youth: and pornography, 211, 237–38, 288n17; queer, 157–58

www.ingramcontent.com/pod-product-compliance
Lightning Source LLC
Chambersburg PA
CBHW021848230426
43671CB00006B/312